Shades of Sovereignty

Shades of Sovereignty

Money and the Making of the State

Paul Wilson

ROWMAN & LITTLEFIELD
Lanham • Boulder • New York • London

Published by Rowman & Littlefield
An imprint of The Rowman & Littlefield Publishing Group, Inc.
4501 Forbes Boulevard, Suite 200, Lanham, Maryland 20706
www.rowman.com

6 Tinworth Street, London SE11 5AL, United Kingdom

British Library Cataloguing in Publication Information Available

Library of Congress Cataloging-in-Publication Data

Names: Wilson, P. A. (Paul Anthony) author.
Title: Shades of sovereignty : money and the making of the state /
  Paul Wilson.
Description: Lanham : Rowman & Littlefield, 2021. | Includes
  bibliographical references and index.
Identifiers: LCCN 2021011186 (print) | LCCN 2021011187 (ebook) |
  ISBN 9781538154014 (cloth) | ISBN 9781538154021 (epub)
  ISBN 9781538156926 (pbk)
Subjects: LCSH: Money. | Currency question. | Monetary policy. |
  International finance--Law and legislation. | Monetary unions.
  | State, The.
Classification: LCC HG221 .W775 2021 (print) | LCC HG221 (ebook)
  | DDC 332.4--dc23
LC record available at https://lccn.loc.gov/2021011186
LC ebook record available at https://lccn.loc.gov/2021011187

In memory of my parents
John and Anne Wilson

Contents

Chapter 1: Introduction   1

Chapter 2: The Money of Nation Builders   9

Chapter 3: International Monetary Unions in the Nineteenth Century   37

Chapter 4: Money and Empire   47

Chapter 5: The End of Empire   89

Chapter 6: Secession   117

Chapter 7: Accession   163

Chapter 8: Countries and Currencies in Waiting   173

Chapter 9: Modern Multinational Monetary Unions   195

Chapter 10: Monetary Sovereignty and the Making of the State   221

Bibliography   231

Index   249

Acknowledgments

The author wishes to thank Robert Pringle and Professor Paola Subacchi who, having read the typescript in full, made a number of corrections and suggestions, most of which have been incorporated in one form or another into this final version of the book. They have saved the unsuspecting author from traps of inconsistency and errors of omission. Any remaining errors will of course be entirely the responsibility of the author.

I am grateful to Norman Lamont (Lord Lamont of Lerwick) for his commentary on the events of September 1992 and sterling's exit from the Exchange Rate Mechanism.

Thanks are also due to Professor Forrest Capie and John Plender for their repeated and generous encouragement toward a rank amateur.

Both Jonathan Callaway, director of the International Banknote Society, and Pam West, president of the same society, have been helpful in sharing their expert knowledge and kindly offering assistance.

And last, but certainly not least, I remain ever grateful to Leslie Gardner of Artellus, who continues to promote my books, perhaps out of a sense of adventure, or curiosity, or sympathy. Who knows? But it is appreciated.

Glossary

Arbitrage

The international trade in currency—particularly specie—where bullion values in one country would differ from those in another country. Silver or gold coins might be shipped to a country where the bullion is more valuable and melted down to be reused at a profit.

Bimetallic System

The unit of currency is fixed to a specific weight of gold and to a specific weight of silver. This kind of arrangement could be particularly vulnerable to shifts in the relative value of silver and gold in the marketplace.

Currency Adoption (Dollarization)

A country may adopt the currency of another country with or without that country's agreement. In recent years this step has usually been taken by countries suffering extreme monetary instability—perhaps in the form of hyperinflation.

Currency Board

A currency board is an arrangement whereby a central monetary institution issuing national notes and coins chooses to "fix" its own currency to another "anchor" currency at a set exchange rate, forgoing its discretion to influence exchange rates and surrendering the competitiveness of its own currency to the policies of another country for the sake of stability.

The "anchor" currency is recognized as a more stable currency, and fixing the exchange rate to the anchor will serve to stabilize the more unstable currency. The rate of exchange between the local and the reserve currency will be written into the constitution of the currency board to ensure there is no deviation. And, to guarantee the integrity of this arrangement, the currency board concerned can issue its own currency only at a rate for which it has adequate "cover" in the anchor currency. That is to say, for every one unit of its own currency, it would be able to exchange a fixed number of units or fractions of units of the anchor currency. Reserves of the anchor currency should amount to 100 percent (or even more) of the value of the national currency issued.

To guarantee adherence to the fixed exchange rate, it should be fixed by law, and any alterations to the exchange rate would likewise require a change to the law.

Exchange Rate

Fixed exchange rate: In the strictest sense, the exchange rate of one currency to another is set for the long term and may be established in legislation or in the constitution of, for instance, a currency board.

Floating exchange rate: No attempt is made to peg or fix the currency to another reserve currency.

Pegged exchange rate: A situation where the exchange rate of one currency to another is set but perhaps only for a shorter period than is the case in a fixed exchange rate and may deviate within set limits from the original rate

Free Banking

Commercial banks are permitted to issue their own banknotes without restraint.

Free Minting

An arrangement whereby members of the public could deliver silver or gold in any form to a mint and have it minted into coin.

Gold Exchange Standard

Central banks could hold as reserves banknotes that were themselves convertible to (or exchangeable for) gold. Under the Bretton woods agreement, currencies were fixed to the US dollar.

Gold Standard

In the strictest sense, management of a currency system where a unit of the national currency is fixed to a set weight of gold and is convertible freely to that gold.

Inflation

Extreme inflation: At least 15 percent per month.

Hyperinflation: Increases in the Consumer Price Index of at least 50 percent per month for at least three consecutive months.

Legal Tender

A legal term defining the type of currency that is acceptable in settlement of debts within a given country. As described by the Bank of England:

Legal tender has a narrow technical meaning which has no use in everyday life. It means that if you offer to fully pay off a debt to someone in legal tender, they can't sue you for failing to repay.

The concept of legal tender only really comes into action in a court of law.

Moral Hazard

The temptation to act imprudently, taking risks in the knowledge that the consequences will be covered by insurance or by a government bailout.

Seigniorage

The profit made by government or a central bank on the issue of currency. This profit used to be based on the difference between the cost of production of currency and its nominal value. In modern economies, seigniorage is created when money, issued by the central monetary authority, is used to purchase government debt and other bonds. The seigniorage is now based on the yield (interest) on that debt paid by the government to the central bank.

Chapter 1

Introduction

INTRODUCTION

This book is about the political dimension of monetary sovereignty and its role in the creation of states. It does not attempt to investigate specific monetary policies or instruments in depth—topics that have received close attention from generations of economists. Rather, the focus is on the relationship between monetary sovereignty and political sovereignty. Is monetary sovereignty a vital component of political independence? Or is it something that can be modified or even dispensed with in certain circumstances without compromising political sovereignty? Does an insistence on "monetary independence" always serve the best interest of a state? Is the meaning of monetary sovereignty fixed, or is it mutable and dynamic? Such questions are raised in urgent form by several contemporary developments, including the emergence of the global internet, the ongoing revolution in cross-border payments systems, and, linked to this, the emergence of new would-be private monies. Many central bankers appear to view these as posing direct long-term challenges to monetary sovereignty. A close examination of the historical evidence suggests, however, that the underlying issues are much more nuanced than often thought. Given the wide diversity of countries' experience and circumstances, there is no easy or unqualified answer to such questions.

But what is monetary sovereignty? Some guidance was offered by the Nobel Prize–winning economic theorist Robert Mundell, who suggested that monetary sovereignty is framed by a country's policy and legal sovereignties. Policy sovereignty was, in Mundell's description, the ability of a country to devise and implement its own policies in respect of the currency in circulation without reference to other countries. The legal sovereignty was, similarly, a government's ability to make laws without interference from any outside authority.[1] With these conditions in mind, monetary sovereignty is the ability of a government to pass laws and develop policies relating to the operation of its monetary system unconstrained by the laws and policies of other countries or authorities. The sovereign power is, then, the highest authority in the creation of monetary laws imposed on the population of a state. Within this wider framework—but only within it—the monetary authority (which will usually be a central bank) has a degree of autonomy in the use of its powers and mechanisms to achieve monetary targets that will ultimately be set by government.[2]

Mundell's interest in this dimension of monetary government ties in closely to his concept of the Optimal Currency Area (OCA). He described an OCA as a geographic region in which a group of countries with economies that already work closely together and enjoy a degree of similarity in the operation of their economies would benefit from the use of a single currency with the aim of facilitating trade and helping to integrate capital markets. Mundell identified a group of requirements to ensure that an OCA can work properly. These included the free movement of labor and capital and risk-sharing arrangements that would involve fiscal transfers from wealthier members to poorer ones at times of stress. This concept has provided a theoretical, economic basis for the decision by various countries or jurisdictions to surrender some degree of monetary sovereignty in combining to share a common currency beneficial to all participants. The practical application of Mundell's principle can be seen at work in currency unions in one form or another in Africa, Europe, and the Caribbean, demonstrating that some countries are prepared to surrender their monetary sovereignty or some part of it in return for other benefits (often, but not always, economic).

Further examples are furnished by experience following the breakup of the Soviet Union, beginning in 1990, which led to the reintroduction of independent currencies, first in the Baltic states and then in the other countries that seceded from Moscow's control. One of the newly independent states, Estonia, had once had an independent currency in the form of the kroon, which had existed for a period between the two world wars, until the country fell under the control of the Soviet Union in 1940. At independence, Estonia moved to reintroduce the kroon as a vital symbol of independence, but after less than twenty years it was ready to surrender monetary sovereignty again in return for what was perceived by the Estonians to be a greater prize—deeper integration into the European Union and the accompanying sense of greater security that integration offered. Thus, there were and are some matters more important to governments than the absolute and uncompromised freedom to manage all aspects of their own currency. Sometimes, these reasons would be economic and, sometimes, purely political.

This recent history demonstrates that monetary sovereignty is a dynamic issue. What was appropriate in terms of monetary independence or otherwise for a country last year may not be so this year. As circumstances and problems change, so may the solution. And what may suit one country now may not be right for another country at the same time. Nation-states may now choose to surrender or recover monetary sovereignty according to the prevailing circumstances. Who is to say that circumstances in the Euro zone in the future might not lead Estonia to conclude that membership in the Euro confers fewer benefits than expected?

To begin with, though, there is the question of where the sovereign authority over currency lies within a country. From earliest times, authority over money more often than not rested in the hands of a monarch. When the first coinage of the Western world appeared in what is now western Turkey in the sixth and seventh centuries BC, local rulers adopted the measure of stamping the coins as a way of reassuring the populace that the quality of the precious metals used was of a reliable standard of fineness. The impress of the ruler's symbols was therefore a guarantee of value offered by the central authority in the land. And yet for princes or powerful office holders in republics such as Athens or Rome, money was not solely an economic issue. For these, money was first and foremost a means of exercising power. When power was seized, or empires extended, the sovereign authorities then—and, indeed, now—take control of the issue of money as a matter of some priority. Whoever controlled the supply of money commanded the army, the civil service, and other public services. In this way, control of the money supply was immediately essential to the exercise of authority. In some cultures, authority over the production of currency has been specifically reserved to the prince. Thus, in the Islamic east, the striking of coinage was an important right, known as sikka, reserved to the ruler as a particular symbol of his sovereignty and power. Over time, however, debasement of the coinage meant the ruler's guarantee itself lost value. A successful currency enhanced a ruler's prestige; a failed one undermined it. The stability of the money system and of prices in the marketplace reflected not only good economic and monetary policy but also a confidence in the political stability and durability of the regime.[3]

Currency, therefore, has always had a propaganda value. A ruler's tenure of power might be underpinned by the widespread distribution of his coinage to the further reaches of his realm, by his insistence that only his coin might be acceptable. The Lex Cornelia (testamentaria nummaria) of the Roman dictator Sulla (81–80 BC) reinforced the authority of the state by means of the official currency. By this decree it was forbidden to reject any coin that bore legitimate symbols of the republic and, subsequently, the image of the emperor.[4] In this way the establishment of a currency system widely recognized and accepted by the population was important in consolidating power not only in Rome itself but also in securing its widespread provinces. Currency at that time was then vested with powers beyond that of an instrument for trade. However, this approach could also be exploited by ambitious individuals challenging the rightful emperor. Thus, the Roman admiral Carausius, who seized power in the province of Britain in 286 and declared himself emperor, began by issuing his own coinage, which bore his own imperial image but was initially somewhat mediocre in design, execution, and silver content. But, four years later, Carausius and his supporters issued a coin of finer design and execution and with significantly higher silver content than the debased silver coinage issued by Rome. The objective was to score a propaganda point over Rome: The better the silver content, the more credible the coin; the more credible the coin, the more credible the authority that issued it.[5] In another era, signal failures in these matters could lead to removal of currency from the powers of the prince as happened in Sweden in the seventeenth century. Such examples show that power over the issue of money is in some circumstances considered too important to be trusted to the sovereign.

Peoples colonized by Rome were also conscious of coinage as an effective medium for propaganda and an assertion of an independent national identity. A rebellion in Israel against Roman rule during the reign of the Emperor Hadrian, which began in 132 AD and lasted for several years, was accompanied by an issue of "insurrection coins," which bore the name of the leader of the insurrection, "Simon, Prince of Israel." Some commemorated the "Liberation of Israel," and others, the "Liberation of Jerusalem" and were stamped with "year 1" or "year 2," marking a new era.[6] Even today, many are convinced that money is a potent tool for independence movements, even somehow vested with powers conferring international recognition on a new country and therefore a vital step on the path to full sovereignty.

The monetary regime might also reflect a country's fundamental philosophy of government. Following the American colonies' successful War of Independence against Britain, the leading political thinkers in the colonies, including the founding fathers Jefferson, Madison, and Hamilton, aligned themselves variously with two conflicting political positions: one that held that control and issue of money would be led by the federal government and another according to which money would be a matter for the newly independent states. Power over money was in the view of some observers one of the central issues defining the relationship of the colonies to the federal government, which would bind them. If postrevolutionary America was a laboratory for the exploration of options in government, the shaping of its currency regime was a major element in the experiment.

Two generations later, nationalist movements in continental Europe culminated in the creation of the nation-states of Switzerland, Italy, and Germany with their accompanying national currency systems. The discovery of a national identity in these countries also coincided with rising middle-class liberalism and moves toward an internationally coordinated and standardized monetary system (the gold standard). Combinations of these movements served to produce different solutions to the question of money according to the circumstances applying to different countries. In Germany, conservatives created the new state and dominated foreign and defense policy but compromised with liberals to allow the latter the lead on economic and monetary matters. Germany's subsequent adoption of the gold standard was inevitably linked to the interests of a rising mercantile middle class, but it was also a potent symbol of the country's coming of age as a single, unified power of the first rank.

In Japan, during an era of modernization spanning the last quarter of the nineteenth century and the first thirty years of the twentieth, economically cautious liberals confronted a conservative party bent on building a Japanese state with an Asiatic empire funded by an expansive issue of money. The direction of Japan's development, economic prosperity, and imperial destiny would be argued in debates over monetary policy and in particular the adoption and management of its gold standard. Its history shows how at various times in different countries money is vested with ideological and nationalistic significance; indeed, it is seldom a purely economic matter. The exercise of national monetary sovereignty therefore is typically driven not only by the need to adapt economic policies to national priorities but by all sorts of wider political demands, including that of underpinning political sovereignty. It is somehow symbolic of the politicized connection between sovereignty and monetary independence that the UK Independence Party, which at a populist level launched the campaign to withdraw the United Kingdom from the European Union, included the pound sterling sign as a prominent element in the party's logo.

Over the past 150 years, conventional notions of monetary sovereignty and the belief that it is necessarily tied to national independence have, however, been challenged.

Early experiments in the international coordination of monetary policies in the second half of the nineteenth century gave rise to the Scandinavian and Latin monetary unions. These experiments are often cited by skeptics as evidence that currency unions without fiscal and political union are destined to be short lived. But despite the relatively short life span of these unions, they were precursors of international attempts to coordinate money, which extended throughout the twentieth century well into the twenty-first, ranging from diplomatic—and largely unsuccessful—conferences in Brussels (1920) and Genoa (1922), to formal multinational monetary unions such as those that now operate in Francophone Africa, the Caribbean, Southern Africa, and, best known of all, the euro. As the era of empire has given way to an era of self-determination, a country might now surrender its sovereignty over currency not because it is compelled to do so by a superior power but as a matter of choice. It is in fact the right to exercise choice that is the essence of monetary sovereignty. Indeed, I shall argue that monetary sovereignty is no longer an indispensable adjunct of political sovereignty.

Control of currency by national agencies has, indeed, come under threat from several fronts. Private ownership of the means of issuing money is nothing new. Private control of monetary operations has been a matter of public debate and changes in government policy into our own times. As recently as the 1940s, the Bank of England was owned by private shareholders until nationalized by the Labour Party government of Clement Atlee in 1946. Until this point, one argument in favor of private share ownership insisted that it protected independence of action from government interference. But by the mid-1960s this argument—especially in countries of the British Commonwealth—was largely dead and very few central banks now have private shareholders.[7] But now, in what might be seen as a swing of the monetary pendulum in the direction of private issue, the emergence of so-called cryptocurrencies is seen by many central bankers as a direct threat to monetary sovereignty as currently understood. Indeed, there is some evidence to suggest that cryptocurrencies beyond the control of central government and monetary authorities could be of interest to aspiring national independence movements.

Any discussion of the true meaning and significance of monetary sovereignty must also consider the degree to which any currency is truly independent. The currency of a country may, for instance, bear all the symbols of an independent state but perhaps be issued on currency board principles where its value is fixed in law to the currency of another country (almost exclusively now that of the dollar). In such cases the country concerned forgoes all ability to influence the value of its currency by the monetary operations available to a central bank, thereby ceding a large part of its monetary independence. And yet, assuming the country adheres strictly to the currency board principles, the arrangement in almost all cases confers reliable price stability.

In other cases, a currency may be subject to market forces, the rise or fall in that currency's value linked for example to international demand for an export commodity such as oil. External shocks of this sort to a national currency may make it very difficult for a central bank to manage the currency effectively using the various operations at its command. In those cases, where the market may have more influence on a currency than the central bank issuing it, to what extent can it be true that the country's currency is independent? A clear example of the susceptibility of currencies to market movements can be seen in the September 1992 effect of market activity in forcing Britain's sterling out of the European Exchange Rate Mechanism. This particular case goes some way to demonstrate, for example, that an attempt to fix the exchange rate of a national currency and at the same time maintain the free flow of capital will compromise any independent monetary policy.

But as Norman Lamont, Britain's Chancellor of the Exchequer at the time, points out:

The devaluations of sterling and seven other currencies in 1992 were not caused by capital flows or speculation alone but by a combination of financial and political conditions including the French Maastricht referendum. . . . Every country is to some extent affected by other countries. Even the Federal Reserve System may find its ability to sustain a given level of the dollar, if that is what it wants, affected by the interest rate policy of the European Central Bank and vice versa. No one is completely free ever from the influence of other countries.[8]

Viewed from a different perspective, some currencies might seem not only to be independent but to be vested with power that goes beyond the limits of their own geographic borders. Once, this might have been sterling, which was held by many countries as a reserve currency convertible into gold. In our times, it is plainly the US dollar that has a reach well beyond America's jurisdiction, forming about 60 percent of global reserves and being used as the currency of denomination for important commodities (confirming its desirability as a reserve currency). A measure of the power of the US dollar is reflected in the ability of the US government to deny or severely limit the access to that currency for countries under sanctions. If the power of a national currency has been clearly recognized in the case of the US dollar and, previously, the pound sterling, many can be forgiven for concluding that the possession of a national currency is an indispensable component of a country's sovereignty. Further, some public figures claim powers for currency that are entirely unproven, such as the ability to attract international recognition for a claim of independence or the power to prevent war. I hope to show that these claims are at best confused and at worst deliberately misleading.

How did we reach the point where the issue of a national currency is seen an indispensable building block of sovereignty?

NOTES

1. Robert Mundell, "Money and the Sovereignty of the State," https://www-ceel. economia.unitn.it/events/monetary/mundell14.pdf. See this paper also for a more extensive discussion of the meaning of sovereignty.

2. W. F. Crick, *Commonwealth Banking Systems* (Oxford: Clarendon Press, 1965), 15–18, for a view of the relationship between autonomous central banks and government, particularly in the states that were newly independent in the late 1950s and early 1960s.

3. Jonathan Williams, ed., *Money: A History* (London: British Museum Press, 1997), 91.

4. Elio Lo Cascio, "The Function of Gold Coinage in the Monetary Economy of the Roman Empire," in *The Monetary Systems of the Greeks and Romans*, ed. W. V. Harris (Oxford: Oxford University Press, 2010), 171.

5. Richard Reece, *The Coinage of Roman Britain* (Stroud: Tempus Publishing, 2006), 51.

6. Martin Noth, *The History of Israel* (London: Adam and Charles Black, 1972), 452.

7. Crick, *Commonwealth Banking Systems*, 38.

8. Author's personal conversation with Lord Lamont.

Chapter 2

The Money of Nation Builders

The inability of the colonists to get power to issue their own money permanently out of the hands of George III and the international bankers was the prime reason for the Revolutionary War.

—Benjamin Franklin

From the early modern era to the nineteenth century, experiments in the creation of new states took place that tested the ability of nation builders to establish efficient monetary regimes suitable for entirely new forms of government. The federal nature of some of these new countries required a compromise to balance a degree of autonomy of the constituent states with a need to ensure they did not issue separate competing currencies. Other states forged in the nineteenth century from the unification of smaller sovereign territories were spared this complication. In the cases studied here, we look at the nature of the problems and the solutions adopted.

THE UNITED PROVINCES OF THE NETHERLANDS

The Union of Utrecht of 1575 created the United Provinces of the Netherlands at a time of rebellion against the sovereign power, Spain. For more than twenty-five years after its creation, the federated nature of the new state permitted each province and some cities to issue coin from their own mints, leading to a competition between those mints to compete by debasing coinage, reducing the production cost of a coin, and yielding short-term seigniorage (profit), but in the long run reducing the attractiveness of this coin to the public. By the beginning of the seventeenth century, fourteen mints competed for the benefits of seigniorage. Attempts to standardize coinage to counter this problem failed.[1]

Laws of 1603 and 1609 attempted to impose uniform standards to prevent differences in bullion content, which would in turn lead to the best coinage being melted down for use in new, debased coinage with lower silver content but identical face value, yielding a greater seigniorage. In 1609, the authorities took a further step to resolve the issue by creating the Bank of Amsterdam in response to representations by the merchant class for whom the variety of increasingly debased coins together with the presence of foreign coinage complicated trading conditions. The bank acted as a source of creation of so-called bank money—a client's credit on the books of the bank—as an alternative to the classical work of the mints. Merchants trading in bank money would value the convenience and security of this alternative to settlement in coin, which might be clipped or debased, and bank money could command a premium against coinage. Offering convenience and security, bank money provided, on a local basis, the same benefits offered by bills of exchange over long distances.[2] Although this development was driven by the lobbying of the merchant class and was not primarily a decision taken for political reasons with the purpose of binding the states together, it did show that competitive monetary authorities seem not to sit comfortably together within a political union. The experiences of the United Provinces in devising a monetary arrangement that would work for a union comprising various states immediately following a war of independence would be curiously echoed in the arguments surrounding the establishment of a monetary regime in the United States of America at a later time.

THE PROBLEM OF CURRENCY IN
BRITAIN'S AMERICAN COLONIES

Britain's inability to supply valid currency to its earliest colonies in the New World and then to its further colonies in Asia and the Antipodes speaks to the vast distances involved and the time it took to send anything anywhere in the age of sail. But it also serves to highlight the resourcefulness of people deprived of currency by their own governments. And it also highlighted the question of who exactly held power over the issue of money.

In the middle of the seventeenth century, Massachusetts, one of England's earliest colonies in America, defied the mother country's prohibition on colonial minting to produce a so-called pine tree shilling. The primary purpose of this minting was to provide a medium of exchange when barter was no longer a practicable method.[3] In a gesture of rebellion, or perhaps simply as a measure of desperation, the coinage was approved by the colonial legislature and launched in 1652, three years after the execution of the English King Charles I and the establishment of the republican commonwealth in England. The overthrow of monarchical power in England opened the way for some local autonomy in monetary matters. Despite the approval of the colonial legislature, a body of opinion in Massachusetts opposed the pine tree shilling on various grounds. Some were opposed for financial reasons in that the locally minted coins were debased and produced at a higher rate of seigniorage which prompted price inflation. Other, more political opposition, was based on the fact that the new currency challenged the royal prerogative; in other words, one community in the American colonies remained loyal to the principles of monarchy some years after the king's execution and expressed its opinions by taking a stand against the local production of an independent currency.[4]

In February 1690 the Colony of Massachusetts turned to the issue of bills of credit, which they ordered would be "in value equal to money" to fund preparations for a military campaign in Canada. These bills of credit and a second issue produced in 1691 were not, in the thinking of the time, legal tender, but rather promissory notes—a promise to pay real money—although the colonial treasury was obliged to accept them when presented for redemption. After a year, however, the colonial authorities decreed that, in all but certain exceptional contracts, bills of credit would be legal tender. This was the beginning of a period of excessive and uncontrolled monetary issue in the colonies, which took the paper money in circulation from 30,000 pounds in 1692 to 400,000 pounds in 1728. Together with the circulation of counterfeits from New Hampshire, Rhode Island, Connecticut, and Massachusetts, the paper money in circulation swelled, forcing the government in London to take a series of actions to rein in the increasing money supply.[5] Colonial governors could no longer authorize the issue of bills of credit, and existing bills were to be withdrawn. Taxes had to be paid in coins only.

Instructions to the Crown's governor in Massachusetts to reduce the amount of paper money in circulation brought protests from the colonial House of Assembly. Under this unenlightened policy, total money in circulation, including coinage, was reduced from about 400,000 pounds to a little less than 200,000 pounds, about half of which was based on notes issued by private banks and backed by silver. Ultimately, with such an inadequate money supply, the governor as the Crown representative was forced to accept payment of taxes in commodities rather than in the preferred coin.[6] Further attempts by the House of Assembly to increase the money supply by permitting the circulation of bills from the other neighboring colonies was similarly blocked in the 1740s, bringing with it deflation and a slowdown in trade. Appeals to Parliament in London fell on deaf ears.

Discussion of Britain's loss of the American colonies always focuses on the issue of taxation and rarely if ever focuses on the matter of money supply. In fact, the faulty system for the supply of money in the American colonies became one of the key issues that drove the colonists to their ultimately successful armed confrontation with the British government.

The use of paper money was of direct interest to no less a figure than Benjamin Franklin, the elder statesman among the founding fathers and a printer by training, who had been a key figure in the production of paper currency for the state of Pennsylvania. In his paper "A Modest Enquiry into the Nature and Necessity of a paper currency" of 1729,[7] Franklin contended that while an excess of money would be of *"no advantage to trade"* (to understate the dangers of inflation), an insufficiency of money would be *"exceedingly detrimental to it."* Although Franklin's self-interest in promoting the increased printing of money has not gone unremarked—even by Franklin himself—his contention that an increased money supply would hold down interest rates on credit agreements and therefore would make credit more easily available to support trade chimes with the view that when money is available, so is credit. Franklin further specifically attributed the scarcity of currency in Pennsylvania to the activities of English merchants who, in exporting to America, were drawing stocks of gold and silver out of the colonies; he went on to argue that the local production of paper money would be of benefit to English merchants keen to continue exporting to Pennsylvania and other American states at a time when there was no silver or gold coinage to be had. Plainly Franklin's campaign for more printed money in Pennsylvania worked. When Alexander Hamilton, first Secretary of the Treasury of the newborn United States of America, issued his report to the House of Representatives on the creation of a national bank in 1790, he singled out Pennsylvania for special attention because it had nearly a million and a half dollars of paper money in circulation. To put this money supply for one state alone into perspective, Hamilton's proposal set out a maximum capital stock of no more than 10 million dollars for a federal central bank serving all of the colonies.[8]

As Franklin had noted in 1729, what gold and silver there was tended to be drawn out of the colonies in return for imports from Britain under the closed imperial trading system. Previously, much of the coinage circulating in the English colonies originated in Mexico and South America, with which the colonies had a trade surplus. However, regulations imposed on the colonies by the mother country restricted trade with the Spanish colonies, closing off one of the few means of earning specie. With the ending of this trade avenue and its source of minted coins, other means of improving the money supply were sought. Inevitably, paper emerged as a cheap and convenient solution.

Individual colonies such as Massachusetts and Franklin's Pennsylvania produced their own paper currency to make up the shortfall. Excessive note issue had, of course, led to inflation which held its own attractions for small farm holders who would find it so much easier to pay off fixed debts to their creditors in heavily inflated, devalued notes. But the case for paper issue in, for instance, Rhode Island, was upheld even by establishment figures such as the governor of that colony who in 1740 cited paper money as the reason

Rhode Island flourished commercially in comparison with other colonies.[9] The opposition to locally issued paper included communities, such as merchants and wholesalers, who needed adequate access to sterling to trade with England and for whom local paper offered few advantages. The governor of Massachusetts sided with this latter group and against paper, the support for which he attributed to an excess of democracy. He observed that "the ignorant majority . . . always sought to tamper with sound money."

The settlement of transactions in paper money rather than specie was, despite Franklin's arguments, unattractive to those British (as well as colonial) merchants, whom he identified as part of the problem. As a result of their lobbying, legislation was passed in London in the form of the Currency Act of 1764, forbidding the production of paper currency in the colonies and setting out a program for the retirement of the existing paper currency. Demands for the payment of taxes to England in sterling, restrictive trade regulations, and an atrophied money supply were together the major factors destabilizing the relationship between England and its colonies in North America.[10]

Some thirty-six years after his "Modest Enquiry" and a year after the introduction of the Currency Act, Franklin found himself in London, a representative of the disgruntled colonies, for negotiations with the British government. There, Franklin proposed to the government in London an intriguing plan as an alternative to the government's heavy-handed schemes of taxation. Bills of credit, printed in the colonies, would be issued to borrowers prepared to pay the colonial treasuries 6 percent interest. The bills would act as "running cash," that is, to all intents and purposes, banknotes. While the 6 percent interest would be remitted to the British government in lieu of tax revenues, the colonies would benefit by the substitution of these bills of credit for absent gold and silver coinage.[11] Franklin, as a printer, of course had a personal interest in the promotion of printed paper as a solution to the problem but nevertheless had struck on a solution that was hardly more radical than the "running cash" notes issued by the Bank of England from the late seventeenth century, even if the Bank of England's running cash was based on certificates of deposit rather than on bills of credit. The British government rejected the proposal, preferring to stick to taxation as a means of raising revenue. It may also be that the government in London had concluded that, because the colonies were struggling to raise enough good coinage to settle the usual taxes and costs of imports, they would be unable to finance the interest payable to Britain on these bills in sterling or other quality coinage.

US FEDERAL CONTROL OF CURRENCY

During the American colonies' revolutionary war, the new nation's leaders had sought to finance their military operations by issue of the continental dollar. Although this expedient was in wartime understandable, the monetary basis of the new republic needed a more secure footing. The right to coin and issue money, which had for so long been a power exercised by the individual states, was withdrawn from them and allocated to the federal government by the Constitutional Convention, which opened in Philadelphia in 1787.

Regarding the issue of money, the Constitution declared:

Section 8 The Congress shall have power—

To coin money, to regulate the value thereof, and of foreign coin and fix the standard of weights and measures;

To provide for the punishment of counterfeiting the securities and current coin of the United States;

To make all laws which shall be necessary and proper for carrying into execution the foregoing powers, and all other powers vested by this constitution in the government of the United States, or in any department or officer thereof.

And to be explicit, the Constitution goes on to withdraw the currency issue powers from the state:

Section 10: No State shall . . . coin money; emit bills of credit; make anything but gold and silver coin a tender in payment of debts.[12]

The Federalist Papers, a series of essays written by Alexander Hamilton (the first Secretary of the Treasury) and James Madison (subsequently, fourth president of the United States), were published to explain the decisions of the Continental Congress and to promote the appropriate division of powers between the federal government and the individual states. Writing in Federalist Paper No. 44 of 1788 under the name Publius, Madison contended:

The right of coining money, which is here taken from the States, was left in their hands by the Confederation, as a concurrent right with that of Congress, under an exception in favor of the exclusive right of Congress to regulate the alloy and value. In this instance, also, the new provision is an improvement on the old. Whilst the alloy and value depended on the general authority, a right of coinage in the particular States could have no other effect than to multiply expensive mints and diversify the forms and weights of the circulating pieces. The latter inconveniency defeats one purpose for which the power was originally submitted to the federal head; and as far as the former might prevent an inconvenient remittance of gold and silver to the central mint for recoinage, the end can be as well attained by local mints established under the general authority.

So Madison objected to the strange arrangement whereby the federal government would set the fineness or alloy standard and the nominal value, while the individual states could set the weight and design of the coin, fearing that it would lead to a wide variety of coins in circulation. He accepted the idea of having a distributed set of production sites or mints for practical purposes but insisted that they should remain under federal authority to achieve a homogeneous currency.

He goes on:

> *The extension of the prohibition to bills of credit must give pleasure to every citizen, in proportion to his love of justice and his knowledge of the true springs of public prosperity. The loss which America has sustained since the peace, from the pestilent effects of paper money on the necessary confidence between man and man, on the necessary confidence in the public councils, on the industry and morals of the people, and on the character of republican government, constitutes an enormous debt against the States chargeable with this unadvised measure, which must long remain unsatisfied; or rather an accumulation of guilt, which can be expiated no otherwise than by a voluntary sacrifice on the altar of justice, of the power which has been the instrument of it.*

In other words, the damage wrought by the inflationary effect of the depreciating continental currency during the war and paper currency issued by individual states since the war was so corrosive of the social and economic foundations of the country that the right to issue paper money had to be withdrawn from the individual states. He also rejected the authority of the states to issue their own paper money on the grounds that such devolved powers would simply result in a variety of currencies that would in turn prove an obstacle to trade between the states, possibly even leading to disputes between states:

> *In addition to these persuasive considerations, it may be observed, that the same reasons which show the necessity of denying to the States the power of regulating coin, prove with equal force that they ought not to be at liberty to substitute a paper medium in the place of coin. Had every State a right to regulate the value of its coin, there might be as many different currencies as States, and thus the intercourse among them would be impeded; retrospective alterations in its value might be made, and thus the citizens of other States be injured, and animosities be kindled among the States themselves.*

In making this point, Madison was foreseeing possible "currency wars" between the states. Worse still, should an individual state issue its own paper currency that subsequently was devalued, Madison feared that it could lead to difficulties with foreign countries; a single state might therefore by imprudent management of its own paper currency create problems between the entire Union and one or more foreign countries:

> *The subjects of foreign powers might suffer from the same cause, and hence the Union be discredited and embroiled by the indiscretion of a single member.*

Finally, to reinforce the prohibition on paper money and to limit the states' flexibility in monetary decisions, they were not to permit anything other than gold or silver as legal tender.

> *No one of these mischiefs is less incident to a power in the States to emit paper money, than to coin gold or silver. The power to make any thing but gold and silver a tender in payment of debts, is withdrawn from the States, on the same principle with that of issuing a paper currency.*

With considerable logic Madison had set out a program for the abolition of paper currency, reduced the individual states' authority to issue currency of any kind, and established gold and silver as the only legal tender, a program perfectly consistent with the aims of the hated British Currency Act of 1764 and at odds with the views of Benjamin Franklin. In his defense though, it is clear that Madison's support for gold and silver coinage as the only legal tender was based on the assumption that those coins or at least some significant proportion of them would remain in America and not be drained from the colonies back to Britain.

In 1790, only two years after Madison's Federalist Paper was published, Hamilton, as Secretary of the Treasury, submitted his "Report on the Subject of a National Bank" to the House of Representatives. The remit of Hamilton's national bank was broad: it was not formed purely to regulate money supply but would also act as banker and lender to both the government and the private sector, handle the multiplicity of foreign currencies circulating, and manage debt and revenue collection. Its role was based broadly on the facilitation of trade and promotion of the economy rather than the narrow function of sole issuer of a national currency. Taking the Bank of England and the Bank of Amsterdam as models, the new national institution would be funded by private money but would trade on the confidence of its public, governmental status. Exploiting private deposits as the basis for a fractional reserve banking system, the National Bank would multiply the effect of those deposits to expand the money supply.

Considering the desirability of issuing paper money, Hamilton resisted the idea of a purely fiat issue and insisted on a convertible currency that could be redeemed for gold and silver coin, an arrangement that would place a natural limit on the issue of paper money. Hamilton may have had in mind here the lessons of John Law's Banque Royale seventy years earlier where the convertibility of the currency forced the bank's administrators to take (albeit, half-hearted) measures to slow down the redemption of paper for coin. A more recent and pertinent lesson, however, was the failure and massive depreciation of revolutionary America's own inconvertible paper currency, the "continental dollar," issued during the revolution.[13]

Other notables of the revolutionary movement shared Hamilton's view of the need to constrain the issue of paper money. Thomas Paine, the English radical author who had immigrated to Pennsylvania two years before the start of the revolution set out his view in "Dissertations on Government, The Affairs of the Bank and Paper Money" of 1786. The circulation of paper money unbacked by specie would occupy the place of gold and silver, which would then not be attracted into the colonies. Indeed, if inconvertible paper money were to be allowed to compete with gold and silver, the latter would be sent abroad in keeping with Gresham's law: why settle transactions in America with good silver and gold when transactions could be carried out with the intrinsically worthless paper? Ship the valuable coins abroad.[14] Writing of paper money as a possible legal tender, Paine declared that, under a republican government, no institution—specifically no "Assembly"—could declare fiat paper money to be legal tender because such a move would amount to "an attempt at arbitrary power." Any committee or individual proposing such a measure "deserves impeachment."[15] Paine did, however, draw a distinction between a pure, fiat money unbacked by specie and issued by political authorities, on the one hand, and, on the other hand, of promissory notes redeemable for coin at a bank of which he approved. Like other leading thinkers of the new republic, Paine's overwhelming preoccupation was with the restraint of arbitrary power. For him, a fiat currency was nothing more than the expression of such power by monetary means.

Although Hamilton shared Paine's distrust of money printed at the whim of government and also held the view that convertibility to coin in a bank would restrain any temptation to overissue money, in some respects his view differed from Paine's. Paper money was a perfectly acceptable form of circulating currency as long as it continued to oil the wheels of commerce. Consistent with his era, he did not deny that gold and silver occupied a quite different position in the matter of currency because they were "*the money of the world*"—that is, they were acceptable for trade with other countries, could be used to settle international debts, and could be used by the government to fulfill any other international financial obligations it might have. But, if as a result of a circulating paper currency some gold and silver left the country, that was less important than that sufficient money—of some sort—should circulate in the domestic economy. In any case the amount of gold or silver present in America was more dependent on the ability of the new country to export goods and to earn gold and silver by means of its own skills, manufactures, and produce.

Hamilton's proposal for the creation of a national bank attracted opposition from some of the leading lights of the revolution who disapproved of the whole culture of finance as opposed to what they saw as a more legitimate basis for the economy in agriculture and manufacturing. Thomas Jefferson, the secretary of state (foreign minister), and John Adams, Washington's vice president (and, subsequently, second president of the United States), were among the most prominent and vocal opponents of the wider world of banking and finance. While Adams was firmly opposed to private banking, he was, curiously, in favor of a public bank with a network of branches. The issue was so bitterly debated that, in the view of one historian and eminent chief justice, the creation of the Bank of the United States was the single most important factor in forcing the establishment of the Republican and Federalist parties.[16] This may or may not have been the case, but the argument over the centralization of public finances through a national bank reflected the fundamental disagreement between those who wanted a strong federal government and tended to be aligned with northern, commercial, nonagricultural interests, on the one hand, and the Republicans who hailed from Southern agricultural states, which wanted the greatest possible power to be reserved for individual states.

In his report on a national bank, Hamilton explained why central authorities might have a duty to monitor and audit the performance of any bank authorized to issue money. *"If the paper of a bank is to be permitted to insinuate itself into all the revenues and receipts of a country; if it is even to be tolerated as the substitute for gold and silver in all the transactions of business; it becomes, in either view, a national concern of the first magnitude."* Indeed, one of the articles of Hamilton's proposal for a national bank was that the notes issued by the bank would be receivable as payments to the United States (that is, as payment for taxes, inter alia).

The extent of opposition to the creation of a national bank and to any national bank's right to issue banknotes as part of a centralized authority can be measured by a letter from Jefferson to Hamilton's erstwhile friend and collaborator James Madison, the author of Federalist Paper No. 44, setting out the benefits of a centrally administered federal currency above that of the states. In that letter, Jefferson asserted that anyone signing or issuing banknotes of a federal national bank and anyone recognizing those notes was equally guilty of treason to the individual state.[17] Thus, for some Republicans, a national federally issued currency was not only *not* legal tender but was a strong symbol of a foreign power and of the federal government's attempts to undermine and subvert the power of individual states. For the federal government, Hamilton's report on a national bank lays out the counter position that "*The emitting of paper money by the authority of government is wisely prohibited to the individual states by the national constitution.*" It is easy to see why, in the opinion of at least one well-placed historian, the controversy over the federal versus state issue of money was a—perhaps *the*—most important reflection of the irreconcilable differences between Federalists and Republicans.

Despite the opposition of Jefferson and Madison, the bill for the establishment of a Bank of the United States as proposed by Hamilton passed the Senate and was signed into law by President Washington in February 1791.[18] Twenty years later, the bank's charter was to be renewed by a vote in Congress, which, however, it failed to secure due to opposition by small commercial banks and ardent opponents of Hamilton's own Federalist party, notwithstanding the fact that, Madison, by now president, and his treasury secretary Gallatin, both opponents of Hamilton, had come round to thinking the bank was useful.

Rather less controversial was the establishment of a national mint in line with recommendations set out by Hamilton and made law by the Coinage Act of 1792. Incorporating a decimal system, which divided each dollar into a hundred cents, the new system would be based on a formal bimetallic ratio accepting gold and silver as legal tender in payment of unlimited amounts (and copper coins as legal tender payment up to a limit). Foreign coins would be relieved in due course of their legal tender status, and a national mint would operate on the principle of free minting, that is to say citizens could take silver and gold to the mint for coining without incurring a seigniorage charge.[19]

On the expiry of the charter of the First Bank of The United States, the government granted a twenty-year charter to its successor, the Second Bank of the United States, in 1816. Alexis de Tocqueville, a minor French aristocrat of liberal leanings, whose magisterial survey *Democracy in America* records American society in the 1830s, wrote favorably of the bank as "*the great monetary tie of the Union, just as congress is the great legislative tie.*" De Tocqueville noted with particular approval the fact that notes issued by the bank were accepted on the western frontiers of the country "*for the same value as at Philadelphia, where the Bank conducts its operations.*"[20] In the eyes of this well-informed foreigner, the national bank performed an important function in helping to bind the country together through its issue of a currency that was recognizable and trusted throughout the country.

THE BANK WARS

But, under Nicholas Biddle, who became president of the bank in 1823 and remained there until its charter too expired in 1836, the Second Bank eventually became a focus of animosity for the government of Andrew Jackson, seventh president of the United States. Biddle had set out his own position as early as 1824 when instructing the head of the Washington branch of the bank that the head's first responsibility was to follow the requirements of the bank's board and Biddle himself, its president, even if it meant conflict with the president of the United States. Biddle, although by personal inclination a Jeffersonian Republican, found himself in sympathy with the sixth president, John Quincy Adams, who, as a Federalist of the Hamilton school and therefore closely aligned with business and finance interests, should have been a personal opponent. Jackson, whose support base among the electorate was populist and opposed to the wealthier, elite classes, saw the bank as a pillar of a "*young nobility*" system. He considered that the creation of a new central bank, for all intents and purposes, would be neutered. It would have no rights to issue notes or make loans and would be under the control of the treasury. De Tocqueville noted that Jackson was aided in his campaign by newspapers collaborating with the management of other note-issuing banks that resented the Second Bank's ability to constrain rival note issue. While smaller provincial banks were unable to issue notes to a value beyond a proportion of their relatively limited capital value, the Second Bank of the United States benefited from being the depository of federal funds and was therefore able not only to issue many more notes but also to buy up notes of other banks, convertible to gold or silver, which it could present for redemption at such a time as to drain the competing note-issuing banks of their reserves. This was a classic game known as note dueling.[21] Many note-issuing banks had, therefore, an interest in bringing down the bank. While such a situation might be unthinkable today, this was a time when federal institutions in America were by no means fixed as pillars of the Constitution. De Tocqueville went on to recognize in the conflict between the Bank of the United States, on the one hand, and the allied forces of provincial banks, newspapers, and a populist president, on the other, an episode in the rivalry between federal and state power already evident in the polemics of Hamilton and Madison some forty years earlier.[22]

The president's attempt to veto another chartering of the Second Bank of the United States failed, but the arguments in favor of his point of view were skillfully presented, certain to appeal to the electorate and probably a major factor in his successful reelection. Jackson's antipathy toward the bank was only aggravated by his belief that, in the runup to the 1836 election, the bank might construct a financial crisis to undermine his bid for reelection. Jackson also labored the point that a large proportion of shares in the bank were held by foreigners; if the majority of shares were to end up in the hands of citizens of a foreign country and that country were to go to war with the United States, what would be the consequence for the bank?[23]

Political groups confronted each other over the question of banknote issue. In a remarkable contrast with monetary life during the colonial era, paper money was now seen as the favored medium for the business classes. Laboring classes with powerful support in the Senate formed up on the side of bullion.[24] While it might seem curious that small farmers and laborers, for whom inflationary paper might be an easy route to settling debts, should favor bullion, another way of looking at it was that the working man was all too often paid in depreciating paper money.[25]

Following his election to a second term—notwithstanding the presumed opposition of the bank—Jackson pressed ahead with his plans to dissolve it. The first step was the removal of public funds and their distribution to state banks in which Jackson had confidence, his so-called pet banks. Two successive secretaries of the treasury, McLane and Duane, doubtful of the wisdom of transferring public funds to banks that had insufficient silver backing to the banknotes that they issued and were therefore insecure, opposed the president's plans, only to find that they were moved on to other posts.

The process of transferring public funds from the Second Bank of the United States to Jackson's pet banks appears to have caused a nineteenth-century credit crunch because Biddle's bank sharply reduced the number of loans it was making, called in existing loans, and presented for redemption banknotes issued by state banks, with the objective of coping with the transfer demands. The speed and scale of this operation led to the bankruptcy of merchants who appealed to the government. Roger Taney, Jackson's placeman as Secretary of the Treasury and subsequently a (very) long-term member of the Supreme Court, spoke out against the bank's actions as a challenge to democracy, highlighting the rivalry between an elected government and an unelected central bank leadership, a tension still evident in many countries today. Jackson, as he had always intended, allowed the bank's charter to lapse without renewal. So ended the second central bank of the United States, bringing to an end a period known as the "Bank Wars." It was followed by the period of free or wildcat banking. There was to be no central bank structure in the United States until 1913.

THE FEDERAL RESERVE SYSTEM

America's monetary history had for a hundred years been a drama in which the power of the center and the federal government was pitted against more libertarian, decentralizing forces. At times of crisis, when either the state faced an existential threat, as it did during the Civil War, or its monetary and financial system looked close to implosion, as it did during a widespread banking collapse in 1907, the authorities were prompted to take action. Powerful figures in America's financial world pushed for a central authority to regulate the banking system. Various ideas for a central bank or at least reserve "system" were proposed against opposition from those who feared the concentration of too much power in the hands of a single institution. America, true to its history of independent thinking, created not a single central bank along the lines of the banks in Sweden, the Netherlands, and England, but rather settled on a proposal put forward by a Democrat faction in the Senate led by the immensely influential Senator Carter Glass. The proposal, put forward in 1913 and passed into law in December that same year by President Woodrow Wilson, neutralized the fundamental objection to a single central monetary authority by setting out a plan for a number of regional federal banks that would be run by local bankers. The entire system would be overseen by a Washington-based Federal Reserve Board whose members would be appointed by the president. It was, then, a creative compromise to the challenge of controlling money involving a balance of power between the states (or at least regions) and the center.[26]

NATION BUILDING IN EUROPE: THE RISING
TIDE OF LIBERALISM AND GOLD

If America, as an experiment in nation building and a country freed of the narrower social and political traditions constraining development in the Old World, was free to search out new paths in its approach to money, the European states had to contend with conventions reaching back hundreds, if not a couple of thousand years. The great landowning classes of Imperial Rome, which were also the most powerful political classes, had stored their wealth in gold. Tenant farmers, in debt to the landed aristocracy of the Middle Ages, benefited when debts, denominated by nominal value of a coin, could be paid in currency of debased silver, which was easier for them to come by. Any interested party that received its income through fixed payments from those tenant farmers, based on long-term agreements, wished naturally enough to receive that income in something that held its value. Renaissance governments willing to entertain or indeed encourage debasement of silver coin would nevertheless preserve the high standards of gold coinage. As late as 1811, at the height of the Napoleonic Wars, the British parliamentarian Lord King declared that he would reject Bank of England notes and accept payment of debts owed to him by his tenant farmers only in gold, forcing the government to establish Bank of England notes as legal tender. At this point, then, there was a decoupling of the interests of some of the landed classes and the immediate war aims of the British government. The merchant classes, on the other hand, had notably come to the aid of the government and the Bank of England by affirming publicly their support for Bank of England notes, first during the Jacobite invasion of 1745 and then in 1797 in response to the French revolutionary wars, both of which events had prompted runs on the Bank of England. In this sense, the trading classes were more supportive and closer to the government policy in emergency circumstances than were the conservative landowning classes. But this was a temporary willingness to eschew gold.

If gold was good enough for great landowners, it was also good enough for the up-and-coming middle classes, in most normal circumstances. International transactions had always best been settled by gold, which was much more portable, traditionally tended not to be debased, and held its value. Gold was therefore most acceptable for the international transactions conducted by traders. Throughout the eighteenth century, trade in manufactured goods increased, particularly from England, which had successfully established excellent access to gold, both directly from Brazil and indirectly in arbitrage trade against high-quality English silver coins on the continent. Thus, commercial traders, an increasingly powerful bloc in British society, became ever more interested in the use of gold as the basis for the British economy. As the nineteenth century wore on, the balance of monetary power started to shift away from major landowners and toward urban, commercial, industrial, and financial communities associated with liberal political movements facing the traditional conservative politics of the land. The process had already begun in England at the start of the century but then got under way on the continent in the middle of the century. Even further back in time, we see an interesting parallel to these urban versus rural preferences for gold over silver in the way that the trading cities of Northern Italy were first to introduce gold coins in the Middle Ages, while the agrarian communities and nations clung to silver.

By the middle of the nineteenth century, silver, with its tendency to depreciate and inflate prices, had come to be associated with certain sectors of the agrarian classes, strongly influential in the southern states of Europe, while the urbanized, developed business communities of Northern Europe preferred gold, which held its value. In the nineteenth century, the balance of monetary power shifted from landowning classes to an urban, industrial and financial elite. Liberal, middle-class politics dominated the Swiss cantons before and after confederation, ensuring a pro-business, pro-gold inclination in the Swiss federal parliament in the middle of the century. The growth of liberal political movements and the consequent increase in political influence of their supporters in the business world in Denmark, Sweden, and Holland in the 1840s and in Italy in the 1860s and 1870s inevitably led to the adoption of a gold standard, although this happened faster in some countries than in others.[27] In France, the origins of the members of the legislature in 1852, for example, clearly confirm the change in the balance of power away from landowners, who constituted 18 percent of the Assembly, to the middle classes, primarily former civil servants and the bourgeoisie, which together made up 50 percent of the Assembly.[28] Notwithstanding this growth in middle class, liberal, mercantile influence in France, Italy, and Switzerland, silver remained the basis of their currency systems largely due to French political influence in neighboring countries.

THE UNIFICATION OF SWITZERLAND

The long-independent cantons of Switzerland were forged for the first time into a unified Helvetic Republic by the force of invading French revolutionary armies in 1798. The French also imposed for a time a unified monetary system.[29] But, from 1803 until unification in 1848, authority to mint and issue coins reverted to the cantons, resulting in a patchwork arrangement of monetary standards that might have been recognizable to inhabitants of the United Provinces of the Netherlands at the end of the sixteenth century or the American colonies until authority over coinage was vested in a central government by the Continental Congress.

Following unification in 1848, Article XXXVI of the Federal Constitution of 1850 allocated authority over minting and issuance of coinage to the federal government. Notwithstanding Switzerland's experience of invasion by French forces at the end of the eighteenth century, it was still to France that the cantons looked when they sought a model for the new national currency. Although German-speaking cantons had proposed the country should adopt German models for its currency system, the French-speaking cantons countered by pointing out that there was no single, unified German currency system, an argument that won the day for a French model. The Federal Coinage Act of 1850 ensured that Switzerland's silver coinage would be modeled on the specifications of size and fineness of the French silver franc, but there was no provision for gold coins, despite an apparent inclination toward gold on the part of Swiss federal parliamentarians. Switzerland was not alone in deferring to French leadership in monetary matters. In June 1852, the silver coins of France, Belgium, and some Italian states were decreed to be legal tender, and in 1865 Switzerland became a full member of the Latin Monetary Union (see chapter 3).[30]

Banknotes, typically for the time, were treated differently. In 1881 a single, standardized banknote design was imposed, but issue by various private banks was permitted.[31]

THE UNIFICATION OF ITALY

Italy's currency, once unified under the rule of Rome, had, following the collapse of that empire, fragmented into as many different systems as there were states—and more—and remained fragmented until French armies under Napoleon invaded in 1793 and introduced the civilizing benefits of the franc. In 1814, however, with the collapse of Napoleonic France's power and influence, the franc was forced out of circulation in Italy except for the states of Piedmont and Parma. A period of revolutionary turbulence greeted the return of the old reigning dynasties in Naples and Sicily in the period from 1820 to 1821. Other revolts took place a decade later in Modena and Parma, both of them suppressed by the reactionary forces of Austria, while papal troops did the same for a revolt in the Papal States. Piedmont, the northern state with the most advanced economy on the peninsula, harbored political ambitions to lead Northern Italy out from under Austria's hegemony. By 1861, Naples, Sicily, and Lombardy were, by force of arms, incorporated with Piedmont into a unified Kingdom of Italy.

The leaders of Piedmont—King Victor Emanuel and his prime minister, Cavour—had been reluctant to absorb Sicily and Naples into this new Italian state, recognizing the economic differences between the south and the north of the peninsula, but were presented with a fait accompli by Giuseppe Garibaldi, the most flamboyant and successful commander of this period in Italian history, known as the *Risorgimento*. Sicily and Naples were both incorporated into the new, unified Italy.[32]

Even if there was no way of escaping this incorporation, the concerns of the king and his prime minister were justified in purely economic terms. The disparity in the economies of north and south continued into the twentieth century. In 1911, the agricultural south was lagging 40 percent behind the industrial north in terms of GDP per head.[33] The difficulty of bringing together states with quite divergent economies was to be encountered again in quite different circumstances in Germany and Yemen in the late twentieth century.

In Italy the challenge of merging many different states with such divergent economies was difficult enough, but the fragmented monetary arrangements added to the complexity.

A plethora of monetary systems existed in the peninsula prior to unification. In states and even towns, a variety of coins of different weights and fineness circulated. Piedmont was on a bimetallic (based on the use of both gold and silver standards) system, while Venice and Lombardy under Austrian control, the Two Sicilies (Naples and Sicily), and Tuscany were on a silver standard. In Tuscany alone, twenty-four different families of currency were in circulation. Not all Italian states had banks issuing notes. But of those that did, the notes issued by Tuscany were as a rule convertible into specie, while those of Sardinia and Rome were not. Nothing more clearly exemplifies the fragmented nature of Italian statehood at the time than this multiplicity of monetary systems.[34]

The process of integrating this galaxy of currencies began shortly after the Austro-Italian War of 1859. There was an intermediate stage of consolidation when, for a short period, currencies of Piedmont, Parma, the Papal States, and the Austrian coinage circulating in Lombardy replaced many of the other provincial and town currencies. Then, after unification in 1861, Piedmont-Sardinia was rewarded for its political leadership of the Risorgimento by the adoption of its currency, the lira, as that of a unified Italy. Although the economic and transactional benefits of a unified currency were not lost on the political leadership that introduced it, the political symbolism was even more important for the generation that was forging a new country.[35]

Because of the few note-issuing authorities in Italy, it has been suggested that there may have been as many as nine times more coins than banknotes in circulation at unification. The process of retiring some of these coins as part of the currency reform went on for decades. Some of the silver piastres of Naples, for example, were withdrawn only in the last decade of the nineteenth century in payment of taxes.[36] The poorer, undeveloped areas of the south and the conservative rural communities there clung to the old money, long after the wealthier, industrialized north had embraced the new lira.

The bimetallic French system, in which the value of the franc was fixed to a certain amount of either gold or silver, had for a time operated in Italy during the Napoleonic period but had subsequently been dropped. It was, however, formally readopted following unification in 1861. Political considerations were influential in this decision. France had played a key role in the process of unification. Italian unification had been bought at the cost of a war against Austria in which French troops had fought alongside those of Piedmont-Sardinia. In terms of both its military and political support, France was the godfather of Italian unification, and Piedmont recognized the debt in transferring to French sovereignty the Province of Savoy (together with its note-issuing bank) and the county of Nice in accordance with the Treaty of Turin, which had been agreed between Napoleon III of France and Victor Emmanuel II of Piedmont. It is hardly surprising that Piedmont should turn to France for ideas as to the optimal currency system for the new state, just as the Swiss cantons had.

The lira, just like the franc, was to weigh five grams and would be 90 percent fine silver. The gold-to-silver ratio was at one to 15.5, also identical to that of the original germinal franc issued in France in 1803. Following the decision of the Swiss ten years earlier to allow legal tender status for Belgian and French coinage, Italy went one better, accepting the circulation of the coins of both states as well as those of Switzerland.[37] Running high levels of spending immediately after unification, the government of the day required a greater supply of money. Financing of a new war with Austria was a major factor in this public sector spending as was the central government's assumption of the debt of Italy's member states. Specie left the country, and commercial banks' reserves were drained. The government suspended convertibility into specie—a so-called corso forzoso, or forced circulation of banknotes—and declared the notes of other issuing banks to be legal tender. While those notes could not be converted into specie, they could be converted into notes issued by the Bank of the Kingdom of Italy (the Banco Nationale nel Regno d'Italia, or BNR), which were not themselves convertible into those of other issuing banks. As a result, BNR notes assumed the role of a reserve for other banks. Until 1870, the monetary system fundamentally consisted of three tiers of medium of exchange: (1) gold coins, silver five franc coins, and French banknotes; (2) other depreciated silver coins; and (3) Italian banknotes not considered true money and consequently subject to heavy discount.[38] In 1884, Italy returned to convertibility and the gold standard. Although such a development would have normally instilled confidence in the lira, prices in fact rose, and the exchange rate of the lira declined.[39]

When convertibility was resumed on the gold standard in 1884, note-issuing banks had an incentive to ensure that they held high volumes of convertible notes. The notes of these banks exchanged at par (one for one), so any bank overissuing its own notes could convert those notes into those issued by other banks and these, in turn, could be converted into specie. A group of six of these note-issuing banks calculated that the government would have to turn a blind eye to overissue because, in the short term, it produced the liquid cash necessary to keep the economy going. And, sure enough, matters came to a head in 1891 when the high volumes of notes on issue far exceeded the reserves held in the banks. In response, the government simply lowered the legal requirements for reserves to be held against issued notes.[40]

This state of affairs was recognized as unacceptable in the long term, and reforms were instituted following a review in 1893. Note-issuing banks of

Tuscany were merged with the BNR to form the Banca d'Italia. The Banca di Napoli and the Banca di Sicilia came under supervision of the central government, while the Banca Romana went into liquidation and disappeared altogether. Nonetheless, underlying problems remained. Specie flowed out of the country and, perhaps to make up for the failing money supply, notes continued to be issued in excessive volumes. With shrinking volumes of specie and increasing volumes of paper in circulation, the only option was to suspend convertibility again in 1894.[41]

Consolidation of note-issuing banks into a single national bank proceeded slowly alongside the consolidation of monetary systems. The National Bank of the Sardinian States incorporated the banks of Genoa and Turin by 1850. Upon unification, it became the National Bank of the Kingdom of Italy, and in the next six years absorbed, among others, the state banks of Parma and Venice. The process of absorbing the remaining note-issuing banks into the Banca d'Italia went on for decades, the Bank of the Papal States and two note-issuing banks in Tuscany in 1893 and the banks of Naples and Sicily not until 1926, shortly after Mussolini had assumed dictatorial powers and embarked on the consolidation of fascist power in Italy. The concentration of issuing powers at the Bank of Italy, while perfectly consistent with the international trend toward the creation of central banks in the 1920s, had for the Italian leadership an additional purpose in supporting Mussolini's drive toward a strong lira.[42]

GERMANIA SUI GENERIS

Until the unification of a German Empire under Prussian hegemony following its overwhelming defeat of France during the Franco-Prussian War of 1871, the region of German-speaking peoples in Northern Europe was divided into many different states, some monarchical, some, such as Hamburg and Frankfurt, republican city states. During this period before unification, early steps had been taken toward harmonizing fiscal and currency arrangements, including the eradication of customs barriers in 1834, creating the Customs Union, or Zollverein. Common standards were also proposed for the independent currencies to facilitate trade between the various states. In 1837 the Munich Coinage Treaty established common specifications for the South German medium of exchange, the gulden. A Prussian-led currency standard, the thaler, to which twenty-one North German states of the Zollverein, or Customs Union, subscribed, emerged for the first time a year later at the Dresden Convention on July 30, 1838. A requirement of this convention was that German states would choose either the gulden or the northern thaler as the unit of exchange with fixed silver content and consequently a fixed rate of exchange between the two.[43] While some people see these steps as the start of monetary unification, the fact is that at this stage there were two currency standards with a fixed exchange rate between the two, with the coinage being issued by the individual states rather than some central authority. Nevertheless, the fact remains that, while Italy's progress toward a unified currency took decades to achieve and began only after unification, the German states had already embarked on a project to harmonize currencies prior to fiscal and political unification. In this sense, Germany's journey toward currency unity has much in common with the euro project, the establishment of which has predated full political and fiscal union among its member states.

From the middle of the nineteenth century, an economic boom, fed by increased international production of gold during the 1840s and 1850s, the expansion of trade, and the development of the railways, had been underway in various German states. Answering a demand for finance to support this rapid economic development, note-issuing banks were licensed by individual states.

From 1851 to 1857, the number of banks across Germany issuing banknotes increased from nine to twenty-nine and then thirty-three by the 1870s. The proliferation of note-issuing banks in Germany in the third quarter of the nineteenth century echoes that of note-issuing banks in England in the 1830s, a generation earlier, but was clearly not at the same rate of increase as that taking place in the United States at the same time. Immediately before unification, something like forty different families of banknotes were in circulation in various parts of Germany. For the banks, there was a particularly profitable opportunity in the issue of low-denomination notes—much as English banks had moved to fill a gap created by the Bank of England when it ceased to issue notes smaller than five pounds. And, just as the Bank of England and government eventually sought to restrain the overissue of low-denomination notes with an attendant and problematic increase in redeemable liabilities and expansion of money supply, the Prussian government tried to ban the issue of small-denomination notes.[44]

Despite Prussia's opposition, commercial banking enthusiasm for the overissue of low-denomination banknotes was encouraged by the government of some small states, adding to the confusion and expansion of paper money in circulation. By the 1870s, an estimated 1.3 billion paper marks, or 8 percent of net national product, were in circulation, a total value of paper money that the issuing banks would have been unable to redeem in full due to insufficient reserves of specie.[45] Boom periods, stimulated by an overissue of paper money, were followed by banking crises in 1857, 1866, and 1873 when a number of banks failed. When the Bank of Prussia, as the principal monetary institution of the Prussian heart of the new empire was fittingly subsumed into the Reichsbank, other state banks, such as those of Bavaria and Saxony, retained note-issuing rights.

The creation of the North German confederation in 1867 and a federal parliament represented two more steps forward toward the goal of German unity. By 1868—the year of the fourth German Trade Assembly in Berlin—a monetary "unity" (if not union) was seen as "important and desirable" across all German states.[46] But the individual currency systems of the petty princedoms were seen as not up to the task of a currency of national unity, to the extent that in 1869 the English financial and constitutional commentator Bagehot thought it most likely that the French bimetallic system would be adopted by a united Germany.[47]

If indeed Napoleon III had hoped to extend France's monetary influence beyond Belgium, Switzerland, and Italy to Germany, Prussia, under the leadership of the Chancellor Bismarck, was having none of it. Despite the fact that there was no unified German state until 1871, the Liberal party, associated with the bourgeoisie, was already the dominant party in the Reichstag by 1874, obliging the towering figure of the political right, Bismarck, the Reichskanzler or prime minister, to find a compromise that facilitated a liberal, bourgeois domestic economic and monetary policy in return for acceptance of conservative leadership of the national government. That domestic policy, harnessed as it was to industrial, commercial interests, meant that gold was favored above silver.[48]

Under Prussia's leadership, Germany was determined to adopt the gold standard, which seemed to be an important factor in Britain's economic success. The five billion gold franc reparations paid by France to Germany at the end of the war of 1870–1871 was used by the latter as the foundation of its new gold standard monetary system. The five billion franc reparations imposed by the victorious Prussians on France following the latter's defeat in 1871 equated to a third of France's gross national product and was sufficient to provide much of the basic reserve that Germany needed to convert from a silver-to a gold-based monetary system.[49]

About 5 percent, or 273 million francs, of the reparations from France, defeated in the Franco-Prussian War of 1871, was to be paid in gold and contributed to the plan to convert Germany to a gold standard. Over a billion marks' worth of silver coins in the various constituent states of the new German Reich were withdrawn from circulation, nearly 400 million marks of which were recoined as minor silver denominations from 1873–1876, while the remaining seven hundred million marks' worth of silver was steadily unloaded onto the market, mostly after 1876, in return for gold, further depreciating the silver price, which had already been in decline.[50] Germany's policy and its execution were perceived as the single biggest factor in moving Europe toward a gold standard.[51]

Careful measures were adopted to smooth the passage from the individual currency systems of the constituent states to a unified currency for the new German Reich. The legacy coinage of the states would continue to circulate and enjoy legal tender status for some time after the unification process had begun. As a further concession to the sensitivities of the constituent states, gold coins and silver coins with a face value over two marks would display the Imperial Eagle on the obverse and the portrait or emblem of the individual state on the reverse, an approach adopted also for the coinage of the modern euro. Silver would officially circulate until 1907, the official date for final transition to a gold coinage only.[52]

Coinage acts of 1871 and 1873 created a common unit of account, the gold mark. But the permitted circulation of foreign coins and paper notes issued by the individual states of the Reich, both of which constituted 10 percent of the total money supply, was necessary to compensate for a continuing shortage of money into the 1870s, presumably because the conversion from silver to gold was not moving fast enough. At this point, then, there was still no central bank controlling issue. This was to be the subject of serious political debates in the years from unification to the Reichsbank's foundation in 1876.

Notwithstanding all of Germany's efforts to buy gold in the period immediately after unification, converting the gold francs of France's reparations into Reichsmarks, using the paper bills transferred as the major part of the reparation arrangement to buy gold on the London market, and using Germany's silver coinage to buy gold, there was still a massive net outflow of new gold Reichsmarks in 1874. Between 900 and 950 million gold marks left Germany in that year, more than the value of all the gold coins issued up to 1873.[53]

Not even Germany, whose adoption of the gold standard in the early 1870s had significantly contributed to the collapse of bimetallism, was immune to the effects of an international competition for gold. Some senior officials in the German government wondered whether a single silver standard had not provided some protection against the most extreme, destabilizing cross-border flows in specie. Bimetallism, fixing the unit of currency to a specific amount of gold and silver, offered entrepreneurs excellent opportunities to exploit varying gold-to-silver ratios in different countries to make a profit. Even countries such as Germany, firmly committed to the gold standard, were unable to prevent gold from being exported to markets where it attracted a higher premium. Supporters of the gold standard concluded that only the creation of a central bank would offer a means of managing monetary issues and stemming the outflow of specie. In the view of the Reichsbank's first president, the role of the bank was simply "providing for the currency and sustaining monetary circulation in the country."[54]

The idea of the formation of a Reichsbank was promoted, among others, by the liberal politician and businessman, Ludwig Bamberger, during debates in the Reichstag, while Bismarck and his staff, who were aligned with Prussian landowning interests rather than the liberal business bloc in parliament, were relatively indifferent to the idea. Bamberger's proposals enjoyed the support of southern liberal states such as Baden and Hessen, which saw in the Reichsbank a means of influencing policy that otherwise might have been solely in the hands of the dominant Prussian leadership of the Reich. Not all liberals, however, were in favor of a Reichsbank regulating the monetary system. One faction favored a laissez-faire approach and furthermore liked the idea of free banking.[55] Bizarrely, this group of liberals found itself allied on the Reichsbank issue with Bismarck and his supporters, including the Prussian Finance Minister Camphausen, who pointed out that the Bank of England shared its note-issuing rights with Scottish and Irish banks.

At least one leading liberal politician, Eugen Richter, opposing the creation of the Reichsbank, found fault not only with the idea of a monopolistic control of money but equally feared that it would amount to a political tool in the hands of Bismarck.[56] When it came to the issue of the creation of a central bank, there were liberals against it for economic and commercial reasons, others who opposed it primarily for party political reasons, and other liberals, like Bamberger, who were positively insisting on the need for it. It cannot be said, then, that there was a homogeneous liberal point of view on the issue of monetary control.

Richter proved to be right. The Reichsbank, created out of the Prussian Bank in 1875, was indeed subjected to political interference by the chancellor, who presided over its directorate and used it to further the interests of the state outside the economic arena, for example, as a tool of foreign policy. In 1887, relations between Germany, Austria, and Russia were particularly tense as Russia sought to exercise greater influence over parts of Eastern Europe that Austria-Hungary believed were within its own sphere. Secret negotiations between Germany and Russia concluded with an agreement by which Germany would not oppose Russia's expansion of influence in the Balkans in return for an undertaking that, in the event that France were to attack Germany, Russia would not intervene. It is no doubt against this backdrop of secret realpolitik that Bismarck prohibited the use of Russian state bonds as security for loans from the Reichsbank, perhaps to reduce the exposure of Germany's banking system to a possible default by Russia.[57]

The fact that the Reichsbank was privately owned was cited by some as a defense against possible party-political manipulation, an argument that we have previously seen in respect of the Bank of England. State ownership would have enabled easy and relatively frequent exploitation by the government as a lender of last result. It would have been able to bail out any foundering financial institution, which threatened financial instability. The argument today might be seen as one of moral hazard. If commercial banks know that high levels of risk will be underwritten by a central bank willing to act as lender of last resort, they will take more risk. In late nineteenth-and early twentieth-century Germany, there was a view, particularly on the political left (ironically), that a privately owned central bank would be less susceptible to government manipulation than a nationalized one under Prussian control. The respect shown to the privately owned Banque de France by Prussian troops during the War of 1870–1871 was also cited as evidence of the advantages of a privately owned central bank.[58]

Indeed, there were grounds for thinking private status could enable the principal note-issuing bank to take an independent stand against government policies. The Bank of England's status as a privately owned institution was to lead at least two of its governors in the twentieth century to exercise independence from government to an extent that was nothing short of high-handed.[59] The Reichsbank, on the other hand, did fall under greater political control in the runup to the First World War, despite the hopes of those liberals who had called for an institution free of government manipulation and as Richter had predicted.

In the wider context of the relationship between the state and the economy, the arrangements for monetary issue and the independence (or otherwise) of note-issuing authorities in the runup to the First World War reflected a difference between the dirigiste states of the continent and the liberal economy of Britain where the Bank of England resisted attempts to bring it under the state's control. A good example of this difference in outlook is presented by the relative preparation under government direction of the French and German central banking institutions for the First World War compared to the unpreparedness of the Bank of England.[60]

Commenting on the subordination of monetary policy to purely political and national ends in the nineteenth century in the context of the unification of Italy, Foreman-Peck concludes:

1. economics will generally play second fiddle to politics.
2. money as a symbol of national unity matters much more than as a possible instrument of economic policy.[61]

These are interesting comments of wider significance for our themes. The importance of money as a medium of national identity certainly did gain weight during the period of nation building in nineteenth-century Europe and for most of the twentieth century. As we will see, this function of money as a reflection and symbol of sovereignty and a means of binding together component parts of newly formed states remained important through the majority of the twentieth century. However, there are indications that toward the end of the twentieth century and since, the role of currency as a foundation stone of sovereignty is losing ground. Even in the nineteenth-century standard-ized multinational monetary systems, such as the Latin and Scandinavian Monetary Unions, were devised to facilitate trade across national borders, thereby asserting the primary importance of money not as declaration of national individuality but rather as a functioning tool of commerce. We will see how these attempts were made in the nineteenth century to create mon-etary systems that were not defined and constrained by national borders.

NOTES

1. Charles P. Kindleberger, *A Financial History of Western Europe* (London: Routledge, 2006), 48.

2. Ibid.

3. Alexander del Mar, *Barbara Villiers: A History of Monetary Crimes* (Hawaii: University Press of the Pacific, 2004), 49–50.

4. There was an amusing twist to the story of the Massachusetts pine tree shilling. The Boston mint was willing to mint any bullion submitted to it, which encouraged the West Indian buccaneers to submit their ill-gotten gains for minting, which they then promptly exported, leaving the colony short of coinage. See del Mar, *Barbara Villiers*, 51.

5. Del Mar, *Barbara Villiers*, 54.

6. Ibid., 55.

7. Benjamin Franklin, *A Modest Enquiry into the Nature and Necessity of a Paper-Currency* (1729), http://xtf.lib.virginia.edu/xtf/view?docId=legacy/uvaBook/tei/FraMode.xml;chunk.id=d7;toc.depth=100;brand=default.

8. Alexander Hamilton, "Report of the Secretary of the Treasury, Alexander Hamilton, on the Subject of a National Bank: Read in the House of Representatives Dec. 13th, 1790," https://fraser.stlouisfed.org/title/report-secretary-treasury-alexander-hamilton-subject-a-national-bank-3677.

9. Glyn Davies, *A History of Money: From Ancient Times to the Present Day* (Cardiff: University of Wales Press, 2002), 465.

10. Ibid., 462.

11. Walter Isaacson, *Benjamin Franklin: An American Life* (New York: Simon & Schuster, 2003), 222–23.

12. World Digital Library, "Constitution of the United States," https://www.wdl.org/en/item/2708/, and quoted in John F. Chown, *A History of Money from AD 800* (New York: Routledge, 1996), 159.

13. Ron Chernow, *Alexander Hamilton* (New York: Penguin Press, 2004), 347–48.

14. Michael Foot and Isaac Kramnick, eds., *The Thomas Paine Reader* (London: Penguin Classics, 1987), 194.

15. Ibid., 195.

16. Chernow, *Alexander Hamilton*, 351.

17. Ibid., 352.

18. Chown, *A History of Money from AD 800*, 161.

19. Davies, *A History of Money*, 469.

20. Alexis de Tocqueville, *Democracy in America* (Everyman's Library, 1994), 409.

21. Ibid., 409.

22. Ibid., 410.

23. Craig Karmin, *Biography of the Dollar* (New York: Three Rivers Press, 2008), 108.

24. Chown, *A History of Money from AD 800*, 168–71.

25. Ibid., 185.

26. Liaquat Ahamad, *Lords of Finance: The Bankers Who Broke the World* (London: Windmill Books, 2010), 56.

27. Giulio M. Gallarotti, "The Scramble for Gold: Monetary Regime Transformation in the 1870s," in *Monetary Regimes in Transition*, ed. Michael D. Bordo and Forrest Capie (New York: Cambridge University Press, 1994), 29–30.

28. Ibid., 56 n 89.

29. Angela Redish, "The Latin Monetary Union and the Emergence of the International Gold Standard," in *Monetary Regimes in Transition*, ed. Michael D. Bordo and Forrest Capie (New York: Cambridge University Press, 1994), 71.

30. Redish, "The Latin Monetary Union and the Emergence of the International Gold Standard," 71.

31. Eric Helleiner, *The Making of National Money: Territorial Currencies in Historical Perspective* (New York: Cornell University Press, 2003), 35.

32. James Foreman-Peck, "Lessons from Italian Monetary Unification," Working paper 113, Austrian National Bank, 2006, 2. https://www.researchgate.net/publication/4801732_Lessons_from_Italian_Monetary_Unification.

33. Ibid., 7, 14.

34. Kindleberger, *A Financial History of Western Europe*, 136–37.

35. Helleiner, *The Making of National Money*, 107.

36. Foreman-Peck, "Lessons from Italian Monetary Unification," 16.

37. Redish, "The Latin Monetary Union and the Emergence of the International Gold Standard," 71.

38. Foreman-Peck, "Lessons from Italian Monetary Unification," 18.

39. Ibid., 17; and Michael Bordo and Lars Jonung, "The Future of EMU: What Does the History of Monetary Unions Tell Us?," Working paper, National Bureau of Economic Research, 1999, 11, https://www.nber.org/papers/w7365.

40. Ibid., 11.

41. Ibid., 11–12.

42. Kindleberger, *A Financial History of Western Europe*, 138, 362.

43. Harold James, "Monetary and Fiscal Unification in Nineteenth-Century Germany: What Can Kohl Learn from Bismarck?" Princeton Department of Economics, 1997, 6, https://ies.princeton.edu/pdf/E202.pdf; and Bordo and Jonung, "The Future of EMU," 13.

44. James, "Monetary and Fiscal Unification in Nineteenth Century Germany," 10–11; and Bordo and Jonung, "The Future of EMU," 13.

45. James, "Monetary and Fiscal Unification in Nineteenth-Century Germany, 10–11, 17.

46. Ibid., 8.

47. Ibid., 8–9.

48. Gallarotti, "The Scramble for Gold," 28–29.

49. Mark Metzler, *Lever of Empire: The International Gold Standard and the Crisis of Liberalism in Prewar Japan* (Berkeley: University of California Press, 2006), 26.

50. Chown, *A History of Money from AD 800*, 89–91; Galarotti, "The Scramble for Gold in the 1870s," 61.

51. Ibid., 60 n 147.

52. James, "Monetary and Fiscal Unification in Nineteenth-Century Germany, 9.

53. Ibid., 13.

54. Ibid.

55. Ibid., 14.

56. Ibid., 15.

57. Marjorie Deane and Robert Pringle, *The Central Banks* (London: Hamish Hamilton, 1994), 46.

58. James, "Monetary and Fiscal Unification in Nineteenth-Century Germany, 18–19.

59. The two governors were Lord Cunliffe, who clashed with Prime Minister Lloyd George on the use of Britain's gold reserves to pay for US materiel during World War I, and Montagu Norman, who promoted a high degree of central bank independence from government oversight.

60. Paul Wilson, *Hostile Money: Currencies in Conflict* (Stroud: The History Press, 2019), 97–99.

61. Foreman-Peck, "Lessons from Italian Monetary Unification," 21.

Chapter 3

International Monetary Unions in the Nineteenth Century

Although national currencies accompanied the creation of nation-states in Europe and America from early modern times, there was no universal belief in the Middle Ages that the currency circulating in any state must be only that issued by its own central government. Indeed, some currencies issued by one state were widely accepted by others, the Venetian ducat being a leading example. Currencies were at that time judged and accepted by their value in many places, without any legal restriction forbidding the circulation of foreign currencies (although there were exceptions such as that of England where laws from the early Middle Ages forbade the circulation of foreign coins). Usually, the circulation of foreign currency would be a de facto decision by the population, although there is at least one medieval example of a political attempt to coordinate currency systems.

In 1327, the Kings of Hungary and Bohemia agreed on a currency system based on Hungarian gold florins and Bohemian silver groschen. This monetary agreement formed the basis for a general commercial treaty, which Poland also joined in 1335, designed to divert trade in precious bullion around Vienna, which had been profiting from its central European location astride the trade routes leading west from Hungary and south from Bohemia.[1]

But caveat emptor. The arrangement brought with it unintended consequences for Bohemia's domestic industry. As the silver now flowed westward toward Frankfurt, it was traded for cloth from the Low Countries and England and imported in such quantities that Bohemia's own cloth industry declined. The unintended consequence apart, however, this monetary and trade agreement demonstrated more than six hundred years before the commercial and monetary agreements of the European Union that European states could cooperate for a common purpose, even if it was to the disadvantage of another European state.

In the nineteenth century, more structured efforts to coordinate the monetary arrangements of various European states were made with the objective of promoting trade. The Latin and Scandinavian Monetary Unions—which should perhaps be better described as monetary confederations, given the lack of a central authority—relied on the goodwill of independent states to adhere to the agreed-upon rules. It was no doubt this absence of a central overseeing authority that led to the collapse of the two unions.

THE LATIN MONETARY UNION

France's bimetallic standard—fixing the franc to a specific weight and fineness of both silver and gold—was first adopted in 1803 and then imposed on parts of Europe as a result of the expansion of French power on the continent during the Napoleonic Wars. Subjugated territories such as the Netherlands had dropped the standard after the Napoleonic Wars, but others had abandoned it, then readopted it by choice, including Belgium, which had itself seceded from the Netherlands in 1830. Switzerland and Italy adopted the bimetallic standard as one of the features of their drive to achieve their political unions in 1848 and 1861, respectively. In the cases of Belgium and Italy, both countries already owed to some extent their existence as independent, unified states to French intervention: when Belgium broke away from the Netherlands in 1830 an attempt to reassert Dutch authority in 1831 had been blocked by France. In 1848, Italy's efforts to break away from Austrian control was supported decisively and militarily by France. In the case of Switzerland, the decision to adopt the French system over the German approach to money was sealed by the fact that, at that time, there was no single German system but rather two systems, one operating in northern Germany and one in the south. And, in terms of the use of money for purposes of political influence and national identity, Germany was effectively half a century behind France, which had first imposed its monetary system on some of these European countries at the start of the nineteenth century.[2] The adoption of a single unified system, such as that of France, could offer a stable, ready-made system desirable for a fledgling nation-state. Contemporary with this political attraction on the part of some European states for bimetallism was an international enthusiasm for free trade treaties and harmonized standards in weights, measures, and coinage as a means to promote trade.[3] Following a turbulent period of nation building, the spirit in the air was one of international cooperation and harmonization of standards.

But it would be naïve to imagine that there was no mood of national ambition and aggrandizement involved. Much of the drive toward the creation of one of these monetary unions was provided by a man whose very name and family history spoke of ambition. Louis Napoleon, nephew of the great Bonaparte, had attempted, unsuccessfully, to seize power in France by means of coups d'état in 1836 and 1840. Despite this checkered background, he had by 1848 succeeded in getting himself elected president of France and, in December 1851, at the third, this time successful, coup attempt had transformed into Emperor Napoleon III (1852–1870). Determined to live up to his uncle's titanic reputation and to assert his own presence on the international stage, the new emperor's reign was marked by military adventures: assisting Italy to break free of Austria, forming an alliance with Britain to confront Russia in the Crimea, and providing military support for a failed attempt to install an Austrian archduke as emperor of Mexico. At the same time, the emperor was engaged in expanding France's overseas empire, notably in the Far East, and securing France's existing colony in Algeria. His government was dependent on the Banque de France and French commercial banks for funding. Those banks in turn favored the circulation of both gold and silver largely because of the success they had enjoyed in the arbitrage trade of the two precious metals.[4] The emperor's decision to promote a bimetallic system was therefore driven ultimately by the need to finance his imperial ambitions overseas rather than by any fundamentally sound economic thinking.[5]

A conference of the states favoring bimetallism, convened in Paris in 1865, was aimed at the introduction of a "uniform and universal coinage" and was prompted by the fact that somewhat debased Swiss and Italian silver coins, which were only 83.5 percent fine compared to the 90 percent fine coins of France and Belgium, were circulating in the latter two countries, obtaining seigniorage gains for Switzerland and Italy, and replacing in circulation the finer locally produced silver coins of France and Belgium, which in turn were disappearing from circulation in a classic example of Gresham's law. France's initial and unilateral reaction had been to reduce the silver content of most of its own silver coins to 83.5 percent in line with those of Italy and Switzerland. In an additional measure, Swiss coins were not to be accepted in payment of customs dues owed to France.[6] But those were only stopgap measures. The more substantive attempt to resolve the problem was the treaty on the Latin Monetary Union, which came into force on August 1, 1866, with France, Italy, Belgium, and Switzerland as original signatories and Bulgaria, Greece, and the Papal States joining a year later.

The participating states agreed to produce coins to a specific set of denominations and standard of fineness at 83.5 percent, which France had already adopted in line with coins of Italy and Switzerland. Gold was to be coined in face values of five, ten, twenty, fifty, and one hundred francs, with silver minted in denominations of five francs and lower. Thus, both silver and gold five-franc coins existed. Low-denomination coins from any of the signatory countries would be accepted by each and any of the state treasuries in payment of dues up to a maximum of one hundred francs. Each state treasury would also be obliged to exchange into gold or five-franc silver coins any of its own token or low-denomination coins accumulated and submitted for conversion by the other countries.

Although Belgium had proposed the adoption of the gold standard at the conference of 1865, the idea was rejected in favor of bimetallism. While the question of coinage manipulation by means of debasement for the purpose of gathering increased seigniorage had been tackled, no limits on the issue of paper money had been established, a gap that France and Italy both went on to exploit at times of difficulty.[7] In Italy's case, convertibility of banknotes into specie had been suspended during its war with Austria in 1866. Small-denomination privately produced notes were issued, and vast quantities of Italian notes circulated around the union.[8]

In 1867, the restlessly ambitious Napoleon III convened a second conference to promote the expansion of the Latin Monetary Union as a truly international currency. Much attention was given to the possible alignment of the English sovereign, the American half eagle, and a new twenty-five-franc gold coin, which would replace the existing twenty-franc coin of the Latin Monetary Union as the axis around which a new, global monetary system would turn. Other, ancient issues of monetary reform were debated: the right range of gold and silver coins to produce a balanced denominational structure and how to assign new values to coins when changes in the gold-to-silver rate of exchange took place. The most important conclusion of the conference was that an international monetary regime should be based on gold alone rather than on gold and silver, accepting the idea originally put forward by Belgium two years earlier. Certainly, by the 1870s some countries associated general economic success with a gold standard, based on the particular example of Britain, and mistook a correlation for a cause. The gold standard had, moreover, become "*a symbol of sound practice and badge of honour and decency.*"[9] It was associated with the "*civilised, rich and active*" nations, while silver was the established standard for "weaker and poorer" nations. In a strange way, misguided collective attitudes toward certain monetary régimes would be reprised nearly a century later when possession of a central bank came to be viewed as an indicator of national sovereignty and political maturity, while currency boards, associated with imperial monetary management, were abandoned as a relic of colonial subordination.

What is really interesting to us now about this concept of a global unified currency is that not only were Norway, Sweden, and Austria attracted to participating in the next stage of discussions but, most remarkably, given the dollar's current global preeminence, the United States of America was enthusiastic about an international currency. Rather less surprising was the refusal of Britain to participate in the discussions at this stage as anything more than an observer state. In Germany, Bismarck's dismissal of the fundamentally French concept as a "dream" was equally unsurprising.[10]

The debates continued in Britain and on the continent. The majority trend was toward gold, and France's defense of bimetallic standards is interpreted by some as having originally been a tactical ploy, to be surrendered in return for other gains. A second possible explanation revolves around the Bank of France's concerns that transition from bimetallism to a gold standard would involve redemption of silver coins for gold, which would stretch the Bank of France's gold reserves to the limit.[11] (In the event, the Bank of France's gold reserves were to be depleted not by redemption for silver but by indemnity following France's loss of its war against Prussia in 1871.)

For the time being, the free minting of silver in Latin Union countries continued to feed a bimetallic requirement for silver. That metal was drawn into France and other Latin Union territories, and gold flowed out—most notably to north European countries. Conditions were somewhat different in Italy, which increased silver coinage by 20 percent in order to export it to neighboring countries of the Latin Monetary Union, where silver coins, which were now worth less than their face value because of the depreciation of silver, could still be exchanged for gold at the formal gold-to-silver exchange rate.[12] France, determined to sustain the Latin Monetary Union, was prepared to absorb this trade, which for Italy was part of the answer to its fiscal shortfall.

Emergency measures were taken. In 1873, in France and Belgium these measures were restricted to limits on the amount of silver that could be coined in any one day. France suspended free minting of silver; that is, the public was not able to deliver silver in any form to the mint for conversion to coin, thereby slowing down the entry of silver into the monetary system. The minting of silver was limited throughout the Latin Monetary Union to six francs per head of the population.[13] The impact of market pricing on silver as a commodity undermined the principle of bimetallism as a viable basis for international cooperation. A five-franc silver coin now had the same nominal value as a five-franc gold coin, but nowhere near the same bullion value. Tax paid in debased silver on the basis of face value was a bad deal for the respective governments.

Belgium and Switzerland were at this point in favor of winding up the union, although they entertained reservations about Italy's willingness and ability to redeem all its token coins held by the other countries in the union in accordance with the 1865 treaty. France and Italy in any case stood firm against dissolution, fearing the costs of redeeming silver coins for gold.[14] In January 1874, a yearly limit on the coinage of the silver five-franc piece was imposed across the union. The value of silver, however, continued to decline in international markets. Coinage of five-franc silver pieces was suspended first in France and then in Belgium in 1876 and subsequently throughout the entire Latin Monetary Union in 1878, although Italy indicated that it intended to continue coining silver.

As the central protagonist in the Latin Monetary Union's drama, France's conduct of its monetary policy has been subject to particular scrutiny. Even though representatives of Belgium, Switzerland, and Italy favored a gold standard during the discussions on the foundation of the union, as did, indeed, the French representatives themselves, the French Ministry of Finance maneuvered to keep the issue out of the legislature, where there would have been a bias toward gold.[15] The ministry's operations were consistent with strong support for silver at the Banque de France and commercial banks that had successfully participated in the silver arbitrage trade.

More sinister interpretations of France's adherence to the bimetallic standard as an instrument of political power seemed justified when a French official spoke of circumstances where *"France will bring a great influence with her forty millions, or, if expected annexations are realized, her one hundred millions of people using her monetary system."*[16] It may be that the official did not really know what he was talking about, was bragging without substance, or was bluffing in discussions with receptive interlocutors. Either way, the idea that France might enjoy an extended sphere of influence based on her monetary system had occurred to at least one senior official. Perhaps a more pragmatic point of view is expressed by the idea that, although Napoleon III himself needed the banks' financing for his territorial ambitions overseas, he was not inseparably wed to the principle of bimetallism but was waiting for the right moment and conditions to cede the principle in return for other concessions.[17] Eventually even the Banque de France's support for silver caved in when it became aware of the amount of gold that was leaving France in the 1870s.[18] In 1878, France finally dropped bimetallism and converted to the gold standard. Currency issued by member states of the Latin Monetary Union continued to circulate, but the rules of engagement were changing every few years to cope with changing circumstances.

As, during the First World War, government expenses of France and Italy escalated, coinage alone was an inadequate basis for money supply particularly because much of the silver coinage was melted down and exported. Note issue increased in each country, forming the overwhelming mass of money in circulation and remained in circulation after the war. With little coinage to move between the member states and paper notes now having legal tender status only in the country of issue, the Latin Monetary Union de facto had come to an end. Switzerland and Belgium finally drew to an end their involvement in the union in the 1920s.[19]

From its high point of bimetallism through a lengthy period based on the gold standard and finally a wartime acceleration in the issue of fiat money, the principles of the Latin Monetary Union had been compromised under the pressure of external events: the international decline in the value of silver, the decision of Germany and other north European states to adopt the gold standard, and the exigencies of war. The Latin Monetary Union eventually just faded away. It is not difficult to imagine other currency systems following a similar path to oblivion.

THE SCANDINAVIAN MONETARY UNION

Like much of Europe, the Scandinavian states were on a silver standard in the middle years of the nineteenth century, and much of the coinage in any one of the three states had originated in the other two, as had been the case in the Latin Monetary Union. All three states—Norway, Denmark, and Sweden—were using the riksdaler, or imperial dollar, as the unit of account, exchanging at the following rate: one Norwegian specierigsdaler equals two Danish rigsdaler equals four Swedish riksdaler.

The exchange rate of Norwegian and Danish daler was more or less in line with the value of those coins assessed by silver content, ensuring that arbitrage operations were not worthwhile. The silver content of Swedish daler, however, meant that the intrinsic value of the coins was greater than the official exchange rate to Danish and Norwegian coins. It was therefore possible to make purchases with Norwegian and Danish coins in Sweden, while Swedish coins would be melted down or exported.

These conditions led to debates on the ideal monetary standard and system for the Scandinavian states, with all three countries leaning toward the gold standard due to the fact that their principal trading partners, Germany and Britain, were both on the gold standard.[20] The perceived connection between Britain's economic success and its adherence to the gold standard had been a factor leading Germany to begin the process of adopting it in 1871, and evidence to the US monetary commission in 1876 stated that *"the prosperity of England is largely due to its monetary standard."*[21] A belief that one size might fit all—that the gold standard of Britain would work just as well to deliver prosperity and progress in countries with quite different economies, banking, and legal systems—was widespread. If Germany was prepared to adopt the standard, so much more convincing was the argument in favor of gold. The Scandinavian states—Norway, Denmark, and Sweden—followed the German lead in adopting a gold standard on the basis of a convention between them late in 1872, which went on to become the monetary standard of the Scandinavian Monetary Union founded in 1875. The fall in silver values in 1873 and the evident lack of confidence in the bimetallic system evinced by Belgium and Switzerland in that year only made the case for gold more compelling.

From another point of view, the economic attraction of a unified monetary system was reinforced by a political and cultural mood of pan-Scandinavian cooperation favoring closer bonds between the three states, although there were nationalist elements in Norway that were less than enthusiastic about the plan.[22] Conferences over the period of 1863–1872 resulted in the common currency union of 1873 between Sweden and Denmark, with Norway joining two years later.

Replacing the daler as the common unit of account, the new Scandinavian krona had a fixed value in gold, and token coins of silver and copper were to be produced at a fixed 80 percent fineness. The treasury of each country would accept the coins of the other two in unlimited amounts, but there was a limit on coinage acceptable in payment of private debts. Although the union standards did not formally cover banknotes until 1894, those of each country circulated in the others from the beginning.

At the beginning of the First World War, Scandinavian notes were, along with those of most developed countries, declared inconvertible into gold, permitting the money supply in banknotes to increase without constraint. Notes from the various countries no longer traded at par. The export of gold was also prohibited, and gold coins produced by one country ceased to circulate freely among the others. Coins of the participating states ceased to trade one for one.

Although the Scandinavian Monetary Union dissolved under the pressure of the First World War, the internal monetary relationships had fared better than those of the Latin Monetary Union. There was no deliberate attempt by one country to issue excessive volumes of substandard coinage to gain seigniorage advantage over the other members, as Switzerland and Italy had done. A single standard based on gold avoided the difficulties associated with bimetallism and the arbitrage opportunities associated with the gold-to-silver ratio whenever the value of one metal to the other altered significantly in the wider marketplace. Notes from one country of the union were acceptable in the other countries. The Scandinavian Monetary Union, despite the advantages it had over the Latin Monetary Union, nevertheless did not survive the collapse of the gold standard.

Bordo and Jonung point out that the dissolution of the Latin and Scandinavian Monetary Unions was facilitated by the fact that each member state still had its own central bank, which made the transitional process easier.[23] Equally, the fact that each state retained its own central bank points to the reality that the Latin and Scandinavian Monetary Unions were monetary confederations, which were looser than a true union in the way they were administered; member states were obliged to coordinate policies rather than be subject to a single homogeneous policy from above. The success of any such loose monetary confederation lacking a central decision-making body is dependent on the consent of its participants, and the lack of a shared polity makes it all the more easy for participants to withdraw.

But the importance of the existence of these two systems lies in the fact that they embodied the idea that currencies should be coordinated in such a way as to improve trade across borders rather than create another barrier to transactions. The monetary sovereignty of the issuing states was of secondary importance. They were conscious attempts to decouple monetary matters from national sovereignty. That the systems failed due to problems in governance has, unfortunately, lent credence to a supposition that only a currency issued by a nation-state can be truly successful. This was why, at the point when the euro system was under huge pressure during the sovereign debt crisis of 2009–2010, many commentators looked back to the nineteenth-century unions as clear evidence that the euro was doomed to fail.

NOTES

1. Peter Spufford, *Money and Its Use in Medieval Europe* (Cambridge: Cambridge University Press, 1988), 169.

2. John F. Chown, *A History of Money from AD 800* (New York: Routledge, 1996), 84–85; and Eric Helleiner, *The Making of National Money: Territorial Currencies in Historical Perspective* (New York: Cornell University Press, 2003), 134–35.

3. Angela Redish, "The Latin Monetary Union and the Emergence of the International Gold Standard," in *Monetary Regimes in Transition*, ed. Michael D. Bordo and Forrest Capie, 68–85 (New York: Cambridge University Press, 1994), 69–71.

4. Giulio M. Gallarotti, "The Scramble for Gold: Monetary Regime Transformation in the 1870s," in *Monetary Regimes in Transition*, ed. Michael D. Bordo and Forrest Capie, 15–67 (New York: Cambridge University Press, 1994), 22.

5. Ibid.

6. Michael Bordo and Lars Jonung, "The Future of EMU: What Does the History of Monetary Unions Tell Us?," Working paper, National Bureau of Economic Research, 1999, 14, https://www.nber.org/papers/w7365.

7. Bordo and Jonung, "The Future of EMU," 15.

8. Thomas J. Sargent and Francois R. Velde, *The Big Problem of Small Change* (Princeton, NJ: Princeton University Press, 2002), 316.

9. Gallarotti, "The Scramble for Gold," 18–19, quoting Joseph Schumpeter, *History of Economic Analysis* (London: Allen and Unwin, 1954), 770.

10. Chown, *A History of Money from AD 800*, 88–89.

11. Bordo and Jonung, "The Future of EMU," 15 n29.

12. James Foreman-Peck, "Lessons of Italian Monetary Unification," working paper 113, Austrian National Bank, 2006, 18; and Bordo and Jonung, "The Future of EMU," 16.

13. Chown, *A History of Money from AD 800*, 91.

14. Bordo and Jonung, "The Future of EMU," 16.

15. Gallarotti, "The Scramble for Gold," 59.

16. Harold James, "Monetary and Fiscal Unification in Nineteenth-Century Germany: What Can Kohl Learn from Bismarck?," Princeton Department of Economics, 1997, 7, https://ies.princeton.edu/pdf/E202.pdf.

17. Helleiner, *The Making of National Money*, 131, 134.

18. Gallarotti, "The Scramble for Gold," 56.

19. Helleiner, *The Making of National Money*, 144.

20. Denmark's decision-making vis-a-vis monetary systems remains geared to that of its principal trading partners. It has held back from membership in the euro partly because it had received a derogation from its obligation to join that currency system along with the UK. Denmark's policy toward the euro was pragmatic: had either Sweden or the UK, Denmark's principal trading partners, joined the euro, Denmark would have joined (author's personal conversation with the Ambassador of Denmark to the UK, 2009).

21. Gallarotti, "The Scramble for Gold," 20.

22. Bordo and Jonung, "The Future of EMU," 17; and Helleiner, *The Making of National Currency*, 135.

23. Bordo and Jonung, "The Future of EMU," 22.

Chapter 4

Money and Empire

While nineteenth-century Europe wrestled with the challenges of maintaining monetary unions where membership was entirely a question of choice, Britain and other imperial powers (including France, which was also at the center of the Latin Monetary Union experiment) had to come to terms with the challenge of managing currency arrangements and supply for very remote colonies. History had thrown up two fundamentally different approaches to these challenges that might have served as lessons to imperial administrators. Either the sovereign power could try to impose strict control of the currency arrangements in its further possessions, or it could accept that the challenge of doing so was beyond the political power of the imperial center. Regional trading realities, rather than ideology and questions of political sovereignty, would often prove to be the deciding factor in their calculations.

An examination of the currency systems of various empires—and of the British Empire in particular, the most far-reaching geographically of all the empires—explains the starting point for many colonies selecting a currency regime in the postcolonial era. The leadership of some of those states thought the imperial system served them well. More, however, concluded that independence should be accompanied by a complete change in the means and mechanisms by which money should be managed. To understand the decisions of newly independent governments in matters relating to currency, we need to understand the nature of the imperial currency systems that existed, in some cases, until the second half of the twentieth century.

THE OTTOMAN EMPIRE

When the Persian Ilkhanid dynasty lost control of the further reaches of its empire and the last of its governors fled Anatolia in or just before 1326, its Ottoman vassals seized the opportunity to issue coins for the first time bearing the name of their own sultan, Orhan Bey. Their issue of their own coinage was therefore a signal of the Ottomans' assertion of independence.[1] As the Ottoman Empire subsequently expanded into Europe and further into Anatolia, it, like the Ilkhanids, initially pursued a policy of decentralizing the production of coinage. From the fifteenth century to the early part of the seventeenth century, the Ottomans operated about forty mints producing the silver akçe. But, over a period of nearly twenty years, beginning about 1620, the number of mints declined to about thirty and then to about four by the 1640s, almost certainly reflecting a decline in the demand for a depreciated locally produced silver coin and its substitution to some extent by foreign coinage, rather than any political imperative to maintain tighter control over production.[2]

The fact is that the Ottomans did not impose a single, homogeneous monetary system on their newly conquered territories. It is true that the gold coins called sultani were produced according to identical standards of weight and fineness aligned to the Venetian ducat in much of the empire, but the decision to issue them in any one region was dependent on whether that region was considered to be a fully integrated and secure part of the empire. The sultani were not, for instance, minted in the more remote, autonomous regions of Wallachia, Moldova, and the Crimea. At the very edge of Ottoman power—in parts of Hungary—coinage from Poland, the Hapsburg lands, and smaller independent principalities of Hungary circulated more freely than the Sultan's own coins.[3] Surprisingly, in the Balkans, which had been so attractive due to their silver mines, and even in Anatolia, the production of silver akçe slowed down in the early part of the seventeenth century and, eventually, mints in those regions began to close toward the middle of the same century with the inevitable result that the local population adopted various foreign coins for their transactions.[4] Newly conquered territories were allowed to operate varying standards for their silver coinage according to the dictates of local conditions.[5]

Thus, even during periods of tighter central control from Istanbul in the eighteenth century, Egypt appears to have preserved the same degree of independence in coinage standards as it had enjoyed as a subject land of the Roman Empire. Gold coins produced at the mint in Cairo, which were supposed to be produced to standards laid down by Istanbul, in fact were produced with a poorer standard of gold content. Enjoying the same nominal value as the real thing in Istanbul, the coins from Cairo enjoyed strong circulation in Istanbul, driving out of circulation the locally produced, higher-quality coins.

Şevket Pamuk suggests that the Ottoman authority over the monetary regime in its empire was weaker the farther away the province was from the capital.[6] This contention is also supported by the internal disorder in Yemen, aggravated in part by the debased locally issued akçe in the sixteenth and early seventeenth centuries. Pamuk notes that this civil disorder sometimes had to be put down by military intervention.[7] In conditions of weak central control and inadequate supplies of currency from the imperial center, a variety of debased silver and copper coins of local production, as well as Dutch and Spanish trading coins, were allowed to circulate in Yemen.

At the other end of the Ottoman Empire in the Crimea, the monetary autonomy of a khanate, which enjoyed a degree of independence from the sultan, was reflected by the fact that its silver coinage bore the khan's symbols and not the sultan's name.[8] That was the limit of the khan's independence, however. He did not enjoy the sovereign right of minting gold coins.[9] And, because the Crimea was at the very extremity of Ottoman authority, a variety of other coins were allowed to circulate there, just as they were in Yemen: Dutch thaler, Spanish pieces of eight, and Polish coins.[10] Again, foreign "trading" coins circulated in the western extremities of Ottoman sovereignty: in Algeria, Spanish pieces of eight, and in Tunis, Venetian ducats, gold coins from Sicily and Malta, and, in due course, the Spanish eight real piece (piece of eight), which emerged as the most popular of them all.[11]

In the east of the Ottoman Empire, a heavy silver coin called the shahi was set at an unrealistically high exchange rate against other Ottoman coins, such as the akçe or the sultani. The high "nominal" value of these shahi coins, compared to their relatively debased silver content, made them an attractive form of payment—especially when an individual was to pay taxes at face value rather than in accordance with the silver content. One theory for the overvaluation of these coins concerns currency competition with Iran, which was at war with Ottoman Turkey in the late sixteenth century.

Judged by the homogeneity of its monetary policy—or lack of it—the Ottoman state might have seemed more of a confederation, like the prerevolutionary colonial states of America, rather than a centralized imperial state. Foreign coins circulated in various territories—for instance, in North Africa, Yemen, and the Crimea—that owed allegiance to the sultan, and most of those territories were permitted to operate their own mints and monetary systems with a degree of independence even when, in the eighteenth century, the Porte exercised greater centralizing authority than it had done in the seventeenth century. But, before we judge too harshly, it should be recognized that, at the peak of the Ottoman Empire and well after, currencies traveled more freely and foreign currencies operated as media of exchange more commonly than is now the case. Even at the height of Britain's imperial power in the second half of the nineteenth century, London was unable to force sterling on remote colonies, such as Australia, India, and Hong Kong, whenever a much more convenient regional currency presented itself.

INDIA UNDER THE MUGHALS

A different approach was applied by the Central Asian Timurid dynasty in the management of the monetary system of its Mughal Empire (sixteenth to nineteenth centuries) in India. A series of reforms began with the introduction of a new style of coinage in the 1560s reflecting the dynasty's own Islamic religion and Central Asian culture. This was followed in 1577–1578 by an organizational reform of coin production during the reign of the Emperor Akbar. A new cadre of mint masters was appointed accountable for the security and standardization of the currency, and in time the number of operating mints would be reduced, leaving only six mints in northern India authorized to coin gold and silver. A few years later—1580–1581—the mints were further reduced to only two authorized to mint gold and silver, one of them being located at the headquarters of the imperial army. It is, however, unclear as to whether mints were closed down as part of a security consideration or in recognition of changing requirements for capacity, one suggestion being that the coins of the previous Suri dynasty had by that time been fully recoined into Mughal coins, entailing a reduction in the minting capacity required.[12] Mints authorized to produce coins in copper were located close to either the source of the raw material or treasuries where quantities of coins captured from the Suri dynasty were stored, making the recoinage of these obsolete coins that much more convenient.[13]

By creating a centralized imperial department responsible for the coordinated imposition of imperial monetary policies across all Mughal mints, the administration established the footings for a rigorously controlled homogeneous monetary system that lasted well into the seventeenth century. The department also played a vital role as the transmitter of imperial propaganda, using the currency as a means of promoting the emperor's authority by broadcasting his name around the empire and associating it in popular minds with a well-run monetary system.[14]

By 1595, however, a further change of policy reversed this consolidation of minting facilities, such that four widely distributed mints were producing gold coins, fourteen were producing silver rupees and forty-two were minting copper coins. What brought about this reversal of policy? We might speculate that, after thirty years, the Mughal grip on India was sufficiently strong that the administration no longer feared loss of control of money. At the same time, given the distances involved, it could be that a very small number of mints were no longer able to supply enough coins to the farther reaches of the imperial domain. Early empires, including those of Rome, China, and seventeenth-century England, had struggled to supply the farther reaches of the lands under their control with sufficient specie. Some imperial administrations—for example, the Ilkhanids of Persia and the Mughals with varying degrees of success—took steps to establish mints in the more remote areas of their lands, perhaps recognizing that the ability to circulate their own coins in those regions was an integral part of their claim to exercise authority there. Equally, they may have merely found that the security and logistic challenges of distributing large volumes of coin over long distances was most easily avoided by devolving the minting operations to the provinces. The real reason, however, could have been once again the simple requirement for expanded capacity to cope with another major recoining exercise. In the last decade of Akbar's reign—1595–1605—the silver rupee had come to replace the copper *dam* as the principal unit of exchange, and a number of silver mints were opened to cope with the demand for coining facilities. By the end of Akbar's reign, only two of the provinces in his northern Indian empire had no silver mint.[15] It is impossible to ignore the timing: the empire had converted from copper to silver in the era of the sixteenth-century price revolution, when Europe was flooded with New World silver, which in turn made its way eastward along the trade routes to India. With the arrival of vast quantities of silver and the decision to rebase the currency from copper to silver, increased minting capacity was required.

Overall, rigorous control of the circulating currency remained a key feature of the Mughal administration, differentiating it quite clearly from the Ottomans' willingness to permit the circulation of many different foreign coins in their territories. In Mughal India, foreign coins were not accepted as a unit of exchange for transactions but rather had to be recoined as Mughal currency. This approach, however, was not available to the administrators of Britain's empire. The distances involved were too great, the circumstances of overseas markets too diverse, and, at least by the middle of the nineteenth entury, Britain's overseas administrators too free thinking in their approach to the establishment of workable monetary systems.

THE BRITISH EMPIRE AND ITS MONETARY SYSTEMS

Many legislative measures had been taken in England since the tenth century to prohibit the circulation of foreign coins in England. This matter was the subject of legislation late into the nineteenth century. In 1870 the introduction of the Mint Bill expressly removed the power of the Crown to make foreign coins legal tender, thus removing an option last exercised (at least in theory) by Edward IV during the Wars of the Roses. The Chancellor of the Exchequer, in introducing the bill, explained that the Crown's privileges in the governance of coinage had to be stated explicitly lest their absence be interpreted as cancellation of those powers. Pointedly, he noted that the

Crown retained the right to introduce any coin it pleased into British domin-ions.[16] In reality nothing was quite that simple.

Problems of currency supply to the American colonies in the eighteenth century were a foretaste of similar issues that were to challenge London in the management of a widely dispersed maritime empire in the following century. Consisting of between 22 and 25 percent of the world's land surface and embracing more than one fifth of the world's population, Britain con-sumed 20 percent of the world's exports from 1860 to the start of the First World War, and sterling was used to invoice the largest part of world trade.[17] As the financial capital of the world, its position on the gold standard set the benchmark for all other nations aspiring to be countries of some consequence. In these circumstances, the government in London had to consider how the gold standard would work not only in the mother country but perhaps also in far-flung countries whose economies could hardly support the convertibility requirement that underpinned the standard.

At the height of its empire, Britain was operating on the gold standard with a remarkably small reserve cover of gold to banknotes issued by the Bank of England. According to the Palmer Rule, named after one of the bank's gov-ernors, 30 percent of notes issued would be covered by gold and silver, while the remainder would be covered by bonds and other securities. If Britain was unable or unwilling to cover all of its own banknote issue with gold, how could it possibly extend a truly convertible gold standard to all the countries of the empire? An upsurge in gold production in the second half of the nine-teenth century, much of it coming from Britain's colonies in South Africa, Canada, and Australia, helped to keep the wheels turning, but, as European countries followed Germany on to the gold standard, much of the production of these new territories left British control. Some colonies—India and Hong Kong, for instance—had long run their economies on the basis of silver, and attempts to introduce gold failed. A creative solution was required, or those colonies had to be allowed to go their own way in monetary matters.

CANADA AND THE DOLLAR

From the first issue of banknotes by the Bank of Montreal in 1817, Canada displayed a natural tendency to adhere to the unit of value and account of its nearest and most important trading partner, the United States. Notes were issued by a number of banks in New Brunswick, Quebec, Kingston, Nova Scotia, and Toronto in the 1820s and 1830s, many of them still denominated in pounds in a loose arrangement of banknotes issued by commercial banks, which was not out of keeping with the prevailing arrangements in America and Britain at the time. But by the 1830s and 1840s, notes might be denominated in both pounds and dollars, facilitating their circulation in the United States, just as notes issued by US banks could circulate in Canada. US dollar coins also circulated in Canada, particularly again in those areas where trade with the United States was greatest. The absence of a single national currency in both countries and the prevalence of notes issued by private banks made the circulation of notes a commercial matter rather than one of sovereignty. Notes issued by provinces, such as Nova Scotia and Prince Edward Island, with closer trading ties to Britain, rather than the United States, elected to issue their notes in sterling denominations. The diverse nature of currency issue was of sufficient concern to prompt discussion in the Canadian Assemblies in 1820 and 1821 of the possibility of creating a government-owned bank with sole rights of issue.[18]

Attempts to enforce a sterling currency were made by authorities in London and their senior representatives in Canada as early as 1825 when the treasury in London sought to impose the circulation of British silver and copper coinage in the Canadian provinces. These efforts, designed partly to encourage trade with Britain, but also to reinforce the political ties to the imperial center, were, however, not successful against widespread local preferences.[19] In fact both the British sovereign and the US ten-dollar coin, as well as US and Spanish silver dollars, were legal tender in the Province of Canada from its establishment in 1841. That year, proposals were put forward by the governor general to abolish note issue rights by commercial banks, a proposal that was three years ahead of Britain's Bank Charter Act of 1844, which began the long process of abolishing the issue of notes by commercial banks. The provincial assembly was however persuaded to vote out the proposal by the commercial note-issuing banks in a move echoing the opposition of the commercial banks in the United States to the privileged position of the Second United States Bank in the 1830s.

The move toward a dollar-based currency gathered speed in 1851 when an act for the maintenance of provincial accounts in dollars and cents was passed by the Canadian legislature but delayed by the government in London, which was still hopeful of a sterling-based currency. A compromise law of 1853, providing for the use of both sterling and dollars as units in provincial accounts, was the outcome and a clear and early indication that London was unable to dictate monetary policy to the colonies. Even Nova Scotia, previously adhering to sterling, together with New Brunswick had adopted the dollar as the unit of value in 1860, thus pointing the way for the rest of Canada. Despite the limits on London's power over Canada in monetary matters, the 1853 law did result in Canada's currency being fixed to a specific amount of gold, and its banknotes became fully convertible.[20]

When in 1867 the separate provinces in British North America were brought together in an act of confederation, the scene was also set for the replacement of the provincial currencies by a single dominion currency. Even this did not remove the issuing rights of commercial banks, however, because they were allowed to continue to issue notes of no less than four dollars in denomination. US dollars, alongside other foreign coins, also continued to circulate in Canada until, in 1870, legislation addressed the question of US coins in Canada. While steps were taken to eliminate other foreign coins from use in Canada, where their circulation was seen as something of an embarrassment to legislators, American gold coins were granted legal tender status. US silver coins were also granted legal tender status but at a 20 percent discount to their nominal value, which meant that the coin was worth less than its bullion value, with the inevitable consequence that they disappeared out of circulation, to be returned to the United States or melted for the bullion value.[21]

The final step in the consolidation of currency issue in Canada was not to come until 1934 when the Bank of Canada Act was passed, establishing a single central bank of issue and providing for the gradual phasing out of commercial banknotes. Ironically, given the monetary link with America, one of the reasons for the establishment of the Bank of Canada was the desire to lessen the influence of New York's commercial banks on the international value of the Canadian dollar.[22]

In Canada, as in other British dominions, the importance of regional markets and neighboring trading partners carried greater weight in the development of currency systems in the long run than did the preferences of the imperial center in London.

INDIA CHOOSES SILVER

In the early days of the East India Company's trading operations in India during the seventeenth century, it had been obliged to turn over all its imported coins to the Mughal imperial mints for recoining before they could be used to buy luxury products for export to England.[23] Coins in India had to bear the emperor's name and symbols of authority in order to achieve widespread acceptability even if they had been issued by princely states enjoying a degree of autonomy. Attempts to challenge the royal authority to coin—known as sikka—could incur the most drastic response. The Dutch East India Company had managed to produce coins at its mint in Pulicat in the middle of the seventeenth century identical to the Mughal silver rupee in weight but, significantly, bearing the company's insignia.[24] But, in the 1690s when the English East India Company minted coins that were identical to imperial Mughal coins in silver fineness and weight but bearing English monarchical symbols, the Emperor Aurangzeb, stung by this threat to his authority, authorized an attack on the company's settlement at Bombay.[25] By the early nineteenth century, the Mughal government had become less rigorous in enforcing the emperor's rights: coinage was being struck by foreign occupying powers and princely states exercising a degree of autonomy from the center.[26] By 1835 the currency in circulation included East India Company coins bearing the portrait of William IV of England and five years later, the image of his successor, Victoria.[27] From a point when the company could enjoy the right to strike coin only by complying with Mughal restrictions, it had progressed to assume the right of sikka, the issue of coins, traditionally reserved for the emperor and reinforced by the appearance of his image on currency.

The company had also extended its monetary power into the area of banknote issue. Under the administration of the company, there had been a decentralized banknote issue arrangement in India, permitting the banks of the presidencies of Bombay, Madras, and Calcutta to issue notes at a time when Britain itself was moving toward greater reduction of the number of issuing banks.[28] The Indian uprising of 1857 changed everything. The shock to the British government and the East India Company leadership in India of a rebellion against British rule was such that power was transferred from the East India Company to the Crown and a program of reorganization followed. The power of the regional presidencies to create laws independently for the issue of currency was withdrawn in 1861 by the Indian Councils Act.[29] Paper money was issued by the government in that year, each rupee being backed with a fixed amount of silver. Although paper currency was now under the control of the government of India rather than the East Indian Company, this was not to say that there was a single issuing center. Beginning in 1861 for a period of forty years, India (as it was then, which included modern-day Pakistan and Bangladesh) and Burma, annexed to India, were divided into seven regions or "circles," each of which issued currency. The notes of one circle were legal tender only in that circle, a situation reversed only by an act of 1910. At the same time a significant development occurred when provision was made for "*bankers and merchants to make trade remittances between the currency centres by means of telegraphic orders*," a technology that had been pioneered in America.[30]

India's familiarity with silver was of long standing. The country had changed from a copper-based commodity currency to a silver one at the end of the sixteenth century. Its paper notes were now backed by silver rather than gold. But the value of silver on the world market was about to decline. As American cotton came back on the market after the Civil War ended in 1865, India's cotton exports decreased and so, accordingly, did its import of silver. This, together with increased global production of silver and European policies increasingly favoring gold, contributed to the dramatic depreciation of silver. Because the rupee was backed by silver, its value in gold depreciated in step with that of silver to gold. The depreciation of a silver-based rupee was seen as beneficial to exporters, although damaging to other sectors and extremely disruptive to the Indian government's budgeting process. While the country's revenues were earned in silver, government-to-government debts owed to London, including charges for the deployment of troops in India, were paid in gold.[31] The system worked effectively enough until 1893, but by this stage most countries had ceased to mint silver, reducing demand and worsening the depreciation of that metal. By 1872, only three major economies remained on silver: the United States, Mexico, and India (China and Japan were not considered major economies at the time, and both were still on the silver standard). In 1873, the United States switched to the gold standard. In 1893, the mints in India were closed to the free minting of silver (the ability of members of the public to bring silver to the mint to be coined).

From 1892 to 1913, India's monetary system developed gradually as a result of recommendations made by committees and legislation by the governing council of India. The result was the genesis of the gold exchange standard, which was managed, according to J. M. Keynes, who began his career in the India Office in London, by "administrative practice only" in the absence of a single act of parliament regulating the system. Keynes's comment points out an important reality of the development of currency systems in general: where the sovereign power is unable to supply enough currency for the purposes of an expanding economy, alternatives will be developed by those closest to the "front end" of the problem, whether they be commercial operators or, as in the case of India, imperial administrators far from the central seat of power.

Although silver was no longer being minted freely, as late as 1898 rupee banknotes were issued covered not by gold but mostly by silver coin and also by Indian government securities and sterling notes held in London, which were themselves covered by gold and other securities in an arrangement known as the gold exchange standard. Other nonmetallic reserves in the form of sterling-denominated securities could also be held in London as cover for rupee issue. Sterling notes were to play the part of a multiplier of the gold cover. The rupee notes in turn formed the reserves of Indian commercial banks, enabling them to make loans and effectively create money on the basis of fractional reserve lending. In this sense, the assets included not only sterling notes but also rupees, which were backed by sterling (i.e., gold-convertible) notes held in London. Applying the standards of those times when gold was the only real money and paper merely a claim on it, this financial architecture might have seemed little short of a Ponzi pyramid scheme. If each asset holder were to claim their portion of gold at the same time, the entire structure would have collapsed because there was not enough gold in reserve to cover all liabilities.

In 1899 British gold sovereigns were declared legal tender in India, and proposals for minting them at a branch of the Royal Mint in Bombay were far advanced but fell afoul of resistance by the British Treasury and the Royal Mint itself, presumably because this would have drawn gold out of Britain and into India. At the same time, attempts were made to encourage the circulation of gold coinage but without success. The government tried various ploys to push gold convertibility. In 1900, currency offices in Calcutta, Madras, and Bombay were instructed to cash notes for gold unless silver was demanded. By March 1901, 6.75 million pounds in gold had been cashed for paper notes, but, of this, most of the gold ended up going abroad, being paid back to the government in settlement of taxes and other dues and most of the remainder ended up with bullion dealers. As an attempt to establish gold as the basis for India's circulating currency, the exercise was a failure. The remaining gold in India was shipped back to London and held in a special account for India at the Bank of England.

Britain had similarly tried to impose a sterling/gold exchange standard system in 1903 on the Straights Settlements colony, incorporating Singapore and parts of modern Malaysia. However, as in India and, as we shall see, Hong Kong, the population feared that the silver-based currency that they operated and that was prevalent in East Asia would be undermined and protested against the plan.[32]

Writing in 1913, Keynes supposed that the failure of the attempt to force circulation of gold in India in 1900–1901 was due to the fact that the gold sovereign was too high a value for such a poor country.[33] Nevertheless, by 1913, the situation had reversed. Gold had flowed into India in substantial volumes, and the balance of the reserves had altered so that proportionately more backing for the rupee was held in gold in India than in securities, or silver, or gold in London. Be that as it may, the failure of Britain's attempt to force a gold-circulating currency in India should have contained a warning to other imperial powers intending to impose unsuitable currency standards on their overseas colonies: it will work only when or for as long the population wants it—unless of course draconian measures are introduced to support the change.[34]

For India and for the other colonies, the principal value of the gold exchange system was the use of gold for the settlement of international debts, even when the local currency system did not require local convertibility into gold. Indeed, Keynes, surveying the international currency situation, observed that gold-circulating currency in the hands of the general population was not helpful in the event of a crisis or a foreign drain on gold. In such circumstances, Keynes added, the gold reserves of a country needed to be centralized—and held as a reserve. Keynes's warning was to be particularly pertinent at the outbreak of the First World War in 1914.[35]

HONG KONG CHOOSES SILVER

Similar attempts to impose the gold-based pound in Hong Kong in 1845 met with failure because the Chinese, Hong Kong's main trading partners, simply did not want gold. Consequently, gold sovereigns traded at a significant discount—sometimes, as much as 30 percent. The right of the Chinese to determine their own preferences in monetary terms was upheld by Hong Kong's supreme court, which ruled that they would not be obliged to accept gold if they wished to be paid in silver. The issue of paper money in Hong Kong also developed along local lines rather than adhering to a London-imposed structure. Banks that were chartered could issue notes under regulation from the Hong Kong government, with the benefit that their notes would be accepted in payment of taxes, while other unregulated institutions, generally partnerships, would issue unregulated notes, which were not accepted in payment of taxes and consequently commanded less trust among the population. The volume of notes issued was, moreover, determined by the silver reserves held by the relevant bank. An influx of silver acting as a reserve permitted an increase in note issue and as a result an increase in the money supply. In the event of an outflow of silver, the opposite effect pertained. Whatever else was the case in London, in Hong Kong silver ruled. Indeed, the colony's determination to exercise autonomy in monetary matters led to an ordinance according to which a bank chartered by London for note production in Hong Kong would need similar approval from the authorities in Hong Kong.[36]

The value of silver in Hong Kong was reinforced by the fact that it was the basis of the currency of mainland China. A change of policy in China on silver would force the authorities in Hong Kong to adjust. Such a change of policy occurred in the early 1930s. The price of silver in global markets surged as a result of an American policy to buy silver and force up prices. China responded in 1935 by demonetizing silver and selling it on the international market. In other cases (Germany in the 1870s, Japan in the 1890s, and Romania in the 1990s), a silver reserve would be sold off and converted to a gold reserve. However, in the case of China the profits were spent, leaving a fiat currency as the sole basis for its monetary system. Because China was the single most important source of Hong Kong's silver dollars, the Hong Kong authorities had two options: accept a massive deflationary effect caused by the decline in silver stocks or bow to the inevitable by issuing inconvertible notes and withdrawing from the silver standard. This, Hong Kong finally did in December 1935. Note issue was from then on backed not by silver but by noninterest-bearing certificates of indebtedness that could be purchased from the government.

Hong Kong had rejected a gold-backed sterling note issue as early as the 1840s because it did not reflect the local preference for silver and the realities of trade with China, where silver predominated. It had then been forced to abandon silver when its principal trading partner, China, abandoned that metal in response to market incentives.

In an empire over which the sun never set, local factors determined the basis of the monetary regime for widely dispersed colonies with differing regional conditions in trade and resources. The British Empire in currency terms was relatively loose and by no means homogeneous in its monetary regimes.

AUSTRALIA: DOLLAR OR STERLING?

Founded as a British penal colony in 1788, Australia presented its first colonists with the daunting challenge of creating a society from scratch so far removed from the mother country that a journey of 13,000 miles by sea from London to Botany Bay around the Cape of Good Hope might take four months. Even a journey to the nearest substantial British base, that of the East India Company in Madras, 6,200 nautical miles away, required weeks at sea. The remoteness of this most distant of all colonies (at least at the end of the eighteenth century, before Britain had established colonies in Singapore and Hong Kong) meant that the colonists were left to fend for themselves in many ways, in providing food and building materials and in developing their own economic system. Troops guarding the convicts and the colony, as well as the convicts themselves once they had served their sentence, were free to engage in private enterprise, selling produce they had grown themselves or their services to those able to pay. But for payment, the supply of specie and notes was both erratic and improvised.

Coins had been—and continued to be—carried to the colony by troops, immigrants who had freely chosen to make a new life in Australia, the crews of visiting ships, and even the convicts themselves. But, inevitably, paper supplied the gap left by inadequate amounts of coin. Work performed by craftsmen was settled with bills to be paid by the British Treasury, and produce sold to government commissary stores was paid for with store receipts. These two forms of paper became the first circulating currency notes in New South Wales. As with tobacco deposit notes in early colonial America and deposit notes for unwieldy copper "platmynts" in seventeenth-century Sweden, circulating paper currency appeared as a resourceful response to the absence of a more orthodox medium of exchange.

In addition to the store receipts that formed the first paper currency in circulation and that, being issued by government commissariat stores, held the status of a government issue, there were also personal promissory notes issued by traders, craftsmen, and private individuals. Subject to the origin of its issue—either the official bills or receipts, or the privately issued promissory notes—the paper was known as either "sterling" or "currency," respectively. The proliferation of these personal notes and the frequency with which they were being counterfeited prompted action on the part of the local authorities. Attempts by the earliest governors of the new colony to bring the issue of promissory notes under control failed, another instance of the general principle that, where a government fails to supply adequate volumes of currency, the private sector—that is, the general population—will creatively supply the shortfall.[37]

Lachlan Macquarie, the dynamic, reforming governor of the new colony from 1810 to 1821, took the first major step in establishing a regular currency for the colony by buying 40,000 Spanish dollars, which were modified thoughtfully to reduce the possibility of their leaving the country. Silver dollars (as well as copper coins) had been brought to the new colony but often left again rapidly in payment for imports. Macquarie addressed this silver drain by ordering that the center of the dollar be knocked out of the coin, thereby reducing the quantity of silver left in the coin, leaving the coin with a greater nominal value than its bullion value. With its silver content thus reduced, the motive for exporting the coinage was undermined. In an attempt to kill off the circulation of petty "currency," he applied to London for permission to charter a note-issuing bank, a proposal that was rejected by London on no more sound grounds than that Macquarie was not empowered to create such a bank. In so rejecting a proposal that would have provided a basis for proper management of paper currency, the government in London had reacted with a shortsightedness reminiscent of London's obstructiveness toward the introduction of paper currency in colonial America half a century before. But both London and the administrators in the new colony recognized the limits imposed on authority by the distances involved. The administrators in the colony persevered in their plans, and the Bank of New South Wales was born.

In 1822 Macquarie's successor as governor, General Thomas Brisbane, went a step further in exercising local autonomy in monetary matters when he attempted to establish the silver dollar as the basic medium of exchange and unit of account. In 1823, the governments in New South Wales and Tasmania issued decrees formally establishing the dollar as the unit for public accounting and public sector salaries. Regulations set by Macquarie establishing sterling as the unit of account and medium of exchange were rescinded. The project lasted only three years, however, when it was reversed by a decision of the home government in London to impose the circulation of British coins as the medium of exchange and sterling as the unit of account, just as it had attempted in Canada at that time. Even after British coins arrived in the territory in 1825, dollars continued to circulate, with a sterling nominal value, which were widely accepted. Because the colony was still dependent on dollars for coinage, they continued to circulate until about 1830. At about the same time, a number of other note-issuing banks were established, which, along with the notes issued by the Bank of New South Wales, drove out of circulation the petty currency issued by commissariat stores and private traders.[38]

Even these new arrangements were insufficient to supply the requirements of the new colonies for currency. In 1834 the authorities in Hobart, Tasmania, proclaimed the circulation of South American dollars to be legal. In the same year, a bill was passed establishing the sikka rupee of India as legal tender. Significantly, legal tender status for the US dollar was ruled out because the authorities did not foresee any significant trade with North America. Seen alongside trends in Canada toward the use of the US dollar during the same period and Hong Kong's adherence to silver at a later time, it is evident that regional market forces could have just as much, if not more, influence over policies in the colonies toward the circulation of foreign currencies than did direction from London.

But local initiatives were still not able to evade imperial intervention. Lord Glenelg, colonial secretary in London, issued instructions in 1836 to colonial administrators requiring them to submit for royal approval all legislation on circulating currency. All the same, Spanish and Mexican dollars, and briefly, French Francs, were still in circulation in 1847. By 1849, however, the poor quality of Mexican dollars added to the growing reluctance of the banks to accept silver dollars at the established sterling rate (four shillings and four pence to the dollar). By that year, British coinage alone circulated, and it was generally believed that British silver coin was the only legal tender, although people, including those in the banking world who should have known, were unable to point to the legislation conferring legal status.[39]

Within two years, the course of Australia's monetary history changed again. Gold had previously been found in the colony, but the government had discouraged dissemination of the news, fearing it might destabilize the relatively new settlement. But the news of more finds in 1851 could not be suppressed, and it sparked a gold rush. The production of gold in what is now the state of Victoria encouraged the legislative council to seek approval to set up a branch of the Royal Mint in Australia so that the mined gold could be converted locally into specie. The government in London agreed and promulgated an Order in Council and Royal proclamation that stipulated that, although the gold coinage of Australia should be of the same weight and fineness as the gold coinage of Britain, the designs should be different to ensure that the coins would not be returned to Britain to circulate there. These and British gold coins would be legal tender in Australia. Silver coinage from

Britain would, as in the British Coinage Act of 1816, have legal tender status up to a maximum transaction of two pounds.[40]

In fact, the growing confidence of the legislators and administrators in Australia expressed itself in a petition to the secretary to the colonies in 1855 requesting legal tender status for the Australian gold sovereign throughout Britain's overseas colonies, a request that was initially dismissed out of hand. Within two generations, a colony of castaway convicts had grown into a confident settlement of frontiersmen ready to display their economic success through the prestige of their own gold coinage. In 1860 the request was repeated, and, although there was some reservation about granting legal tender status for Australian coins in Canada and Newfoundland, by 1871 gold coins minted in Sydney and in the second mint at Melbourne had legal tender status in the United Kingdom and its colonies.[41]

Commercial banks continued to issue notes except in Queensland, where the only notes having legal tender status were those issued by the state treasury. This state of affairs was finally brought to an end by the Australian Notes Act of 1910, which placed all responsibility for note issue and the resultant benefit of seigniorage in the hands of the commonwealth treasury. The circulation of British coins in Australia also ceased at this time. In 1909 the Australian government had requested a share of the seignorage accruing to Britain on British coins circulating in Australia. When Britain declined, the Australian government passed legislation on the circulation of Australian coinage, thereby securing the seigniorage for Australia. At this point, Australia was truly independent in a monetary sense.[42]

MAURITIUS

Initially a Dutch and then a French colony until it was seized by Britain in 1810 during the Napoleonic Wars, Mauritius, under British administration, was, in the words of one nineteenth-century monetary historian, "*an instructive lesson in the futility of arbitrary, if well-meant endeavours to substitute an alien scheme of currency for that prescribed by trade relations.*"[43] In the early years of British occupation, the currency supply reflected Mauritius's position on international trade routes: Spanish, American, Sicilian, Austrian, British, French, and Indian coins all circulated on the island. From the middle of the century, when gold was discovered in and exported from Australia, there seemed to be a possibility that Mauritius would be drawn onto the gold standard. The pull of trade with India, however, was irresistible, and, although Britain had tried to impose sterling as the legal currency for Mauritius in 1825, at roughly the same time as similar measures had been attempted in Australia and Canada, by 1876 the Indian rupee was established as the legal tender for Mauritius.[44]

As an example of the principle that British colonies were ultimately permitted to align their monetary regimes with regional monetary systems based on trading relationships (true of, for example, New Zealand, Canada, Hong Kong, and India), Mauritius conformed to the trend. The island's long-term importance in monetary history, however, lies in its role as the first territory—colonial or otherwise—to establish a currency board. Note issue had been in the hands of two commercial banks—the Bank of Mauritius and the Commercial Bank—until they both crashed in 1847, as a consequence of which the government of Mauritius decided to establish a single government currency board having a monopoly of note issue.[45]

Under this new arrangement, the currency board was permitted to issue notes only when backed by reserves of which one-third to a half was to be in coins and the remainder in securities, the total value being equal to the value of notes in circulation. In other words, there was to be 100 percent backing for the notes issued by the board. Although the board began by using local securities for this backing, it eventually switched to less volatile British securities.[46] Mauritius's example was increasingly adopted by other British colonies and remains the original model for those countries still operating currency boards today.

NEW ZEALAND

From the 1840s, sterling was the legal tender of New Zealand. A shortage of coins in the 1840s and 1850s led local traders to experiment with the private issue of notes, an experiment that fairly quickly failed, to be succeeded by the issue of private copper coinage, a practice that survived into the 1880s. At the higher end of the denominational structure, gold coins produced in Melbourne had legal tender status by 1869, with gold coins minted in Sydney following suit in 1871. The circulation of Australian coinage in New Zealand reflected the realities of the trading relationship that existed between the two and bore parallels with the circulation of American coins in Canada and vice versa.[47]

What was special about New Zealand's currency system was the creation of the Colonial Bank of Issue in 1847 as the sole bank of note issue (although the Union Bank of Australia, which had hitherto issued notes in New Zealand, was allowed a grace period to continue issuing). Only three years after the establishment of the colony of New Zealand in 1841, the Bank Charter Act of 1844 had been passed in Britain, providing for the gradual removal of issuing rights from commercial banks and the establishment of a monopoly of note issue at a central bank. This development was promoted by Earl Grey, the secretary of state for the colonies, as the new best practice in monetary regimes, and in New Zealand local legislation was passed in 1847 adopting the approach to monopoly public issue. Accordingly, the Colonial Bank of Issue opened its doors in 1850, as a governmental entity with monopoly of note issue, coming into operation second only to the Mauritius Board of Currency Commissioners, although the legislation in New Zealand had preceded that in Mauritius. The Colonial Bank's note issue was also distinguished by the fact that it was managed on the basis of 100 percent cover in securities and coins for the notes issued, as with the Mauritius Currency Board arrangement.

There was still, however, enthusiasm in some quarters for the establishment of chartered commercial banks of issue, and, under political and commercial banking pressure, an act was passed in 1856 winding up the Colonial Bank of Issue while a further local act was passed in the same year permitting the governor to authorize the establishment of commercial banks of issue. While there was resistance to this liberalization of note issue and a campaign was launched to promote the creation of a state bank of issue, which would secure the benefits of seigniorage for the public rather than for individual shareholders in commercial banks, legislation to that effect was not passed. As far as banknote issue was concerned, New Zealand had taken quite the opposite direction to Britain by reversing monopoly note issuing rights in favor of free banking. By the 1890s, there were six banks issuing notes in New Zealand, three of them Australian.[48] Indeed, it was partly to reduce the Australian banks' monetary influence that the Reserve Bank of New Zealand, with its monopoly note-issuing rights, was finally established in 1934.[49]

CURRENCY BOARDS AND THE EMPIRE

During the nineteenth century and the early part of the twentieth century, British colonies, starting with Mauritius, led the way in introducing currency board arrangements. The fact that the first currency boards emerged in some of the most remote outposts of the empire points toward the difficulty of maintaining a single homogeneous currency system across such distances at that time. It is also evident that the first currency boards emerged at a time of change in the currency regimes of Britain and its colonies. Following the introduction of the Bank Charter Act of 1844, which was a turning point in British monetary history, at a time when Hong Kong rejected the gold standard and Canada insisted on dual sterling-dollar accounting for the provincial governments, other colonies came up with their own solutions to the question of monetary management. In some cases—as in Mauritius, for instance—the development of a unique local arrangement was in reaction to a failure of free banking where combined commercial and note-issue responsibilities could threaten the foundations of the monetary regime of the colony. Central government in London also saw the benefits to colonial governments of concentrating seigniorage in the hands of the colonial authorities to help defray the costs of administration. The wide variety of economic conditions across the empire drove a pragmatic acceptance that separate colonies should have media of exchange and units of account of their own, which would be tied at fixed parity to sterling. To issue local currency, each currency board was required to buy or sell sterling at the corresponding parity to its own currency. The link to sterling at the peak of the gold standard, when sterling was dominant, provided exchange rate stability and a bedrock of confidence for inward investment to those colonies.[50] From the middle of the nineteenth century to the 1930s, currency boards were established in various parts of the empire: Mauritius in 1849, the Straits Settlements centered on Singapore in 1897, and British West Africa in 1912.

THE WEST AFRICAN CURRENCY BOARD

The creation of the West African Currency Board had its origins in the fact that the region was using vast numbers of British silver coins for domestic transactions. It has been suggested that in the first decade of the twentieth century almost as many British silver coins were put into circulation in West Africa as had entered circulation in Britain. While this was attractive to British traders importing and exporting between Britain and West Africa, it yielded no seigniorage to the local governments. There was also a growing concern that any large-scale repatriation of these coins to Britain could have a very injurious effect on the British monetary system. Both to protect against this possibility and to provide seigniorage revenues to support the administration of the colonies, a local currency based on a currency board was conceived. Despite opposition from British merchants operating in West Africa who preferred to retain the convenient use of sterling and feared that a new West African currency would not be reliably convertible in the long term (a set of objections reminiscent of the position of British merchants trading with American colonies in the middle of the eighteenth century), the authorities pushed ahead with the project.[51]

The West African Currency Board was significant in that most currency boards had started off by redeeming notes in gold or silver specie and then switched to sterling notes. The West African Board from its very inception redeemed local notes only in sterling notes, thereby placing sterling on the same footing as gold and establishing the sterling gold exchange standard as the basis for the currency board. As with other currency boards, at least 100

percent cover in sterling was required for the local currency issued. The idea
was subsequently adopted in other British territories overseas and then spread
to other countries. The model was also adopted at the end of the First World
War by British forces supporting anti-Bolshevik forces in northern Russia.
Yet another means of constraint, guaranteeing a limit to the issue of money,
was set by an arrangement whereby a very large proportion of the reserve
cover for the currency board notes was held in London, notably for the currency boards of South Rhodesia and the British Caribbean. This proportion of
those colonies' reserves might be used to invest in British government debt.
While those investments yielded interest to the relevant currency board, it
was also a useful source of investment capital for the treasury in London.[52]

In certain of these colonies, currency board reserves could take the form
of government securities issued by Britain or other dominions, but specifically not the securities of that same colony (except it seems in the case of
India). This constraint was designed clearly to prevent the local colonial
government from simply issuing increasing amounts of government debt to
provide the reserve needed to back increasing amounts of currency issue.
Such a situation was specifically forbidden, for instance, to the currency
boards of Ceylon (now Sri Lanka), the Straights Settlements, and the British
Caribbean. Restrictions on other currency boards in this respect were less
specific but more generally stated in that the securities allowed as a reserve
had to be approved by ministers in London.[53] Above and beyond the domestic
regulations governing the use of local securities as reserve backing for locally
issued currency, there was always, after all, a government in London overseeing the fiscal and monetary conduct of its colonies. Colonial governors were
not permitted to authorize legislation on currency matters without first refer-
ring the matter to the secretary of state for the colonies in London.[54]

Further currency boards were established after the First World War—the
East African Currency Board in 1919, Palestine in 1926, Hong Kong in 1935,
British Caribbean Currency Board in 1937, and currency boards in Southern
Rhodesia and Malaysia/Singapore/Brunei in 1938, with their local currencies
pegged purely to sterling.[55] By the late 1940s, some fifty countries, many
of them at the time still under British control, were operating a currency
board system.

As the trend toward the establishment of currency boards in British colonies picked up, there was also a move toward the establishment of central
banks in the dominions: South Africa had enacted legislation to create its
own reserve bank in 1921. Recognition of the special status within the empire
of six countries—Australia, Canada, The Irish Free State, Newfoundland,
New Zealand, and South Africa—was formalized in the 1931 Statute of
Westminster, whereby no law passed in Britain would be accepted in the
dominions unless the individual dominion requested that it be applied to it.

The statute implicitly but effectively guaranteed the monetary independence of those states where Britain's writ on currency matters had in any case not run for very many years.

This constitutional development, the international promotion of central banks in many other independent countries after the First World War, Britain's withdrawal from the gold standard in 1931, and the impact of the depression, provided conditions for the creation of central banks as opposed to currency boards in the dominions. The Bank of Canada and the Reserve Bank of New Zealand were created in 1934; India, while not formally a dominion until 1947, nevertheless acquired a central bank in 1935 in the form of the Reserve Bank of India, perhaps indicating that whatever its constitutional status, in monetary terms, it was already a dominion. The development of a central banking function in Australia was a slower process, starting in 1920 when the Commonwealth Bank took over from the treasury responsibility for the issue of notes. Further central bank powers were extended to the Commonwealth Bank under emergency legislation during World War II, but the entire central bank function transferred in 1959 to the newly created Reserve Bank of Australia.

So gold-producing dominions were comfortable with a gold-based currency; Asian colonies, where silver was long established, resisted attempts to impose a gold-based standard; and currency boards established in the interwar periods were based on sterling notes or sterling-denominated paper as cover for notes issued. In terms of its monetary regime, the British Empire was less a centrally dictated and homogeneous whole and more a federation of differing monetary regimes, varying in nature one from another according to regional preferences, natural resources, and, as in the case of a pure sterling paper-backed currency, prevailing international norms. Only the use of sterling as the ultimate reserve currency to which the others were fixed at parity and into which they were convertible provided a shared point of reference. In this general administrative sense, it might be possible to conclude that it had more in common with the Ottoman Empire's loose approach to currency than that of India's Mughals.

A number of British overseas territories—territories administered by the UK in respect of their foreign and defense policies, but with an enhanced degree of autonomy in domestic matters—continue to operate a currency board system, pegging their locally issued currency to the pound sterling (Falklands Isles, Gibraltar, and St. Helena) or to the US dollar (Bermuda, Cayman Isles).

Sterling's dominance as an international reserve currency tracked downward Britain's status as the global superpower, to the status of aging colonial power with diminishing territorial possessions overseas. Some economists and politicians in London early in the twentieth century had already seen the way the wind was blowing and advocated a voluntary step away from global leadership of the gold standard. Instead, they wished to see Britain settle for economic and monetary leadership of the empire. This approach certainly suited some of the dominions that wanted a system for coordinating currency exchange rates between themselves, but when the issue was debated at the London Imperial Economic Conference of 1923, no conclusions were reached. When in 1931 Britain came off the gold standard, a number of other countries followed it, again raising the question as to how Britain's colonies should relate to Britain's own monetary regime.

The idea of stabilizing the exchange rates of the various dominions was again raised at the Ottawa Conference of 1932, notably by Canada and Australia. But, although Britain had no objections to its colonies coordinating their exchange rates among themselves, Britain itself was not about to participate. Indeed, the sterling bloc developed on the basis of a series of individual decisions by participating states. Canada and South Africa took into consideration the strength of the US dollar as much as that of sterling in setting their own currencies' exchange rates.[56] European states, such as those of Scandinavia, also chose to peg to sterling for the purposes of stability, as did others, such as Argentina and Iran, expanding the sterling bloc beyond the empire.

Britain's reluctance in the 1930s to take a central, coordinating role, much less a commanding one, was a sign of the times: the empire had always functioned on the basis of multiple monetary standards and regimes without an attempt by the center—at least after 1830—to impose a single homogeneous system largely because over the course of the nineteenth century successive governments in London took a pragmatic view of what could and could not work in such a geographically and economically diverse empire. After the economic trauma of the First World War, the burden of war debts, and the failure of the brief return to the gold standard, Britain was even less willing or able to accept responsibility for managing a global economic system. Britain's power over the dominions was shown to have further diminished during the creation of a new world economic order at the end of the next war. But, in reality, its refusal to take a steering role in imperial monetary affairs between the wars was a straw in the wind—an early indication that Britain was already losing the will to administer an empire. The management of various monetary systems of a far-flung empire comprising countries operating in different regional markets and the difficulty, if not impossibility, of imposing a single homogeneous system across an empire was to prove a challenge also for France.

THE EMPIRE OF FRANCE

France's imperial monetary policy, like that of the other so-called "first rate" powers in the nineteenth century, developed by a process of trial and error. The empire was not created according to some calculated template of grand strategy involving a monetary plan applicable in all territories from the moment of their annexation.

Overseas expansion in the post–Napoleonic era began with the seizure of Algiers in 1830, followed by Tahiti in 1843, and continued throughout the nineteenth century, with French colonial activity spreading into West Africa and Indochina in the middle of the century. The pace picked up in the last twenty years of the century, particularly in Africa as France expanded into Congo and Madagascar, but military operations also reached as far as the northern border of Vietnam with China. France's humiliating defeat in the Franco-Prussian War 1870–1871, resulting in the relegation of France to the second position after Germany among continental European powers, prompted the country's political leadership to look beyond Europe not only as a source of economic development and raw materials but also as an outlet for the country's energies and *amour propre*.[57]

Although France's colonial expansion was by and large supported (or at least, after some hesitation, not rejected) by the government in Paris, the annexation of some territories was initiated by the independent action of zealous military officers (an admiral in the case of the seizure of Tahiti). For this class of empire builders, a lack of clear policy direction from the center on matters of colonization and the delays in communicating across long distances were insupportable. In their view, only decisive action on the part of the man on the ground could resolve local problems. Matters were made yet more complicated by the structure of government and ministerial respon-sibilities in Paris. For much of the period of colonial activity, there was no single and central ministry responsible for the administration of the empire: this work was divided at various times between the Ministry of the Marine, the Ministry of Foreign Affairs, and the Ministry of the Interior. It was not until 1894 that a Ministry for the Colonies was established. The administra-tive structures necessary for a centralized coherent monetary policy for the empire were thus absent.[58]

In such circumstances where the center offered unclear direction of and fragmented control over colonial expansion and local administrators were allowed to shape the local colony as dictated by local circumstances or meth-ods as they saw fit, it is hardly surprising that different territories developed in different ways. In parts of France's east Asian territories, the colonies might be administered through local "mandarins"; in Madagascar, French administrators governed through local chiefs representing the island's races. In Senegal, on the other hand, French municipal law was the basis of government, not colonial decree, and the country was represented directly in the French National Assembly.[59]

Beyond the administrative question of the optimal way to run individual colonies, there was a bigger debate underway: should the colonies be assimilated into the French state, or should the association of the colonies to metropolitan France be one of confederation—a halfway house between full integration and independence? If assimilation, then a range of administrative policies, based on the system of metropolitan France, would lead to harmonized policies across the empire; if association, then, inevitably, colonies would be left to develop certain policies, among them monetary regimes, suitable to their own circumstances.

To begin with, monetary policy seemed to militate against assimilation. Initially, currencies of the colonies were not to circulate in metropolitan France, and the French franc was likewise not to circulate in the colonies. This led to administrative difficulties for the exchange authority in France, which was unable to cope with a proliferation of colonial currencies being changed into French francs, so the situation was eventually simplified by imposing the metropolitan unit of account on all territories overseas.

Policy swung in the opposite direction in the second half of the nineteenth century as colonial expansion picked up. The issue of local banknotes was then entrusted to private banks in various parts of the empire, including the Banque de l'Afrique Occidentale, the Banque des Antilles, and the Banque d'Indochine. Demonstrating the ascendancy of association over assimilation as the basis for monetary policy, the governor of French Indochina declared the Piastre de Commerce, pegged to the Mexican silver dollar, to be legal tender in Indochina. This pegging arrangement lasted until 1895, at which point the silver content was reduced to discourage export of piastres. From 1920, the piastre was pegged to the franc at the rate of ten to one, and from 1921–1930, the piastre was convertible to gold, completing the journey from a silver standard to a gold standard modeled on that of British India.

Elsewhere in the empire, locally issued notes were fixed after World War I to the franc at one to one and at that rate were increasingly exchanged for French francs, which in France's Pacific colonies and Sub-Saharan Africa over time became the only circulating currency. So, while France's overseas empire began from the position of association, permitting a greater degree of freedom in the choice of local currency systems to its colonies, the market increasingly moved the currency regime toward assimilation as the century wore on—certainly, in some regions. France, in fact, seemed to be pursuing quite the opposite approach to that of Britain, whose failed attempts to install sterling and gold in its colonies had forced London to take a more accommodating approach to colonial wishes.[60]

In some cases, attempts by France to impose its own currency arrangements on colonized territories were resisted by the local population, which lacked faith in unfamiliar monetary tokens. Burkina Faso—occupied by France in 1897 when it was known as West Volta and formally incorporated into France's West African possessions in 1903—clung to its use of cowry shells as the medium of exchange and store of wealth, despite France's efforts to create what would at the time have been seen as a modernized monetary system.

Initially, local French authorities were not in a hurry to act against the existing cowrie monetary system, believing that it would gradually wither on the vine. But, before long, the movement to replace cowries gained momentum partly because cowries were simply inconvenient to count and partly out of concern that, as cowries were demonetized in other parts of West Africa, they would inevitably be drawn toward West Volta. In 1907, ten years after its first occupation of West Volta, France banned the import of cowries, and local treasuries were forbidden to accept local taxes paid in cowries.[61] In this way, the levying of taxes, it was hoped, would act as the final arbiter of the validity of money. If the cowrie was not acceptable for taxes, its legitimacy as currency would be limited. The reality though was that cowries continued to be preferred in rural areas as a store of value and as a medium of exchange for a range of other transactions.

Other measures to stop their circulation proved equally fruitless. In 1917, the ban on cowries in settlement of taxes was temporarily lifted with the purpose of gathering in vast quantities for destruction in the hope that the cowrie would be completely taken out of circulation. The effect was only to raise the exchange rate to the franc in favor of the cowrie. Other measures to promote the franc at the expense of the cowrie were adopted. Throughout the 1920s, refusal to accept francs in the marketplace was one of only fifteen offenses punishable without trial. Extraordinarily, these hordes of cowries were not completely flushed out until the 1940s. Even then, the cowrie continued to command the respect of the local population. As late as 1946, native officials in the province of Gaoua petitioned the regional commandant with a request that a portion of their salaries be paid in cowrie. Long after they had ceased to be used as currency, the cowrie retained special ritual and medicinal purposes. Just as Britain had found in its attempt to dislodge silver as the preferred basis for currency in India, Hong Kong, and elsewhere, local preferences stubbornly prevailed.

The shock of the Second World War forced monetary reform in substantial parts of the French Empire. The creation of the Caisse Centrale de la France Libre in 1941 for the issue of banknotes in French Equatorial Africa, which

was free of Vichy collaborationist control, was the first step in the nationalization of banknote issue, reversing the colonial policy of devolving banknote
issue to private banks. This de facto wartime nationalization of France's colonial issue was consistent with moves to nationalize the Banque de France in
metropolitan France, a process that was completed in 1945. Furthermore, the
common foreign exchange controls, pooled foreign reserves, and convertibility of the franc zone currency to French francs were imposed on the Sub-
Saharan franc zones after the war but before independence, measures that
laid the foundation for the franc zones in Africa (see chapter 9 on monetary
unions).[62]

The dissolution of France's overseas empire in the 1950s and 1960s led to
fully independent currencies for some countries and for others a system that
was little short of a currency board except that anchor currency reserves in
excess of 100 percent of the currency on issue are not legally required. Initially
pegged to the franc and subsequently the euro, this arrangement formed the
basis for the monetary unions in West Africa and Central Africa comprising a
number of France's former colonies. A monetary echo of France's Empire can
still be heard, albeit faintly, today, as we shall see in chapter 9.

PORTUGAL ABROAD

By the middle of the nineteenth century, Portugal's Empire was past its best.
The oldest of all the European empires with scattered possessions stretching
to the Far East, its colonies were now modest in terms of population and
wealth when compared to the overseas territories of Britain and France in the
Western Hemisphere, Africa, South Asia, or the Antipodes. French, Dutch,
and British possessions superseded Portugal's posts as the key entrepots
in trade with Japan; Portugal's West African territories dwindled in significance as the slave trade with the Americas was closed off by the activities of
Britain's Royal Navy.

Against this backdrop of colonial decline, the National Overseas Bank, or
the Banco Nacional Ultramarino, was founded in 1864 as a joint public–private venture to provide the colonies with stable currency, as well as credit for
businesses, with the intention of breathing new life into the flagging colonial
economies. Unlike French and British models, which established separate
currency-issuing banks or currency boards for each colony or group of currencies, the Banco Nacional Ultramarino was based in Lisbon and supplied
the currency for all of Portugal's overseas territories. Branch offices were
created in the colonies overseas, beginning with Angola and Cape Verde in
1865–1866, followed by other branches in Angola, Goa, and Sao Tome.[63]
Other aspects of the Banco Nacional Ultramarino's constitution distinguished

it from what we would now recognize as a central issuing authority. To begin with, it engaged in both commercial-banking and note-issuing functions at a time when some countries—notably Britain—were seeking to separate the two functions. This combination of commercial-banking and note-issuing functions was to appear in other banks in the Portuguese Empire and would lead in 1925 to the Portuguese Banknote Crisis.[64]

Despite—or perhaps because of—the relative weakness of Portugal's Empire in comparison with those of Britain and France, Lisbon sought and, in 1890, succeeded in expanding its overseas possessions to include Guinea in West Africa and South Nyassa Land, which was incorporated into Mozambique, creating what is known in Portugal as the Fourth Empire. With this expansion and the challenge of managing the vast surface areas of Angola and Mozambique, as well as other, remote and isolated possessions such as Macau and Timor in Asia, changes to the banking and currency-issuing arrangements became necessary. In 1901 new legislation was introduced permitting most provinces to have their own independent note-issuing banks, although there could be only one issuing authority per province. The exception to this arrangement was to be the creation of a single note issuer for all four West African provinces of Guinea, Cape Verde, Sao Tome, and Principe, replicating developments in France's overseas empire at that time when regional note-issuing banks were created to serve a group of countries. It can hardly have been a coincidence that the Banque de l'Afrique Occidentale, founded to serve France's West African territories, had also been established in 1901. Although the new legislation opened up the possibility of different banks serving different territories, in reality it was the Banco Nacional Ultramarino that retained the contracts for all territories.[65] The apparent liberalization of currency issue was in reality a fig leaf for a continued monopoly. Most, but not all, of the various colonial currencies issued by the Banco Nacional Ultramarino were from 1914 denominated as escudos and pegged at one to one to the escudo of Portugal.

In 1919 a new banking law allowed for the granting of sole issuing rights to a single bank for a period of twenty-five years. The possibility of different provinces choosing different note issuers was in effect abolished and a tender held for the exclusive award of rights to produce notes for all of Portugal's colonies, which the Banco Nacional Ultramarino won, with faint competition from one other Portuguese bank. Despite the Banco Nacional Ultramarino's twenty-five-year term of exclusivity of supply to the colonies, the colonial authorities in Angola decided to exercise a little local autonomy. The high commissioner of the colony issued a decree as a result of which the colonial administration contracted with the Banco Nacional Ultramarino for the exclusive issue of notes in Angola in return for two development "grants." The same agreement raised the ceiling for the fiduciary issue of notes (i.e., the notes that could be issued without full cover). The commercial benefits of increased note-issue rights, however, were not to last very long. When the Banco Nacional Ultramarino failed to deliver on its promise of development grants, the colonial administration in Angola created a new Banco de Angola, to which the Banco Nacional Ultramarino was forced to cede its note-issuing rights.[66]

Despite this turn of events, a further set of decrees passed in Lisbon in 1929, under the new national dictatorship government, reassigned to Banco Nacional Ultramarino exclusive banknote-issuing rights throughout Portugal's overseas empire, with the exception of Angola, for a period of thirty years.[67] In 1951 amendments to the constitution of Portugal's Empire converted its colonies into overseas provinces and proposed closer integration of the provinces with metropolitan Portugal. Among other things, this set out the requirement that the headquarters of Portugal's overseas central banks be established in Lisbon and that Banco Nacional Ultramarino escudos should be convertible into Portugal's own escudos and vice versa. As part of this set of reforms, Banco Nacional Ultramarino's rights as lead issuer of banknotes, granted in 1929, were reconfirmed.[68] At a time when Britain was beginning to dismantle her own empire, Portugal's efforts, directed by its long-term right-wing authoritarian prime minister, Antonio Salazar, to bind her colonies closer to her by monetary means, among others, was an attempt to resist the tides of history and the winds of change.

ITALY'S AFRICAN EMPIRE

While some European powers—notably Spain—lost empires in the nineteenth century and others at that time clung on to overseas possessions that they had seized in earlier centuries, yet another set of states, including Germany and Belgium, moved relentlessly to acquire territories overseas, sometimes by negotiation but more often by conquest. Italy, not long unified, sought its own share of the spoils.

Italy's banks of issue—the Banca di Napoli and the Banca di Sicilia retained the privilege of note issue until 1926, when they were finally absorbed into the Banca d'Italia—played an active part in the extension of Italy's power. Bonaldo Stringher, director general of the Banca d'Italia from 1900–1919, actively promoted the idea of Italy's expansion overseas because, in the thinking of the time, it would raise the country to the first division of European nations. The Banca D'Italia, the Banco di Roma, the Banco di Napoli, and the Banco di Sicilia were all encouraged to set up operations overseas in Eritrea, Somaliland, and Libya. In some cases, the function of these banks was to finance Italian trade and expansion, but in others they acted as banks of issue, albeit with mixed success in the early years.[69]

ERITREA

A stretch of Red Sea coastline purchased in 1869 from a local ruler by an Italian steamship company then became the first overseas possession of the Italian state by purchase in 1882. Over the next twenty-five years, Italian authority spread inland and farther along the coast. During this period of expansion and consolidation, lands were incorporated where a variety of currencies and currency substitutes (including salt bars, glass beads, and cartridges) circulated, foremost among them Maria Theresa dollars, but also rupees from India and currency from Egypt.[70]

Although the Italian authorities were not happy about the circulation of Maria Teresa dollars, they recognized their importance for the purpose of regional trade and therefore resisted the temptation to withdraw them from circulation. Indeed, quite to the contrary, the Italian authorities imported from Austria significant volumes to Eritrea for official use. Before too long, however, Italian authorities chose to introduce a new family of silver coins in 1890, the Eritrean thaler, produced in Italy, rather than pay Austria for production of Maria Teresa dollars.

Each silver Eritrean thaler was worth five Italian lira, but was of poorer quality silver than the Maria Teresa dollar and recognized as inferior by the indigenous population. Moreover, this was a period of particular volatility in the Italian economy and banking system, aggravated by the overissue of banknotes by various banks of issue. It was also a period of low demand for silver internationally because many countries had converted to gold. Consequently, the value of the Eritrean thaler would fluctuate in line with the market for silver. By 1898 Italian authorities had recognized the general failure of the Eritrean thaler and had withdrawn the coins from circulation, leaving the Maria Teresa dollar as the main circulating coin until the end of the First World War. Attempts to supplement the inadequate volumes of the Maria Teresa dollar with a new "Italian" thaler were similarly unsuccessful because again they were seen by the local population and trading partners in the region as substandard.

And, in the estimation of the local population, banknotes were even less credible than the Italian thaler. Banknotes shipped from Italy had been available in Eritrea since 1885, but shipments were suspended when authorities there reported back to Italy that the local population was unwilling to accept paper money. All attempts therefore to impose an Eritrean thaler, an Italian thaler, and banknotes had failed against the natural conservatism of the local population when it came to currency matters. A second shipment in 1885, which included notes from both the Banca d'Italia and Banco di Napoli, hardly fared any better because the colonial authorities observed that two different banknote designs aroused the suspicions of the local population. The Banco di Napoli notes were duly returned to Italy. Not until the outbreak of World War I did banknotes finally achieve greater acceptance in Eritrea, some thirty years after the first attempts to circulate them. Even then, acceptance was more marked in the urban settlements dominated by Italian immigrants than among the rural population.[71]

SOMALIA

Extending its territorial possessions in the Horn of Africa, Italy seized the port of Mogadishu in 1908. Two years later, the Italian authorities introduced the silver rupee as the local currency, pegged simultaneously to the pound sterling and to the Italian lira. A rise in the value of silver in the period after World War I led, predictably enough, to the hoarding and covert smuggling of the silver rupee abroad. Consequently, in 1920 the Italian government authorized the Bank of Italy to print Italian rupee banknotes in Rome for issue in Somalia that were initially supposed to be convertible to silver, presumably in an attempt to flush hoarded silver out and into circulation. Given the shortage of silver rupees and the internal and external drain of that silver, it was clearly impossible to honor that promise, and convertibility was suspended shortly after issue.

The Italian rupee notes were to remain legal tender only until July 1925, six months after Mussolini had assumed dictatorial powers, when by royal decree the Italian lira became the legal tender for Somalia. This was no indication, however, of a wider fascist policy to impose the currency of metropolitan Italy on its overseas territories, and in any case the Italian lira was in turn replaced by a colonial lira launched in 1938.

LIBYA

Caught up in the late nineteenth-century race for empire, Italian nationalism was disadvantaged by the fact that the country had not long been unified and was therefore slow off the starting blocks. The country's opening moves in the game of colonization in the Horn of Africa spoke volumes; France and Britain were not keen to take on more territory in the area, and even Egypt was content to cede the port of Massawa to Italy. Only Ethiopia had any real interest in competing with Italy for control of the area. Libya was a different matter. Italian nationalists looked across the Mediterranean and saw in Libya a land that had been conquered by their Roman forefathers. It was, for some Italians, a land that they should "take back."

The opening gambit in Italy's foray into North Africa was not, though, military. Instead, commercial companies were encouraged toward the end of the nineteenth century to acquire enterprises in Libya and to develop links through the export of products from Africa. In 1905 the Italian government followed these first tentative steps by instructing the Banco di Roma to establish branches in the principal cities in Libya, although its function there was to finance trade and not to assume the right to issue banknotes locally.[72]

Pressure from the irredentist, or nationalist, movement to expand Italy's overseas territories to include all those that had formed a part of the Roman Empire in the Mediterranean mounted, and provinces of the evidently weak Ottoman Empire, such as Libya and Tunisia, attracted particular attention. In 1911 Italian Prime Minister Giolitti declared war on the Ottoman Empire with the aim of seizing Mediterranean portions of its empire. As a result of the peace negotiations at the end of the Italian-Turkish War settled by the Treaty of Ouchy, Italy was awarded both Libya and the Dodecanese Islands in the Aegean. In December 1911 the Italian government authorized the Banco di Roma, the Banco di Sicilia, and the Banca d'Italia to open branches in Tripoli, Benghazi, and elsewhere in Libya. In contrast to her colonies in East Africa, Italy saw Libya as somehow an integral part of the homeland perhaps because Libya, unlike Somaliland and Eritrea, had been a part of the Roman Empire. For this reason, Libya was not provided with its own, separate currency but rather used the Italian lira.[73]

ETHIOPIA AND ITALIAN EAST AFRICA

In 1935 Fascist ambitions for an Italian Empire took another aggressive step forward when a short and brutal war against Ethiopia led to the absorption of that proudly unique country and culture into Italian possession, forming, together with Somaliland and Eritrea, the expanded colony of Italian East Africa. The invasion and occupation of Ethiopia became a cause celebre at the League of Nations and a test case of its effectiveness as a means of resolving conflict. Outraged international opinion looked toward France and Britain, leading members of the league with more reason than most to strive for peace following their experiences in the Great War, as the two states that might force Italy to withdraw. Although some leading politicians—notably Britain's Foreign Minister Anthony Eden—tried to bring resolution to the conflict by proposing mediation at the League of Nations, Italy rejected their efforts. Eden's suggestion that the League embargo oil sales to Italy was not taken up.

As early as August 1926, Italy's fascist leader, Benito Mussolini, committed his government to preserving an unnaturally strong lira, contrary to the best interests of Italy's export industries. In 1927, during the period of the resumed gold standard, the exchange rate of the lira was officially fixed at nineteen to the dollar or ninety-two to the pound sterling, and the minimum gold reserve, equating to 40 percent of the value of notes in circulation, was suspended. While many states, beginning with Australia in 1929, had withdrawn from the gold standard by 1931, Italy, together with a few other countries—France, Poland, and the Netherlands—held out until 1934. Mussolini's obsession with a strong lira betrayed a sentimental, rather than realistic, monetary outlook: a belief that a strong currency necessarily indicated a strong country and a strong leadership. To sustain these exchange rates and a gold standard, the country was obliged to obtain substantial foreign loans, cut back on budgeted public projects, force the population to hand over its holdings of foreign exchange, introduce currency controls, and withdraw silver coinage from circulation.[74]

Against this background, the Ethiopian war placed an unbearable pressure on Italy's gold reserves and monetary system. Italy's preparations for and actual expenditures in the opening stage of the war in Ethiopia beginning in October 1935 amounted to 3.5 billion lira; between that October and New Year's Eve 1935 the country's gold reserves fell from 3.9 billion lira to just over 3 billion lira. Kirshner[75] concludes that Italy lost between a third and a half of its gold reserves in the first six months of the invasion. In this precarious position, it is doubtful that Italy could have withstood sustained political, economic, and monetary intervention by France and Britain. The fact of the matter, though, is that Ethiopia was simply not seen as being of sufficient strategic importance to risk war with Italy or to push Italy further into the arms of a resurgent Germany. Italy's fragile monetary system was not put to the test.

The currency of this new African empire was the Africa Orientale Italiana (AOI) lira, printed in 1938 and issued by the Bank of Italy. It was at par with the Italian lira and indeed was identical in appearance to the lira except that there were some color variations, and, at the top of the note, the words "Italian East Africa Special Series" had been stamped, presumably to prevent quantities of these notes from being returned to metropolitan Italy, where they would have contributed to inflation. So, even though the AOI lira looked very similar to that of the homeland lira and was valued at par with it, it nevertheless fell short of the monetary status that Libya enjoyed purely by virtue of its history as a one-time Roman colony. But, as with so many of the other currency experiments in Italy's overseas possession, it did not last long, being abolished by force of arms as a result of the successful British campaign in 1941–1942 to oust Italy from East Africa.

Elsewhere, Italy's short-lived empire gave rise to a number of equally short-lived currencies. In Albania, a gold franc had been legal tender since 1936. When Albania was invaded by Italy in April 1939 before the general European war had broken out, a new national bank was formed under Italian control, and gold convertibility ceased. A series of banknotes, called the franc, with lower denomination notes, and coins called the lek, were issued bearing Albanian images overlaid with fascist symbols. The new franc was pegged to the lira at one to 6.25, and francs on issue were covered by Italian lira rather than gold. When in 1943 Italy withdrew from the Balkans and Germany's Reichswehr moved into Albania, the national bank was required to cover German military expenditures by expanded money supply. Albania's foreign reserves and gold were in due course transferred to Berlin. Italy's control of Albania's money supply was a short-lived affair.[76]

Two years later, Italian possessions in the Mediterranean were extended to include the Ionian Islands and an Ionian drachma issued, valued at par with the previous Greek drachma. The designs of the notes incorporated text in Italian, but the notes were denominated as drachma rather than lira, and in almost all designs the predominant theme was the glory of ancient Greece. At one and the same time, then, the design of these notes represented a nod toward local Greek sentiments and a wink toward Italy's expansionism. In the Italian-occupied province of Montenegro, in southern Yugoslavia, prewar dinar notes were allowed to circulate as long as they bore a stamp. Farther north, in the area that is now Slovenia, which had been absorbed by Italy as the Province of Lubiana, there was no attempt to install a new currency reflecting a combination of Italian and local imagery and symbolism. Instead, the lira of the homeland was allowed to circulate in that country, which, like Libya, had once been a province of Rome.[77]

Italy's brief conquest of these territories, culturally disparate yet generally geographically close to the motherland, occupied largely during the political and military turmoil of the Second World War, meant that the imperial power had little time to establish and nurture a coherent set of monetary policies. As we have seen from the examples of Italian East Africa and France's West African colonies, the monetary systems imposed by a conquering power would face resistance from the local population and require a surprisingly long period to achieve full acceptance.

GOLD AND THE AMERICAN EMPIRE

The basic principle of a gold standard was only instituted by law in the United States in 1900. In the same year, the US Bureau of Insular Affairs, tasked with managing America's administration of territories that had been surrendered by Spain at the end of the Spanish–American War in 1898, set about the introduction of a gold exchange standard in Puerto Rico and the Philippines. Emulating Britain's sterling-based gold exchange system, the imposition by the United States of the gold exchange standard on its newly acquired colony of the Philippines was the first projection of the US dollar overseas as a serious international currency.

Under this version of the gold exchange system, individuals and entities in the Philippines would use US gold dollars for overseas transactions, but, as with the sterling exchange system in many of Britain's colonies, the coins in domestic circulation were silver. The currency reserve was to be held in private banks in New York, positioning that city as the center of the gold dollar exchange system, in the same way that London was the hub of the sterling gold standard. The effect was to detach the Philippines from its ancient trading relationship with China and the silver standard, which had predominated in Asia, an outcome that British-administered Hong Kong had avoided. Equally problematic was the fact that revenues were gained in volatile silver, while debts to the United States were payable in gold, a difficulty encountered by the British administration in India.[78]

In a similar way, a gold exchange standard was established in Panama, which required that country to open an account in New York to receive payments in gold from the US government for the lease on the Panama Canal. These payments would become the founding reserve for a gold exchange standard for Panama, but the reserve was held in New York.[79] The British model of the gold exchange standard in Egypt was studied in detail as an example of how a financial model could be settled on a country not formally under another country's control, the Suez/British case offering an obvious model for the Panama/United States administration.

When the Philippines achieved independence in 1946, a central bank with all the associated freedom of monetary maneuver replaced the currency board, which had operated during the period of US administration. In this respect, the Philippines' decision to establish a central bank rather than stick with the old currency board arrangement was in step with the decisions of the majority of British colonies gaining independence in the postwar period. In the thinking of the time, currency boards were for colonies, and central banks were for independent states, even if experience had subsequently shown that it was the currency board that was more effective in securing price stability.[80]

THE GOLD EXCHANGE STANDARD AT
THE SERVICE OF JAPAN'S EMPIRE

Japan, which itself had been subject to unfavorable commercial treaties as a result of unwanted intervention by the naval forces of America in the 1850s, sought in its turn to open up other closed Asiatic states to its own advantage. In 1876, in a deliberate act of provocation, a Japanese battleship entered Korean waters, prompting an armed reaction by Korean forces on the Island of Ganghwa, the so-called Ganghwa incident. The consequent Treaty of Ganghwa obliged Korea to open up to trade with Japan and established a number of privileged advantages for Japanese merchants and individuals in Korea. One step too far for the Korean authorities at this point was the circulation of Bank of Japan notes, prompting a diplomatic protest to the Japanese government, which soft pedaled for the time being on any attempt to force the circulation of Japanese notes in Korea.[81]

By stages, Japan reinforced its position in Korea, leading toward occupation and a protectorate status, followed by formal colonization. Monetary administration formed a part of this process, and in 1902 Japan's Minister of Finance authorized the Dai-ichi Bank to issue its own banknotes in Korea. Although Korean authorities, prompted by Russia, tried to ban this issue, counterpressure by the Japanese authorities undermined Korea's resistance. By the end of 1904 Dai-ichi Bank notes, with a value of more than 3 million yen, were circulating in Korea, backed by Japanese yen notes, as the intermediary reserve in a gold exchange standard.[82]

Japan's developing control of Korea's monetary system also involved the appointment of a Japanese financial advisor (in reality more of an economic proconsul) in 1904, who arranged in 1905 for the closure of Korea's mint, the import of coins from Japan, and the introduction of a gold standard to be implemented by the Dai-ichi Bank, which was already operating in Korea. In mid-1905 the yen gold exchange system was launched with legal tender Korean yen notes issued by Dai-ichi bank, now effectively Korea's central bank, backed by a reserve of Japanese yen notes and securities held in Japan. The Japanese yen notes used to back the Korean yen issue were themselves issued on the basis of reserves of sterling notes owned by Japan but held in London. A relatively modest quantity of gold-supported sterling notes, which in turn supported the Japanese yen, were backing the colonial Korean yen. Very little of the reserve that backed Korea's notes therefore was in the form of gold specie. The notes carried vignettes of Korean scenery to convey a sense of Korean identity as a concession to local sensitivities.[83]

The Korean mint having been closed in 1905, a token coinage imported from Japan was introduced, and the old Korean nickel and copper coins that were still circulating were at last demonetized, the population being required to exchange them for no more than half their face value. The population in general thus lost half of their wealth in an inequitable currency demonetization process. That same year following a coup d'état, Korea became a Japanese protectorate until, in 1910, it was formally annexed. In 1909 the Bank of Korea (subsequently renamed the Bank of Chosen) was created to finance the new colonial government's projects and transactions.[84]

Similar monetary measures were taken to project Japan's power in other parts of Asia. Taiwan, which had been ceded to Japan by China at the end of the war of 1895, became the first colony in its overseas empire. In 1899 the Bank of Taiwan was established as the sole note-issuing authority for the new colony and subsequently tried to move Taiwan off the silver standard and onto gold in line with Japan's own system. As Britain, France, and Italy had found, it was no easy matter to shift a colony from its monetary preference. By 1906 Taiwan's circulating currency included old Chinese and Japanese silver coins, gold Japanese yen coins, and gold yen-denominated paper notes. A global shift upward in the value of silver, however, accelerated the transitional process, causing silver coins to leave Taiwan, leaving the gold yen-based paper notes to fill the void.[85]

Extending Japan's monetary reach, the Yokohama Specie Bank, which had already opened a branch in Shanghai in 1893, was able from 1902 to issue notes from the Shanghai branch but also from two other branches in mainland China. Notes were denominated in silver dollars, gold yen, and *tael* (silver ingots, a traditional Chinese currency format and value). Through the first two decades of the twentieth century, the Yokohama Specie Bank issued more than eighty different types of notes in China. During the years from 1915–1916, as China was coming to terms with the disappearance of the Qing Empire and the emergence of provincial warlords, public confidence in Chinese note-issuing banks collapsed when the convertibility of their notes was suspended. The Yokohama Specie Bank stepped in to offer alternative notes. The value of its notes in circulation increased from seven million to eighteen million yen over that same period. By 1917, the value of its notes on issue had increased threefold since 1915, significant enough an indication of Japan's growing power to attract negative opinion among politically active Chinese who launched a boycott of Japanese notes issued in China.[86]

The Yokohama Specie Bank also established a branch in southern Manchuria in 1900 and began to issue silver-backed notes there in January 1903, performing the same role as the Dai-ichi Bank in Korea as a proto central bank. It was also tasked with redeeming military scrip issued in Korea during the Russo-Japanese War by the Japanese army to purchase local produce. To compensate for the cost of this exercise, the Yokohama Specie Bank was given the mandate to unify Manchuria's currency on a Japanese silver yen standard.[87]

Japan's creation of different issuing banks for different colonies may not appear so different from Britain's establishment of separate currency boards for colonies in different regions. The disadvantage of creating independent issuing banks in the colonies, however, was the negative impact that had on Japan's own earnings. Yen issued by the colonial banks were used to pay for imports from Japan. In this way, Japan was denied the opportunity to sell products in exchange for gold-backed foreign exchange.[88]

Japan's use of currency-issuing banks as a means of financing military expenditures in its nascent overseas empire in the late nineteenth and early twentieth centuries was perhaps the most aggressive example of its kind, certainly overshadowing Italy's relatively weak use of currency issue as a tool of empire. It was able to impose its currency policies on overseas territories that were relatively close at hand in ways that Britain, lacking the same ruthless determination, was unable and unwilling to achieve over its own far-flung empire. But, it was ultimately the single-minded determination of Japan's military adventurers and their insatiable requirement for funding that would set radical conservatives on the path of violent action against leading liberals who favored the rigorous classical gold standard in the runup to the Second World War.

While states in Europe during the late nineteenth century were trying to establish coordinated currency systems that would enable the money issued in one country to circulate freely in another, thereby separating the circulation of currency from national boundaries, imperial powers were grappling with the challenges of monetary systems for remote colonies. There, local traditions and the powerful logic of regional markets hampered attempts by imperial governments to assert their will. These realities tested to the limit the geographic range of sovereignty over money and indeed over the colonies.

As the imperial power of Britain waned after the First World War, its willingness to exert authority over its dominions failed it. They in turn learned to go their own way on monetary matters. From this point on, there was a growing recognition in Britain's colonies that full monetary sovereignty would accompany or might even precede political independence. In the 1930s, the dominions still recognized Britain as the imperial power but knew that, when it came to monetary policy, they were independent. Other colonies that did not enjoy dominion status were able to issue their own currency but only on the basis of currency board rules. Similarly, different degrees of control were exercised by Italy and France over their own colonies.

As the empires of the European powers dissolved in the decades following the Second World War, the acquisition of an independent currency became an article of faith for almost all countries achieving independence.

NOTES

1. Şevket Pamuk, *A Monetary History of the Ottoman Empire* (Cambridge: Cambridge University Press, 2000), 30.

2. Ibid., 145.

3. Ibid., 92.

4. Ibid., 131.

5. Ibid., 88–89.

6. Ibid., 89.

7. Ibid., 100.

8. Ibid., 105.

9. Ibid., 106.

10. Ibid., 107.

11. Ibid., 110.

12. John S. Deyell, "The Development of Akbar's Currency System and Monetary Integration of the Conquered Kingdoms," in *The Imperial Monetary System of Mughal India*, ed. John F. Richards (Delhi: Oxford University Press, 1987), 33–34.

13. John F. Richards, *The Mughal Empire* (Cambridge: Cambridge University Press, 2008), 72–73; and Deyell, "The Development of Akbar's Monetary System," 22.

14. Ibid., 44.

15. Ibid., 38.

16. Alexander del Mar, *Barbara Villiers: A History of Monetary Crimes* (Hawaii: University Press of the Pacific, 2004), 82–83.

17. Paola Subacchi, *The Cost of Free Money* (New Haven and London: Yale University Press, 2020), 52–53.

18. R. Neill, "Central Banking and Government Policy: Canada, 1871," University of Prince Edward Island, accessed November 21, 2020, http://people.upei.ca/rneill/web_papers/1871_notes.html.

19. James Powell, "A History of the Canadian Dollar," Bank of Canada, 18–20. https://www.bankofcanada.ca/wp-content/uploads/2010/07/dollar_book.pdf.

20. Ibid., 22–23, 33; and Eric Helleiner, *The Making of National Money: Territorial Currencies in Historical Perspective* (New York: Cornell University Press, 2003), 112.

21. Powell, "A History of the Canadian Dollar," 26–32; and Helleiner, *The Making of National Money*, 21.

22. Ibid., 153.

23. Richards, *The Mughal Empire*, 198.

24. Om Prakash, "Foreign Merchants and Indian Mints in the Seventeenth and the Early Eighteenth Century," in *The Imperial Monetary System of Mughal India*, ed. John F. Richards (Delhi: Oxford University Press, 1987), 184.

25. Richards, *The Mughal Empire*, 241.

26. Jonathan Williams, ed., *Money: A History* (London: British Museum Press, 1997), 122.

27. Ibid., 122.

28. John Maynard Keynes, *Indian Currency and Finance* (Cambridge: Cambridge University Press for the Royal Economic Society, 2013), 26.

29. Indian Councils Act, 1861, clause 43(2). https://archive.org/details/indiancouncilsac00grearich/page/20/mode/2up?q=currency.

30. Benjamin Tsoi, "The Constitutions (Founding Laws) and Comparable Features of Select Currency Boards in the Former British Empire," working paper, Johns Hopkins University, October 2014, https://sites.krieger.jhu.edu/iae/files/2021/02/Benjamin-Tsoi-Working-Paper-2-21.pdf; and Keynes, *Indian Currency and Finance*, 29, 31.

31. Keynes, *Indian Currency and Finance*, 1–2; and Helleiner, *The Making of National Money*, 165.

32. Mark Metzler, *Lever of Empire: The International Gold Standard and the Crisis of Liberalism in Prewar Japan* (Berkeley: University of California Press, 2006), 43; and Keynes, *Indian Currency and Finance*, 21–22.

33. Giulio M. Gallarotti, "The Scramble for Gold: Monetary Regime Transformation in the 1870s," in *Monetary Regimes in Transition*, ed. Michael D. Bordo and Forrest Capie (New York: Cambridge University Press, 1994), 63 n182.

34. Metzler, *Lever of Empire*, 36, 38; and Keynes, *Indian Currency and Finance*, 33–34.

35. Keynes, *Indian Currency and Finance*, 51–52.

36. Kurt Schuler, "Episodes from Asian Monetary History: A Brief History of Hong Kong Monetary Standards," *Asian Monetary Monitor*, September–October 1989.

37. S. J. Butlin, "Foundations of the Australian Monetary System 1788–1851," University of Sydney, 2002, 21, http://setis.library.usyd.edu.au/pubotbin/sup2pdfall?id=sup0003; and Robert Chalmers, *A History of Currency in the British Colonies* (London: HM Stationery Office, 1893), 244.

38. Butlin, "Foundations of the Australian Monetary System," 21, 155, 162; and Chalmers, *A History of Currency in the British Colonies*, 246.

39. Butlin, "Foundations of the Australian Monetary System," 173–74, 521.

40. Chalmers, *A History of Currency in the British Colonies*, 253–55.

41. Ibid., 263–67.

42. Reserve Bank of Australia, "Origins of the Reserve Bank of Australia," 1–3, https://www.rba.gov.au/education/resources/explainers/pdf/origins-of-the-reserve-bank-of-australia.pdf?v=2021-04-11-13-24-22; and Helleiner, *The Making of National Money*, 94.

43. Chalmers, *A History of Currency in the British Colonies*, 360.

44. Ibid., 360; and W. F. Crick, *Commonwealth Banking Systems* (Oxford: Clarendon Press, 1965), 501.

45. Chalmers, *A History of Currency in the British Colonies*, 367.

46. Svetoslav Pintev, *Currency Board Arrangements: Rationale for Their Introduction, Advantages and Disadvantages: The Case of Bulgaria* (Diplomica Verlag, 2002), 7.

47. Ken Matthews, "The Legal History of Money in New Zealand," Reserve Bank of New Zealand, https://www.rbnz.govt.nz/-/media/ReserveBank/Files/Publications/Bulletins/2003/2003mar66-1matthews.pdf?revision=20608ae6-d484-4ad0-a30c-822c9be13de6.

48. Chalmers, *A History of Currency in the British Colonies*, 287–90.

49. Helleiner, *The Making of National Money*, 151.

50. Crick, *Commonwealth Banking Systems*, 3–4, 11.

51. Helleiner, *The Making of National Money*, 166–68; and Chibuike U. Uche, "Banks and the West African Currency Board," in *Money in Africa*, ed. Catherine Eagleton, Harcourt Fuller, and John Perkins (London: British Museum Press, 2009), 50.

52. Pintev, "Currency Board Arrangements," 7; and Helleiner, *The Making of National Money*, 178.

53. Tsoi, "The Constitutions (Founding Laws) and Comparable Features of Select Currency Boards in the Former British Empire"; Keynes, *Indian Currency and Finance*, 33; and Crick, *Commonwealth Banking Systems*, 4–5. This last reference notes that restrictions on currency boards investing in local government securities were in any case relaxed in 1954.

54. Crick, *Commonwealth Banking Systems*, 5.

55. Chwee-Huay Ow, "The Currency Board Monetary System: The Case of Singapore and Hong Kong" (PhD diss., John Hopkins University, 1985); and Helleiner, *The Making of National Money*, 168–69.

56. Charles P. Kindleberger, *A Financial History of Western Europe* (London: Routledge, 2006), 387.

57. Frederick Quinn, *The French Overseas Empire* (Westport: Praeger Publishers, 2000), 107, 113.

58. Ibid., 116, 143, 149.

59. Ibid., 155–156.

60. Banque de France, "Fact Sheet No. 127: The Franc Zone," July 2010, https://www.banque-france.fr/sites/default/files/media/2016/11/02/the_fact_sheet_n_127_july-2010.pdf; Keynes, *Indian Currency and Finance*, 25; and University of Quebec at Montreal, "Currency, French Indochina," http://indochine.uqam.ca/en/historical-dictionary/333-currency-french-indochina.html.

61. Mahir Şaul, "Money in Colonial Transition: Cowries and Francs in West Africa," University of Illinois, http://faculty.las.illinois.edu/m-saul/documents/SaulMoneyinColonialAA.pdf.

62. Banque de France, "Fact Sheet No. 127: The Franc Zone."

63. A. B. Nunes et al., "Banking in the Portuguese Colonial Empire (1864–1975)," Working paper 41, University of Lisbon, 2010, 6–9, accessed November 22, 2020, https://ideas.repec.org/p/ise/gheswp/wp412010.html.

64. Paul Wilson, *Hostile Money: Currencies in Conflict* (Cheltenham: The History Press, 2019), 26–29.

65. Nunes et al., "Banking in the Portuguese Colonial Empire (1864–1975)," 11.

66. Ibid., 14–16.

67. Ibid., 18.

68. Ibid., 20–24.

69. Donatella Strangio, *The Reasons for Underdevelopment: The Case of Decolonisation in Somaliland* (Berlin-Heidelberg: Physica Verlag, 2012), xiv.

70. Arnaldo Mauri, "Eritrea's Early Development in Monetary and Banking Development," Working paper 28, University of Milan, 2003.

71. Ibid., 12.

72. Saima Raza, "Italian Colonisation and Libyan Resistance: The Al-Sanusi of Cyrenaica," *Journal of Middle Eastern and Islamic Studies* 6, no. 1 (2012): 87–120, http://mideast.shisu.edu.cn/_upload/article/43/90/71b453574410bb697d5766774f85/11caa68a-4eae-413c-a0ce-8c6101d7dd85.pdf.

73. John E. Sandrock, "Italy's Colonial Empire: A Paper Money Trail," The Currency Collector, http://www.thecurrencycollector.com/pdfs/Italys_Colonial_Empire_-_A_Paper_Money_Trail.pdf.

74. Ben Bernanke and Harold James, "The Gold Standard, Deflation, and Financial Crisis in the Great Depression: An International Comparison," in *Financial Markets and Financial Crises*, ed. R. Glenn Hubbard (Chicago: University of Chicago Press, 1991), 33–68.

75. Jonathan Kirshner, *Currency and Coercion* (Princeton, NJ: Princeton University Press, 1995), 230–231.

76. Arta Pisha, Besa Vorpsi, and Neraida Hoxhaj, "Albania: from 1920–1944," in *South-Eastern European Monetary and Economic Statistics from the Nineteenth Century to World War II*, 355–378, https://www.bnb.bg/bnbweb/groups/public/documents/bnb_publication/pub_np_seemhn_02_09_en.pdf.

77. Sandrock, "Italy's Colonial Empire: A Paper Money Trail."

78. Helleiner, *The Making of National Money*, 5.

79. Metzler, *Lever of Empire*, 42–44; Keynes, *Indian Currency and Finance*, 25. Keynes states that the gold exchange standard was introduced by the United States in the Philippines in 1903 and that it was based on the system first introduced in India.

80. Helleiner, *The Making of National Money*, 189–90.

81. Ibid., 182; and Niv Horesh, *Chinese Money in Global Context: Historic Junctures between 600 BCE and 2012* (Stanford, CA: Stanford University Press, 2014), 197. Horesh states that the reigning Yi dynasty of Korea had as early as 1878 (two years after the Ganghwa incident) invited Japan's Dai-ichi Bank to take responsibility for the issue of notes in Korea.

82. Metzler, *Lever of Empire*, 52.

83. Helleiner, *The Making of National Money*, 182.

84. Metzler, *Lever of Empire*, 53–54; Helleiner, *The Making of National Money*, 175; and Horesh, *Chinese Money in Global Context*, 197.

85. Horesh, *Chinese Money in Global Context*, 202–203.

86. Ibid., 186–187, 192.

87. Metzler, *Lever of Empire*, 57; and Horesh, *Chinese Money in Global Context*, 186.

88. Metzler, Lever of Empire, 254; and Horesh, Chinese Money in Global Context, 200.

Chapter 5

The End of Empire

In the twentieth century, and especially since the end of the war, the processes which gave birth to the nation states of Europe have been repeated all over the world. We have seen the awakening of national consciousness in peoples who have for centuries lived in dependence upon some other power.

—Harold Macmillan, Prime Minister of Great Britain, "Wind of Change Speech" February 3, 1960

A parting of ways, when one nation or region decides to separate from another and to declare independence, will, more often than not, result in an abrupt transition to a new and independent currency with monetary institutions that reflect and guarantee the newly found independence in a monetary regime. But there have been exceptions. Following the dissolution of France's Empire, a number of countries in Sub-Saharan Africa that had been French colonies agreed on independence to maintain currency unions pegged to the franc (and later to the euro), with the Banque de France continuing to play an important part in the management of reserves. And sterling's lingering importance as a reserve currency ensured that some countries newly independent of Britain maintained a large part of their reserves in that currency until it was gradually replaced by the US dollar. At least one country, however, maintained a link to sterling long after it had become independent. It was especially interesting that the country concerned, Ireland, had had the longest period of monetary subordination to England of all of its colonies.

The dissolution of empires in the second half of the twentieth century gave birth to dozens of new states, each having to make decisions as to which currency regime it would adopt. In this chapter we examine a range of cases that demonstrate that, although some general trends were observable among countries gaining independence after the Second World War, the factors involved in decision-making subsequently have become increasingly varied. While countries achieving independence in the postwar period more often than not chose the central bank and independent monetary policy as the right and proper means of managing the currencies of a sovereign state, more countries now consider alternatives to the central bank in the form of currency boards, dollarization, or membership in a currency union.

THE IRISH FREE STATE AND THE IRISH REPUBLIC

In 1922 the Irish Free State came into existence as a self-governing dominion within the British Empire with the same status as Canada. The new Irish Free State initially opted to continue to use sterling notes and coins, primarily in recognition of the fact that Britain remained Ireland's main trading partner. However, plans for a new coinage were put before the Dail, the Irish parliament, in 1926. The new coins would replicate the British denominations already in circulation but would be of a significantly higher silver content than their British counterparts. As the report of the second reading of the bill for the introduction of the national coinage recorded, the government of the Free State saw a new coinage with national symbols as a natural accompaniment to the country's newly won independence. Beyond that immediate recognition, however, the debate circulated around the issue of the composition of the coins, the profits to be made from the minting operation, and the question as to whether Free State coins would be accepted in Britain. The Dail addressed the question in this second debate largely on pragmatic and financial grounds: pragmatism, rather than the burning passion of nationalism, set the tone of the parliamentary debate, although the designs chosen for the new coins did become a matter of heated and public controversy when the new coins were issued in 1928.

The decision had been made to use images of farm animals as representative of Ireland's primary products and exports. In the eyes of those Republicans who opposed the compromise agreement with Britain that had given birth to the Free State, the new coins, which had been produced at the Royal Mint in London and held to the same denominational structure and names as British coins, proved that Ireland remained an economic dependency of Britain. Other lines of attack had focused on the absence of images representative of Ireland's Christian inheritance or cultural past. Even more telling, perhaps, was the belief that the choice of farmyard animals played to past British prejudices about the Irish and would attract mockery.

The Free State government resisted. At the launch of the new coinage, the minister of finance, Ernest Blythe, stated that "*the possession of a distinctive coinage is one of the indications of sovereignty.*" In this, he was not only asserting the independence in monetary matters of the new state from Britain (yet ignoring the fact that Ireland's currency would remain pegged to sterling for many years to come) but was also making a point for the benefit of the more zealous republicans. Unlike the coinage of the other dominions—South Africa, New Zealand, Australia, and Canada—none of the Irish coins bore the image of the king, and all were struck with inscriptions in the Irish language alone. With the benefit of hindsight, these characteristics indicated the direction Ireland would take in breaking sooner and more completely from Britain than did the other dominions.[1]

Even after Ireland had taken a further step toward complete independence by a change of constitution in 1937 and the establishment of a nonexecutive presidency in that year, it remained for many years within Britain's sphere of monetary influence purely by virtue of the close trading relationship between the two states. After the 1926 Coinage Act, the banking fraternity in Ireland sought assurances that the link to sterling would be upheld. Political independence was one thing, but monetary independence quite another.

The Free State now moved to address the matter of paper notes in circulation. Proposals for a new system of paper currency were set out in a report in 1926 by a commission headed by Professor Parker-Willis of the University of Columbia in the United States. That an American was invited to chair this commission was hardly remarkable given that American experts were advising China and several countries in Latin America and elsewhere at the time. The conclusions of the report provided for the continued but limited issue of banknotes by commercial banks and suggested that Ireland would remain within the British economic system "for a long time to come" because of Britain's importance as Ireland's primary trading partner. The new Free State pound was to be backed 100 percent by British government securities, gold, or sterling, and the Parker-Willis commission recommended that the new Irish currency should be freely convertible to sterling at a rate of one for one to guarantee its acceptability among the Irish population and make the transition simple to handle. It was, in effect, to be run on currency board principles. This convertibility at par would also be guaranteed in London at the Bank of England, acting as the agent of the Currency Commission. Indeed, the new banknotes were printed with the inscription "Sterling payable to bearer on demand in London."[2] This confidence-building measure would prevent a flight of capital, an issue of some sensitivity because nearly 30 million pounds had been withdrawn from commercial banks out of a total of 192 million pounds of deposits since the signature of the treaty establishing the new Free State. The Free State pound would be on the sterling exchange standard, but seigniorage would accrue to the Irish government based on the yield earned on British securities held as part of the reserve.[3]

Acting on the recommendations of the commission, the Free State government passed the Currency Act of 1927, creating a Currency Commission, which began to issue legal tender notes in 1928. The Currency Act also began the process of limiting the rights of the commercial banks to issue their own notes in regulated volumes in the Free State. A new series, known as consolidated notes, would be printed with the names of the individual issuing banks, which would deposit securities at the Currency Commission up to the full value of all their notes issued under this arrangement. Because notes of the commercial banks had circulated freely in Northern Ireland, which remained within the United Kingdom, legislation was also passed in London to limit the volume of notes that those commercial banks could issue in the north.[4]

So the currency issued was backed one for one by sterling and would be fully convertible. Although the money-issuing authority became the Central Bank of Ireland in 1943, it continued to operate as a conventional currency board for some years after its establishment: the requirement for 100 percent cover was relaxed only in 1961, when the "payable in London" inscription was removed from the notes. Lending to government did not begin immediately but started on a small scale before 1965. Furthermore, the requirement that the one-for-one parity of the Irish and British pounds could be changed only by legislation, very much in line with classic currency board requirements, remained in force until 1971. The issue of consolidated notes by commercial banks was gradually phased out after the creation of the central bank. In the following years, more powers consistent with central bank status were adopted. After five years of double-digit inflation in Britain in the 1970s, which was being conveyed to Ireland through the link to sterling, the bank finally severed that link in 1979, and Ireland joined the European Monetary System. In 2002 the Irish pound was replaced in circulation by the euro.[5]

Although Ireland continues to import more by value from Britain than from any other country, the experience of sterling's unreliability as a peg in the 1970s and Ireland's long memories of its difficult relationship with its larger neighbor made the euro an attractive option. Even the sovereign debt crisis of 2009–2010, which threatened the continued existence of the euro and was particularly traumatic for Ireland together with another handful of euro members, did not prompt Ireland to leave the euro in the way it had abandoned sterling in 1979. This was partly due to the fact that the European Central Bank and the European Union (EU) were both willing and able to take steps to keep Ireland afloat, including the provision of substantial loans (to which Britain had also contributed). Ireland's discipline in recovering from the economic crisis at that time has rewarded the EU's support and confidence, and even the financial difficulties that may impact Ireland as a result of Britain's withdrawal from the EU are unlikely to shake Ireland's commitment to the euro. Indeed, the solidarity of the EU member states in backing Ireland's position in the withdrawal negotiations with Britain are likely, if anything, to confirm to many Irishmen that the decision to adopt the euro was the right move.

Ireland's own monetary and political history in the hundred years since its independence from Britain supports the proposition that a country does not need monetary independence to guarantee political sovereignty. So long as a country maintains its political sovereignty, it can choose a monetary regime to suit its objectives. Ireland continued to peg its currency to sterling long after it had ceased to be a dominion and had left the commonwealth, assessing the British currency to be best suited to its economic interests. When it did abandon its link to sterling and subsequently joined the euro system, it was a matter of choice, a freedom of maneuver guaranteed by its political sovereignty.

BRITAIN AND THE WIND OF CHANGE

When Britain's Prime Minister Harold Macmillan delivered his "Wind of Change" speech in February 1960 in South Africa, he was doing no more than recognizing the tide of decolonization that was already sweeping over the British and French Empires. In the fifteen years between the end of the Second World War and his speech, India, Ceylon, Ghana, Malaysia (including at that time Singapore), Burma, and Pakistan had become independent, and Nigeria and Cyprus were to become independent within the year. And by the end of 1960 even more colonies had gained their independence from France: Cote'Ivoire, Benin, Mali, Guinea, Mauritania, Niger, Burkina Faso, Togo, Chad, Central African Republic, Republic of Congo, Gabon, Cameroon, Madagascar, and France's remaining possessions in the Indian subcontinent. The wind of change had developed into a storm by 1960, bringing with it a shift in monetary governance structures.

It is hardly surprising that newly independent states would want their own currencies as an expression of national identity, but independence in monetary terms meant more than just having a distinctively printed banknote bearing national symbols and local languages. It also involved the freedom to decide on monetary policy and the machinery with which those policies would be executed, a freedom of maneuver denied under the currency board arrangement, which was associated with the imperial past. Among British-administered territories, India had already established its own reserve bank in 1935, a reflection of the true status and significance of that empire within an empire. At the separation of India and Pakistan, the latter established its own central bank in 1948, arguably having even more reason to assert its national identity in the machinery of government, having secured independence not only from Britain but also from India at one and the same time.

SRI LANKA

Representative of this move away from colonial monetary systems was the decision of Sri Lanka to opt for a central bank. Sri Lanka—then Ceylon—had run its money on a currency board basis from 1884 until independence in 1948, but then opted for a central bank as being more consistent with its newfound independence. A central bank would have the ability to intervene in support of its own currency, to set interest rates and buy and sell reserve currencies in the marketplace to strengthen or weaken the national currency, measures of monetary autonomy denied under a currency board regime.

Further reflecting its determination to break with the British colonial past and recognizing the United States' dominant position in the new monetary order, Sri Lanka had invited an expert from the US Federal Reserve Bank, rather than the Bank of England, to draw up plans for the creation of the new central bank.[6] When Sri Lanka became independent in 1948, it did so as a dominion until it became a republic in 1972. Dominion status within the empire had on the whole been associated with possession of a central bank, as in other cases, such as Australia, New Zealand, Canada, and South Africa. So Sri Lanka's decision to replace its currency board with a central bank was perfectly consistent with the mood of independence of the time, but also with the perception that dominions had central banks, not currency boards.

BURMA

The decolonization process in Burma as it affected that country's currency regime was particularly complicated. Burma had been annexed to India in 1886, and Indian rupee notes, slightly modified, had circulated until the Japanese invasion in 1942. While the war was still under way, however, the Reserve Bank of India was already indicating that it was unwilling to resume its role as Burma's issuing bank. Senior banking advisers to the Burmese government in exile in India could foresee a separate Burmese currency in the postwar period but would not go so far as to believe in the possible success of a Burmese central bank. As in some other colonial administrations, the presiding belief was in the efficacy of a currency board.

Under Japanese control, vast amounts of Japanese-issued notes had been put into circulation, creating conditions of inflation. At Japan's defeat, British authorities were faced with an administrative challenge as to how to withdraw from circulation those Japanese notes. Following the completion of this currency "mopping-up" operation, the British governor's executive council (which did include some Burmese members, although not representatives of the leading party of independence, the Anti-Fascist People's league) made the decision in 1946 to establish the Burmese Currency Board.[7] In the transitional period to independence, during which direct government was carried out by an executive council, the currency board was established. But, in an indication of Britain's continuing power and influence—or at least its determination to claim that power and influence—the currency board was established in London, held tightly to the heart of the sterling zone.[8]

Burma achieved independence in 1948, its decision to skip the transitional phase of dominion status, no doubt pointing toward a wish to sever the link to Britain immediately and conclusively. Although work began on the relocation of the currency board to Rangoon, the capital, it was not long before the Burmese government opted for the transfer of note issue-responsibility to a central bank. As plans for the design of the Union Bank of Burma developed (with assistance from an American adviser, as in Sri Lanka), British experts were consulted and expressed concern at the freedom the bank would have in setting exchange rates, rather than fixing by legislation the new currency to an anchor currency (i.e., sterling). In the view of those leading British financial administrators, such a move would undermine the confidence of the public in the stability of the currency. But Britain's influence in Burma was at an end. In 1952 the Union Bank of Burma began operations as the country's central bank in succession to the Currency Board of Burma.[9]

ISRAEL, TRANSJORDAN, AND THE PALESTINE CURRENCY BOARD—THE BRITISH MANDATE

Israel

As Britain began the process of dissolving its empire, its mandate over Palestine, granted by the League of Nations in the aftermath of the First World War, also came to an end. As defined by the League, the British mandate of 1922 was designed to *"secure the establishment of the Jewish National Home"* at the same time *"safeguarding the civil and religious rights of all the inhabitants of Palestine."*[10] UN General Assembly Resolution 181 of November 29, 1947, called for the mandate to end by August 1, 1948, and for Palestine to be partitioned into separate Jewish and Arab states and an internationally administered Jerusalem. Under the General Assembly Resolution, a Joint Economic Board would issue currency for the two separate states. It was to be political partition with economic union, a solution unique in the postwar monetary world, but reflecting the unique circumstances surrounding Palestine.[11] This requirement, like other provisions of UN General Assembly Resolution 181, was never to come to fruition. Britain accelerated the process of withdrawal, announcing in December 1947 its intention of ending the mandate on May 15.

Formed in response to UN General Assembly Resolution 181, the United Nations Palestine Commission was tasked with implementing the measures required by the resolution, taking over the administration of Palestine in the immediate aftermath of Britain's withdrawal. But security had been a major problem for the commission's ability to implement those measures. Both Arabs and Jews had risen against the British mandate, the former during the 1930s and the latter over the period 1944–1947. But now, Jewish and Arab militias, the latter supported by Arab states, confronted each other in armed conflict. The Palestine Commission, in its First Special Report on the Problem of Security, noted that "powerful Arab interests both within and outside Palestine" were opposing the partition by force and refused to cooperate with the commission. The same report noted that the Jewish militias, although supporting the planned partition, were also committing "irresponsible acts of violence"; the prevailing circumstances were described as "virtual civil war." Any prospect for a unified economic system serving two partitioned entities could not be realized in the face of Arab opposition to the partition itself.[12]

During the period of the mandate, the Palestine Currency Board had acted as the issuing authority for the Palestinian pound, which was fully backed by sterling currency and securities held in London. By December 1947 Britain's thinking on withdrawal from Palestine was well advanced. Officials concluded that at the end of the mandate exchange controls would collapse and sterling (or at least Palestine pounds, which were redeemable ultimately for sterling) would leave the mandated territory in significant sums. The decision was therefore made to exclude Palestine from the sterling zone and to block Palestine's sterling balances in London, allowing only enough sterling to be available for the purposes of maintaining trade.[13] On February 22, 1948, all but three million pounds of the sterling assets backing the Palestine pound were blocked, and Palestine was excluded from the sterling zone. Blocked accounts in London had also been credited with funds in settlement of British military expenditures in Palestine during the war. On March 2, 1948, the Chancellor of the Exchequer (the Minister of Finance), Sir Stafford Cripps, confirmed in parliament that no negotiations had been held with the beneficiaries of the blocked assets prior to the announcements.[14] A United Nations note published in April 1949 recorded the value of the sums blocked in London as 56 million pounds, representing more than a half of all Palestine's sterling balances. Ironically and somewhat ludicrously, the Chancellor of the Exchequer, speaking in parliament in July 1949, refused to confirm the value of the blocked accounts, a value that had already been declared to the foreign nationals forming the UN Palestine Commission. The British position, as recorded in the United Nations note, was that the funds would remain blocked until a successor—then envisaged to be the Joint Economic Board—to the Palestine Currency Board was set up. As far as the UN Palestine Commission was concerned, in taking over the administration of Palestine from the British mandated power, it would also be assuming responsibility for the issue of currency for Palestine, which in turn meant that it would take over the "current income and assets" of the London-based currency board after the end of the British mandate.[15]

In March 1948 the Palestine Commission reported that the British government had decided to release seven million pounds of the blocked currency. And four days before the end of the British mandate—that is on May 11—the United Kingdom passed a note to the UN Commission for Palestine in which it confirmed that the British government would be willing to discuss the redemption of large quantities of Palestine pounds coming into the possession of the commission.[16] The question of the redemption of Palestine pounds and the return of the blocked assets would also be raised in the UK Parliament in July 1949 when a member of parliament asked Cripps what portion of the blocked sterling balances were to be allocated to the areas of Palestine to be under Arab sovereignty. Cripps responded by confirming that the value of the sterling balances was being discussed with the Israeli government and would be discussed with *"any Arab successor government."*[17] This point would be remembered by the most prominent Palestinian leader more than four decades later. On a more mechanical level, coins that had been produced for circulation toward the end of the mandate were melted down at the end of the mandate by order of the Palestine Currency Board.

But events were to overtake the Palestine Commission's efforts to assume responsibility for transition. On May 14, 1948, unable to secure an orderly transition from the mandate power and struggling to cope with the ethnic conflict, the United Nations decided to dissolve the Palestine Commission, which was wound up on May 17. On the same day—the day before the British mandate ended—David Ben-Gurion, the head of the Jewish Agency, proclaimed the creation of the State of Israel. In the same month the UN's Palestine Commission observed that the supply of currency already in Palestine would be insufficient in the event of a run on the banks during the withdrawal of the mandate power and that a general breakdown in security would increase the demand for cash. Indeed, the commission had already noted on March 12 that there had been a run on the Anglo Palestine bank in Tel Aviv on February 22 of that year—the day on which Britain had excluded Palestine from the sterling zone.[18] The general officer commanding British troops in Palestine arranged for the shipping of all remaining Palestine pounds and records relating to them from the Port of Haifa back to the United Kingdom on June 10 under conditions of utmost secrecy, reserving only enough for the remaining troops' needs.[19] The supply of currency to the new Israeli state and to the Arab areas of Palestine looked to be woefully inadequate.

But some people had already decided to act independently. In March 1948—prior to the announcement by Ben-Gurion—the Jewish Agency in New York had informed the Palestine Commission that reports in the *New York Times* suggesting that the Jewish Agency was planning to issue a currency based on the US dollar (that is, not linked to sterling) were misleading. The agency stated that the press had misunderstood comments that merely listed a range of currency options. Indeed, consistent with what was happening in other countries emerging from British administration, discussions had taken place among the Israeli leadership in 1948 on the establishment of a central bank, rather than a currency board, but the discussions were shelved due to the ongoing conflict. An interim solution was adopted.[20]

Prior to the expiry of the British mandate, the Anglo-Palestine bank, originally founded in 1902 by the Jewish Colonial Trust, had already been tasked by the Israeli leadership to procure and issue banknotes for Israel, and it began negotiations with the American Banknote Company. It is difficult to avoid the conclusion that the Jewish Agency based in New York had arranged the link between the bank and the American Banknote Company. That Israel was planning its own currency prior to the withdrawal of the mandate power and before the dissolution of the Palestine Commission plainly points to the fact that Israeli leaders knew by then that there was no chance that the Joint Economic Board would take over responsibility for the issue of currency for two separate states.

To avoid charges of supplying currency to an unrecognized state, the American Banknote Company insisted that its name would not appear on the notes (the inclusion of the printing company's name on notes it produced was at that time quite common), and the words "legal tender for any amount" were subsequently overprinted as an afterthought. As the notes were being printed for the Anglo-Palestine bank, the name that would also appear on the notes, the design avoided the possible accusation that the notes were being produced for a national bank before the nation existed. In fact, because US President Truman had unilaterally recognized Israel on the same day that Ben-Gurion had declared an independent Israel, the American Banknote Company would have had a degree of political "cover" from the White House. All the same, the company could not have foreseen the speed of Truman's actions, which had not been the subject of consultation with his own State Department, and the company could hardly have been blamed for taking precautionary measures. As no name had yet been decided for the new currency, the existing designation "Palestine pound" was used. The notes arrived from America in July 1948.[21]

On August 17 the provisional council of the State of Israel promulgated the Banknotes Ordinance of 1948, officially chartering the Anglo-Palestine Bank (which had in any case already ordered and taken delivery of the banknotes), as the bank with sole responsibility for issuing the new currency. The population was given one month (August 17–September 15) in which Palestine mandate pounds could be exchanged for the new Israeli pounds at a rate of one for one. After that, Palestine mandate pounds were no longer legal tender, and exchanges were to be made only at the discretion of the Anglo-Palestine Bank. The new currency was to be backed by a combination of gold, foreign currency notes, Palestine mandate notes (themselves redeemable for sterling), and treasury and commercial bonds.[22] Palestine pounds taken out of circulation by the process of exchange for the new Israeli pounds at the Anglo-Palestine Bank (subsequently renamed Bank Leumi) would be redeemed by transferring them to Britain and exchanging them for sterling, which would then be paid into Israel's own sterling number two account—the blocked account.[23]

A major complication arose when the new Israeli authorities blocked the local bank accounts of Palestinian Arabs who had fled Palestine. A report by the United Nations Conciliation Commission for Palestine on its 206th meeting held on March 6, 1951, in Jerusalem recorded the views of the Arab League: The Palestinian pounds blocked in those accounts were convertible to sterling through the Palestine Currency Board. But the account holders who were resident as refugees in neighboring Arab countries were not Israeli citizens in the view of the Israeli authorities, who would not permit Arab refugees to return to Israel to access their money in the blocked accounts. The Arab League observed that the refugees were thus deprived of money to assist their settlement in other Arab states. In fact, the economic adviser to the UN Conciliation Commission noted in a report on the possible unfreezing of assets that in effect the Palestinian refugees' funds were blocked twice: in the first place they could not access their blocked accounts in Palestine and then, because Palestine's membership of the sterling area had been suspended, conversion to sterling would not be possible.[24]

In April 1949 the Conciliation Commission requested the Israeli authorities consider releasing the blocked accounts. A similar request was made by the Arab League in the following month, to which the Israeli authorities responded that the accounts would be available to the owners on the conclusion of peace. Proposals for the unfreezing of some limited amounts from the blocked accounts were discussed in October 1949, leaving the question of the majority of the funds in refugees' blocked accounts in Israel outstanding.[25]

Two years later the matter was still under discussion. The Arab League representative consulted by the Conciliation Commission was concerned that Palestinian pounds—amounting to some four or five million pounds sterling in value in the blocked accounts—would be converted to sterling by the Israelis. But the fear was that Palestinians claiming the value of their blocked accounts would be paid not in sterling but in Israeli pounds, which those refugees would not be able to use in their new states of domicile and which would not be redeemable for sterling. The Arab League representatives called on the United Kingdom to bear in mind the position of the Palestinian refugees when converting Palestinian pounds for sterling. Some thirteen million pounds sterling had been released by Britain not long before the March 1951 meeting in final settlement of the issue of the blocked Palestinian accounts, but it was unclear that that sum had completely exhausted Palestine's sterling reserves.[26] Attempts by lawyers acting on behalf of the Palestinian refugees to sue the banks responsible for blocking the accounts in the courts in London failed, but were eventually successful in Jordan. Finally, buckling under the pressure of repeated legal processes, the commercial banks that had blocked the accounts at the direction of the Israeli government sought a compromise. In return for a very soft syndicated loan from the commercial banks to Israel, the government in Tel Aviv authorized the unblocking of the Palestinian refugees' accounts.

Unlike so many other countries emerging from British administration, Israel's newly independent currency would be issued neither by a central bank nor a currency board, but rather by a commercial bank. In the context of armed conflict, the new Israeli government had taken the easiest practical solution, placing the task on the bank, which was fully under the control of the Jewish Agency. While the Anglo-Palestine bank during a provisional period discharged its responsibilities as the issue department, all other central bank responsibilities, including monetary policy, remained with the Finance Ministry. In March 1951 a Committee for the Establishment of a State Bank was created and submitted its findings in September 1952. The Palestine pound was replaced by the Israeli lira in 1952, and the Palestine Currency Board was formally dissolved on June 17 of that year. In August 1954 the Knesset passed the Bank of Israel Law, and the bank came into being on December 1 of the same year.

While Palestine pounds were being redeemed in 1951 by the Israeli government in exchange for sterling, the Palestine pounds held in the Gaza Strip, then occupied by Egypt, were to be exchanged for Egyptian pounds and then redeemed in London. While the government of Egypt, like that of Israel, accepted that the sterling paid in return for redeemed Palestine pounds would be paid into a sterling number two (or blocked) account, it "reserved the right" to transfer it in due course to its sterling number one (unblocked) account.[27]

TRANSJORDAN

With the collapse of the Ottoman Empire, Britain had been granted a mandate by the League of Nations to administer Transjordan, the region to the east of the Jordan River and the Dead Sea, as well as Palestine. At the time of the granting of the mandate, a memorandum was submitted by the British to the Council of the League of Nations in which it was noted that a number of provisions of the Palestine mandate—specifically those applying to the creation of a Jewish homeland—would not apply to the mandated territory of Transjordan. The proposals contained in this memorandum were accepted by the Council of the League of Nations on the same date as the main mandate on Palestine was promulgated—September, 16, 1922.[28] As far as the mandated British government was concerned then, there were differences between Transjordan and Palestine both geographically and politically, and this position had been accepted by the Council of the League at the time of the granting of the mandates. Between 1928 and 1946 a series of treaties between Britain and Transjordan gave increasing independence to the latter, while Britain retained authority over Transjordan's defense, foreign affairs, and finances. A final treaty in March 1946 transferred full independence to Transjordan, and in May of that year, Transjordan became the Hashemite Kingdom of Jordan.

When it came to money, however, Jordan and Palestine were linked. Like Palestine, Transjordan used the Palestine pound backed by blocked sterling assets in London.[29] According to the United Nations Conciliation Commission for Palestine, the funds administered by the Palestine Currency Board in London during the mandate period had been invested in treasury securities, and the profits were divided between Palestine and Transjordan according to the proportions of notes in circulation in each territory. To give a sense of the relative currency circulation in both countries, during the first years of the Second World War circulation of notes in Transjordan amounted to only 6 percent of that in Palestine.[30] When Britain announced its decision to suspend Palestine's membership in the sterling zone in February 1948, the suspension was also applied to Jordan, although it was confirmed that discussions were underway to support Jordan's return to the sterling zone. Successor organizations to the Palestine Currency Board, it was noted, would be in a position to redeem the sterling backing in return for Palestine pounds returned to Britain.[31]

But the political distinction between Transjordan and the Arab parts of Palestine as referred to above was further reflected in British official thinking when it came to the matter of supply of Palestine pounds to the Palestinian Arab areas. It had been suggested in official circles in London that the currency due to be reserved for Palestinian Arabs—who, it was assumed, would eventually have their own separate Palestinian state—should be transferred not to Israel but to the Ottoman Bank in Jordan. But a foreign office letter to the colonial office on March 18, 1948, rejected the idea on grounds that "this could only have the effect of suggesting to King Abdallah that we wished him to take over the Arab areas." There was also a fear that such a move might give this impression to the world and "provide a handle for criticism." Plainly, the objection indicated that there was no intention on the part of Britain that the new Hashemite Kingdom of Jordan should have any claim to the assumed Arab state of Palestine. British officials therefore took steps to ensure that the settlement of the currency question could not be interpreted as conferring a claim by Jordan on sovereignty over the Arab areas of Palestine. An alternative plan was proposed to transfer money through a roundabout route (via Arab lands) to Arab banks in Palestine.[32]

And yet, if Jordan was not to absorb the Arab areas of Palestine, it did have to absorb large numbers of Palestinian Arabs seeking refuge from the new Israeli state. In the period 1948–1951 Transjordan's sterling balances increased by twelve million Palestinian pounds due to the influx of Palestinian refugees, but these funds had been rapidly exhausted to cover the vital imports of food and other necessities in which Jordan was not self-sufficient.

After independence, the Jordan Currency Board was established in 1949—based in London, notwithstanding Jordan's independence—and tasked with issuing the Jordanian dinar with sterling as the anchor currency. The Jordanian dinar began to be issued in July 1950.[33] At this point Transjordan rejoined the sterling area and its note issue was based on 100 percent sterling cover. Palestine pounds were exchanged for the new Jordanian dinars until June 1951 and then redeemed for sterling, which would also be held in the blocked sterling accounts. (The Palestine pound did, however, continue to circulate in the Western Province of Transjordan, reflecting trade with Palestine). A law establishing the Central Bank of Jordan was passed in 1959, and the bank started operations in 1964.[34]

In the turmoil of postwar Britain, when the new Labour Party government of Clement Atlee was trying to balance the demands of rebuilding Britain and managing an orderly withdrawal from an empire that had been three hundred years in the making, its winding down of Palestine Currency Board commitments could hardly have been managed better, especially where Arabs and Israelis themselves were unable to find a satisfactory modus vivendi.

WEST AFRICAN CURRENCY BOARD

Even the model West African Currency Board, which had acted as the example for so many other currency boards in British territories overseas (and indeed for the Caisse d'Emission operated by Britain during military operations in North Russia in 1917), did not survive the enthusiasm for national currencies and national central banks.

In Ghana, which became independent in 1957, the first calls to replace the West African Currency Board with a central bank dated back to 1947, at the point when Sri Lanka was planning its own transition from currency board to central bank. In much the same way, the assumptions of that post-imperial time led people to believe that the creation of a central bank was an indispensable part of the machinery of government for an independent state, like a national airline, a "symbol of political maturity."[35] British responses to these developments were not entirely passive. No objection could be made to the trappings of national currency in the form of distinctive notes and coins appropriate to each country. Separate national entities for the management of those currencies would also be perfectly understandable, but it was the potential policies to be adopted that gave the British side cause for concern. Colonial administrators urged newly independent states, such as Ghana, to be cautious in setting up their central banks, advising 100 percent reserves and convertibility to sterling—in other words, almost a currency board (as then understood) by another name. Although this point of view was apparently based on a concern that central bank arrangements and poorly backed currencies had not always been successful elsewhere, it is a fact that at this time Britain was desperately worried about a drain of sterling balances from London. For this reason, the government and the Bank of England were anxious to prop up the sterling area by persuading former colonies to hold sterling as the primary reserve currency. In a Bretton Woods world where the dollar had become the premier global currency and sterling had taken a battering in the period immediately following the war and then again during the Suez crisis (and the United Kingdom was committed to maintaining a par value for its currency under the rules of the International Monetary Fund), British officials did everything they could to maintain international demand for sterling. The moves by newly independent states, such as Ghana and Nigeria, to establish their own central banks threatened this demand, and the operations of the West African Currency Board declined accordingly.

As the constituent states of the West African Currency Board withdrew from the arrangement, Britain took steps to wind it up altogether, posting officials to the four countries (Nigeria, Ghana, Sierra Leone, and Gambia) to arrange for redemption of banknotes and repatriation of coins to the United

Kingdom. Attempts were made to identify lessons from the dissolution of the Palestine Currency Board. Nigeria soon followed Ghana out of the board in 1958, followed by Sierra Leone in 1963 and Gambia in 1964. At the end of June 1963, notes and coins in circulation in the remaining currency board areas were valued at about fifteen million pounds, when they had amounted to about one hundred million pounds in value five years earlier.[36] By 1965 the board had been wound up.[37]

EAST AFRICAN CURRENCY BOARD

As the West African Currency Board was winding down, a review of the operation of the East African Currency Board was underway, advised by Dr. Erwin Blumenthal, a representative of the Deutsche Bundesbank. Blumenthal's 1962 study, invited by the government of what was then called Tanganyika, concluded that, although the currency board had made efforts to perform the functions of a central bank, it would soon reach the limits of what it could do in that respect. In other words, if the aspiration was to have a monetary authority that would perform the functions of a central bank, it should no longer operate as a currency board. Blumenthal, however, went further, suggesting that the appropriate replacement would be a regional central bank (based in Arusha, Tanganyika) having the sole right to issue legal tender currency for the four participating countries of Uganda, Kenya, Tanganyika, and Zanzibar (the last of which was at that time a British protectorate and not yet a part of what is now Tanzania). The Blumenthal proposals also set out the idea that each of the participating countries should have its own state bank to handle national operations. Nearly forty years before the birth of the euro, Blumenthal was proposing a monetary governance structure not dissimilar to that of the Eurosystem.

The senior administrators of the currency board itself recognized that such a structure would have required a degree of political federation post-independence.[38] Yet political federation was not to come to fruition at that time. For various reasons, mostly internal and national in character, the political leaders of the countries involved in the 1960s could not find common ground for the establishment of a federation. But efforts to maintain a regional intergovernmental framework were established in 1967 in the form of the East African Community, the member states of which now include the former participants in the East African Currency Board as well as Burundi, Rwanda, and South Sudan. Mirroring the development of the European Union, the East African Community countries have signed protocols covering the establishment of a common market and customs union, and, in 2013, a further agreement on the creation of a common currency was signed.[39] National interests could still impede the development of this project, but it is not now impossible to imagine Blumenthal's vision of the early 1960s coming to fruition.

ITALY'S TRUSTEESHIP IN SOMALIA

At the end of the First World War, the loss of territories by the defeated imperial powers of Germany and Turkey led to the establishment of new states moving toward independence under a temporary "mandate" granted to the victorious powers. In these circumstances, the latter were authorized by the League of Nations to govern those territories until they were ready for complete independence. The former Ottoman territories, governed under a League of Nations mandate, included Palestine and Transjordan, administered by Britain, and Syria, administered by France. Former German territories in Africa and in the Pacific were similarly administered after the war under League of Nations mandates, granted to France, Belgium, and Britain. At the end of the Second World War, the United Nations decided that ten of these territories administered under a League of Nations mandate were now to be administered under a UN trusteeship. Somalia, which had not been a League of Nations mandated territory, was added to the list of UN trustee territories. The question was now, which country would be best placed to act there on behalf of the United Nations?

After the Second World War Italy lost the overseas territories formerly under its control. In the unique case of Somalia, however, the United Nations paused for thought. In contrast to the winning powers' mood at the end of the First World War, neither Britain, France, nor America were interested in taking on a mandate for the government of Somalia for as long as it took to decolonize the country. France and Britain, it will be remembered, had had minimal territorial interest in the Horn of Africa during the heyday of imperial expansion in Africa. The experience of the Second World War left both countries economically drained and less certain of their position in the world, even less likely to extend their overseas commitments. And, with no history of territorial ambition in Africa and a declared foreign policy in opposition to colonialism, America was even less inclined to accept the responsibility. Faute de mieux, the defeated former colonial power, Italy was granted the "trusteeship" of Somalia for a ten-year period from 1950 to 1960, at the end of which Somalia was to obtain complete independence. Adding to the unique nature of this case, Italy was not even a member of the United Nations when the trustee period began. This, together with Italy's wartime record as a fascist state, led the United Nations to impose particularly strict governance conditions for the Italian trusteeship.

During this period of trusteeship, Italy was charged with developing the political, social, and economic institutions of Somalia to prepare the country for independence. In its attempt to prepare Somalia for self-government, Italy unsurprisingly sought to emulate the institutions familiar to its own political and cultural experience. An inclination to graft Italy's own governmental structures onto Somalia, where a deep-rooted clan system overlay regional rivalries, was reinforced by the fact that thousands of Italian settlers remained in the country during the period of the trusteeship. Their presence and the prospect of a new relationship with Somalia as a potentially attractive export market invited the establishment of structures—including a monetary system—with which the Italian state was familiar and which would facilitate a successful transition and trading relationship.[40]

The Banca d'Italia had played a central role in Italy's earliest African ventures as supplier of currency since 1885. Bonert Stringher, the director general of the Banca D'Italia during the first two decades of the twentieth century, had been an active proponent of territorial expansion and of the bank's potential for aiding that expansion. It had established its first branch in Mogadishu as early as 1920 and was consequently familiar with Somalia as a place in which to operate. In 1948, the Banca d'Italia conducted a study on the possibilities for Somalia's new monetary arrangements. Ruling out the introduction of Italy's own monetary system, as well as the possibility of a separate currency linked to the Italian system, both on the grounds that, should Somalia's new monetary system founder, it would also have implications for Italy's own currency, the study concluded that an entirely independent currency would be most suitable. In fact, the preponderance of Somalia's trade with its neighbors pointed toward a pegged exchange rate to the East African shilling. The creation of a currency board–like mechanism in the form of a Casa per la Circolazione Monetaria della Somalia would guarantee stability of the new currency. The casa was to be based in Italy and directed largely by representatives of key Italian institutions, including the Banca d'Italia. Its responsibilities would be limited to the issue of currency and advice to the authorities in Somalia on currency matters. The administrative execution of the casa's policies, the ordering of the notes and coins, storage of the monetary reserves, withdrawal of worn notes and coins from circulation, and general accounting tasks rested with the Banca d'Italia. However, the key difference between Somalia's casa and a classical currency board was that the former would not be based on a single currency for convertibility purposes, but rather the casa would hold a variety of currencies as well as gold. Reserves equaled the total amount of currency in circulation so that, in this sense, the system more closely resembled a currency board than the rather less stringent arrangements that applied to the leading foreign currencies during the gold standard era when reserve holdings of the anchor currency might equate to only 40 percent of the currency on issue.[41]

The Somalo, the new currency for Somalia, was introduced by the Italian authorities in May 1950. Its nominal gold standard value as set by the International Monetary Fund gave it parity with the East African shilling. Because Britain had introduced the East African shilling into Somalia following its defeat of Italy in Eastern Africa in 1941, the replacement of the shilling by a Somalo at the rate of one for one offered a simple rate of exchange at par for the population needing to exchange their old shilling notes. It also removed an opportunity for traders to inflate prices during the transitional period. Those who held legacy Italian lira notes surrendered them at a rate of 87.5 lira for one Somalo.[42]

The process of converting East African shillings into Somalo was to take place over two months between May 22 and July 22, 1950, and was carried out by three banks in Mogadishu and five mobile offices operating in the provinces. In stark contrast to Italy's earliest attempts to impose European currency in the Horn of Africa, which had been met with resistance, the local population now welcomed the introduction of the Somalo and moved enthusiastically to convert their holdings of shillings. It had been three decades since the Banca d'Italia had first opened an office in Mogadishu, so a generation had grown up used to the circulation of notes in the country. This and a one-for-one exchange rate to the shilling together with the designation Somalo, which clearly pointed toward the coming independence of the country, created conditions favorable for the changeover. In fact, the parity of the Somalo to the shilling led to the local population's continuing to refer to the new currency as the shilling.[43]

Toward the end of the trusteeship period, Italy agreed with the emerging government of Somalia that the casa would be converted to a central bank and transferred to Mogadishu well before the end of the trusteeship, which was scheduled for December 1960. This would enable the local authorities to become used to the currency-issuing operation, but also enabled Somalia's government to make an early start on exercising control over what for them was a key instrument of sovereignty. In fact the date of independence was brought forward to July 1, 1960, and full responsibility for the currency was transferred to the new Somali central bank as of June 30. Noting that the population had continued to refer to the Somalo as a shilling, the new government, in an early assertion of its authority, had passed legislation in 1959 changing the name of Somalia's currency to the shilling. The decision may also have owed something to a pragmatic belief that Somalia was likely to trade more with British East Africa than it would with Italy.[44] Various measures were introduced in 1961 to remove East African shillings from circulation, and the Somalo itself, replaced by the Somali shilling at the rate of one to one, ceased to be legal tender in December 1963. By introducing a currency at the rate of one to one with the East African shilling, the Italian authorities enabled a smooth transition to the new currency and recognized the realities of Somalia's local trading relationships. That it was replaced by a new currency that differed from the Somalo only on the basis of its name was a testament to the fact that the Somalo did what was required of it as a transitional currency.[45]

INDOCHINA 1945–1954—THE
AFFAIR OF THE PIASTRES

Few countries demonstrate in their recent history as clearly as Vietnam the willingness of a small but nevertheless determined country to resist foreign control and foreign currency regimes. An overseas French colony since 1887 when various provinces of modern Vietnam were formed together with Cambodia into French Indochina (Laos being added to the union in 1893), the country was permanently in a state of conflict from the end of the Second World War to 1975. Briefly seized by Japan in March 1945 and held until Japan's surrender in August of that year, French Indochina's currency regime was destabilized by Japanese policy, but not by the introduction of military scrip as had been the case in Burma, Philippines, and Indonesia. In those cases, while Japan had the initiative and the belief in its own ability to create a new empire, it planned ahead to produce and issue military scrip. By the time of the March 1945 coup d'état, by which Japan overthrew French control of Indochina, the senior commanders in Japan and in the key theaters knew they were facing defeat and were on the back foot. Rather than attempt to issue military scrip in Indochina, they simply exploited the existing local colonial note-issuing arrangements. During the three months of Japanese control, the Banque de l'Indochine and the Institut d'Emission were forced to issue abnormally high volumes of five hundred piastre notes, promoting high levels of inflation.[46]

France's attempt to reassert control over Vietnam at the end of the war did not attract the support of America, which had insisted on a postwar commitment toward self-determination and decolonization (at least in so far as the old European empires were concerned). And for many Vietnamese, the successive collapse of the French and Japanese colonial powers in 1945 provided the opportunity to nationalists and communists to assert the country's independence. In September 1945—less than a month after Japan's surrender—Ho Chi Minh declared an independent Democratic Republic of Vietnam and introduced a national currency called the *dong*. Although the dong circulated in competition with the piastre, rebels determined to overthrow the French colonial power were still happy to accumulate piastres. The excessive issue of five hundred piastre notes by the Japanese provided a ready supply of notes for anti-colonial forces, but they were also in wide use among the population and even among Chinese troops liberating the north. Unable to resist the opportunity to exploit the situation, the commander of Chinese forces in the north of the country unilaterally devalued the piastre against the Chinese currency known as the customs gold unit. Where the Chinese currency unit had previously been exchanged for a piastre at one to one, it was now worth 1.5 piastres, giving Chinese troops a serious advantage over the local population in the market for produce, commodities, and even land. The Chinese commander in the north, Lu Han, also demanded that the Banque d'Indochine redeem for francs the Japanese-issued five hundred piastre notes.

With inflationary stocks of five hundred piastre notes convertible to francs and in the hands of both the opposition Viet Minh organization and Chinese troops, the French authorities had to take urgent action. In November 1945 the five hundred piastre notes were demonetized with next to no compensation, somewhat along the same lines as the British had done with Japanese-issued rupees in Burma at the end of the war. In Burma, the demonetization plan had as one of its objectives the punishment of those who had collaborated with the Japanese and had profiteered during the war; in Indochina under resurgent French control, however, the purpose had been to starve the anti-French forces in the north of currency and to close off a massive potential liability in francs being exploited by the Chinese.[47]

France's monetary administration of Indochina post-1945 was hardly designed to endear it to the local population. Since the 1930s, the piastre had been worth ten francs, but following Bretton Woods, France devalued the franc against colonial currencies in 1945 to boost French exports to its overseas territories; the piastre was strengthened from ten to seventeen francs to the piastre. The sole note-issuing authority, the Banque d'Indochine, supported the move because each piastre note it issued was now worth seven francs more than it had been previously. In reality the market in Indochina continued to value the piastre at its prewar rate of one to ten francs. Because the Office Indochine des Changes was obliged to exchange a piastre at the official rate of one to seventeen francs, French troops stationed in Indochina would buy one piastre with ten francs at the market rate and then cash it in for seventeen francs at the official rate. The profits could be even more substantial if the exchange chain involved US dollar exchanges for piastres on the black market. In fact, it later emerged that American Embassy and aid officials had been playing the black market to keep prices down, buying piastres at the reduced rate with US dollars, which in many cases were finding their way to the Viet Minh forces and helping to pay for their armaments.

The unnaturally high exchange rate of the piastre during this period and the enormous exchange rate trade—doubling in value every two years from 1948—was sucking more francs into Indochina and contributing to the spiraling cost of the war. Many of the largest sets of transactions, however, were then returned to France so that the exchange in Indochina was acting as a revolving door. In at least one case, the beneficiary of the transactions was the Gaullist Party in France, which was going through difficult financial times.

A 70 percent profit (at least) in francs on each piastre was a major incentive for soldiers and bureaucrats to serve in Indochina and to maintain France's authority there. In much the same way that American officials supported currency advantages for American troops in European theaters during the Second World War,[48] proponents of the strong piastre asserted that it was only fair that French troops should benefit in some way from their arduous and dangerous service in Indochina. When this situation was exposed in 1952 as the "Affair of the Piastres," it became one of a handful of scandals dogging France's Fourth Republic and forced the French government to restore the old exchange rate of one piastre to ten francs, bringing the official rate into line with the market rate and saving the military budget an estimated fifty to seventy billion francs per year. Whether this revaluation was economically disadvantageous to Indochina or not, the fact that the revaluation was unilateral without prior consultation angered local Vietnamese political leaders, adding impetus to the drive for independence. At home in France, the scandal was a major factor in a growing disillusion with what was being seen as a dirty war, hardly worth supporting, and indeed France pulled out of Indochina in 1954.[49]

THE FRANC IN SUB-SAHARAN AFRICA

In the postwar readjustment to a new world based on American political hegemony and a dominant new reserve currency in the form of the dollar, existing European powers—or at least some of them—understood that their empires were facing dissolution. Some countries adjusted more effectively to the coming changes than others. After setbacks in Indochina and Algeria, France's policy in this respect was one of skillful adaptation to the new world, especially in Sub-Saharan Africa, without quite the resignation of Britain to loss of empire.

Until the Second World War the locally issued colonial francs circulating in France's Sub-Saharan territories were pegged at one to one with the French franc. In 1945 in the aftermath of the Bretton Woods conference, the French franc was devalued to boost French exports and stimulate the country's economy. The CFA (Colonies Francaises d'Afrique) franc was created in response to the devaluation of the French franc designed to help France's economic recovery by boosting exports. Recognizing that a devalued franc would have constrained the exports of its colonies to their main market, France, Paris agreed to create the CFA franc.

In 1958 the establishment of France's Fifth Republic under Charles De Gaulle included a revision of its colonial establishment. Two years later a number of France's Sub-Saharan African colonies became independent, and the Colonies Francaises d'Afrique became the Communaute Francaise d'Afrique, a gathering of countries independent of France but still tied in monetary matters in the same way that many of Britain's colonies remained in the sterling zone after independence. Because the former African colonies remained important export markets for France, it was crucial for France's commerce with the region that the former colonies' currencies should be stable with respect to the French franc.

For those former colonies in Sub-Saharan Africa, two monetary unions were created and a regional bank established for each of them. Former colonies were invited to choose whether they would participate or not. The two monetary unions continued to use the legacy monetary unit of the CFA franc, which had existed since 1948 and was originally pegged to the French franc at fifty to one. Backing for the CFA franc was in due course relaxed below the requirement for 100 percent cover in gold, French francs, or other convertible currency so that securities issued by the local governments were acceptable. Currency was issued by each of the two zones, and, although one of the central banks proposed individual currencies for each of the countries within its zone, the proposal met with no enthusiasm among the participating governments (although issue by individual states of the Central African franc zone did indeed take place between 1975 and 1993). With only a few exceptions, the political leadership of the newly independent states was generally conservative in outlook and not disposed toward a complete break with France. Only the emergence of a new generation of educated, professional leaders in places such as Guinea, Mali, Madagascar, and Mauretania would lead to a complete rupture with France's currency hegemony in some but not all of its former African colonies.[50] Nevertheless, two franc zones survive in Sub-Saharan Africa and, along with a handful of British Overseas Territories, form the last vestiges of the European monetary empire. France's management of the decline of its monetary influence in Africa has so far been skillful. But nothing lasts forever, and further major changes are now underway in the franc zone, again reducing France's monetary influence in the region (see chapter 9).

In this overview, we have only been able to sample some of the many instances of monetary management in a post-imperial era. Over seventy countries have obtained independence from European empires in the postwar period. In the overwhelming majority of cases, they have introduced their own currencies, with most establishing a central bank and some adhering to the currency board principles that worked for them during their period as colonies. Yet others have adopted the currencies of other countries for the sake of convenience or pooled their monetary sovereignty to create currency unions, proving that political independence offers the right to choose from among a variety of options.

NOTES

1. Dail in Committee, Coinage Bill, 1926, second-stage debate, January 27, 1926; Ewan Morris, "Devilish Devices or Farmyard Friends?," *History Ireland* 12, no. 1 (2004), accessed January 9, 2020, https://www.historyireland. com/20th-century-contemporary-history/devilish-devices-or-farmyard-friends/.

2. I am grateful to Jonathan Callaway, director of the International Banknote Society, for drawing to my attention this printed inscription.

3. Eric Helleiner, *The Making of National Money: Territorial Currencies in Historical Perspective* (New York: Cornell University Press, 2003), 154–155; John L. Pratschke, "The Establishing of the Irish Pound: A Backward Glance," *Economic and Social Review* 1, no. 1 (1969): 70–72, http://www.tara.tcd.ie/bitstream/handle/2262/68789/v1n11969_3.pdf?sequence=1&isAllowed=; and Patrick Honohan, "Currency Board or Central Bank? Lessons from the Irish Pound's Link with Sterling 1928–1979," Economic and Social Research Institute, 1994, 6, https://www.researchgate.net/publication/4836435_Currency_Board_or_Central_Bank_Lessons_from_the_Irish_Pound percent27s_Link_with_Sterling_1928-79.

4. Pratcshke, "The Establishing of the Irish Pound: A Backward Glance," 52, 63.

5. Michael Bordo and Lars Jonung, "The Future of EMU: What Does the History of Monetary Unions Tell Us?," Working paper, National Bureau of Economic Research, 1999, 21, https://www.nber.org/papers/w7365; and Honohan, "Currency Board or Central Bank?," 7, 9–10.

6. Central Bank of Sri Lanka, "The Bank's Beginning," https://www.cbsl.gov.lk/en/about/about-the-bank/bank-history; Helleiner, *The Making of National Money*, 195.

7. Sean Turnell, *Fiery Dragons: Banks, Moneylenders and Microfinance in Burma* (Copenhagen: Nordic Institute of Asian Studies Press, 2009), 142.

8. Ibid., 144–146.

9. Ibid., 163.

10. "The Palestine Mandate, Article 2," Yale Law School, Avalon Project, http://avalon.law.yale.edu/20th_century/palmanda.asp.

11. "Termination of the Mandate for Palestine (1948)," Economic Cooperation Foundation, https://ecf.org.il/issues/issue/945; "Creation of Israel 1948," Office of the Historian, US Department of State, https://history.state.gov/milestones/1945-1952/creation-israel; "UN General Assembly Resolution 181," Truman Library, https://www.trumanlibrary.org/israel/unres181.htm.

12. Report of the Palestine Commission to the Second Special Session of the General Assembly of the United Nations, April 10, 1948, Part 3B and C, https://unispal.un.org/DPA/DPR/unispal.nsf/0/BCE2BD823185E523802564AA0056DAEA.

13. "Future of the Palestine Currency Board," Cabinet Office File CO 537/2307, The National Archives, Kew, London, prepared in response to a parliamentary question posed by Sir Edward Keeling, MP, on the future of the Palestine Currency Board, https://discovery.nationalarchives.gov.uk/details/r/C1250833.

14. "Parliamentary Debate of 2 March 1948," HC Deb, 2 March 1948, c207, https://www.theyworkforyou.com/debates/?id=1948-03-02a.205.10#g207.5.

15. Report of the Palestine Commission to the Second Special Session of the General Assembly of the United Nations, Introduction, paragraph F3, https://unispal.un.org/DPA/DPR/unispal.nsf/0/BCE2BD823185E523802564AA0056DAEA.

16. "The Question of Palestine," United Nations Palestine Commission, Communication Received from the United Kingdom Delegation Concerning the Palestine Currency Board, May 11, 1948. https://www.un.org/unispal/document/auto-insert-210581/.

17. "Sterling Balances (Palestine) 12 July 1949" House of Commons, TheyWorkForYou, https://www.theyworkforyou.com/debates/?id=1949-07-12a.202.3.

18. United Nations Palestine Commission, Report dated 10 March from the Advance Party concerning discussion with Finance and Currency Officers, https://www.un.org/unispal/document/auto-insert-211073/, and Memorandum dated 12 March from the Advance Party concerning Currency and Foreign Exchange, https://www.un.org/unispal/document/auto-insert-211808/.

19. "Palestine Currency Board to Undersecretary of State, Colonial Office 11 June," Cabinet Office File 537/3878, The National Archives, Kew, London.

20. "History of the Bank, Bank of Israel, https://www.boi.org.il/en/AboutTheBank/History/Pages/Default.aspx.

21. "Anglo Palestine Bank Series," Bank of Israel, https://www.boi.org.il/en/Currency/PastNotesAndCoinsSeries/Pages/Default.aspx. A rather confused article in *Haaretz* dated April 13, 2018, states first that the notes were to be produced in America and then shipped to Europe and flown on to Israel. Two paragraphs later, the report states that the notes arrived from Ceylon. The same report suggests that the notes were based on Ceylon's own designs of the time, but a cursory glance of images available online shows that Ceylon's notes on issue in 1948 were quite different from those issued by the Anglo-Palestine Bank. "Forgotten Stories from 70 Years of Israeli Economic History," *Haaretz*, https://www.haaretz.com/israel-news/business/forgotten-stories-from-70-years-of-israeli-economic-history-1.5994597; "U.S. Recognition of the State of Israel," US National Archives, https://www.archives.gov/education/lessons/us-israel.

22. St. Louis Federal Reserve Bulletin, 1948, citing the Ordinance in translation: https://fraser.stlouisfed.org/files/docs/publications/FRB/pages/1945-1949/30313_1945-1949.pdf.

23. "Foreign Office Letter to Bank Leumi, 20 June 1951, "Foreign Office File 371/91388, Palestine Currency Board, The National Archives, Kew, London.

24. "Status of the Question of Unfreezing of Assets, November 23, 1949," United Nations Conciliation Commission for Palestine, https://www.un.org/unispal/document/auto-insert-211947/.

25. Ibid.

26. "Summary Record of the Two Hundred and Sixth Meeting, 6 March 1951," UN Conciliation Commission for Palestine, https://unispal.un.org/DPA/DPR/unispal.nsf/.

27. Letter from Egyptian Ministry of Finance, Cairo to Foreign Office, London, 24 August 1951, Foreign Office File FO 371/91388, The National Archives, Kew, London.

28. League of Nations Mandate of Palestine and Article 25 of the Palestine Mandate, Memorandum by the British Representative, https://dl.wdl.org/11572/service/11572.pdf.

29. "The Making of Transjordan," Hashemite Kingdom of Jordan, http://www.kinghussein.gov.jo/his_transjordan.html. Some people have inferred from the fact that Jordan used the Palestine pound that it was part of the Palestine mandate; in other words, Transjordan was a part of Palestine because it used the same currency. From this it has been inferred that Transjordan was intended to be the Arab area of Palestine. The flaw in this argument is that Britain had circulated one currency for multiple political entities under its administration in other regions. (See following sections on West African Currency Board, East African Currency Board, and Malaysia/Singapore). The circulation of a single currency in multiple jurisdictions did not, in the British administrative system, indicate a shared polity or national identity. See also W. F. Crick, *Commonwealth Banking Systems* (Oxford: Clarendon Press, 1965), 159, on this point.

30. "Note on Currency and Banking in Palestine and Transjordan, 18 July 1949," United Nations Conciliation Commission for Palestine, https://www.un.org/unispal/document/auto-insert-211494/; A. Basch, Development Projects in Jordan, June 25, 1951, International Bank for Reconstruction and Development, World Bank Documents.

31. "Note on Palestine Assets," United Nations Conciliation Commission for Palestine, https://www.un.org/unispal/document/auto-insert-210827/; "Communication Received from the Jewish Agency for Palestine Concerning Currency Arrangements, March 18, 1948," United Nations Palestine Commission, https://www.un.org/unispal/document/auto-insert-211493/; and International Bank for Reconstruction and Development, Development Projects in Jordan, June 25, 1951.

32. Beith, J G S (Foreign Office, London) to Higham, J (Colonial Office) 18 March 1948, Cabinet Office File 537/3878, The National Archives, Kew, London.

33. "Jordan: Selected Issues," International Monetary Fund, https://www.imf.org/external/pubs/ft/scr/2008/cr08291.pdf; "All About the Jordanian Dinar, April 20, 2015," Treasury Vault Blog, https://treasuryvault.com/blog/all-about-jordan-dinar/; Steve H. Hanke and Kurt Schuler, "Currency Boards and Currency Convertibility," *Cato Journal* 12, no. 3 (1993), 687–727, http://latlibre.org/wp-content/uploads/2019/02/99Schuler02.pdf.

34. "Central Bank of Jordan: 50 Years of Achievements," 1–4, December 2017, https://www.cbj.gov.jo/EchoBusv3.0/SystemAssets/PDFs/EN/50th%20 acheivements.pdf.

35. "Information about Bank of Ghana," Bank of Ghana, https://www.bog. gov.gh/about-the-bank/; Helleiner, *The Making of National Money*, 201; Crick, *Commonwealth Banking Systems*, 15.

36. Crick, *Commonwealth Banking Systems*, 6.

37. Helleiner, *The Making of National Money*, 204.

38. Crick, *Commonwealth Banking Systems*, 404–405.

39. Elias Biryabarema, "East African Trade Bloc Approves Monetary Union Deal," *Reuters*, November 30, 2013, https://www.reuters.com/article/ us-africa-monetaryunion-idUSBRE9AT08O20131130.

40. Donatella Strangio, *The Reasons for Underdevelopment: The Case of Decolonisation in Somaliland* (Berlin-Heidelberg: Physica Verlag, 2012), 8–12.

41. Ibid., 16.

42. Ibid., 18.

43. Ibid., 21.

44. Ibid., 22–25.

45. Peter Symes, "The Banknotes of Somalia, Part 2," http://www.pjsymes.com.au/ articles/somalia(part2).htm.

46. "Currency, French Indochina," University of Quebec at Montreal, http:// indochine.uqam.ca/en/historical-dictionary/333-currency-french-indochina.html.

47. Ibid.

48. See Paul Wilson, *Hostile Money: Currencies in Conflict* (Cheltenham: The History Press, 2019), 181.

49. "Currency, French Indochina"; and Jonathan Marshall, "Dirty Wars: French and American Piaster Profiteering in Indochina, 1945–75," *The Asia-Pacific Journal* 12, no. 32 (2014).

50. Helleiner, The Making of National Money, 210, 212–13.

Chapter 6

Secession

Following decolonization after the Second World War, some countries underwent further reordering of their sovereignty and monetary allegiance. In some cases, a country that had recently become independent might find that one of its constituent parts then sought independence for itself. Thus, Pakistan separated from India in 1947, and the move was reprised when Bangladesh separated from Pakistan in 1971. British Somaliland, briefly united with Italian Somaliland (Somalia), then broke away again. Although the African Union resists the alteration of colonial borders as a threat to opening a Pandora's box of border problems that had been for a time avoided by European colonial policy and administration (and indeed Somaliland, for this reason, remains largely unrecognized by multinational and international communities), the African Union did endorse the decision of South Sudan to break free of Sudan. Both Somaliland and South Sudan now have their own currencies, regardless of whether those currencies are recognized elsewhere or are working to the benefit of the countries concerned. This was also the case with Singapore in 1966, which left the Malaysian federation, and, after a failed attempt to forge a common currency with Malaysia, settled for its own currency.

In other cases, one monetary union was abandoned, only for the newly independent country then to form a monetary allegiance elsewhere as if a reorientation of monetary allegiance rather than complete monetary independence was the objective. This was much the case in Estonia, Slovakia, and East Timor. There could be other outcomes as well. Hong Kong, free of Britain after a little over 150 years, was handed back to China, but not obliged to adopt the yuan. But, more often than not, new countries have given birth to new currencies, even if only for a short period.

In this chapter we shall examine a number of countries the governments of which at independence had to make decisions as to the monetary regime that would most suit their individual circumstances. In some cases, the choice of one monetary regime or another was based overwhelmingly on economic calculations. In other cases, the decision was based less on economic and more on political considerations. We will also observe other instances where a monetary regime was selected purely because it was administratively convenient. The evidence points toward a conclusion that there is no single solution to the question of which currency regime should a new country adopt.

SINGAPORE 1965: SOVEREIGNTY AND RESERVES

In 1957 the Federation of Malaya, consisting of the Straits Settlements of Penang and Malacca together with nine Malay states, gained independence from Britain. In Singapore, which was similarly moving toward independence but had not quite reached that point, leading political figures of the governing People's Action Party (PAP) believed that Singapore's economic development and, indeed, the state's survival depended on merger with Malaya. But there were reservations among Malaya's political leaders. The conservative United Malays National Organisation (UMNO), the governing party in Kuala Lumpur, perceived Singapore's PAP as pro-communist and feared the ethnic Chinese majority in Singapore would become dominant in the federation. UMNO therefore opposed a merger with Singapore alone on both political and ethnic grounds. One possible solution to the problem of the ethnic Chinese becoming dominant was proposed by Tungku Abdul Rahman, the prime minister of the Federation of Malaysia in May 1961. This proposal sought to counterbalance the Singapore Chinese by incorporating into Malaya the states of Sarawak and North Borneo, where the populations were ethnically Malayan. In 1963, Singapore, North Borneo, and Sarawak joined the federation, which then became known as Malaysia.

The merger, however, got off to a poor start. Malaysians in Singapore hoped that it would lead to preferential employment for themselves in the new Federation of Malaysia but were disappointed by the local PAP policies, which did not accommodate Malayan aspirations. Stirred up by some UMNO politicians, ethnic riots broke out between Chinese and Malayans in Singapore in 1964. There were differences, also, over Singapore's level of contributions to the state's defense costs at a time of hostilities with Indonesia. As reported in retrospective articles in the Singaporean press fifty years after the events, the Malaysian federal finance minister sought significant increases in tax receipts from Singapore, amounting to some 35 percent of all of Malaysia's revenues when Singapore's population amounted to 17 percent of the whole of the federation at most.[1]

Tensions increased when UMNO and PAP decided to field candidates in elections in Singapore and Malaysia, respectively, fostering a belief that both parties were interfering in the local politics of Singapore and Malaysia.

Given the prospects for a continuing deterioration in the relationship between Malaysia and Singapore, the former's prime minister, Tungku Abdul Rahman, took the unusual step, perhaps unique in postwar politics, of deciding to separate Singapore and Malaysia.

On August 9, 1965, the Malaysian parliament voted unanimously (in the absence of the Singaporean members) for separation. The prime minister of Singapore, Lee Kuan Yew, declared Singapore independent the same afternoon. Some commentaries note that Lee, who was personally committed to the idea of union with Malaysia, had tried to find a compromise with the government in Kuala Lumpur prior to the vote. Other reports—based on the recollections of Singaporean politicians involved in the negotiations with Malaysia—suggest that Lee had already reconciled himself to separation and authorized representatives to discuss it with the government of Malaysia as early as July 26, with the agreement to separate being signed on August 7. If these recollections as to chronology are correct, Singapore was not expelled from the Malaysian Federation by the vote on August 9. It was more a case of an agreement to separate, which the Malaysian parliament then endorsed.[2]

The period between the intergovernmental negotiations for Singapore's departure from the federation and the declaration of independence was so short that there was no time to prepare a new currency for Singapore. But the issue of a new currency for an independent Singapore was not, perhaps, a matter of immediate urgency. There had been a lengthy period during which the currency of Malaya had circulated in Singapore even when the two British colonies were quite separate jurisdictions. From 1938 the British colonial authorities had merged the currency-issuing arrangements of Malaya and the Straits Settlements, a group of colonies including Singapore south of the Malayan states. Following the wartime occupation of Singapore by Japan, Japanese notes were withdrawn from circulation, and from 1950, during the last phase of its colonial period and before Singapore had joined the Federation of Malaysia, Singapore continued to share its currency with Malaya under the Board of Commissioners of Currency, Malaya and British Borneo. Currency issued by this entity circulated in Malaya and Singapore, but also in North Borneo (now Sabah), Sarawak, and Brunei. This shared currency arrangement had even continued following Malaya's independence in 1957. Thus, Singaporeans had been used to sharing their currency with Malaya under various states of political independence since 1938. Some continuity in currency matters following independence might even have been desirable. The Singaporean leadership did not therefore start from the position that independence from Malaysia necessarily meant the end of a shared currency.

Two months after Singapore left the federation, the governor of Bank Negara Malaysia—the central bank—was authorized to hold discussions with Singaporean authorities to explore the options for operating a common currency. His initial proposal was to have two separate designs—one for Singapore and one for Malaysia—each of which would be permitted to circulate in both countries. The Singaporean side sought to limit Bank Negara's freedom of maneuver in issuing Singaporean currency by asserting that it should act as Singapore's agent and only at its direction.

Negotiations continued into the summer of 1966. The idea of two separate designs was set aside, replaced by the idea of one design, notes being identified only by the series prefix *M* as belonging to Malaysia or *S* for Singapore. But Singapore's most serious concerns centered on the control of reserves backing the common currency: quite understandably it wished to control its own reserves. Malaysia appeared to concede this point. All progress, however, ground to a halt over the apparently administrative assertion by Bank Negara that it would own the title to the property designated as the Singapore branch of the common bank because the Singapore branch, not being a legal entity in its own right, could not own assets. A seemingly minor point, but with more serious implications. If the Singapore branch could not own title to its own building, how could it own reserves?

Singapore made several counterproposals: either reserves could be lodged with a third party, such as the Bank of England, or the legal status of the Singapore branch could be modified to permit control of assets. But neither proposal succeeded in unblocking the impasse. The plan for a common currency fell apart because both parties were unable to reach agreement on the control of Singapore's reserves.[3] Both sides agreed that from 1967 Malaysia and Singapore—as well as Brunei—would issue separate currencies.[4]

Thus ended the idea of a shared currency relationship between Malaysia and Singapore, which had been a de facto and de jure currency union since 1938 with the exception of the period of Japanese occupation. But unlike virtually all former British colonies, Singapore looked back to the colonial era currency board system as one that could work for them. According to the recollections of Singapore's former finance minister, Goh Keng Swee, Singapore's cabinet ministers had all concluded that the currency board system was the right approach for the newly independent country. Their thinking was conditioned by events in major economies overseas, which included the devaluation of the pound in 1967, attributed by Goh to the British government's policies of spending and stimulating employment via credit policies of the Bank of England.[5] The cabinet concluded that the best means of combating inflation was to adopt a convertible currency that would remain strong, ensuring that the prices of goods imported to Singapore would be stable. Because Singapore had to import many of its requirements, this objective was a priority. But there was also a philosophical motive to adopting the currency board system. As recalled by Goh, Singapore's cabinet respected the economic approach of the German and Japanese governments: growth should not be stimulated by "loose" economic policies, dependent on a weak currency. Government budget deficits should be covered by taxes rather than central bank assistance. Although Singapore had little respect for the results of Britain's economic mismanagement in the 1960s, the government did recall the effectiveness of the colonial currency board system. Adopting the currency board system, the Singaporean government fixed the exchange rate of the Singapore dollar to the US dollar and passed a law requiring more than 100 percent cover in reserves (either foreign assets or gold) for all banknote issue.[6] By 1973, however, Singapore had moved away from the currency board system and allowed the Singaporean dollar to float. Further changes in the country's monetary regime have occurred since then, but the currency is still backed fully (at least 100 percent) by foreign assets or gold. This legacy feature of the colonial era currency board is still seen as a prudent element in managing Singapore's currency.

While many of Britain's former colonies established central banks at independence perhaps most commonly for reasons of prestige, Singapore notably elected to maintain a currency board regime, which its leadership considered to be the most reliable means of managing the new state's currency. Although Singapore has moved away from classic currency board principles, its continuing 100 percent cover of money on issue retains one of the key confidence-building measures of the currency board. That Singapore favored the currency board system for the reasons that it did might be seen as a reflection of the general disciplined approach to many issues adopted by the Singaporean government, which have made the former colony an economic success.

THE COLLAPSE OF THE RUBLE ZONE

Putting to one side for the moment the dismantlement of the empires of Britain, France, Belgium, and Portugal between the 1940s and the 1970s resulting in the birth of dozens of new independent states and currencies, the past twenty-five years have seen numerous instances of secession from some established and internationally recognized unions. Of these, the breakup of the Soviet Union, creating fifteen new republics, yielded the largest number of secessions in one go. The conditions for that fragmentation had been provided by new domestic policies of *perestroika* (restructuring) and *glasnost* (openness) introduced by the Soviet leader Mikhail Gorbachev in the mid-1980s. This attempt to liberalize both the politics and the economics of the Soviet Union was seen in "conservative" quarters as a dangerous loosening of the tight grip of the Communist Party on the Soviet Union and in both liberal and nationalist quarters as a signal that dissent would be tolerated. Protest movements and demonstrations flourished in the late 1980s, and tech-nocrats of a nationalist bent in various Soviet Republics began to think and plan for a new world in a way that would not have been previously tolerated.

The decision by the Baltic states—first and foremost, Lithuania in March 1990—to declare independence from the Soviet Union in the early 1990s triggered the wider dissolution of that union. The Russian parliament was quick to see the way the wind was blowing and declared Russia's sover-eignty three months later on June 12, 1990. Six months later, the State Bank of the Russian Federation began to take over the administrative functions of branches of the State Bank of the Soviet Union within Russia. The decisive split between Russia and other republics on the one hand and the Soviet Union on the other was exemplified by the former withholding tax revenues from the latter throughout 1991. Russian national institutions and leaders were pitched against Soviet hardliners, a conflict resolved only by the failure in August 1991 of a coup led by the latter. From this point onward, the Soviet State Bank had lost control over monetary policy. This and other functional failures spelled the end of the union. In December 1991 the Soviet Union was dissolved and all its constituent republics became independent.[7]

The collapse of the union did not mean the immediate end of the ruble zone. From the beginning of January 1992, the ruble continued to circulate in the newly independent republics, administered by the central banks of each of the independent republics and not by a single central authority. Even if Moscow was still in control of the production of physical cash, the other central banks issued ruble-denominated credit and in some cases—notably, Belarus, Moldova, and Georgia—also issued ruble-banknote substitutes in the form of ruble-denominated "coupons," of which the volume in circula-tion increased during the first half of 1992 when Russia failed to supply enough banknotes. The extension of ruble-denominated credits to enterprises in the former Soviet Republics encouraged large-scale imports from Russia, initially beneficial to Russian exporters, but in the longer term worrying for the Russian authorities, who would take steps to bring it under control in the second half of 1993.

At the same time, pricing policies introduced by the liberalizing govern-ment of Boris Yeltsin were designed to ease government control of prices and to cut the dependence of industry on state subsidies. After so many years of restrained pricing within a command economy, this liberalization released a surge of inflation. In the year from December 1991 to December 1992, retail prices increased sevenfold. The issue of local coupons, which were not convertible and valid only for transactions in the republic where they were issued, was increased to capture seigniorage.[8]

While some of the newly created republics emerging from the Soviet Union—the Baltic states and Georgia—immediately set about the introduction of their own currencies as a natural expression of independence, some decision-makers in the Russian Federation made efforts to preserve the ruble zone. Energy and some raw materials, which Russia itself was able to produce, were offered at great discount to republics that remained within the ruble zone.[9] In June 1992 twelve of the republics of the former Soviet Union—that is, all except Georgia and the Baltic states—agreed that they would give the other countries three months' notice of a decision to introduce an independent currency. Other provisions of this agreement covered the procedures to be followed in converting ruble holdings into new national currencies. In the event that a signatory failed to comply with these and other clauses, the other states would "take steps" to protect the ruble zone economies. Nevertheless, that same month, Kyrgyzstan announced its intention to introduce an independent currency, and in September 1992 Azerbaijan followed suit.

Despite various attempts on the part of Russia to form a consensus on a ruble zone with its former republics at conferences in Kyrgyzstan in October 1992 and in Moscow in May 1993, further cracks appeared in the arrangement. Ukraine failed to sign the June agreement and in October 1992 announced the introduction of its own currency, followed not long afterward by similar declarations by Moldova and Belarus. In the wake of these defections from the ruble zone, some leading conservatives in Moscow, notably Prime Minister Viktor Chernomyrdin, sought to hold together a shrunken ruble zone of Armenia, Belarus, Kazakhstan, Tajikistan, and Uzbekistan. Liberals wishing to concentrate on the reform of Russia's economy without external distractions opposed Chernomyrdin's position. A condition of membership of this final and much reduced incarnation of the ruble zone was the deposit in Moscow of hard currency amounting to 50 percent of the value of the rubles circulating in each of the remaining member states, a requirement not dissimilar to that applied to France's postcolonial franc zone in Sub-Saharan Africa. It was this requirement that was the last straw for some of the most loyal supporters of the ruble.[10]

Different republics of the former Soviet Union looked at the ruble zone in different ways: some sought to escape it as swiftly as possible for economic reasons to avoid the prospect of uncontrolled inflation imported from Russia or for reasons of national identity or indeed for a combination of the two reasons. Some of these countries also doubted the willingness of other republics to implement economic reform at a suitable pace. Other territories clung on to the ruble well beyond its natural end as a means of preserving the economic or political link to Russia or to avoid disruption to continuing trade between the former Soviet Republics. Just as there were (at least) two schools of thought within Russia regarding economic reform, the former republics

found themselves inclined either toward radical change or to a general conservatism. Domestic political factors could also form part of a government's
calculations. In the case of Kazakhstan there were concerns at the highest
level in government that a complete rupture with the ruble zone could have
negative effects on the economic well-being of the Russian population in the
north of Kazakhstan, with the potential consequence of civil disorder.

But in July 1993, Russia complicated an already difficult situation by carrying out a currency exchange, replacing the old series notes with a completely
new set, in order to neutralize the potential effect on the Russian economy
of the vast holdings of rubles in the former Soviet Republics being used to
make large scale purchases in Russia. The remonetization operation prompted
a flight from the ruble in the former Soviet Republics. A final attempt to
persuade the now reduced number of countries still using the ruble to accept
Russia's monetary hegemony was made in September 1993. An agreement
on the "New style ruble area" set out an uncompromising position where
Russia would determine money supply, interest rates and reserve requirements. Taken together with the flight from the ruble and the demand for hard
currency to be deposited in Moscow, this agreement was no more likely to
succeed as the basis for a working system than previous efforts. By the end
of November 1993 all the former Soviet Republics had abandoned the ruble
except Tajikistan which, in a state of civil war during which it was receiving
vital military support from Russia, continued to use the ruble until 1995.[11]

Secession has monetary implications not only for the newborn state, but
also for the remaining rump that it has left. The trauma of separation for a
great country may in some cases echo the economic shocks that beset an
imperial power separated from overseas colonies that are a vital source of raw
materials. Thus, Russia's loss of its Soviet satellites in 1991 brought with it
economic consequences that would have been recognizable to some conservative economists in Germany after the First World War. Hjalmar Schacht,
one-time president of the Reichsbank in the 1920s and one of Germany's
delegates to the various reparations conferences held in the interwar years,
bemoaned Germany's loss of its colonies in the postwar settlement because
it cut off his country's access to vital raw materials for German industry.
Similarly, large-scale Russian enterprises, separated from their easy access
to Tajikistan aluminum, Azerbaijan oil, Uzbek cotton, and Armenian copper
by the collapse of the union, struggled to adjust to the new situation, and
production dropped.

Among the various instances of countries abandoning the ruble, the case of
Estonia is particularly worthy of study.

ESTONIA 1992: THE BEGINNING OF
THE END FOR THE RUBLE ZONE

Throughout the late 1980s, the Soviet Union's grip on its constituent republics was loosened by demonstrations and protest movements from the Baltic to Central Asia and by a growing inclination for greater democratization at the highest decision-making levels in the Soviet Union. The Estonian Popular Front was in the vanguard of this movement, pressing from 1988 for the flying of the blue, black, and white national flag and the legalization of Estonian as the national language. In November 1988, the National Assembly—then, still the Supreme Soviet—declared that Estonian laws would take precedence over the laws of the Soviet Union. Although Lithuania was the first of the Soviet Republics to declare independence on March 11, 1990, the supreme council of Estonia began the move to complete independence at the end of the same month. It was not, however, until August 20, 1991, during the dark days of an attempted but ultimately unsuccessful coup in Russia by hardliners opposed to reform that Estonia, along with another nine former Soviet Republics declared its independence. On September 17, 1991, Estonia, Latvia, and Lithuania were all admitted as full members of the UN, sealing their independence.

First thoughts on an independent Estonian economy and a national currency had already been formulated as early as 1987, before the protest movements got underway across the Soviet Union. Among the principal concerns of the small group of social scientists who developed proposals for a new currency were the desire to protect the country against inflation imported from its main trading partner, the Soviet Union, and the need to avert repeated cash crises. In identifying these objectives, the team working on the original plan had correctly forecast the economic concerns. Russia's liberalization of prices of January 1992 had unleashed hyperinflation in the wider ruble zone. The inflation rates transmitted thereby to Estonia in the early months of 1992 were recorded at 87 percent in January, 74 percent in February, and 30 percent in March. While prices were expanding at inflationary or even hyperinflationary rates, the money supply was proving less than adequate, presumably because the supply of rubles from Moscow was failing. In extreme circumstances, the private sector often steps in to fill the gap, and indeed private enterprises began to issue money substitutes. The authorities also took exceptional measures to permit a local currency in Estonia's second City Tartu and to allow foreign currencies to circulate in parallel to the ruble. Action had to be taken before the combination of inflation and money supply problems could lead to serious social disorder.[12]

Although it was alleged that Russian authorities had threatened to seize any new currency being imported to Estonia, it had relaxed its position on national currencies by spring 1992 largely because of concern at the monetary policies pursued by some of the newly independent republics that remained within the ruble zone. In view of these unpredictable factors, the government of Russia became more interested in a smaller (and no doubt more controllable) ruble zone, although the Russian Central Bank pursued a different policy, continuing to extend credits to former Soviet Republics. Conditions had become favorable in both Estonia and Russia for the introduction of an Estonian national currency. Indeed, the International Monetary Fund (IMF) noted the existence of agreements between Russia and Estonia on monetary issues that provided for the retirement of rubles (rather than their return to Russia) as the kroon was introduced.[13]

On June 20, 1992, Estonia became the first of the former Soviet Socialist Republics to introduce its own currency. The following day President Yeltsin announced that the Soviet ruble was from that date the Russian ruble. Given that inflation was reaching 1,000 percent annually at the end of the Soviet period, authorities in Estonia sought to establish a currency that would above all offer price stability. The problem was that Estonia had no foreign reserves to back its new currency. In an interesting echo of the land bank principle put forward by John Law in the eighteenth century and propagated by the French revolutionary authorities, who cited church land as backing for assignats, the Estonian parliament allocated a large tract of forest as collateral for the new currency. But, as with those earlier essays at the creation of a land bank, there was a gap between concept and realization. Land could not rapidly be turned into foreign currency or gold on demand. Another more liquid form of backing would be desirable to instill confidence in the kroon.

The solution was to be found in Tallinn's gold reserves shipped to Britain, Sweden, and Switzerland prior to the Soviet Union's invasion of Estonia in 1940. A portion of these reserves were held by the Bank of International Settlements (BIS) at its accounts in London, New York, and Berne. Fortunately, the BIS had refused to transfer the gold to the Soviet Union's account when it received requests to do so from Eesti Pank (then, under Soviet control) in July 1940. Britain had similarly refused to hand over gold belonging to Estonia (as well as that of the other Baltic states) held at the Bank of England in the postwar period. When Estonia requested the return of its gold in 1992, Britain recognized its responsibility to comply. These gold reserves and those held in Sweden and Switzerland, amounting altogether to 11.3 tons, were returned to Estonia either as bullion or hard currency, providing the initial backing worth more than $130 million at 1992 gold prices for the new currency.[14]

This provided some reassurance on the matter of reserves. But currency flows between Russia and Estonia also posed a problem. Both countries were concerned at the prospects of cross border flows of rubles that might result from the remonetization operation. Russia's concern was that rubles in excess of the sum that Estonian citizens would be permitted to exchange for kroon would be spent in Russia by Estonians wanting to get rid of them. On Estonia's part, the concern was that rubles held in Russia and elsewhere would be brought to Estonia by people wanting to take advantage of the exchange. Both countries therefore took steps to limit the potential fallout. Estonia limited the number of rubles that could be exchanged for kroon, while Russia blocked the import of rubles from Estonia altogether.

Unlike Latvia and Lithuania, Estonia did not run its own currency in parallel with the ruble during a transitional period but rather opted to replace the ruble with the kroon outright. To instill confidence in the new currency, the leading banking authorities concluded that it would need to be both stable and convertible.[15] Although Eesti Pank had been established as a central bank, the mechanism chosen to achieve the desired stable currency was that of the currency board. In implementing the withdrawal of rubles and their replacement with kroon, Eesti Pank selected an exchange rate based on the prevailing rate between the Soviet ruble and the Deutsche Mark at eighty to one. Circulating rubles were redeemed for new Estonian kroon at the rate of ten to one, thereby setting a kroon to Deutsche Mark rate of eight to one. It was this exchange rate that formed the basis of Estonia's Currency Board until the Deutsche Mark was replaced by the euro, which then became the new anchor currency for the kroon. During the currency board period, only the Estonian parliament could formally alter the fixed rate, although the central bank was granted some minimal room for maneuvering within 3 percent of the fixed exchange rate. In this way, the kroon was pegged, rather than fixed, to the Deutsche Mark, leading some people to question whether it was a currency board in the true sense of the term. Further criticisms of the exchange program included the charge that the exchange rate undervalued the kroon and made imports more expensive. The cost of living was also seen to increase, and inflation continued at an unacceptably high rate for several years after the adoption of the currency board regime.[16]

So determined was Estonia to introduce its own sovereign currency as a further step in asserting its independence that it appears that it resisted or ignored IMF warnings against doing so. In the IMF's view, Estonia was not yet ready to introduce and manage its own currency and that certain other economic measures, such as price liberalization and a balanced budget, needed to be complete to provide the right foundation for monetary reform.[17] But Estonia's decisions in adopting its own currency initially on a currency board basis where it was to begin with being pegged to the Deutsche Mark and then later to the euro (prior to adopting the euro altogether) have, with the benefit of hindsight, been seen as remarkably successful. Between 1992, the year in which the kroon was introduced, and 1997, annual inflation in Estonia came down at an impressive rate from over 1,000 percent to 11 percent as a result of the country decoupling itself from the Russian ruble and realigning itself with the Deutsche Mark.[18] It is, however, important to note that, while the kroon reached the much lower levels very quickly, by 1996 Russia had also come down to a similar annual level of inflation.

Confidence in Estonia's currency, founded on the convertibility guaranteed by the currency board arrangement, quickly spread beyond its borders. The kroon would be traded in other Baltic and Scandinavian states within months of the introduction of the new currency.[19]

Estonia's drive to distance itself politically from Russia took another step forward when it became the first of the former Soviet Republics to begin negotiations to join the European Union, resulting in full membership in 2004. The economic benefits of membership of the European Union for Estonia appear clear: Estonia's GDP per capita had doubled in the ten years since joining the European Union.[20] Despite the sovereign debt difficulties in the eurozone following the banking crisis of 2008, integration into the European project for Estonia led next to adoption of the euro in 2011. Although all countries negotiating to join the European Union undertake to adopt the euro (only Denmark and Britain enjoyed a derogation of this obligation), some have embraced the currency faster than others. Estonia was among those that moved swiftly to sign up to it.

In preparing public opinion in the late 1990s to support the adoption of the euro, by no means at the time a forgone conclusion, the pro-euro lobby in Estonia emphasized not only the economic benefits but also asserted that membership would reinforce national security by supporting its realignment from the Russian to the Western European sphere. The euro was not simply an economic question, but one also of security and defense. Membership of the euro would deepen the process of integration into the European Union, with all the implications that carried for long-term national security. As stated by Andrus Ansip, prime minister of Estonia in 2013: "The euro is a security instrument for Estonia. The main aim in our foreign policy was to join all kinds of international institutions. It was really important for us to be integrated." The anti-lobby was in favor of maintaining the kroon, which had proven an economic success, and the same lobby pointed out that the adoption of the euro would represent a loss of sovereignty and some surrender of national identity. Similar considerations—the pragmatism demanded of national security versus the sentiment attached to national identity—featured in the calculations of Lithuania, which joined the euro on January 1, 2015.[21]

YUGOSLAVIA–SLOVENIA, 1991

The mood across Eastern Europe in 1989 was one of excitement, a growing belief that things could and would change and that the Communist Party of the Soviet Union and its satellite states were losing their grip. In June 1989, Poland held elections in which the opposition Solidarność party was spectacularly successful, removing the Communist Party's grip on power. Parts of the Iron Curtain came down in Hungary, offering many Eastern Europeans an exit to the west. The Berlin wall fell in November of that year.

The general sense of liberation was not confined to the Soviet Union and its allied Warsaw Pact states. Indeed, there are grounds for thinking that the first movement for change in Eastern European communist states originated in Yugoslavia in 1981 when ethnic Albanians in the autonomous region Kosovo agitated for full constituent republic status within the federation. The federal and individual republic governments of Yugoslavia were also struggling throughout the 1980s to cope with increasing economic difficulties and national debt levels. In Slovenia reformist leaders took control of the Slovene Communist Party in the 1980s and edged the republic toward some liberalization of the economy and a measure of political freedom. Intellectuals and journalists agitated for further freedoms and even discussed the possibility of independence for Slovenia. An independent trade union was created by factory workers. By September 1989, Slovenia's National Assembly had asserted the country's right to self-determination, going as far as demanding full independence. A monetary alternative to the Yugoslav dinar was one of the many issues under discussion. As early as February 1991, authorities in Slovenia had thought about the possibility of introducing a parallel currency to the dinar, pegged to the Austrian shilling: a historical echo of Ljubljana's orientation toward Vienna. But this idea was jettisoned for fear of antagonizing the federal authorities, a concern that helped to shape the currency solution that Slovenia eventually adopted.

Slovenia's move toward asserting its sovereignty was, to some extent, justified by political decisions in Serbia. In 1990, the government in Belgrade had abolished the autonomy of two provinces. This act threatened to create an imbalance in voting coalitions with the federation: the two provinces that had previously had a degree of freedom to form alliances with other republics when voting on economic matters would now be more thoroughly under the control of Serbia and yet would retain a vote in federal debates. Criticisms of this Balkan gerrymandering were rejected by Serbia on the grounds that this was entirely an issue of sovereignty of the Republic of Serbia. Belgrade had, in this way, unintentionally given Slovenia the cover it needed to declare its own sovereignty, which it did in June 1990. In September, this political declaration was followed by legal amendments to the republic's constitution, and toward the end of the year Slovenia held a referendum on independence. As a result of the referendum, the government of Slovenia was obliged to declare independence within six months. Although the constituent republics were still talking about a new form of confederation in the first half of 1991, Slovenia had concluded by the middle of the year that there was no other option than a unilateral declaration of independence, which took place on June 25, 1991.[22]

The reaction of Europe and America toward Slovenia's declaration of independence was not as enthusiastic as might have been expected. There was none of the euphoria that greeted the fall of the Berlin Wall. Instead, foreign governments worried about the consequences of the complete collapse of the Yugoslav state into its constituent republics. Who would take responsibility for the legacy debts of the federal state? Would the country dissolve into armed conflict? Bearing these concerns in mind, the international community on the whole chose to support the federal government. And taking this as endorsement, the federal legislature declared Slovenia's declaration of independence illegal, and federal forces and police were deployed to the borders. Among the other measures imposed on Slovenia by the government in Belgrade was a restriction on Slovenia's access to foreign exchange. Heightened tensions broke out into full-on armed conflict lasting ten days in June 1991, but when federal forces withdrew after only ten days, Slovenia's independence was looking probable.[23]

Responding rapidly to deteriorating developments, the European Union offered to act as mediator, seeking to bring the two parties to the negotiating table. The European Union threatened to withdraw from the process if the protagonists failed to negotiate, and at the same time indicated that it would levy penalties on the Yugoslav federal authorities should they fail to step back from military action. As a result of the European Union's efforts, both sides agreed in July 1991—the Brioni Agreement—to a three-month cooling-off period during which Slovenia's move toward independence would be frozen. During the cooling off period, the Bank of Slovenia continued to use the Yugoslav dinar. Although little real progress was made to settle the dispute during the period when the July Brioni Agreement was in force, the important point was that, following the June withdrawal of Yugoslav forces after only ten days of conflict, Slovenia's participation in an international agreement brokered by the European Union to all intents and purposes confirmed its sovereignty. In October, at the end of the cooling-off period, but before the new country had been recognized by any other, Slovenia took another step toward independence by introducing its own currency, the tolar.[24]

When federal Yugoslav forces entered Croatia and fought fierce battles to control the town of Vukovar, capturing it in October, decision-makers at the European Union concluded that recognition of Yugoslavia's constituent republics as independent states could help to bring the fighting to an end. The European Union's Declaration on Yugoslavia of December 1991 recognized Slovenia as an independent state as of January 15, 1992, although some states, including Iceland, Sweden, and Germany, had already recognized it as sovereign before that.[25]

Slovenia's decision to break with the dinar in October was fraught with difficulty. As early as June 27, the remaining governors of the National Bank of Yugoslavia had agreed that Slovenia would be excluded from supplies of banknotes and coins as well as foreign exchange from Belgrade. The refusal to supply foreign exchange was particularly troubling because the new country's central bank, the Bank of Slovenia, had no foreign exchange reserves of its own, the only reserves in the country at the moment of independence being those held in Slovenia's commercial banks totaling about $170 million—somewhat more than the reserves Estonia could call on at about the same time, but nevertheless, not very much. While Estonia had been bold enough to opt immediately for a currency board and the very rigorous regime that went with it, Slovenia chose a softer path. For the Slovene leadership, the very limited foreign exchange reserves in the country ruled out the possibility of a fixed exchange rate of any new Slovenian currency to the reserves backing it.[26] Yugoslavia's position on dinars circulating in Slovenia was no less problematic. Some 8.6 billion Yugoslav dinars were held in Slovenia during the period that the Brioni Agreement was in force and constituted a claim on the National Bank of Yugoslavia.[27] This liability transferred to the Bank of Slovenia because the tolar was introduced to replace the dinar. But after the expiry of the Brioni Agreement in October 1991, a claim was made by the National Bank of Yugoslavia on the Bank of Slovenia for the return of twenty-three billion dinars' worth of Yugoslav dinars in notes and coins (almost three times the value actually held in Slovenia) or its equivalent in hard currency. This claim and a counterclaim by Slovenia to an equal amount remained unsettled until 2001.

A more immediate challenge and one that could not be kicked into the long grass was the preparation for the introduction of the new tolar currency. The earliest preparations had been underway before the National Bank of Yugoslavia severed its currency supply relationship with Slovenia in June 1991 and thus at a time when Slovenia was still bound by federal laws relating to currency supply. To avoid accusations of a deliberate breach of those laws, simple coupons, also known as "provisional payment notes," were printed, which bore no name or other designator identifying the note as a currency. The new coupons were signed by the minister of finance of Slovenia rather than the president of the central bank and were to be described as a security rather than a banknote. With this fig leaf of protection in place, the

Slovenian government and central bank could feel confident that they possessed an interim solution to the currency requirement that stopped short of a breach of federal currency laws. At the end of the Brioni Agreement period, several laws were passed establishing the tolar as the new unit of currency and authorizing the use of the coupons in place of the tolar until the latter was ready for issue a year later.[28] By introducing coupons, rather than fully fledged banknotes, during the transitional phase, Slovenia avoided charges of having breached regulations by which it was still bound.

The changeover from the dinar to the tolar (at least in its transitional coupon form) took place over the period October 8–11, 1991. During those four days, dinars could be exchanged for tolars at a rate of one for one, and sums held in bank accounts were converted at the same exchange rate. Limits were imposed on the amount that could be exchanged in a direct cash-for-cash transaction, while larger sums could be converted as long as they were immediately deposited in a bank account. The tolar remained the currency of the new independent state of Slovenia from October 1991 to January 2007, when it was replaced by the euro.

Slovenia had applied for membership of the European Union in 1996 and after years of negotiating the membership process held a referendum in 2003 in which 86 percent of those casting a vote did so in favor of membership. A significant factor in this strong support for European Union membership was the perception that membership of the European Union and NATO would bring valuable security guarantees, a view very similar to that driving Estonia's decision to integrate into the European Union. But, unlike some of the other Eastern European states, Slovenia, during the second half of the 1990s, had not attracted foreign direct investment to the same extent and had failed to compete with countries such as Slovakia, the Czech Republic, and Poland in terms of exports. Economic opportunities within the European Union were therefore particularly attractive to Slovenia by the year 2000, and enthusiasm for membership had grown, resulting in the overwhelmingly favorable referendum vote.[29] In the following year, Slovenia acceded to the European Union.

Its progress toward membership of the euro was rapid. Within two months of joining the European Union, it joined the Exchange Rate Mechanism, governing exchange rates between the tolar and the euro. Less than two years after that, the European Central Bank and the European Commission confirmed that Slovenia had attained the so-called Maastricht criteria for membership of the European Union. On January 1, 2007, Slovenia became the thirteenth member of the eurozone. The Bank of Slovenia had last carried out a currency conversion exercise sixteen years earlier. Much of the adult population was therefore familiar with the process, even though on this occasion the public was not likely to find the exchange rate of 236 tolars to the euro so easy as the one-to-one exchange rate used for the dinar and tolar exchange. There were fears that there would inevitably be price inflation. While analysis by the European Union and the Slovenians suggested that price increases were no more than 0.24–0.3 percent, a survey indicated that less than 50 percent of the population believed the conversions had been fair.

As with the 1991 currency conversion, all bank deposits were automatically converted on January 1, 2007, the first day of the changeover. Although the transitional period for conversion of cash in 2007 lasted significantly longer than the comparable operation in 1991, Slovenia's approach, described as that of a "big bang," was noticeably shorter than that of other countries going through a similar transition. Nevertheless, the public perception was that the mechanics of the changeover had been well run.[30]

Has the adoption of the euro been a success for Slovenia? It is difficult to say. The financial crash of 2008—only a year after Slovenia's adoption of the euro—together with the sovereign debt crisis that followed it have made it difficult to make a clear judgment. The impact of those events has had a distorting effect on any attempt to understand the benefits and disadvantages of the Eurosystem and have led to major differences of opinion on monetary policy among its members. The Slovenian government's own website notes that inflation in Slovenia was the highest in the eurozone over the years 2007 and 2008, although by 2015 the economy experienced deflation of 0.8 percent. According to the same source, exports over the same years increased over 40 percent, but GDP grew a relatively modest 19 percent over the nine years from 2006 to 2015. Other key statistics for Slovenia show that debt to GDP rose from just under 30 percent to 50 percent in the period between 2008 and 2011.[31] By 2015, this debt figure had risen to 82 percent of GDP, a breach of the Maastricht requirement that caps debt to GDP at 60 percent (although it had slipped back again in two subsequent years). Weak economic reform progress and poor export performance were among the causes of the problems, but members of the Slovenian government exonerated the euro from any blame. At least one view that deserves to be considered as balanced suggests that, while the euro could hardly be blamed for the origins of Slovenia's problems, the inability to determine Slovenia's own monetary policies could constrain the country's attempts to escape its economic difficulties. This view in particular notes that Slovenia was not at liberty to engage in quantitative easing as practiced by the United States and Britain relatively quickly after the financial crisis began to bite.[32]

The arguments over the economic benefits of membership of the Eurosystem continue among interested parties, both those who find themselves members of the euro and those yet to join. But just how significant was monetary independence to the political sovereignty of Slovenia? It has been suggested that the introduction of the tolar prior to Slovenia's recognition by any other country was a necessary precondition for that international recognition.[33] In fact, there is absolutely no evidence that that was the case. The view indeed looks like a distorted form of the "post hoc, propter hoc" fallacy, the erroneous belief in this case that, because the introduction of the independent currency preceded international recognition, the latter must have been a consequence of the former. Nowhere else in recent or more ancient history in fact is there any evidence that the creation of an independent currency can be a prerequisite for international recognition. Why should, for instance, the introduction of a national currency prior to international recognition be necessary for that recognition when that same sequence of events had not been necessary for Estonia as we have already seen? Equally, the circulation of its own national currency has made not an iota of difference to the international recognition (or rather lack of it) of an independent Somaliland. This idea that the creation of a new currency might help to create a unified state where none had existed previously has become a part of the myth of the euro as a precursor to and prerequisite for the foundation of a super state, as will be seen in chapter 9.

Other commentators saw the introduction of the tolar as marking "full" independence.[34] This careful use of "full" may have more to say for itself. Recent cases, such as those of Ecuador, East Timor, and El Salvador, all of which have adopted the US dollar as their national currency, demonstrate that it is perfectly possible to surrender monetary sovereignty without giving up political and legal independence. If monetary sovereignty is something that thus can be voluntarily surrendered without giving up legal and political sovereignty, it is clear that it forms a part of the complete sovereignty package, but not one so vital as to be an existential question, unlike, for instance, a country's freedom to make its own laws. Slovenia's decision to enter the Eurosystem was more obviously an economic one, not, as it was in the case of Estonia, one designed to reinforce national security. This being the case, it is possible to imagine that, should the euro prove to be an economic failure at some point in the future, Slovenia will have a relatively easy decision to make as to whether to remain a member or not.

CZECHOSLOVAKIA: THE VELVET DIVORCE, 1993

As Soviet control over Eastern Europe dissolved, the power of the communist parties governing the satellite states faded fast. Demonstrations in Czechoslovakia in 1989 went unsuppressed, and free elections were held in 1990. But this auspicious start belied the underlying differences between the Czech and Slovak constituent regions. The Czech region had long enjoyed economic advantages, based on its more diversified economy, while Slovakia, with abundant mineral resources and hydroelectric power, had forged a niche industry based on armament production. The Czech region absorbed about 50 percent of all Slovakia's trade. Slovakia, in contrast, accounted for about a third of all Czech trade, but was nevertheless the Czechs' largest single trading partner.[35]

Overlaying the economic and industrial facts, there were differences of opinion between the leaders of the Czech and Slovak regions on the future economic direction of the unified state. As far as the Czechs were concerned, socialism had held back development over the years. On the other hand, Slovaks felt that socialism had worked for them, promoting industrialization, which had narrowed the economic gap with the Czechs.[36]

On a political level, Czechs, of whom there were approximately twice as many citizens as Slovaks in the unified state (ten million as opposed to five million), had always dominated the federal administration and resented the minority Slovaks having anything like an equal part in the decision-making for the combined nations (even though ethnic equality had been the stated objective of a political program dating back to 1945). From another perspective, Slovaks, as the minority, had always known themselves to be the junior partner and consequently felt less commitment to the Czechoslovak state. Further differences of political opinion revolved around the question of federal versus constituent state power, the Slovaks demanding greater autonomy, while the Czechs favored a stronger federal authority. During discussions in 1990 Slovakia had made significant progress toward autonomy, even securing agreement to establish its own ministry of foreign relations. Conflicting views between Czechs and Slovaks on the sharing of political power and management of political institutions have been identified by some analysts as the principal reason for the separation of the two countries, although there were also significant differences in economic outlook, as would become clear.[37]

Parliamentary elections in the summer of 1992 served only to highlight the differences. In the Czech region, the elections were won by a center-right coalition of the Civic Democratic Party and the Christian Democratic Party, taking a radical approach to free-market reforms. In Slovakia, the elections were won by the left-of-center Movement for a Democratic Slovakia, which was opposed to accelerating free-market policies. These differing outlooks made it well-nigh impossible for the Czech and Slovak sides to agree to a government with a common program. Both Czechs and Slovaks rapidly accepted the inevitable and agreed to dissolve the federation with effect from January 1, 1993. To minimize the effect of any shock to the economies of the two countries, which were, after all, major trading partners, it was agreed that there would be a long-term commitment to free movement of labor and a customs union. Moreover, there would be a short-term monetary union, scheduled to last until the middle of 1993.

Perhaps the Czechs and Slovaks always suspected that a monetary union was going to be subject to insupportable strains. Rather than tie the two economies to each other in all and any circumstances, they agreed to certain conditions under which the monetary union could also be dissolved sooner than the middle of 1993. In the event that fiscal deficits of either republic or interrepublic capital transfers were to exceed agreed levels or foreign exchange reserves of either country were to fall to less than one month's worth of imports, the monetary union would be over. And if those conditions were not breached, the union could still be dissolved prior to summer 1993 if the joint Czech–Slovak Monetary Committee could not agree on essential monetary policies. Given the fundamental differences in economic philosophy between the governments in Prague and Bratislava, it must have seemed more than likely that there would also be divergence on monetary policy.

In the event, the divergence developed more quickly than perhaps either side had expected. Economic trends in late 1992 to early 1993 pointed toward a poor outcome for Slovakia. Slovak commercial banks and individuals, fearing a devaluation in Slovakia, were transferring money to what seemed a safer haven in Czech banks. Czech exports to Slovakia increased by 25 percent, while Slovak exports to the Czech region increased by a smaller proportion. Money seemed to be flowing in only one direction, and the decline in foreign exchange reserves, one of the key criteria for dissolution of the monetary union, progressed rapidly over the same period. Even in the Czech Republic, the stronger of the two economies, foreign currency reserves shrank from $847 million to $483 million in the first three weeks of the year. Both parties agreed to end the monetary union in early February 1993.[38]

To stop the flow of currency from Slovakia to the Czech Republic, payments between the two countries were halted on February 3. A short period of four days, from January 4–7, was agreed, permitting citizens of both countries to exchange the existing currency of Czechoslovakia for the currency of the two new separate states. The nascent Czechoslovak state in the period after the First World War had, of course, already had experience of separating currencies in short order. The solution in 1918 had been to apply Czechoslovak tax stamps to the legacy Austrian currency until the new Czechoslovak currency was ready for issue. The idea of applying stamps to currency as a short-term expedient to denote a new issue of currency or new currency for an entirely new political entity was again employed in Czechoslovakia in 1944 by Soviet occupation forces.[39] Thus, it is hardly surprising that the Czechs and Slovaks resorted to tried-and-tested methods of carrying out a currency conversion with very little notice. Czech or Slovak stamps were applied to the existing higher-denomination Czechoslovak notes, identifying the country in which the currency would circulate.

As many Slovaks had suspected, their new country was forced to devalue its currency in 1993, but the consequence of that was to boost the country's growth and exports to the Czech Republic. The Czech Republic's advantage in having a more diversified economy that could compete more effectively in Western Europe has been reflected in its unemployment figures, which have remained lower than Slovakia's since the so-called Velvet Divorce and the end of the monetary union. The Czech Republic's GDP per capita has also remained consistently higher than that of Slovakia over the same period.[40] It is not possible to attribute this difference in GDP and employment rates exclusively to the adoption or otherwise of the euro. But with regard to the relative success of the two economies, the fact that the Slovaks have adopted the euro and the Czechs have not has not resulted in the former catching up with the latter in economic terms.

Perhaps the Czechs always expected to outperform the Slovaks economically. During early discussions between the two countries, the Slovaks had proposed a single currency to be issued by two separate national central banks. But because the Czechs were determined to have two separate currencies, the Slovak idea did not come to fruition.[41] This was an early indication of different attitudes to currency, which would be demonstrated by different responses toward the euro.

Following the separation of the two countries and their currencies, the Czech Republic pushed on with its radical economic liberalization, privatizing state-owned companies, encouraging free-market trade policies, and liberalizing prices. The Czech Republic seemed to be making a rapid and comfortable adjustment to a Western European free-market economy. Although there were signs of economic slowdown in 1996, this did not place an obstruction in the way of the republic's progress toward membership of the European Union. Economic growth in Slovakia, on the other hand, was based on public sector spending and private sector consumption. The economic architecture of the country was not being structurally liberalized as it was in the Czech Republic. But the political orientation and economic policies of both republics "flipped" in reaction to recession in 1998: the right-of-center government in Prague was replaced by the Czech Social Democratic Party, while the legacy socialist government in Bratislava was replaced by a right-of-center party with an interest in an economic reform program. Under this new government, Slovakia moved quickly to achieve the various economic criteria expected of candidates for membership of the European Union. In 2004 both republics acceded to the European Union.[42]

New entrants to the European Union, with very few exceptions (Denmark and Britain) have been required to commit to join the euro currency system but have some leeway in the timing of that accession. Although a right-of-center government had been elected in the Czech Republic in 2006, that government remained committed to health care and pension reforms as a priority and on that basis deferred any decision on membership of the euro. When, following the financial crash of 2008, a sovereign debt crisis among weaker members of the eurozone ensued, leading figures in Prague, including the president, Vaclav Klaus, who had always been a Eurosceptic, expressed serious reservations about the benefits of joining the Eurosystem. Although the Czechs have achieved the necessary economic criteria set by the European Union for membership of the euro, the principal stumbling block is the lack of political will to join it. At the time of writing (2020) the Czech Republic still had not set a date for membership of the euro.[43]

The Slovaks perceived membership of the euro quite otherwise: they liked the idea of reduced transaction costs and considered that reduced exchange rate uncertainty and price stability would be likely to lead to improved foreign direct investment. Successive Slovak governments of different political hues had maintained the momentum of progress toward euro membership and on January 1, 2009, Slovakia became a member of the Eurosystem. The Slovaks had originally been keen on the idea of a common currency serving independent Czech and Slovak nations, so they had previously demonstrated a belief that there were benefits to be had in surrendering a degree of monetary sovereignty. This, we know, foundered on the Czechs' determination to operate an independent currency. The respective attitudes of the Czechs and Slovaks toward monetary sovereignty have therefore been consistent across the past twenty-five years: determined independence on the part of the Czechs and willing dependence on the part of the Slovaks.

Has membership of the euro been positive for Slovakia? And has the Czech Republic been right to abstain? The respective levels of unemployment and GDP per capita have not moved in relation to each other over the past twenty-five years, which includes periods when the two currencies were linked to each other and then entirely independent and separate and, more recently, since Slovakia's membership of the eurozone. Unemployment levels in Slovakia in the period from 2009–2014 were, though, twice those of the Czech Republic. Debt to GDP rates and budget deficit levels of the two countries between 2009 and 2014 did not diverge significantly. Membership of the euro certainly removed Slovakia's ability to adjust exchange rates to promote exports. During the financial and sovereign debt crisis following 2008, the country's employment levels suffered, and the country fell into a recession deeper than that of the Czech Republic. On the other hand, Slovakia's growth rate in the period of 2010–2014 immediately following the crisis consistently outperformed that of the Czech Republic.[44]

The outlook of the political leaders in both countries toward the euro simply might be characterized as either that of pessimists or optimists. Slovaks could be forgiven for thinking that the financial crisis was a unique event and that in general the euro was serving them well. For the Czechs, however, it might have seemed a serious indicator of the dangers inherent in tying national currencies together in this way. In this view, the euro might have survived on this occasion, but it was all too possible that a second similar shock could bring the system down altogether. The general trend of incomes in the Czech Republic would seem to support the view there that life outside the euro can be good. It would be a very confident observer who could dismiss the Czechs' caution out of hand.

ERITREA, 1997

Eritrea had been Italy's first overseas colony, acquired from an Italian steamship company in 1882 and then integrated with Italy's other East African colonies during the interwar fascist era to form Italian East Africa. At the end of the Second World War and following lobbying by the then Emperor of Ethiopia, Haile Selassie, the United States and the United Kingdom supported the idea of a federation of Eritrea with Ethiopia. As a result, UN Security Council Resolution 390A of December 1950 ensured that a British postwar transitional administration was succeeded by the federation of Eritrea with Ethiopia, much against the wishes of Eritrean activists who pressed for a referendum on the future of the country. In 1961 the emperor dissolved the federation, annexing Eritrea formally and sweeping aside any pretense of autonomy. At that point, Eritrean separatists took up arms against the government first of the emperor and then against the regime of the communist Derg ("Military Coordinating Council"), which had overthrown the emperor in 1974.

Eritrea's thirty-year armed struggle for independence drew to a close in 1991, when the repressive regime of the Derg's leader, Colonel Mengistu Haile Mariam, was overthrown by the combined efforts of the Eritrean People's Liberation Front (EPLF) and the Tigrean People's Liberation Front (TPLF), whose leader, Meles Zenawi, became the president of the transitional government of Ethiopia from 1991–1995.[45] During this transitional period, the central government, led by Zenawi, agreed to the Eritrean leadership's proposal for a referendum on the question of independence. From 1991 to 1993, a transitional government formed by the EPLF ran Eritrea until at the end of that period a referendum, endorsed by the UN, resulted in a vote for independence. In May 1993, the UN recognized Eritrea's independence by admitting it as a full member.[46]

Despite the collaboration between the TPLF and the EPLF in the fight against Mengistu and a direct professional relationship between the two leaders, Meles Zenawi and Isaias Afewerki who had, to some extent, been brothers in arms in that struggle, tensions arose between the two countries. Minor border incursions had already taken place when, in 1997, Ethiopian troops crossed into Eritrean territory in pursuit of rebels from the Afar region with the approval of the authorities in Asmara but had then occupied land in Eritrea.[47]

It was against this backdrop of tension that the two states took divergent economic paths. Since independence, Eritrea, by mutual agreement with Ethiopia, had used the birr as its currency, even though, during the transitional period after Mengistu had been overthrown, Eritrean officials negotiating with their Ethiopian counterparts complained that Eritrea had been given little influence over matters such as currency policy at a time when Eritrea was still using the birr.[48]

In early 1997 Eritrea put forward to Ethiopia proposals for its own currency, the nakfa, which, they suggested, should be exchanged at par with the birr. Apparently, it took some eight months for Ethiopia to respond to these proposals, presumably while the TPLF leadership in Addis Ababa evaluated the proposal and weighed the pros and cons.[49]

For Eritrea, the immediate advantages would include seigniorage revenues as well as full control over the issue of notes. These objections were not in themselves unreasonable. While Ethiopia's birr circulated in the newly independent Eritrea, the seigniorage accrued only to Ethiopia. But the proposed one-to-one rate of exchange to the birr was a problem. The Eritrean side might produce excessive quantities of nakfa to be exchanged for birr, which could then be used to buy goods and produce in Ethiopia. There was no suggestion that the nakfa would be issued under the disciplined conditions of, for instance, a currency board, and indeed it was widely believed that Eritrea did not have foreign currency reserves or gold to back the issue of notes. Under those circumstances, it was reasonable to assume that the nakfa would soon depreciate, making a one-to-one exchange rate unrealistic. At least one Ethiopian report suggests that Eritrea also proposed that the nakfa be fully accepted as a medium of exchange in Ethiopia.[50] If true, this would mean that there would be no need to exchange nakfa for birr. An uncontrolled issue of nakfa and one-to-one exchange rate with birr together with full circulating currency status in Ethiopia would have provided every opportunity for Eritreans to buy up Ethiopian produce and goods at advantageous prices and export them to Eritrea. Like so many other aspects of the buildup to war, however, the claim that Eritrea requested one-to-one parity has been contested.

A different interpretation of the Eritrean approach exists. In this explanation (by the late Professor Tekie Fessehazion, an Eritrean citizen), Eritrea wished to promote free movement of the nakfa and of goods, people, and capital in order to promote peace and cooperation between the two countries. The Ethiopian position on the other hand, insisting on payments in hard currency and capital controls, would in the Eritrean view, inhibit the economic prosperity of both countries.[51]

For the Ethiopians, there were other reasons to object to the free circulation of nakfa in Ethiopia. Eritrea's decision to name the unit of its currency "nakfa"—the name of a town in Western Eritrea that had been the site of Eritrean resistance to military assaults by Derg Forces from 1978 onward—was seen as a slap in the face for the Ethiopian leadership. In October 1997 Ethiopia rejected the proposals and upped the stakes by proposing that future transactions should be settled in hard currency based on letters of credit.[52] In November 1997, Eritrea began to issue the nakfa. Unable to comply with Ethiopia's demand for cross-border transactional settlements in hard currency, Eritrea in its turn raised the stakes by embargoing trade with Ethiopia. Given that the latter's main export and import route was through the Eritrean port of Assab, this in the longer term has had the effect of forcing Ethiopia to seek alternative routes to the sea, notably through Djibouti, but also through Berbera in Somaliland. It has also had the effect of decreasing commercial activity at Assab port. Tensions tipped over into outright hostilities.

In May 1998 Eritrea invaded the border regions of Ethiopia, precipitating a war lasting two years, which, at the time was held to be the worst conflict anywhere on the globe. Estimates suggest that, when Ethiopian troops drove deep into Eritrea in a massive counterattack in 2000, one in three of all Eritreans were displaced from their homes. In December 2000, a peace deal was signed by the two countries providing for UN peacekeeping forces to patrol a buffer zone between the two opposing forces and creating a commission to settle the border dispute.

The exchange rate value of the nakfa to the dollar halved between 1997 and 2002. At the start of the conflict, the nakfa-to-dollar exchange rate was eight to one. At the peak of Ethiopia's military success and Eritrea's military failure in June 2000, it more than halved, falling to eighteen to one, before recovering to thirteen to one in early 2001, shortly after the peace agreement had been signed and UN peacekeepers deployed. At the peak of the war in 2000, inflation reached 26 percent before dropping back in 2001 to 7.7 percent, although in 2002 it climbed back up to 23.8 percent. The poor quality of Eritrea's land, drought, and the weakness of the nakfa among other things following the war combined to produce dreadful conditions for the supply of food. By 2004 some 70 percent of food requirements had to be imported, a particular concern given Eritrea's poor foreign reserves.[53]

The situation in Ethiopia during and after the war was quite different. The birr-to-dollar exchange rate declined modestly from 7.5 to one to 8.3 to one over the period 1999–2003. Between 1998 and 2000 the inflation rate moved from 3.9 to 6.2 percent. Surprisingly, between 2000 and 2002 there was a period of deflation while Eritrea was experiencing double-digit inflation, although in 2002–2003 inflation in Ethiopia did reach 15 percent. Throughout the period of the war and just after Ethiopia's foreign reserves amounted to two to three times those of Eritrea.[54]

Expert commentators investigating the causes of this war find it difficult to understand the true reasons for its outbreak, but some ascribe its origins to a permutation of factors ranging from internal Eritrean politics through conflicting models of state and governance, to rival economic models and eventually to mutual rivalry between the leaderships of the two countries. The consensus, however, seems to be that, while the introduction of the nakfa was not the sole cause—or perhaps even the main cause of the hostilities—it added significantly to the tensions between the leadership of the two countries, making it yet more difficult for them to defuse the tensions building over border disputes and economic rivalry.[55] As the charge brought against the introduction of the new nakfa currency as a cause of war must at worst be described as "not proven," there seem to be no known historical incidents of countries going to war on currency matters alone. The important part played by Eritrea's demands for special treatment of the nakfa in Ethiopia simply added one more factor to the deteriorating relationship between the two states.

TIMOR-LESTE, 1999

Until 1975 Timor-Leste (East Timor) had been a Portuguese overseas possession for over four hundred years. Portuguese traders and Dominican monks had been present from the early sixteenth century. By the early years of the seventeenth century, Portugal's presence and control of the trade in local commodities was being challenged by the Dutch East India Company. The two rivals eventually reached an agreement in 1661, as a result of which Portugal's dominance in the eastern area of the island of Timor was recognized by the Dutch in return for Portuguese recognition of the Dutch settlement of Kupang in the far west of the island. No formal governor of the Portuguese colony was installed, however, until 1702. Local resistance to Portuguese rule erupted into rebellion at various times in the eighteenth, nineteenth, and twentieth centuries, although relations between the native Timorese and the Portuguese authorities were relatively peaceful during the period following the Second World War.

There were few obvious signs on the part of Indonesia following its independence from the Netherlands in August 1945 of any intention to absorb Timor-Leste into the Indonesian state. Sympathies and encouragement on the part of Indonesia's leaders for Timor-Leste's aspirations for independence from Portugal did not amount to more than just that: sympathy and encouragement.[56]

Portugal's "Carnation Revolution" of April 1974, which ended the forty-eight-year rule of that country's authoritarian Estado Novo regime, was to change all that. Negotiations between the new Portuguese government and the liberation movements in overseas colonies were followed by the withdrawal of Portuguese military and civil administrators. In Timor-Leste, political parties, hitherto banned, were formed in May. In July 1975 Portugal announced its decision to decolonize Timor-Leste.[57]

Between March and November 1975 Indonesia's military regime, headed by General Suharto, sought to persuade Portuguese authorities to transfer sovereignty over the colony to Indonesia. Suharto himself successfully persuaded US President Gerald Ford to support Indonesia's absorption of Timor-Leste on the grounds that one of its leading, newly created parties, Fretilin, was communist in sympathy and likely to destabilize the region. From September 1975 the Indonesian military launched a series of incursions into the Portuguese colony, prompting the Fretilin party to declare the Democratic Republic of Timor-Leste independent in late November. This step triggered a full-blown invasion by Indonesian naval, air, and ground forces on December 7, 1975, forcing the evacuation of the last Portuguese citizens the following day.[58] Indonesia had moved to occupy Timor-Leste.

Throughout the 1980s the Indonesian occupation of East Timor was marked by guerrilla resistance, while the worst excesses of the Indonesian military in suppressing resistance prompted occasional but not sustained international concern during the 1990s. In the event, Timor-Leste's best chance for independence was catalyzed by Indonesia's own internal weaknesses. When in 1997 the Asian economic crisis led to the overthrow of General Suharto, his successor, the civilian politician Jusuf Habibie, announced a "special status" for Timor-Leste. Unsatisfied with this placatory declaration, Timorese students demanded a referendum on self-determination. What was eventually granted—a "consultation" rather than a referendum—invited the people of Timor-Leste to vote for autonomy within the Indonesian state. Rejection of that proposal meant that the electorate would be voting for independence and that indeed was the result announced by the UN on September 4, 1999. Analysis after the event has recorded a growing sense among senior decision-makers in Jakarta that Timor-Leste was in any case proving to be more a liability than an asset. Indonesian military officers, particularly senior commanders on the ground, who had never been enthusiastic about the civilian Habibie and his rise to power, were not, however, willing to relinquish their hold quite so easily, fearing that it could begin a general dismemberment of the Republic of Indonesia.[59] Violent reactions to the result in favor of independence by pro-Indonesian militias supported by the Indonesian military evoked condemnation by, among others, US President Bill Clinton. When President Habibie backed down in the face of international pressure, agreeing to the deployment of an international peacekeeping force, the Australian-led INTERFET force landed in the capital Dili in September.[60]

In the following February (2000), the administration of Timor-Leste devolved to UN Transitional Administration in East Timor (UNTAET). On January 24, 2000, that is, before UNTAET formally took control and while INTERFET was still operating as the de facto administration, Regulation 2000/7 was promulgated, declaring that the new currency of East Timor would be the US dollar, although public information brochures issued by UNTAET in February confirmed that the people of East Timor could in the future choose their own currency arrangements. The regulation provided for the use of other currencies, such as the Indonesian rupiah, in day-to-day transactions, for instance, in retail purchases. Indeed, quantities of Thai baht, Singaporean dollars, and Portuguese escudos were all circulating in Timor-Leste at the time. Payment of taxes and utility bills would, however, have to be paid in dollars. Because the US dollar was at this stage being adopted, there was no requirement for a central bank or currency board performing the functions associated with those institutions. Instead, a Central Payments Office (CPO), responsible for managing the inventory of banknotes and coins and receiving and disbursing UNTAET funds, was established.

UNTAET clearly set out one unusual aspect of the currency regime: anyone working in government employment would be paid in dollars, while those in the private sector would be paid in whatever currency would be agreed between employers and employed. In those circumstances it should have seemed likely that private sector employers would insist on paying their employees in weaker currencies, while government or UN employees paid in dollars would be advantaged. According to one online press report, as early as January 2000 there were complaints that UN and aid workers were using Portuguese escudos or US or Australian dollars, while the indigenous people were tending to use Indonesian rupiah. The same report noted that the IMF economist Luis Mendonca suggested that the US or Australian dollars, or perhaps even the euro, were the most likely candidates for Timor's future currency but that the IMF would make the decision as to which currency would be used based on the realities of Timor's trade.[61] Was this apparently high-handed statement a revealing slip, a piece of journalistic misrepresentation, or a case of a local IMF representative talking up his authority beyond what had been agreed between the IMF and representatives of the newly independent state? We may never be entirely sure, but IMF representatives at that time were perceived by some particularly acerbic commentators as displaying an almost colonial attitude in their dealings with emerging world economies. One comparable example indeed involved the IMF's stringent bail-out deal for Indonesia in 1998 following the Asian financial crisis, where the attitude of the IMF's managing director seemed to some as unfortunately domineering.[62] And yet, in the IMF's defense, the Asian financial crisis was a very recent memory and its ability to overwhelm larger, stronger, better resourced economies than East Timor must have acted as a harsh but salutary lesson. Timor's political leaders had expressed to the IMF their wish for an independent national currency to be introduced at the time of independence, and, although the IMF staff members were "receptive to their views," they nevertheless recommended that the introduction of a national currency should be deferred until the country had a proven legal framework and effective financial policy to support such a currency.[63]

Seen through the IMF's monetary lens, only a strong currency, all things considered, could have provided a solid monetary foundation for such a fragile state. The IMF's November 30, 2000, report on recent developments and macroeconomic assessment noted anecdotal evidence that the US dollar was increasingly preferred among the wider population as a store of value. Predictably, private sector employees were beginning to demand payment in US dollars. In this report, the IMF urged the CPO "to continue to encourage NGOs, Diplomatic Missions, UN agencies, and other institutions to make their disbursements/payments in U.S. dollars, without prejudice for the freedom of private parties to settle contracts in the currency of their choice."[64]

The decision to favor the US dollar as the official currency for transactions was explained in the UNTAET brochure:

- The US$ was chosen because it is a strong and stable currency and is widely accepted around the world.
- The decision to adopt the US$ was made by the National Consultative Council (NCC).
- The NCC represents East Timorese in all of UNTAET's major decisions.[65]

Eleven of the fifteen NCC members are East Timorese delegates: seven represent the CNRT (National Congress for Timorese Reconstruction), three represent non-CNRT groups, and one represents the Catholic Church.[66]

In a power-sharing arrangement in which UNTAET officials and representatives of Timor-Leste formed a transitional government cabinet, UNTAET retained responsibility for peacekeeping, foreign affairs, managing elections, and drawing up the constitution. Elections to a constituent assembly took place in August 2001, after which day-to-day administration devolved to a cabinet of Timorese representatives.[67] Full independence and membership in the UN followed in 2002.

The choice of currency for Timor-Leste was the subject of the usual considerations plus some. The country's national and economic circumstances complicated the decision-making. The country was then one of the poorest in

Asia with, according to one estimate at the time, a per capita income of about $380. More recent World Bank figures indicate that in 2000 Timor-Leste's GDP per capita was in fact US $415 and that it had almost doubled to US $806 by 2010.[68] By 2013, GDP per capita had increased by a further 50 percent to US $1,210. Latest available World Bank figures for 2019 record a GDP per capita of US $1,560—well over three times the GDP per capita of 2000.[69] The dollar has not altogether delivered the sort of stability in consumer prices over the same period that might have been expected. In each of the years, from 2011–2013, annual consumer price inflation was recorded at over 10 percent. But, since 2014, prices have returned to stable levels. Overall, and on the basis of these figures, East Timor has been served well by its dollarization.

East Timor's principal export is oil, together with gas, forming 90 percent of all exports. Coffee, sandalwood, and marble represent the main remaining exports. World Bank figures for 2017 indicate that East Timor's number one trade partner was Indonesia, which accounted for just over $187 million worth or 30 percent of Timor-Leste's imports. On the other hand, Timor-Leste exported only $6 million worth of goods and services to Indonesia.[70] Thus, Timor-Leste's main trading partner and leading source of imports is the country that it was so keen to break away from, a situation that has not changed in the nearly twenty years since independence. Indeed, at least one credible report in 2001 noted that the Indonesian rupiah was the most widely accepted currency among the general population of the country because it was familiar and, unlike the US dollar, could be used for the smallest transactions. It is possible, then, that the wider population was using the rupiah as a preferred medium of exchange, while trying to hold some dollars as a store of value.[71]

Another factor in any decision on the selection of a new currency related to the country's state-building capacity. In 2001 East Timor's population was believed to be about 800,000, of whom about 340,000 formed the labor force. Educational levels were a particular weakness in what was already a small labor force. Moreover, because Indonesians had performed most administrative tasks during their occupation, little to no experience in administration had developed among the indigenous people. The view was that the country simply did not have the human resources to run a central bank and that this would be an obstacle in managing a floating exchange rate where the country's main exports are limited to a few volatile commodities.

A further factor in planning the currency for East Timor, it seems, may have been a perceived prospect for political instability in the country, which in turn would weaken the currency severely. De Brouwer, looking back on the failure of Papua New Guinea's monetary regime in the mid-1990s when the central bank there was pressured into funding the government's budget deficit, concluded that a successful monetary regime needed to be able to resist pressures of various types. This included pressure from the government demanding monetary support for its own economic program.[72] For the Australian government, which had led the INTERFET peacekeeping force in East Timor and its officials, the experiences of Papua New Guinea must have seemed apposite. The country, like East Timor, is a geographic neighbor of Australia and indeed was administered by Australia for nearly sixty years. Although the population of Papua New Guinea is about eight times that of Timor-Leste, the state-building capacity of the two states would have appeared very similar to the Australians. Moreover, the experience of Papua New Guinea and the fragility of its currency board system under sustained pressure from government seemed to be echoed in the Cook Islands in the mid-1990s. There, a currency board in name only fell apart under a reduction of the fundamental requirement of 100 percent foreign currency, backing down to 50 percent, and persistent requirements by the local government to fund spending programs.[73]

Argentina's Currency Board, instituted in 1991, fell in 2001 when the country's economic failure resulted in riots and three changes of government in quick succession.[74] To be fair, Professor Steve Hanke has explained that Argentina's currency board was not a currency board in the proper sense because it "maintained a mixture of currency board and central banking features."[75] The problem was that, in 2001, the Central Bank of Argentina had started to operate discretionary monetary policies beyond the usual remit of a currency board.[76] In 2000–2001, then, the IMF could have been forgiven for thinking that some countries had not displayed the disciplines required under political pressure to adhere to a currency board regime and could not be confident that Timor-Leste would not fall into the same trap. Full dollarization appeared to be the only guaranteed means of securing monetary stability. Moreover, if Timor-Leste were to avoid currency instability and did not have the resources to manage a currency itself, the obvious thing to do was to adopt another currency that would be resistant to political and economic upheavals. A straightforward dollarization seemed to present a more reliable solution to achieve price stability. The fact that certain Pacific Islands, such as Nauru and Kiribati, were using the Australian dollar seemed to indicate that, for some independent but small states, the adoption of a foreign currency was a sensible solution.[77]

Various options were considered. The Indonesian rupiah had been the only currency in circulation in Timor-Leste during the Indonesian occupation, so it was familiar to the local population. It had an additional benefit in that denominations were sufficiently small to suit the very small transactions typical in Timor-Leste. But Indonesia was not exactly a model of political stability, and its money was also susceptible to swings in value. At one point during the Asian economic crisis, the rupiah had lost 30 percent of its value.

More compelling than either of these points, however, was the powerful emotional need to reject the currency of the country that until recently had been the occupying power, notwithstanding the economic ties that make Indonesia its primary trading partner to this day.[78]

The euro was rejected, partly on the grounds that supplies of, for instance, euro coins would have a long way to travel. The European Union's long-term commitment to Timor-Leste was, moreover, uncertain, and a further complication stemmed from the fact that the union was opposed to the use of the euro by countries that were not its members. The logistical issues of supplying banknotes and coins across long distances similarly applied to the US dollar. But the dollar was perceived to bring with it many more advantages than disadvantages. Coffee and oil, both important exports for Timor-Leste, are denominated in dollars. There also appeared to be at the time a trend toward adoption of the dollar, as had recently happened in Ecuador (2000) and El Salvador (2001). In 2001 the IMF had proposed that Afghanistan adopt the dollar after the American-led invasion of that country. The proposal was resisted by the US treasury on the grounds, among other factors, that the dollar was at the time systemically overvalued and likely to be a hindrance to Afghanistan's competitiveness in the market place.[79] The same concern was thought to apply to Timor-Leste should it adopt the dollar, although there was a counterargument to make: if the dollar was recognizably substantially overvalued, there was room for it to depreciate (and that is precisely what happened over the following ten years, with the dollar generally declining in strength).[80] One further argument proposed in favor of US dollarization was that it might help to maintain US political focus on East Timor, an argument that somehow did not apply to the European Union.[81]

The Australian dollar was also considered as a possible currency to be adopted by Timor-Leste, just as it had been by Nauru and Kiribati. But at the time of the UNTAET decision to adopt the US dollar, the Australian dollar was seen to be substantially depreciated, with a strong likelihood that it would appreciate in the near future. It was thus a reciprocal of the US dollar. But, while some commentators thought that a future decrease in the value of the US dollar was a positive, the prospect of an increase in the value of the Australian dollar was presented as a negative, although it must be acknowledged that the assessments of experts as to the likely changes in relative strength of the US and Australian dollars were absolutely right over a ten-year period.[82] On a positive note, the proximity of Australia to Timor-Leste would at least make the supply of notes and coins relatively easy. Moreover, there were strong trading links in the period immediately after independence between the two countries, and, for smaller private transactions—those not by UNTAET decree required to be paid in US dollars—the Australian dollar was the second most popular after the Indonesian rupiah.

And yet, over and above the stark economic factors bearing on the use of the Australian dollar, either as an anchor for a national currency for Timor-Leste or as an adopted currency, there were also political issues to bear in mind. Some concern was felt that some sort of official status for the Australian dollar would be received badly in Indonesia as a possible extension of Australian influence in the region. Moreover, there was concern in Australia that the adoption of the Australian dollar in some way together with substantial and continuing Australian aid to Timor-Leste might create a sense of dependency of the latter on the former.[83] Thus, in this view, it was desirable to maintain US focus on Timor-Leste, but to lessen Australia's political links to the country.

So Timor-Leste's circumstances were unique. The country was emerging from conflict with Indonesia, which was in fact (and remains) its main trading partner. The population was small in number and, at the time of independence, was not ready to run a central bank or currency board, and experiences in any case of the latter elsewhere at the time were not encouraging. Unlike some of the tiny island states in the Eastern Caribbean (see below), there were no nearby states of shared cultural, legal, linguistic, and administrative background with which East Timor could pool both human and economic resources. The economy was not diversified, relying largely on oil and coffee to raise revenue, both commodities that traded in US dollars. The Asian economic crisis of 1997–1998 was a very recent memory and a bad one at that, pointing toward the need for a stable currency above all other considerations for this very vulnerable new state. Against this backdrop, international advisers concluded that adoption of the US dollar offered a stable currency that obviated the need for a highly skilled and well-resourced central bank or currency board.

The IMF's decision-making role in East Timor, coming not long after it had attracted criticism for its operations during the Asian economic crisis, was bound to seem high handed. The dollar is hardly a perfect solution, moreover. But it is difficult to see a better solution for a country in East Timor's position at independence and indeed up to the present.

SOUTH SUDAN, 2011

After two decades of war, the government of Sudan and the leadership of the Sudanese People's Liberation Movement (SPLM), a largely Christian movement fighting for the independence of South Sudan from Sudan, moved by staged agreements beginning in 2002 toward a final Comprehensive Peace Agreement signed at Naivasha in Kenya in 2005. In addition to the signatures of Ali Taha, the vice president of Sudan, and John Garang de Mabior, leader of the SPLM, the Comprehensive Peace Agreement was witnessed by the presidents of Kenya and Uganda and by representatives of the governments of Egypt, Italy, Norway, the Netherlands, the United States, the United Kingdom, and others. The agreement brought together protocols and agreements negotiated between the two sides during meetings in Kenya over the period 2002–2004.

The various agreements established the responsibilities and authorities of the national government of Sudan and of an autonomous, but not, at that stage, fully independent government of South Sudan. Most importantly, the Comprehensive Peace Agreement established the right of the people of South Sudan to self-determination by means of a referendum. Prior to any referendum taking place, there would be an interim period during which the administration of the national currency (along with many other functions of state) would remain with the national government with its capital in Khartoum, although the government of South Sudan would enjoy autonomy in the matter of taxation and revenues in South Sudan.[84]

When, in January 2011, South Sudan voted in a referendum to separate from Sudan, it was for many observers a significant break with the African Union's long held policy of promoting the maintenance of borders, which were a legacy of the colonial powers in Africa. To encourage secession would, in the view of the African Union, lead to a widespread redrawing of Africa's borders along tribal lines, with who knew what consequences for peace on the continent. For this reason, Somaliland (formerly British Somaliland), which had formed a federation with Somalia (formerly Italian Somaliland) after the Second World War but had then declared independence in 1991 has not been recognized as an independent state by the African Union or by any other international organization (although it does maintain its own currency). But there had been another precedent in the region for secession, that of Eritrea from Ethiopia in 1993. So, from the moment when the government of Sudan had conceded, under international pressure, South Sudan's right to self-determination, independence was a distinct possibility, even though the signatories to the Naivasha Comprehensive Peace Agreement were categorically committed to working toward making national unity attractive. A measure of the probable outcome of a referendum on self-determination was indicated by the Bank of Southern Sudan's low level of engagement with the government of Sudan and the Bank of Sudan, of which it was still legally a member during the interim period. It was rather, in the eyes of some observers, clearly preparing for its new role as the central bank of a new, independent state.

On independence, the government of South Sudan chose to adopt a central bank, rather than currency board regime, fixing the South Sudanese pound to the Sudanese pound one to one, which would make the currency changeover more acceptable and easier for the population in the south.[85] In this respect, the choice of a one-to-one exchange rate had similarities with Italy's introduction of the somalo in 1950. Where it differed from the case of the proposed one-to-one exchange of Eritrean nakfa for Ethiopian birr was, of course, that, in the case of South Sudan, there was no suggestion that its new currency should be accepted in Sudan. One-for-one exchange of the new South Sudanese and Sudanese pounds was the plan for the immediate change-over. In the longer term, the idea was that the South Sudanese pound would be allowed to find its own way in the market, floating but with interventions from the central bank when necessary, although, in the event the pound was pegged to the US dollar, immediately after independence.

But nothing is that simple. After the referendum of January 2011, tensions arose between Sudan and South Sudan over the question of currency. On July 9 South Sudan became independent and was admitted to the UN as a full member on July 14. The introduction of South Sudan's pound had been planned for August 2011. But it was brought forward to July 18, 2011, only nine days after independence, because the South Sudanese authorities became increasingly concerned at the possibility that Sudan would withhold supplies of enough currency to see the new country through to independence. The British company producing the currency was at pains to ensure no currency was delivered until South Sudan's independence had been formally and inter-nationally recognized. Ten days later, Sudan itself introduced a new currency, effectively blocking the repatriation of Sudanese currency to Khartoum from South Sudan. Khartoum had no intention of redeeming something like three billion Sudanese pounds with hard currency to the benefit of South Sudan and to the detriment of Sudan's reserves to the tune of one billion US dollars at the 2011 exchange rate. Seen in this light, it is hardly surprising that Sudan wished to carry out a demonetization program rendering the pounds in South Sudan obsolete and preventing a "backwash" effect. South Sudan, however, claimed it was a breach of an agreement that no new currency would be introduced by Khartoum until six months after South Sudan's own currency had been introduced.[86]

Matters went from bad to worse when Sudan and South Sudan fell out over the question of payments for the export of oil from South Sudan (which had been the source of some three quarters of the unified Sudan's oil reserves) transiting Sudan. South Sudan had failed to pay transit royalties to the govern-ment in Khartoum and, by December 2011, Sudan's patience had been tried to the point where it started to confiscate a proportion of the oil crossing its territory. In the calculation of South Sudan, the action of its northern neighbor in syphoning off oil had deprived the government in Juba of at least $350 million worth of oil revenues. Khartoum's unilateral action attracted inter-national criticism and, in an escalation of economic sanctions reminiscent of the runup to the Eritrea–Ethiopia conflict of 1998, South Sudan instructed oil companies to stop pumping oil.[87]

The World Bank predicted disastrous consequences for South Sudan as a result of this act of self-denial. GDP would collapse, foreign reserves would shrink, the South Sudanese pound would depreciate, and inflation would increase. At the extreme, imports of food would be jeopardized, some 80 percent of the population would be living below the poverty level of two dollars a day, and infant mortality would double. Indeed, the South Sudanese pound, which had been pegged to the US dollar immediately after independence, fell to more than five to one US dollar from its official rate of less than three to one US dollar; prices were impacted. By early 2012, prices in general were double those in the period prior to the referendum, although the rate of inflation was slowing in the last few months of that period. By June 2012, annual inflation had settled to 80 percent. But matters were made worse by the fact that the South Sudanese pound was not trusted in neighboring countries and therefore tended not to be convertible there, a major drawback for the import of food. Access to dollars was therefore that much more important, but, because of the depreciation of the South Sudanese pound, dollars were increasingly difficult to obtain at reasonable rates, especially as black-market practices flourished.[88]

Oil production was resumed in April 2013 when the disagreements with Sudan over transit fees were settled. But in December of that year South Sudan received another buffeting when civil war broke out between competing factions of the SPLM. Although it would be simplistic to describe this civil war as an ethnic struggle along the same lines as the Bosnian Civil War, there has clearly been a pronounced element of tribal hostility between the government of Salva Kiir, who is from the Dinka tribe, and his principal opponent, the leader of the SPLM-in-Opposition faction, Riek Machar, of the Nuer tribe. The country had not had time to recover from the damage caused by the self-imposed oil embargo when the internal conflict broke out, further forcing downward the exchange rate of the South Sudanese pound. In the following summer, the price of oil on international markets began its steep decline from a price of $105 per barrel to a low point in February 2016 of $26 per barrel. The South Sudanese pound reached 11.6 to the dollar in May 2015. Some reports suggested that the exchange rate fell even further to seventeen to one elsewhere in the country. National reserves fell from more than $800 million at the end of 2013 to $108 million in July 2015. With government spending rising to cover the costs of the internal conflict and revenues severely constrained, the Bank of South Sudan was required to support government spending through the issue of money, which in turn fed depreciation and inflation.[89] The collapse in oil prices hit national revenues, making it well-nigh impossible to build up reserves. By the end of 2015, the government of South Sudan bowed to the inevitable and dropped the official peg to the US dollar, allowing the pound to float down to levels consistent with the unofficial market rate of 18.5 pounds to the dollar.[90]

Circumstances have not been kind to South Sudan in its early years. After decades of armed struggle to achieve independence, it had nevertheless remained dependent on its erstwhile enemies in Khartoum to facilitate the export of the one commodity underpinning South Sudan's economy. Less than a year after it had resolved differences with Khartoum over transit royalties, civil war had broken out, and the global oil price crashed. Had the government in Juba been able to foresee these circumstances, would it have chosen to fix its currency to the dollar to begin with and then allow it to float as it did, or would it have perhaps adopted a currency board regime? It is difficult to see what would have been the optimal currency arrangements in such unfavorable conditions. A currency board using as its anchor currency the dollar, in which South Sudan would earn its oil revenues, would have guaranteed price stability and confidence in the pound. But South Sudan's reliance on oil revenues and the collapse in oil prices in the summer of 2014 together with the eruption of a civil war in late 2013 would have challenged the determination of the government of South Sudan to adhere to a currency board discipline. At the time of writing (December 2020), the South Sudanese pound, originally set at less than three to one US dollar at independence, trades at fifty-five to one US dollar.

BOUGAINVILLE

South Sudan's position as the world's newest independent state was challenged in December 2019 when the electorate of the South Pacific Island state of Bougainville voted at referendum for independence from Papua New Guinea. Although the referendum was nonbinding and required Bougainville to secure Papua New Guinea's agreement for separation, a voter turnout of 87 percent and a 98 percent vote in favor of independence would be impossible to ignore. An earlier attempt to break away from Papua New Guinea led to a vicious civil war during the 1990s, which only came to an end in 1998. A period of autonomy for Bougainville followed a peace agreement that had been negotiated by New Zealand.

Various factors have played a part in Bougainville's drive for independence, among them a sense that the population of Bougainville have more in common with the Solomon Isles than with Papua New Guinea. But the region's drive for independence has also been fueled by frustration at its inability to secure adequate benefits from the resources on and around the island group. This was not to say that the population of Bougainville was evidently struggling in comparison with other provinces of Papua New Guinea. One report noted that it enjoyed the second highest per capita educational levels and income of all Papua's provinces and the best life expectancy figures. Plainly, however, Bougainville felt that it could do even better as an independent state. The local economy of the islands has been based hitherto on copper, gold, and fishing, but lessons are being learned from the case of East Timor, where overdependence on a single set of resources (oil and gas) has failed to create enough employment.

Other aspects of East Timor's secession from Indonesia seem to be replicated in the immediate aftermath of the Bougainville referendum. Just as President Habibie of Indonesia had offered East Timor a "special status" in 1997 to try to persuade the island to remain a part of the Indonesian federation, James Marape, the prime minister of Papua New Guinea, is proposing a compromise solution that will consolidate Bougainville's "self-rule" while preserving Papua New Guinea's desire for national unity.[91]

Assuming Bougainville and Papua New Guinea can reach agreement on separation following discussions on a range of issues, what might we expect by way of a monetary regime for the new state? One of the arguments against a central bank or currency board arrangement for East Timor was based on the latter's limited capacity to run one or the other organization. If East Timor, with its estimated population of 800,000 was unable to summon the necessary skilled human resources, how much more difficult might it be for Bougainville, with an estimated population of 250,000, to set up and run a monetary agency of some sort? The most likely option would be adoption of the US dollar, a tried solution suitable to the trade in copper and gold, which would form Bougainville's main source of revenue. Other possibilities exist. Bougainville's stated sense of a shared ethnic and cultural identity with the Solomon Islands and its geographic proximity to the latter might logically encourage adoption of the Solomon Islands dollar without political merger. The volatility of that currency, however, would not work well for Bougainville's copper and gold exports.

One solution, however unlikely, that deserves consideration is adoption of the renminbi. Media reports indicate that Bougainville's leaders have been offered an attractive infrastructure investment package by China in return for privileged access to Bougainville's mineral resources. China is already the number one trading partner of neighboring Solomon Isles, and at present it must seem likely that it will also become the main partner of Bougainville, making the renminbi a logical choice on grounds of trade alone. Such a choice, however, would buck the convention of pricing commodities in US dollars and, moreover, would run counter to China's policy of avoiding the promotion of the renminbi as a major trading currency. The choice of this currency would be a wake-up call for countries in the region and those, like the United States, that have regional interests.

NOTES

1. Edmund Lim, "Behind the Scenes: What Led to Separation in 1965," *The Straits Times*, August 5, 2015, https://www.straitstimes.com/opinion/behind-the-scenes-what-led-to-separation-in-1965.

2. "Singapore: The Road to Independence," http://countrystudies.us/singapore/10.htm; and Cheah Boon Kheng, "The Separation of Singapore," Malaysian Bar, July 25, 2007, https://www.malaysianbar.org.my/article/news/legal-and-general-news/general-news/the-separation-of-singapore.

3. "Second Separation: Why Singapore Rejected a Common Currency with Malaysia," *The Straits Times*, May 14, 2016, https://www.straitstimes.com/singapore/second-separation-why-singapore-rejected-a-common-currency-with-malaysia.

4. Stephanie Ho, "History of Singapore Currency," https://eresources.nlb.gov.sg/infopedia/articles/SIP_2016-03-09_114438.html; and A Survey of Singapore's Monetary History, January 2000, 19–20, https://www.mas.gov.sg/-/media/MAS/resource/publications/staff_papers/MASOP018_ed.pdf.

5. Goh Keng Swee, "Why Singapore Chose a Currency Board over a Central Bank," EconomyNext, November 6, 2015, https://economynext.com/why-singapore-chose-a-currency-board-over-a-central-bank-3071/.

6. Ibid.

7. Marek Dabrowski, "The Reasons of the Collapse of the Ruble Zone," Center for Social & Economic Research, Warsaw 1995, 13–14, 16, http://case-research.eu/sites/default/files/publications/3460035_058e_0.pdf; C L Melliss

8. Dabrowski, "The Reasons of the Collapse of the Ruble Zone," 17–18, 26.

9. Y. Bokarev, V. Kuchkin, and V. Stepanov, *History of Monetary Circulation of Russia* (Moscow: Bank of Russia, 2010), 361, 366; Rawi Abdelal, "Contested Currency: Russia's Ruble in Domestic and International Politics," *Journal of Communist Studies and Transition Politics* 19, no. 2 (2003): 60; Dabrowski, "The Reasons of the Collapse of the Ruble Zone," cites that the agreement signed in Kyrgyzstan in October 1992 between Russia, Armenia, Belarus, Kyrgyzstan, Moldova, Tajikistan, and Uzbekistan reaffirmed the ruble as a common medium of exchange for the signatories' countries, but did not preclude the introduction of surrogate currencies. Other authors note the introduction by Kyrgyzstan and Azerbaijan of their own independent currencies a month before the signature of this agreement.

10. Bokarev et al., *History of Monetary Circulation of Russia*, 366–68; and Abdelal, "Contested Currency: Russia's Ruble in Domestic and International Politics" 63.

11. Abdelal, "Contested Currencies," 68; Dabrowski, "The Reasons of the Collapse of the Ruble Zone," 5, 19, 21; C. L. Melliss and Mark Cornelius, "New Currencies in the Former Soviet Union: A Recipe for Hyperinflation or the Path to Price Stability?," Working Paper 26, Bank of England, September 1, 1994, 18, https://www.bankofengland.co.uk/working-paper/1994/

new-currencies-in-the-former-soviet-union-a-recipe-for-hyperinflation-or-the-path-to-price-stability.

12. M. Soerg, "Estonian Currency Board and Economic Performance," University of Tartu, Estonia, *South African Journal of Management and Economic Sciences* 1, no. 3 (1998): 465, https://www.researchgate.net/publication/334892209_Estonian_currency_board_and_economic_performance.

13. "World Economic Outlook," International Monetary Fund, October 1992, 52, https://www.elibrary.imf.org/doc/IMF081/14367-9781451944563/14367-9781451944563/Other_formats/Source_PDF/14367-9781455261710.pdf; and Seija Lainela and Pekka Sutela, "Introducing New Currencies in the Baltic Countries," Bank of Finland, Institute for Economies in Transition, 1993, 10, 13, https://helda.helsinki.fi/bof/bitstream/handle/123456789/12997/0893SLPS.PDF?sequence=; Abdelal, "Contested Currency: Russia's Ruble in Domestic and international politics" 61.

14. Ardo H. Hanson, "Transforming an Economy While Building a Nation: The Case of Estonia," Working paper 113, World Institute for Development Economics Research, United Nations University, July 1993, 10, https://www.wider.unu.edu/sites/default/files/WP113.pdf; and Gianni Toniolo and Piet Clement, *Central Bank Cooperation at the Bank for International Settlements, 1930–1973* (Cambridge: Cambridge University Press, 2005), 218–19.

15. Lainela and Sutela, "Introducing New Currencies in the Baltic Countries," 6; Soerg, "Estonian Currency Board and Economic Performance," 468, quoting Siim Kallas, then the president of Eesti Pank, on stability and convertibility.

16. Soerg, "Estonian Currency Board and Economic Performance," 466, 471; Lainela and Sutela, "Introducing new currencies in the Baltic Countries," 16–17.

17. Lainela and Sutela, "Introducing New Currencies in the Baltic Countries," 7–9. The authors also point out that, while the IMF was cautious about the introduction of national currencies in newly independent former Soviet Republics in 1992, by 1993 their policy had changed to the extent that the IMF was urging more cautious states, such as Kazakhstan, to make the leap.

18. Soerg, "Estonian Currency Board and Economic Performance," 467, Table 2.

19. Hanson, "Transforming an Economy While Building a Nation," 11.

20. "GDP per capita, PPP (current international $)—Estonia," https://data.worldbank.org/indicator/NY.GDP.PCAP.PP.CD?locations=EE.

21. Mait Talts, "Eurodebate in Estonia: Pros and Contras in Estonian Press," Paper presented at *Estonia and Finland in the Process of Euro Integration Joint Seminar*, Laulasmaa, Estonia, November 6–7, 1998, https://www.ies.ee/061198paper.html; and Andrius Sytas, "Lithuania Joins Euro as Tensions with Neighboring Russia Rise," *Reuters*, December 31, 2014, quoting Central Bank Governor Vitas Vasiliauskas, https://www.reuters.com/article/us-lithuania-euro-idUSKBN0K918E20141231.

22. Mojmir Mrak, Matija Rocek, and Carlos Silva-Jáuregui, eds., *Slovenia: From Yugoslavia to the European Union* (Washington, DC: The World Bank, 2004), 36–40, http://documents.worldbank.org/curated/en/197621468776951986/pdf/283760PAPER0Slovenia.pdf.

23. Ibid., 41–42.

24. Ibid., 92.

25. Ibid., 43–44, 92.

26. Jože Mencinge, "Financial Regulation in Slovenia," 8, http://www.sinteza.co/wp-content/uploads/2016/01/Zakaj-je-potrebna-revizija5-MENCINGER-ENG.pdf.

27. Mrak et al., eds., *Slovenia: From Yugoslavia to the European Union*, 92, 93.

28. Ibid., 93, 94; and Mencinge, "Financial Regulation in Slovenia," 6.

29. Mrak et al., eds., *Slovenia: From Yugoslavia to the European Union*, 355.

30. "Slovenia Joins the Euro Area," European Commission, http://ec.europa.eu/economy_finance/articles/euro/slovenia_joins_the_euro_area_en.htm.

31. Luka Oreskovic, "Slovenia's Membership of the Euro Is Only Partly to Blame for the Country's Economic Problems," *London School of Economics and Political Science Blog*, December 5, 2012, accessed January 9, 2012, http://blogs.lse.ac.uk/europpblog/2012/12/05/slovenia-eu-economy/; "Euro: 10 Years of the Single Currency in Slovenia," December 23, 2016, Republic of Slovenia, Office of Statistics, https://www.stat.si/statweb/en/news/index/6414.

32. "Slovenia," Focus Economics, https://www.focus-economics.com/countries/slovenia; and Oreskovic, "Slovenia's Membership of the Euro."

33. "Then and Now: 25 Years of National Currency," http://www.slovenia25.si/i-feel-25/timeline/then-and-now/25-years-of-the-national-currency/index.html. This website makes the claim that "monetary independence was a precondition in gaining the young country's international recognition."

34. Mencinge, "Financial Regulation in Slovenia," 2.

35. Jan Fidrmuc, Julius Horvath, and Jarko Fidrmuc, "The Stability of Monetary Unions: Lessons from the Breakup of Czechoslovakia," *Journal of Comparative Economics* 27 (1999): 768–74, http://cms-content.bates.edu/prebuilt/fidrmuc,horvath&fidrmuc.pdf.

36. Fidrmuc et al., "The Stability of Monetary Unions," 754; and Klara Cermakova, "Brief History of Currency Separation: Case Study of Czech and Slovak Koruna," *International Journal of Economic Sciences* VI, no. 2 (2017): 31–32.

37. Fidrmuc et al., "Stability of Monetary Unions," 13; Elisabeth Bakke, "The Principle of National Self-Determination in Czechoslovak Constitutions, 1920–1992," 10, 16, https://www.researchgate.net/publication/342572105_The_principle_of_national_self-determination_in_Czechoslovak_constitutions_1920-1992; and Kieran Williams, *The Break-Up of Czechoslovakia and Scottish Independence* (London: History & Policy, 2013).

38. Fidrmuc et al., "Stability of Monetary Unions," 14; and Adrian Bridge, "Czechs and Slovaks Split Their Currency," *The Independent*, February 3, 1993, https://www.independent.co.uk/news/business/czechs-and-slovaks-split-their-currency-1470651.html.

39. Arnold Keller and John Sandrock, "The Significance of Stamps Used on Banknotes," *The Currency Collector*, http://thecurrencycollector.com/pdfs/The_Significance_of_Stamps_Used_on_Bank_Notes.pdf.

40. Cermakova, "Brief History of Currency Separation," 30–44, quoting OECD figures.

41. Williams, *The Break-Up of Czechoslovakia and Scottish Independence*.

42. Jiang Li, "Analysis of the Czech and Slovak Different Strategic Choices towards the Eurozone," *Romanian Journal of European Affairs* 16, no. 1 (2016): 73–74.

43. Ibid., 76.

44. Ibid., 75–85.

45. Paul Henze, "Introduction," *Eritrea's War: Confrontation, International Response, Outcome, Prospects* (Addis Ababa: Shama Books, 2001).

46. Ibid., 10–11.

47. Ross Herbert, "The End of the Eritrean Exception?" Country Report No. 8, South African Institute of International Affairs, 2002, 8.

48. Bereket Habte Selassie, 2006, "Dreams That Turned to Nightmares: The Ethio-Eritrean War of 1998–2000 and Its Aftermath," in *The Search for Peace: The Conflict between Ethiopia and Eritrea*, Proceedings of Scholarly Conference on the Ethiopia–Eritrea Conflict, Oslo, July 6–7, 2006, 26. The author of that paper had been party to the conversations with the Eritreans during which the latter complained about the currency issue. Ravinder Rena, "Historical Development of Money and Banking in Eritrea from the Axumite Kingdom to the Present," *Journal of African and Asian Studies* 6, no. 1–2 (2007): 10.

49. Seyoum Yohannes Tesfay, "Eritrea-Ethiopia Arbitration: A 'Cure' Based on Neither Diagnosis nor Prognosis," *Mizan Law Review* 6, no. 2 (2012): 176.

50. Tekie Fessehazion, "Eritrean and Ethiopian State of Economic Relations: A Nakfa/Birr/LC Analysis," Denden, http://www.denden.com/Conflict/newscom/com-tek98.htm.

51. Ibid.

52. Haile Selassie Girmay, "Ethiopia-Eritrea Border Conflict: The Role Nakfa Played," Ethiopian Embassy to the United Kingdom, 2010. This article obviously puts across the Ethiopian point of view. Habte Selassie, "Dreams that turned to Nightmares," 27.

53. Herbert, "The End of the Eritrean Exception?," 17; IMF figures quoted by Temesgen Kifle, "Can Border Demarcation Help Eritrea to Reverse the General Slowdown in Growth?," Institute of World Economics and International Management, University of Bremen, 2004, 11, 12, http://www.iwim.uni-bremen.de/files/dateien/1613_b090.pdf; "Eritrea: Selected Issues and Statistical Appendix," IMF Country Report 03/166, 2003, International Monetary Fund, 19, 20, https://www.imf.org/external/pubs/ft/scr/2003/cr03166.pdf.

54. "The Federal Democratic Republic of Ethiopia: Selected Issues and Statistical Appendix," IMF Country Report No. 05/28, 2005, 45, International Monetary Fund, https://www.imf.org/external/pubs/ft/scr/2005/cr0528.pdf.

55. Herbert, "The End of the Eritrean Exception?" 9, 13, 16.

56. Paul Hainsworth, "From Occupation and Civil War to Nation-Statehood: East Timor and the Struggle for Self-Determination and Freedom from Indonesia," Institute for British–Irish Studies, IBIS Discussion Paper No. 5, University College Dublin, 3, accessed January 7, 2020, https://www.ucd.ie/ibis/filestore/p_hainsworth.pdf.

57. Frederic Durand, "Three Centuries of Violence and Struggle in East Timor (1726–2008)," 2011, SciencesPo, https://www.

sciencespo.fr/mass-violence-war-massacre-resistance/en/document/three-centuries-violence-and-struggle-east-timor-1726-2008.

58. Ibid.

59. Hainsworth, "From Occupation and Civil War to Nation-Statehood," 8–9. Hainsworth (10) lists some interesting sources analyzing the decision-making of states that decide to give up their control of territories. These themes are unfortunately beyond the remit of this book.

60. Durand, "Three Centuries of Violence and Struggle in East Timor (1726–2008)"; "Modern Conflicts—East Timor-Indonesia (1975–1999)," Political Economy Research Institute, University of Massachussets, Amherst http://www.peri.umass.edu/fileadmin/pdf/Easttimor.pdf.

61. Sonny Inbaraj, "East Timor: Language, Currency a Sore Point for New Nation," *Inter Press Service*, January 21, 2000, http://www.ipsnews.net/2000/01/east-timor-language-currency-a-sore-point-for-new-nation/.

62. Joseph Stiglitz, *Globalisation and Its Discontents* (London: W. W. Norton and Company, 2002), 40–41.

63. Luis Vadivieso, Toshihide Endo, Luis Mendonca, Shamsuddin Tareq, and Alexandro Lopez-Mejia, "East Timor: Establishing the Foundations of Sound Macroeconomic Management," International Monetary Fund, https://www.imf.org/external/pubs/ft/etimor/timor.pdf. One of the authors is of course the IMF economist mentioned earlier in the paragraph.

64. "East Timor: Recent Developments and Macroeconomic Assessment," Section VI, Paragraph 18, November 30, 2000, https://www.imf.org/external/np/et/2000/eng/113000.htm.

65. "Explaining the Currency of East Timor: Questions and Answers about Using the United States Dollar (US$)," UNTAET currency brochure, https://peacekeeping.un.org/mission/past/etimor/untaetPU/currency.pdf.

66. Gordon De Brouwer, "Currency and Monetary Arrangements for East Timor," Australian National University, April 5, 2001, 12, https://crawford.anu.edu.au/pdf/staff/gordon_debrouwer/GdB01-01.pdf.

67. Louis Aucoin and Michele Brandt, "East Timor's Constitutional Passage to Independence," in *Framing the State in Times of Transition: Case Studies in Constitution Making*, ed. Laurel E. Miller (Washington, DC: United States Institute of Peace Press, 2010), 250.

68. "Gross Domestic Product, 2019," World Development Indicators Database, World Bank, February 12, 2021, https://databank.worldbank.org/data/download/GDP.pdf.

69. "GDP per capita (current US$)—Timor-Leste," World Bank, accessed April 20, 2021, https://data.worldbank.org/indicator/NY.GDP.PCAP.CD?locations=TL.

70. "East Timor Trade Balance, Exports, Imports by Country and Region 2017," World Integrated Trade Solution, World Bank, accessed November 29, 2020, https://wits.worldbank.org/CountryProfile/en/Country/TMP/Year/LTST/TradeFlow/EXPIMP; and "Timor-Leste: Country Brief," International Trade Centre, accessed November 29, 2020, https://www.intracen.org/country/timor-leste/.

71. De Brouwer, "Currency and Monetary Arrangements for East Timor," 2.

72. Ibid., 2–3, 5, 7.

73. Richard C. K. Burdekin, "Currency Boards vs. Dollarization: Lessons from the Cook Islands," *Cato Journal* 28, no. 1: 101–15, https://www.cato.org/sites/cato.org/files/serials/files/cato-journal/2008/1/cj28n1-7.pdf.

74. Laurence Ball, "Hard Currency Pegs," in *Handbook of Monetary Economics*, vol. 3B, ed. Benjamin M. Friedman and Michael Woodford (Amsterdam: North-Holland, 2011), 1328–30.

75. Steve Hanke, "Argentina's Peso: Nothing but Trouble," *Forbes*, March 16, 2019.

76. Steve Hanke, "Argentina Should Scrap the Peso and Dollarize," *Forbes*, June 29, 2018, https://www.forbes.com/sites/stevehanke/2018/06/29/argentina-should-scrap-the-peso-and-dollarize/?sh=5ad2ffad393e.

77. De Brouwer, "Currency and Monetary Arrangements for East Timor," 10–11.

78. Ibid., 13.

79. Paul Wilson, *Hostile Money: Currencies in Conflict* (Cheltenham: The History Press, 2019), 219.

80. "U.S. Dollar Index—43 Year Historical Chart, Macrotrends, accessed November 29, 2020, https://www.macrotrends.net/1329/us-dollar-index-historical-chart.

81. De Brouwer, "Currency and Monetary Arrangements for East Timor," 14.

82. Ibid., 10–11; and "Australian Dollar to US Dollar Exchange Rates," Trading Economics, https://tradingeconomics.com/australia/currency.

83. De Brouwer, "Currency and Monetary Arrangements for East Timor," 17.

84. "Protocol Between the Government of Sudan (GOS) and the Sudan People's Liberation Movement (SPLM) On Power Sharing," Naivasha, Kenya, May 26, 2004, Part V Schedules, Schedule A National Powers, https://reliefweb.int/sites/reliefweb.int/files/resources/2FABFAF9185C311485256EA60071784A-gossplm-sdn-26may.pdf.

85. Matthew Arnold and Matthew LeRiche, *South Sudan: From Revolution to Independence* (London: C. Hurst and Co. Ltd., 2012), 175.

86. Ibid., 176; "South Sudan accuses Khartoum of 'currency war'" quoting Pagan Amum, South Sudan's Minister for Peace, BBC Africa 25 July 2011. Author's personal recollection, having been involved in De La Rue PLC's consultations with the Foreign and Commonwealth Office to establish the date of independence and recognition by UN and other countries prior to supply of currency.

87. James Copnall, *A Poisonous Thorn in Our Hearts: Sudan and South Sudan's Bitter and Incomplete Divorce* (London: Hurst, 2014), 97.

88. Ibid., 99; "Inflation in South Sudan," South Sudan Economic Brief Issue No. 1, 2012, World Bank, http://documents1.worldbank.org/curated/en/833711468169442089/pdf/774280BRI0SS0e00Box377296B00PUBLIC0.pdf; and Irina Mosel and Emily Henderson, "Markets in Crises: South Sudan Case Study," Working paper, Humanitarian Policy Group, October 2015, 18, 21–22. https://cdn.odi.org/media/documents/9920.pdf.

89. Mosel and Henderson "Markets in Crises," 2; and Keith Jefferis, "Monetary and Exchange Rate Management: Policies and Processes for Stability and Growth," International Growth Centre, October 8, 2015, http://www.theigc.org/event/monetary-and-exchange-rate-management-policies-and-processes-for-stability-and-growth/.

90. Amadou Sy, "The Implications of South Sudan's Decision to Float Its Currency," *Africa in Focus* (blog), Brookings Institute, December 18, 2015.

91. Ashley Westerman, "Trying to Form the World's Newest Country, Bougainville Has a Road Ahead," National Public Radio, December 30, 2019, https://www.npr.org/2019/12/30/789697304/trying-to-form-the-worlds-newest-country-bougainville-has-a-road-ahead?t=1577958856861; Patrick Elligett, "From Treasure Island to World's Newest Nation: What Is Happening in Bougainville?" *Sydney Morning Herald*, December 11, 2019, https://www.smh.com.au/world/oceania/from-treasure-island-to-world-s-newest-nation-what-is-happening-in-bougainville-20191127-p53eph.html.

Chapter 7

Accession

Fundamental decisions on monetary matters must be made not only in the case of secession but also in the case of accession, probably the most significant of which in the period after the Second World War has been the accession of East Germany to the Federal Republic of Germany.

REUNIFICATION OF GERMANY

Following the fall of the Berlin Wall in 1989, the reunification of Germany seemed to be only a question of time. Early steps toward a plan for reunification—notably, the West German government's ten-point program of November 1989—did not focus on monetary unification. But, on February 6, 1990, West German Chancellor Kohl announced to the press his intention to start negotiations on a currency union. On May 18, 1990, prior to full unification, the two Germanys signed a pact on "Currency, Economic and Social Union between the German Democratic Republic and the Federal Republic of Germany." The currency union came into effect on July 1, 1990, when the population of East Germany was able to exchange its existing currency for that of the Bundesrepublik, three months before the formal unification of the two Germanies on October 3, 1990. There was then a sense in which monetary union—or at least coordination—could precede full-blown political union, a distant echo of the monetary coordination that existed among German states prior to full unification of the country under Prussian leadership in 1871 and, at a stretch, a precedent (perhaps the only precedent) for the euro experiment. A further factor in Germany's bid for unification was the need to secure for this momentous shift in Europe's postwar configuration the support of France, the country that above all others had reason to harbor misgivings. In this calculation, a greater monetary union of Germany with France and other European Union states presented itself as a reassuring quid pro quo. Germany's independence of action would be constrained by being part of a closely knit group of states bound together by monetary union; Germany in return would achieve unification. Just as the European Coal and Steel Community agreement of 1951 was designed to make European war impossible by sharing control of the most important material assets of arms production, a shared currency could prevent any one country (in this case, Germany) from achieving hegemony in Europe.

For some political leaders in France, a European unified currency had also seemed attractive as the means of challenging the dollar for the position of a leading reserve currency. On a domestic level, also, monetary union could bring benefits to bear on France's economy by importing Germany's monetary discipline.[1] The German monetary union was therefore seen in France and elsewhere as a precursor to a grander project.

In the new German monetary union, the Bundesbank became the sole central bank for the unified Germany, and rules for exchange of East German marks for Deutsche Marks were put in place. Under these rules, citizens over the age of sixty were permitted to exchange up to 6,000 marks at an exchange rate of one to one; adults below that age could exchange up to 4,000 marks, and children up to 2,000 marks at that one-to-one exchange rate. Savings beyond those figures were exchanged at half the rate as were debts. Different exchange rates were applied to wages and pensions on the one hand and savings on the other.

Differing approaches to the implementation of monetary union by the West German government and the Bundesbank reflected their respective political and technocratic motives. While the government in Bonn was anxious to deliver early monetary union, seeing it as an essential means of improving the poor East German economy, the Bundesbank took a far more measured approach. Believing the parlous state of East Germany's economy to be the result of poor productivity and an absence of private ownership associated with a free market rather than a pure monetary problem, the Bundesbank advocated an attempt to address the root problem based on gradual economic convergence. The West German government's position was influenced by the need to find an exchange rate that would be attractive to the population of East Germany, giving the working population of East Germany an incentive to remain in the east of a unified Germany and discouraging a mass migration to the west. By extension, an exchange rate that would be attractive to the population would be easier to sell to the East German government. That was not, however, the view of the Bundesbank, where price stability was the overriding, indeed sole, concern. An overgenerous conversion rate would lead, in Bundesbank assessments, to rising labor costs, which in turn would make the East German economy even more uncompetitive. This in turn would produce rising unemployment and consequently lead to the mass migration westward, which was after all the West German government's worst fear. Tensions arose also when Bundesbank representatives suggested that the cost of reunification would probably lead to raised taxes, contrary to the message that the government had been putting out.[2]

In an extraordinary but clear demonstration of the Bundesbank's independence, representatives of the bank publicly criticized the government's position in press and television interviews as a threat to the stability of the Deutsche Mark.[3] Despite the near-theological belief in the Bundesbank's freedom from political interference on monetary matters, the question of Germany's reunification was too important to leave in the hands of the technocrats. Elected politicians had their way, and the Bundesbank was forced to comply with the politicians' agenda and timetable. There was a limit to the Bundesbank's independence on the most important political issues.[4]

The unjustifiably high premium placed on the "ostmark" in this exchange obliged West Germany to pump out more Deutsche Marks to complete the currency exchange operation in addition to the large amounts of money that were poured into the East in what was effectively internal aid. Deutsche Marks issued by the Bundesbank increased by about 10 percent by July 1990. As a result of these actions, inflation crept toward 5 percent, prompting Bundesbank President Helmut Schlesinger to raise interest rates to bring inflation under control. In addition to the concern that the exchange rate created in West Germany would become a source of inflation, there was a direct and very negative effect on enterprises in East Germany, which, poor in productivity as they were, could not afford the new wages in Deutsche Marks, resulting inevitably in a major drop in employment in East Germany within two years of unification. Despite the Bundesbank's concerns, the economic impact of the exchange rate imposed by the West German government did not lead to mass migration because the negatives were neutralized by fiscal transfers from the West German state to East Germany.[5]

If there is merit in looking at historical experience as a means of determining the best monetary arrangements for new political entities (i.e., states), the West German leadership might have considered satisfying Bundesbank concerns by running two parallel currencies for West and East Germany. There was after all a useful precedent in circulation of the parallel currencies of the northern thaler and the southern gulden in Germany in the years immediately following unification in 1871. No doubt the West German leadership saw circumstances in 1990 as being quite different. There were only two states to merge on this occasion, not the two dozen or so that had to be bought together in the 1870s, and perhaps the window of opportunity for unification might close. While East Germany continued to suffer from unemployment following the introduction of the currency union, the merger of the two political entities was executed swiftly and without civil disorder. It would be wrong, however, for other countries to conclude that what worked for Germany would necessarily work elsewhere. Germany's monetary unification project benefited from the vital foundation stones of political and internal cohesion, regional stability, and peace, without which monetary projects have little chance of success. West Germany's position as the economic powerhouse of Europe promised a brighter future for the East. The same could not be said for other countries attempting union.

THE UNIFICATION OF YEMEN

Aden (formerly the People's Democratic Republic of Yemen) joined the Yemen Arab Republic, or North Yemen, in May 1990, two months before the two Germanys reunified. And, beyond the coincidence in timing, the unification of the two Yemens contains other interesting parallels with that of the two Germanies.

North Yemen, like West Germany, was more populous than its junior partner, which accounted for only 20 percent of the combined population. And, even though the descriptions of North Yemen as a free-market economy and South Yemen as a socialist, centrally planned one are seen as simplistic, the North certainly enjoyed a greater per capita income. The discovery of oil in the 1980s in the eastern areas of Yemen, where the border with Saudi Arabia was ill defined, prompted Yemen's leaders to conclude that unification would provide a stronger basis for resistance to any Saudi attempt to secure the new oil finds. More positively, leaders in both the North and South felt that unification offered greater possibilities for prosperity, with Aden in the South offering the privileged position of a free port and therefore economic center for the unified state. North Yemen, like West Germany, played the lead role in driving the unification, and it was the North's riyal that was adopted by the South. But here the parallels stop.[6]

The Northern riyal was set at an overvalued exchange rate to its southern partner. And, too soon after unification, the state's economic dependence on remittances from Yemeni workers in the gulf and aid from Kuwait, Iraq, and Saudi Arabia were severely impacted by the Gulf War of 1990–1991. Various states in the Arabian Peninsula punished Yemen's support for Iraq in the latter's invasion of Kuwait by expelling hundreds of thousands, possibly approaching a million Yemeni guest workers. Some estimates suggest that nearly a million Yemenis were at this point out of work. The promise of prosperity had been shattered by Yemen's unwise foreign policy. In the period between unification and early 1991, the Yemeni riyal went from a relatively stable thirteen to twenty-six to the dollar.[7]

Budget deficits increased significantly after unification, and in the four years from 1990 to 1994 the value of the Yemeni riyal to the US dollar

declined steeply from 17.5 to one to one hundred to one. CPI inflation doubled to 62 percent in 1993, and real GDP declined. The North Yemen economy was simply not strong enough to bear the burden of the unification in a
way that West Germany could; the merger of north and south was based on
weak foundations.

Internal politics did little to help the new unified state to get off to a strong
start. Although South Yemen contributed only one in five of the overall
population, its leaders still expected to occupy half of the senior positions in
government. At the same time, they began to feel marginalized by the asser-
tive North Yemeni General People's Congress, led by President Ali Abdullah
Saleh. Full union was starting to look unattractive for the southern leadership,
which began to agitate for federation as a more manageable alternative.[8]

The apparent failure of the economic aspects of unification contributed
to a loss of confidence. The armies of North and South Yemen had, by May
1994, still not been integrated, and the tensions between the parties ensured
that they would not be. In that month civil war broke out followed swiftly
by a short-lived attempt by the South at secession, which the North managed
to reverse by July of that year.[9] From that point until 2007 South Yemen had
been firmly under the control of the North.

Since 2015 the country has descended into a horrific civil war between the
Shia Houthi people of Northern Yemen and the government led by President
Hadi, a Southerner. In 2019 Southern separatists had seized Aden during the
brutal civil war, in which Saudi Arabia and Iran have been backing opposing sides, playing out a regional and sectarian rivalry by proxy. It would be
entirely wrong to assign any significant part to the currency union in Yemen's
civil war. As with South Sudan, internal discontent, tribal rivalry, wider economic problems, and regional discord have created conditions in which a new
currency is simply unable to flourish.

HONG KONG

In 1997, control of Hong Kong was returned to China by Britain, which
since 1842 had controlled the island as a consequence of the First Opium
War. Britain's territorial holdings in the area had increased after the Second
Opium War in 1860 when Kowloon, the area immediately opposite the
island had been absorbed by Britain. Further territories, the so-called New
Territories, were added to British control by lease in 1898. The lease on the
New Territories was to last ninety-nine years, and so return of that land was
to take place in 1997. In 1982 the British government embarked on a difficult
and protracted set of negotiations for the return of the territories, accepting
that the legal end of the New Territories lease also meant that control of

Kowloon and Hong Kong Island would inevitably be returned to China at the same time.[10]

While China knew full well that Britain had little power to shape the long-term future of the territories to be returned, it also recognized Hong Kong's economic success. Because China had, under Deng Shao Peng, begun to adopt free-market policies and because Deng as head of state and government was leading the negotiations for the return of Hong Kong with Britain's prime minister, Margaret Thatcher, it was consistent with the prevailing policies of the Chinese leadership to allow Hong Kong to continue as an economic success on the capitalist model, albeit within bounds set by China. This approach, known as "one country, two systems," promised that, as a Special Administrative Region, Hong Kong would enjoy a high degree of internal autonomy, except in matters relating to defense and foreign affairs, and that this special status would remain in place for fifty years from the handover in 1997. A further motive behind Deng's promotion of the "one country, two systems" idea was to give some degree of reassurance to Taiwan, which would surely have been watching the progress of the Hong Kong transfer of sovereignty.[11]

Yet another consideration for the leadership of the People's Republic of China was the question of maintaining investors' confidence in Hong Kong under Chinese rule. As the negotiations between Deng and Thatcher progressed, the Chinese threat to exercise force to achieve their aims led to a dramatic loss of confidence in the future of Hong Kong. Property and stock markets collapsed, leading to a severe fall in the value of the Hong Kong dollar in September 1983. In only two days in that month, the exchange rate of the Hong Kong dollar to the US dollar fell by 15 percent.[12] It was at this point that the existing policy of permitting a floating Hong Kong dollar was scrapped and replaced by a currency board based on the Exchange Fund (established in 1935), which manages foreign reserves, fully backing the Hong Kong dollar. Under this continuing system, the three commercial banks issuing banknotes—the Hong Kong and Shanghai Bank, Standard Chartered, and the Bank of China—must purchase with US dollars a certificate of indebtedness equivalent at a fixed rate to the value of Hong Kong dollars issued. At the time of writing, the exchange rate is 7.8 to one US dollar. When Hong Kong dollars are withdrawn from circulation, the certificate of indebtedness is redeemed by the transfer of the appropriate funds in US dollars being returned to the issuing bank. In this way, the Hong Kong dollars on issue are fully backed by US dollars held at the currency board. Unlike the currency boards of a previous era, the Hong Kong operation does not commit to convert all banknotes to the backing currency on demand, although the three commercial banks authorized to issue notes must hold enough currency in their accounts at the monetary authority to cover fully the amount of their Hong Kong dollars issued.[13] In 1993 the Exchange Fund and the Office of the Commissioner of Banking were merged and replaced in 1993 by the Hong Kong Monetary Authority, which remains the supervising body of the currency board.[14]

In 1984 the Chinese and British sides issued "The Joint Declaration of the Government of the United Kingdom of Great Britain and Northern Ireland and the Government of the People's Republic of China on the Question of Hong Kong." This joint declaration set out the basis for Hong Kong's status as a Special Administrative Region, noting that it would continue to operate as a free port, an international financial center and a separate customs entity. The Hong Kong dollar would continue to circulate on the basis of Hong Kong's currency board, which had operated since the year before. In its own "elaboration . . . of its basic policies regarding Hong Kong," attached as an appendix to the Joint Declaration, the Chinese government confirmed that the *"Hong Kong Special Administrative Region shall use its own financial revenues exclusively for its own purposes and they shall not be handed over to the Central People's Government."* The Elaboration also confirmed that Hong Kong would continue to determine its own monetary policy. In this Elaboration, China authorized Hong Kong to continue its unusual practice of permitting the three commercial banks to issue banknotes on its behalf, as long as the currency was managed in such a way as to guarantee its stability and to remove progressively from the banknotes any design elements that were "inappropriate" to the status of Hong Kong as a Special Administrative Region of the People's Republic of China. Article 1 of the Elaboration states that "Hong Kong's previous capitalist system and lifestyle shall remain unchanged for 50 years." While this commitment applies to the general market system and lifestyle, neither the Elaboration nor the Joint Declaration made any specific commitment to the maintenance of the currency board for the full fifty years.[15]

Hong Kong's constitution, set out in the Basic Law, which was promulgated in 1990, confirmed that the Hong Kong dollar would continue to be the legal tender of the Special Administrative Region. The Basic Law also confirmed that the Hong Kong dollar would be backed by a one hundred percent reserve fund and that the Hong Kong authorities could authorize banks to issue the currency, as long as appropriate measures were taken to ensure the stability of the currency. Articles 110 and 113 of the Basic Law asserted that monetary policy and the Exchange Fund would be managed and controlled by the government of the Special Administrative Region, not the Monetary Authority. But, because the Basic Law was promulgated in 1990, it predated the creation of the Hong Kong Monetary Authority. Perhaps in response to this—and recalling failed Hong Kong government intervention by means of interest rate hikes to slow inflation in the early 1990s—officials of the Hong Kong Monetary Authority emphasized publicly after the transfer of sovereignty the importance of preserving the currency board operation free from short-term political interference.[16] Ultimately, however, the Basic Law categorically asserts the sovereignty of the central government of the People's Republic of China and empowers the National People's Congress to approve amendments to the Basic Law. The constitutional autonomy of the Hong Kong Monetary Authority can therefore be withdrawn should China's central government choose to do so and is certainly not guaranteed to last fifty years, which a broad interpretation of the Joint Declaration might infer. Indeed, a spokesman for the Foreign Ministry of the People's Republic of China declared in 2017 that the Sino-British Joint Declaration was no longer binding on China.[17]

Will the Hong Kong dollar, the currency board, and the Monetary Authority itself survive the full fifty years to 2047? As long as the Special Administrative Region of Hong Kong remains a valuable economic asset in its current autonomous form, there would be little reason to scrap the existing arrangements, unless, of course, the leadership in Beijing felt that for domestic political reasons or international consumption it might be desirable to project a policy of "one country, one system." This would be easier to countenance if the Chinese economy continues to grow, overshadowing Hong Kong's economic success or even drawing trade and investment away from the latter. The provisions within the Basic Law for changes in the Hong Kong constitution and China's dismissal of the Joint Declaration clear the way for structural changes. Hong Kong's continuing economic success would seem to afford the currency board some measure of longer-term security. That security could, however, be forfeit if the authorities in Beijing decide that the instability wracking Hong Kong in 2019 can be resolved only by a change of the Special Administrative Region's status.

When empires were dismantled in the postwar period, many former colonies chose to establish a central bank as the monetary institution that seemed to enshrine monetary sovereignty consistent with independence. Others maintained the currency board principle, which they felt operated well during the imperial period. More recently, however, newly independent countries—or those joining with other existing states to form a new political entity—have had other options at their disposal, including dollarization and participation in new monetary unions, thereby surrendering monetary sovereignty, but usually for sound reasons. Some peoples who now aspire to an independent state may find useful lessons in the experience of those who have gone before.

NOTES

1. Barry Eichengreen, *Exorbitant Privilege* (Oxford: Oxford University Press, 2011), 74.

2. Matthias Morys, "Was the Bundesbank's Credibility Undermined during the Process of German Reunification?" Working Paper No. 74/03, 2003, London School of Economics, 18, http://eprints.lse.ac.uk/22355/1/wp74.pdf.

3. Ibid., 10.

4. Marjorie Deane and Robert Pringle, *The Central Banks* (New York: Viking Press, 1995), 6.

5. Goohoon Kwon, "Experiences with Monetary Integration and Lessons for Korean Unification," Working paper 97/65, International Monetary Fund, May 1, 1997, https://www.imf.org/external/pubs/ft/wp/wp9765.pdf.

6. Garrett Khourry, "The Original Sin of Yemen," Medium Corporation, March 26, 2015, https://medium.com/the-eastern-project/the-original-sin-of-yemen-fde04ab298e6.

7. Sheila Carapico, "The Economic Dimension of Yemeni Unity," *Middle East Report* 184, no. 5 (1993): 14.

8. Khourry, "The Original Sin of Yemen."

9. Kwon, "Experiences with Monetary Integration and Lessons for Korean Unification"; and Joseph Bosco, "What China's Stance on Hong Kong Means for US-Taiwan Relations," The Diplomat, July 5, 2017, https://thediplomat.com/2017/07/what-chinas-stance-on-hong-kong-means-for-us-taiwan-relations/.

10. For an uncompromising summary of the Chinese perspective on the negotiations, see "The Chinese Government Resumed Exercise of Sovereignty over Hong Kong," Ministry of Foreign Affairs of the People's Republic of China, https://www.fmprc.gov.cn/mfa_eng/ziliao_665539/3602_665543/3604_665547/t18032.shtml.

11. "Hong Kong's Handover: How Britain Returned It to China," BBC News, June 29, 2017, https://www.bbc.co.uk/news/world-asia-china-40426827, commenting on 2014 events; Treaty Series, "Joint Declaration of the Government of Great Britain and Northern Ireland and the Government of the People's Republic of China on the Question of Hong Kong," 3(2), https://treaties.un.org/doc/Publication/UNTS/Volume%201399/v1399.pdf; and "The Negotiations Leading to the Joint Declaration," Gwulo: Old Hong Kong, https://gwulo.com/node/6197.

12. Priscilla Chiu, "Hong Kong's Experience in Operating the Currency Board System," Paper presented at IMF *High Level Seminar on Exchange Rate Regimes: Hard Peg or Free Floating?*, 2001, https://www.imf.org/external/pubs/ft/seminar/2001/err/eng/chiu.pdf.

13. "Review of Currency Board Arrangements in Hong Kong," Hong Kong Monetary Authority, 11, https://www.hkma.gov.hk/media/eng/publication-and-research/reference-materials/monetary/rcbahke.pdf; "How the Link Works," Hong Kong Monetary Authority, https://www.hkma.gov.hk/media/eng/publication-and-research/background-briefs/hkmalin/06.pdf.

14. "The Negotiations Leading to the Joint Declaration"; and "An Introduction to the Hong Kong Monetary Authority," Hong Kong Monetary Authority, 1, 10,

https://www.hkma.gov.hk/media/eng/publication-and-research/reference-materials/
intro_to_hkma.pdf.

15. "The Joint Declaration" 3(7) and 3(8) and Appendix 1 Sections V and VII.

16. "Review of Currency Arrangements in Hong Kong," 4, 9; Basic Law of the
Hong Kong Special Administrative Region of the People's Republic of China,
Articles 110–113.

17. Ben Blanchard, Michael Holden, and Venus Wu, "China Says Sino-British Joint
Declaration on Hong Kong No Longer Has Meaning," Reuters, June 30, 2017. https://
www.reuters.com/article/us-hongkong-anniversary-china-idUSKBN19L1J1.

Chapter 8

Countries and Currencies
in Waiting

Newly independent states choosing their monetary regimes have taken into consideration questions of national security, administrative capacity, and straightforward nationalism as well as purely economic factors. Does this range of factors still hold for those peoples who currently seek to create their own nation-state or are debating the idea?

Following its December 2019 referendum, Bougainville may now be on the cusp of achieving independence. Other small island states in the Pacific could follow, especially if China is able to encourage a series of pro-independence movements in resource-rich microstates in the region. In these latter cases, it must be very questionable as to whether fragmentation into an increased number of smaller states would be the best basis for managing an independent currency. Timor-Leste is a good case in point. Because it is not a very populous state with low levels of literacy, it does not have the human resources to staff a central bank able to conduct the full range of monetary policies and responsibilities. The example of the Eastern Caribbean Central Bank, which we will look at later, demonstrates the value of cooperation by states that would otherwise be too small to manage their own money. The prospect for independence for other states is much more difficult to imagine mainly because they currently form a part of a larger political unit or units that refuse to countenance secession. In one case, the matter of the choice of currency has played a significant part in a decision at referendum to reject independence. In other cases, leaders of independence movements toy with the idea of using digital private currencies as a means of asserting some measure of independence beyond the control of the existing central bank.

PALESTINE

When the Arab states and Palestinians resolved to reject UN General Assembly Resolution 181 proposing the creation of two states and an internationally administered Jerusalem, they must have had little thought that the question of dual Arab and Israeli states would remain a burning issue into the next century. Would they have anticipated the decision of an US government in effect to abandon in 2019 the idea of dual states and, contrary to international convention and the original UN plan, recognize Jerusalem as the capital of Israel? Probably not.

But at least one of the leaders of the Palestinian people had not altogether forgotten the Palestine Currency Board and the circumstances of its dissolution. During a visit to London in 1993, Yasser Arafat, chairman of the Palestine Liberation Organization (PLO), sought to raise the issue of the gold reserves that had backed the issue of Palestinian pounds. At least one British newspaper reported the belief prevalent in Palestinian circles that the gold had been distributed between Israel and Jordan and that Palestinians had been robbed of their share of the gold.[1]

In the same year, the Israeli government and the PLO signed the first of two "Oslo" Accords as the first step in the Oslo process, which was to lead to a peace treaty and Palestinian self-determination. An early result of the Oslo Accords was the establishment of the Palestinian National Authority in 1994. That Authority in the same year issued Decree number 184 founding the Palestinian Monetary Authority. The status of the Monetary Authority was further formalized by Law number 2 of 1997 of the Palestinian National Authority. The law set out the remit of the Monetary Authority, which was to be based in Ramallah, such as oversight of the banking system, regulation of other financial institutions and of foreign exchange transactions, maintenance of monetary stability, and provision of liquidity to banks. The authority was to "issue the national currency and coins in due course."[2]

Also in 1994, representatives of Israel and of the Palestinian National Authority signed the Paris Protocol on Economic Relations between the Government of the State of Israel and the PLO, representing the Palestinian People. Under Article IV of the protocol, the Palestinian Monetary Authority would hold its own reserves (including gold). In this particular respect, the Israelis and the Palestinians had avoided one of the major issues that had come between Malaysia and Singapore. The New Israeli shekel would be accepted in the Palestinian territories as a "legally circulating currency." The protocol also made allowances for discussions on the possible introduction of "mutually agreed" Palestinian currency or temporary alternative currency arrangements for the Palestinian Authority. The careful wording of this clause in the Paris Protocol therefore did not agree to Palestine's sovereignty in monetary matters but accepted that there would be "discussions" on the subject.[3]

The article in the Paris Protocol that insisted on the use of the shekel for trade with Israel and deferred any introduction of a Palestinian currency is interpreted by some as simply a device to deny the Palestinians a potent symbol of nationality in the form of an independent currency. Some go further and see the insistence on the use of the shekel for Palestinian trade with Israel as an attempt to integrate the Palestinians further into the state of Israel. Of course, an additional benefit to Israel of a forced circulation of the shekel was the seigniorage that it would bring in, and some analysts have suggested that was the principal reason for insisting on the shekel as the sole currency for trade between Israeli and Palestinian entities.[4] But probably more advantageous still is the benefit conferred on Israel by its insistence on trade in shekels with the Palestinian territories, integrating into the Israeli monetary system a Palestinian population that may be in the region of 4.5 million people, perhaps as much as half the entire population of historic Palestine. One study published in 2019 estimates that some $977 million worth of shekels—nearly 25 percent of all shekels in circulation—circulate in Palestine.[5]

In reality, the US dollar, Jordanian dinar, and euro now circulate in the West Bank and Gaza, although Palestinians have continued to use the Israeli new shekel, which had been introduced in 1985. The argument made shortly after the 1994 Paris Protocol that the shekel was the appropriate currency for the Palestinian territories because those territories were economically integrated with Israel was logical, but on the other hand a statement of the blindingly obvious. After decades of Israeli government control of the Palestinian territories, there could hardly be anything other than economic integration of the two economies. The same reporting, however, very candidly noted disadvantages for the Palestinians in the same integrated arrangement, noting the transmission of 400 percent inflation from the Israeli economy in 1984 prior to the introduction of the Israeli new shekel. By comparison, inflation rates in Jordan since 1979 peaked at 25 percent in 1989, and in 1984 was a relatively modest 3.8 percent. This does not of course tell the complete story because over nearly forty years the average annual inflation rate for Jordan has been just over 5 percent, while Israel's inflation rate came down to single figures consistently only in 1997.[6]

Between 2000 and 2005, the Israeli shekel lost over 30 percent of its value against the US dollar, and this depreciation, accompanied by a severe three-year recession from 2001 to 2004, obviously impacted Palestinians and the Palestinian Authority as well as Israelis. One solution proposed in reaction to the major depreciation was the abandonment of the shekel and the adoption of the US dollar. According to Sever Plocker, one proponent of dollarization, writing in 2005, the shekel was "neither a source of national pride nor a symbol of Jewish sovereignty."[7] The adoption of the US dollar, Plocker notes, would "strengthen and cement Israel's 'special relationship' with the United States."[8] Thus, there was in this suggestion a political element as well as a purely economic one. It is worth recalling that, since 2000 and prior to the expression of these views, East Timor, Ecuador, and El Salvador had fully dollarized, and some International Monetary Fund (IMF) officials were proposing the adoption of the dollar for Afghanistan following the NATO invasion of 2001. There was at that time a growing attraction to dollarization. The case put forward by Plocker for dollarization in 2004 suggested that Israel had markedly oriented its economy toward the United States and that a transition to the dollar would increase Israel's economic growth. Analyzing the possible Palestinian response to a prospective dollarization, Plocker suggests that Palestinians would welcome the withdrawal of the Israeli shekel as a symbol of Israeli occupation.[9]

An alternative proposal put forward in 2004 suggested that a new Palestinian state might do up to a third of its trade with the eurozone. This same set of proposals asserted that economies of a comparable size have "*mostly opted for a pegged exchange rate regime, but generally not a currency union or a currency board.*" Nevertheless, the same report proposed that an independent Palestine would do best by adopting a currency board arrangement, pegging its currency initially to the shekel, but then to the euro.[10]

Among other proposals was one that suggested that a Palestine Currency Board might return shekels to Israel and request foreign assets in return, as Israel was able to do with Palestine pounds returned to Britain. This proposal of course presupposes that Israel would accede to this request. Yet experiences of remonetization in Estonia in 1992 and in Russia in 1993 and, subsequently, in Sudan in 2011 have in fact shown that original note-issuing countries may equally be prepared to retire their existing currency to prevent a "backwash" of notes returning to their country of origin to be redeemed for hard currency. Moreover, it suggests that the Palestinian pound be backed 100 percent by the Jordanian currency (or any other currency!) as a preliminary step toward gradually becoming a central bank, with full discretionary authority over monetary policy. This proposal foresaw the need to hold reserves at the Central Bank of Jordan, even though the Paris Protocol categorically accepts that the Palestine Monetary Authority could hold its own foreign reserves, presumably at the Palestine Monetary Authority building in Ramallah.

By 2010, interviews with the then head of the Palestine Monetary Authority indicated that the Authority was making plans to introduce a new currency. The timing of these statements was to some extent taken seriously because Barak Obama, at the time president of the United States, was pressing to resolve the question of a separate state for Palestine by urging Israel to cede land to Palestine. At the same time, the prime minister of Israel, Benjamin

Netanyahu, was uncompromising in resisting the US pressure. Prospects for an independent Palestine were further undermined by the rivalry between the two parties controlling separate parts of the Palestinian territories: Fatah in the West Bank area and Hamas in the Gaza Strip. Such circumstances did not bode well for the independence of a unified Palestine, much less an independent currency. Apart from anything else, the introduction of a new currency in the West Bank would quite possibly have encouraged Hamas to introduce a separate rival currency in Gaza, reinforcing separation.[11]

By April 2016, with no progress on an internationally brokered peace deal evident and Obama's second term in office coming to an end, regional media outlets were reporting new thinking in Palestinian circles. The Palestinian National Authority would gradually withdraw from using the Israeli shekel and adopt the US dollar or the Jordanian dinar as a first step in severing relations with Israel. In the view of one senior Palestinian, Israelis would only trade in shekels, but the Palestinian National Authority was free, on the basis of existing agreements with Israel, to use the Jordanian or US currencies. If the senior Palestinian concerned, Dr. Nabeel Sha'ath, Fatah's Commissioner for International Relations, was thinking of the Paris Protocol as the basis for acceptable use of the Jordanian dinar or US dollar, he would have been reading too much into it. As already noted, the Paris Protocol foresaw only *discussions* on the use of a mutually acceptable currency.[12] Other Palestinians nevertheless supported the idea of a gradual transition from the shekel, largely as a political move to start the process of severing relations with Israel altogether, rather than because it was the best economic decision. Thus, the matter of an independent currency had been vested with a power that it did not actually possess.

A year later, the emergence and increasing popularity of cryptocurrencies seemed to offer the Palestine Monetary Authority an alternative solution to the shekel. The Authority was reportedly planning a digital currency called the Palestinian pound to be in use within five years. Digital currency was perceived to be particularly attractive for Palestine given the special circumstances of the Palestinian territories. It would have been impossible for the Palestinians to take delivery of a printed currency across borders controlled by Israel without Israeli agreement, but a digital currency would be difficult to stop.[13]

Debates on the replacement of the shekel continued into 2018. A degree of de facto freedom in monetary matters, which resulted in the circulation of US dollars and Jordanian dinars in Palestinian areas, was constrained by Israeli authorities, which arranged for the gradual withdrawal of those currencies. Some Palestinians, driven by a strong sense of injustice done to them and the frustration of impotence, wished to see the shekel, a prominent symbol of their political subordination to the government of Israel, replaced as a matter of priority. Palestinian technocrats, however, warned against a hasty withdrawal from the shekel, explaining the potential damage that could do to the revenues of the Palestine National Authority, which relied on the Israeli government for seven billion shekels in tax and customs revenues, amounting to 70 percent of the Authority's income. Dependence on the shekel could gradually be lessened by electronic banking. An increase in the use of credit cards, it was suggested, would facilitate transactions in currencies other than the shekel.[14]

The continuing search for an alternative currency system for Palestine seems to be driven more by national sentiment than by economic considerations, with a number of technocrats advising caution, much as Bundesbank officials responded to plans for a German currency union in 1990. But any practical attempt to drop the shekel must be based on the freedom of maneuver secured by political independence. If, for instance, unilateral attempts were made to operate a purely digital currency in the Palestinian territories based, say, on the Palestinian pound, Israel would no doubt see this as a breach of the strict terms of the 1994 Paris Protocol and take steps to assert monetary control within Israel's borders or react by denying the Palestinian Authority the revenues it receives from the Israeli government. Despite the apparent attractiveness of digital currencies as a means of obviating government control of currency, other methods of penalizing use of a Palestinian digital currency would no doubt be developed. Moreover, experiments in the issue of digital currencies by central authorities (in this case, presumably, the Palestine Monetary Authority) have yet to prove successful. Attempts to issue a central bank digital currency in, for instance, Ecuador foundered after four years because the population refused to adopt the system in sufficient volumes. And for as long as the Palestinian economy is integrated with that of Israel and as long as the latter controls the levers of government through transfers to the Palestinian National Authority, an attempt to break altogether with the shekel would probably result in self-inflicted harm to the Palestinians. Central banks around the world are demonstrating an increasing interest in the issue of central bank digital currencies, but they are able to develop such plans as far as they wish because those central banks enjoy the protection of political and legal sovereignty. It is precisely because the Palestinians do not enjoy that sovereignty that they are unable to secure monetary sovereignty.

On balance it would seem that an attempt to exercise monetary independence either by use of a digital currency, a Palestinian pound in banknote form, or the full adoption of another currency altogether as an effective or even symbolic means of asserting a wider political sovereignty would fall foul of Israeli intransigence. An independent currency may be a consequence of political sovereignty, but even then need not necessarily be a corollary of independence. A new Palestinian pound is likely to succeed only in the framework of a new, sovereign, Palestinian state. Until that time, discussion of alternative currencies for the Palestinians will remain an academic and technological debate.

SCOTLAND

The accession of James VI of Scotland to the throne of England in 1603 in succession to Elizabeth I—a political "Union of the Crowns"—was followed by an attempt to unify the currencies of the two countries. Until the thirteenth century, the Scottish economy had been relatively strong, and its coins were valued at par with those of England. From the thirteenth century, however, the value of English coins increased, presumably as the English economy began to flourish due to the dynamic success of the woolen cloth trade; a gap in value with Scottish money developed to the extent that, by the Act of Union in 1707, when Scottish coins were recalled from circulation, they were worth only one twelfth of the value of their direct English counterparts.[15]

One consequence of the Union of the Crowns in 1603 was the introduction of a set of coins common to both countries. A gold sovereign, known as the unite, identical in weight and fineness to the English sovereign coin of Elizabeth I was current from 1604 to 1619 both north and south of the border and was followed by a smaller, lighter gold coin known as the laurel, introduced in 1620. Scottish silver marks were fixed in value for circulation in England at just under double the value of an English silver mark.[16]

Differences in value between Scottish and English currencies, however, prevailed, while the union was purely at the level of the head of state; absent true union of nations and governments, the differences in value between the two currencies remained in place. That was finally addressed by the Act of Union of 1707, by which Scotland lost its independence as a nation-state and as a sovereign issuer of money. The act provided for a coinage "of the same standard and value throughout the United Kingdom." The unification of the currency involved a recoinage at the Edinburgh mint, and shortfalls in coinage during the transitional period were made up by banknotes issued by the Bank of Scotland. On completion of the recoinage, the Edinburgh mint was closed down, whether as a means of controlling money supply in the sense of ensuring that there would be no unauthorized issue of sterling coinage in Scotland, or perhaps to remove an indispensable facility for independent production of coinage, necessary in the event of any attempt to reassert independence.

Some sense of national identity in the currency was, however, preserved by Scotland's special arrangements for the issue of banknotes. Since the introduction of the Bank Charter Act of 1844, English note-issuing banks' privileges in respect of currency issue were gradually surrendered in favor of the Bank of England. The last private bank with the right to issue its own notes in England and Wales finally stopped issuing in 1921. In Scotland, however, some commercial banks have preserved the right to issue banknotes under special conditions. Thus, at the time of writing, three commercial banks—the Royal Bank of Scotland, the Bank of Scotland, and the Clydesdale Bank— retain the right to issue notes, albeit under the supervision of the Bank of England, which sets requirements for the reserves to be held in London by the commercial banks in order to back their own issue of notes. Because the notes often feature images of prominent figures from Scotland's past—including, remarkably, Robert the Bruce, revered architect of Scottish independence in the fourteenth century—they continue to perform a subsidiary function so often expected of a sovereign currency, that of medium of national identity.

In that sense the Scottish notes are quite a remarkable reflection of the nature of the union with England. It is difficult to think of any other country in the world that permits the circulation of notes reflecting the separate national identity of one of its constituent autonomous states. The banknotes produced by Denmark for the Faroe Isles, for instance, differ in design from those of Denmark itself, but currently feature uncontroversial vignettes of wildlife. Hong Kong's current banknotes, which have much historically in common with Scotland's notes in the sense that Hong Kong had been a British colony and has notes issued by three commercial banks under supervision of a central authority, categorically may not display designs that are "inappropriate to Hong Kong's status as a special autonomous region" of China. Remarkably, the question of the currency to be issued in Scotland became a major factor in debates leading up to Scotland's 2014 independence referendum.

The first step toward the 2014 referendum on full independence for Scotland was an earlier referendum held in 1997 shortly after a Labour government had come to power in Britain under Prime Minister Tony Blair. In this first referendum, Scots voters were invited to cast a vote on two questions: Should Scotland have its own parliament, and should that parliament have "tax-varying powers"? The answer from the electorate to both questions was a very clear yes, and on May 12, 1999, a Scottish parliament convened for the first time since 1707.[17] For the Scottish National Party (SNP), it was the first step toward full independence. Although Scotland had been run by the Labour Party for the first eight years of devolution, the SNP overturned Labour's dominance in the 2007 elections to the Scottish parliament but could form only a minority government. In the 2011 elections, however, the party achieved an absolute majority of seats in the parliament and began its campaign for a referendum on independence. In the following year, the United Kingdom and Scottish governments agreed to the terms of an independence referendum, which would be held in 2014.[18] The matter of Scotland's future currency would prove to be an increasingly important issue in the campaigning until then.

The declared preferred position of the SNP on the question of Scotland's future currency in the event of independence was that of a pound sterling currency union with the rest of the United Kingdom. This in itself was an interesting contrast to so many other countries that had left the sterling zone on independence or had rejected Britain's postwar proposals for currency boards based in London. The SNP insisted that a continuing currency union would minimize disruption for businesses both north and south of the border. Pointing toward the example of the currency union of Luxembourg and Belgium, SNP politicians also noted that a currency union would still leave room for divergent tax and spending policies. Tactically, it would have the advantage of allaying the concerns of so-called swing voters who would have doubts about the wisdom of severing Scotland from a currency system that had worked well for it. Indeed, opinion polls in Scotland in February of that year pointed toward the preference of the electorate for a continuing close link with sterling, with a full currency union being the preferred option for 52 percent of those opposed to independence. And even the largest single group polled of those in favor of independence—42 percent—preferred the idea of a continuing sterling union following independence. Monetary stability was a serious consideration for the public, especially against a backdrop of fresh concerns surrounding the durability of the euro after the sovereign debt crisis of 2009.[19]

However, the Chancellor of the Exchequer in the Conservative-led Westminster government, George Osborne, ruled out any currency union between an independent Scotland and the rest of the United Kingdom, declaring that currency unions were "fraught with difficulty."[20] For the government in London, it was difficult to see why it should accommodate the SNP's request for monetary stability through a currency union following a decision to abandon the political union. South of the border there were many who took Scotland's wish for a say in monetary policy following independence as a case of the SNP's wanting someone else's cake and eating it too. Some analysts concluded that it was this rejection of a currency union by Osborne that played a significant role in persuading the Scottish electorate to vote against independence. The swing voters who had been reassured by the idea of a currency union had had that reassurance withdrawn.[21]

Pro-independence campaigners were left with only three credible alternatives to the refused currency union, the first of which would be use of the pound sterling without formal currency union. In other words, Scotland would have no vote on monetary policies. It would have to accept whatever the Bank of England were to decide on interest rates, for example, and would be denied a seat at the decision-making table. There had been precedent for such decisions elsewhere. Bosnia, for instance, had adopted the Deutsche Mark during its civil war in the 1990s without any formal agreement with Germany. Montenegro, although not a member of the European Union, uses the euro without any vote on monetary policy at the European Central Bank. El Salvador has adopted the US dollar as its national currency, but in doing so has surrendered its ability to make decisions on currency policy to the US Federal Reserve. Use of the pound in this way by Scotland would at least be consistent with the SNP's argument that it would ease trade between a newly independent Scotland and its principal trading market, the rest of the United Kingdom. But some observers were puzzled by the prospect that in such circumstances Scotland would be prepared to surrender control of a key instrument in the management of its economy, a freedom of action that after all was an important objective of the independence movement. From the SNP's point of view the idea that Scotland would have no seat at the decision-making table for monetary policy was difficult to swallow. Unilateral adoption of sterling seemed to make little sense, except to those of the electorate who were anxious to preserve some stability and continuity in the matter of money.[22]

A second alternative would be the introduction of an independent currency. But, if the SNP argument that a shared currency would facilitate trade was right, it stood to reason that a separate currency would be less helpful to trade. But the management of an independent Scottish currency by a Scottish central bank could provide advantages of flexibility in responding to economic shocks. It could also provide some opportunities to accumulate seigniorage, or, in the modern sense, profits on cash issue where the central bank's currency is used to purchase interest-yielding assets, such as bonds.[23] Scotland could choose to peg its initially independent currency to sterling, which would provide some degree of stability, but leave open the door to a change of policy at some later point in the same way that Ireland had broken away from sterling in the 1970s. Furthermore, the example of Estonia had proven that adoption of a separate currency, particularly one based on a currency board arrangement, could provide a stable monetary basis for a newly independent state prior to membership of the euro. (A currency board arrangement, however, would have limited the ability of any Scottish monetary authority to respond independently to economic shocks.)

And it was the euro that was the third option. The SNP had made it clear that it saw Scotland's future after independence as a fully paid-up member of the European Union. But, during the campaign toward the referendum, senior members of the European Union, including the president of the European Commission, Jose Manuel Barroso, stated that there was no provision for Scotland to remain automatically a member of the European Union at independence. The same view was expressed by Hermann Van Rumpuy, the president of the European Council at the time, and had also been set out ten years earlier by a previous president of the European Commission, Romano Prodi.[24] Scotland would need to reapply for membership in the European Union and, as a new member state, would not benefit from the very special arrangements by which Britain (and Denmark) were not obliged to join the euro. Thus, if Scotland were to apply to join the European Union, it would be bound to join the euro at some point, although the question of timing was flexible. Bound in this way to join the euro, an independent Scotland's adoption of that currency would hardly be consistent with the line that a shared currency with Britain would be best for Scotland's trade with the United Kingdom, its main trading partner. In this way, the SNP's strategic political aspiration toward membership of the euro ran counter to its tactical interest in promoting a shared currency with Britain as reassurance to the swing voters. Nevertheless, membership in the European Union is the stated SNP objective, and this would require Scotland to join the euro. As all other states leaving another monetary union to join the euro (Estonia, Latvia, Lithuania, Slovakia, and Slovenia) have done so after a spell of running their own currency in between, an independent currency looks like a sensible intermediary stage. This may in fact be a factor in current (2019) SNP thinking, which foresees a transitional period of continued use of sterling followed by the introduction of a Scottish currency.[25]

The result of the 2014 referendum was a rejection of the independence proposal by the electorate and much of the analysis of the outcome pointed toward the uncertainty surrounding the currency of an independent Scotland as one of the key reasons for the rejection of independence. One poll indicated that more than half of those who voted against independence cited the currency question as one of the three concerns uppermost in their minds.[26]

The SNP was, however, undaunted. Alex Salmond, the leader of the SNP and First Minister of Scotland, had resigned both positions following the electorate's rejection of independence but had continued to describe independence as inevitable. His successor as leader of the SNP and First Minister, Nicola Sturgeon, remained equally committed to independence, but indicated in 2015 that the SNP intended to wait for a clear indication that popular opinion had moved toward support for independence before pushing for another referendum.[27] Until June 23, 2016, there seemed to be no grounds for thinking the mood among Scottish electors toward independence had changed. However, the United Kingdom–wide referendum on continuing membership of, or withdrawal from, the European Union held on that day has undeniably changed the mood in Scotland on the issue of independence. While Scotland itself had voted by a very clear majority to remain within the European Union, a majority of voters—if not a very large majority—across the United

Kingdom as a whole had opted for withdrawal. This divergence of wishes inevitably led to a strong sense among many in Scotland that it was going to be taken out of the European Union contrary to the will of the Scottish people. When the SNP presented its manifesto for the elections to the Scottish Parliament, which took place in May 2016, only a month before the referendum on EU membership, the party declared its intention to seek another referendum on Scottish independence from the United Kingdom should Scotland be taken out of the European Union against the will of the Scottish people. Although an attempt to secure a second referendum on Scottish independence on that basis had been rejected in 2017 by the then prime minister of the United Kingdom, Theresa May, the vote to leave the European Union has given impetus to calls for a second referendum in Scotland. By April 2019, at least one respected poll (YouGov) indicated that support for independence had risen to 49 percent, the highest level since the 2014 independence referendum, largely because of the 2016 United Kingdom–wide decision to leave the EU.[28] Since then, further polls have shown support for independence at greater than 50 percent.

Clearly, the signs were looking more propitious for a second referendum. In May 2019, the Scottish government published a referendum framework bill that would provide the basis for a second referendum should the UK government in London approve it. As discussion of a second independence referendum gathered pace after the result of the European Union referendum, so did public consideration of the currency question. At least one economist suggested (June 2019), that, in the event of a vote for independence and after a transitional period of use of sterling, the country should move to the complete decoupling of currency issue from public sector control. In these circumstances, Scotland would return to a free-banking arrangement where commercial banks would be able to issue their own currency without government control. This proposal assumed that commercial banks would exercise restraint in issuing notes and that monetary discipline would be imposed by the market. But because the Bank of Scotland and the Royal Bank of Scotland had to be rescued from complete collapse by the UK government during the banking crisis of 2008, such a proposal could only be seen as unduly trusting. A more cautious rider attached to this idea suggested that Scottish pounds could be backed one for one with euros or sterling (as are pounds issued by Scottish banks at present) and would be exchangeable at par, in effect a currency board operated by commercial banks, rather than by a publicly owned institution. While such an idea may seem attractive, it is hard to see how an arrangement that currently works nowhere in the world would inspire confidence in an electorate that had already demonstrated its nervousness on monetary matters.[29]

But, by May 2018, newspapers in Scotland were reporting an intention on the part of the SNP to create a new currency for Scotland, confirming that the hopes of a currency union or unilateral use of sterling (i.e., use of sterling without a formal currency union and therefore without a say in Bank of England policies) had been abandoned.[30] In fact it was not quite that simple.

A new plan, put forward in May 2018 by the Sustainable Growth Commission, which the SNP had established in 2016 in reaction to the European Union referendum outcome, recognized the importance of the currency question in the 2014 referendum and the significance of economic stability for the electorate. It set out the intention of moving after independence toward a new Scottish currency pegged to the pound sterling after a possibly extended transitional period during which the pound sterling would be used, albeit without the benefits of a formal currency union with the rest of the United Kingdom.[31] The plan envisages the transfer of sterling held by Scottish banks at the Bank of England to back their own issue of notes to a central bank in Scotland at independence (although the deposits would continue to be the property of the Scottish banks). It accepts that Scottish banks might continue to issue currency for Scotland, in parallel with sterling, until such time as the central bank would be ready to issue its own currency.[32]

The new plan perhaps begs a number of questions. The announcement in the runup to the 2014 referendum by two of the three Scottish note-issuing banks—the Bank of Scotland (owned by the British Lloyds Bank) and the Royal Bank of Scotland—that their registered headquarters would be moved to London in the event of a vote for independence must raise the question as to whether they would agree to shift their reserves north following independence. Commercial banks would of course make their decisions on commercial grounds, and that would mean minimizing risk. The power of the Bank of England as lender of last resort and the treasury as a safety net was well demonstrated at the time of the 2008 credit crunch. The cost then of recapitalizing the Royal Bank of Scotland amounted to twice the estimated GDP of an independent Scotland.[33] If indeed they refused to move their sterling reserves north, would the Scottish government permit the commercial banks' currency to circulate without adequate cover held in Scotland? And, in a newly independent country where two of the three commercial note-issuing banks had been shown to be unreliable (albeit more than a decade ago), would their notes retain the confidence of the population absent the backing of the Bank of England?

A plausible scenario to emerge from the parallel circulation of sterling and commercial notes could see the former hoarded as a store of value, while the latter would be used as a medium of exchange. To counter this possibility, confidence in commercial notes could be underpinned by a clear commitment to convert them for sterling, or indeed for any new Scots pound. But would the population then rush to convert their commercially issued notes for the proven hard currency of sterling? Provided 100 percent sterling reserve cover is held in Scotland, such a "run" on the banks could be managed. But not in the event that the banks insist on keeping their sterling south of the border. In the longer term, the prospects for any future Scots pound backed with sterling will depend on Scotland's ability to earn enough sterling, or hard currency convertible into sterling, from its trade with the rest of the United Kingdom and elsewhere. Nevertheless, the chances of an independent Scotland and an independent Scottish currency becoming reality remain less remote than those of the other aspiring states covered in this chapter.

CATALONIA

Less than two months after Scotland's September 2014 referendum, the electorate of Catalonia, an autonomous community of Spain, participated in a vote on the question of independence. In the case of Catalonia, the drive for independence was motivated by a strong sense of economic grievance. Catalonia had long been economically successful, and many there resented the fact that Catalonia paid more into Spain's central government coffers than it received back in investment. (In 2014, the difference was recorded as ten billion euros net, to the disadvantage of Catalonia.) Because Spain's constitutional court had ruled out a referendum, the vote was described by the Catalan regional government as a "consultation process," and the outcome was legally nonbinding. All the same, the vote of 80 percent in favor of independence pointed toward popular support for independence, and leading separatist politicians insisted that this had earned Catalonia the right to a full referendum.[34]

As with the referendum in Scotland, the question of currency was debated prior to the consultation process. And, also as in Scotland, the preservation of the monetary status quo was perceived to be the preference for the electorate and a vote winner. While in Scotland this meant retention of sterling for the foreseeable future, in Catalonia the desire was for retention of the euro. A year before the vote, Catalan President Artur Mas stated that Catalonia "will have the Euro as its currency whatever happens." There was no possibility, Mas said, that Catalonia would either leave or be thrown out of the euro.[35]

The situation was not, however, quite so straightforward as far as the European Commission was concerned. Earlier in the year, the commission had stated that any region separating from a member state would automatically leave the union and would have to start the process of applying to join *ab initio*. If this position applied to Scotland, it would plainly also apply to Catalonia. It would, therefore, have to wait some time before formally joining the euro and then applying to join the eurozone, a transitional period during which it would have to conform to Maastricht conditions for euro membership: a budget deficit below 3 percent and debt-to-GDP ratio below 60 percent. More conclusively, each existing member state has the right of veto over any new applicant member, and it has been generally assumed that Spain would deploy its veto to prevent an independent Catalonia's accession to the European Union. The question of the Spanish veto had arisen previously in another context. Claims and counterclaims had swirled around the so-called Spanish veto because it might apply to a newly independent Scotland at the time of the latter's 2014 referendum. One argument insisted that Spain would veto Scotland's application to join the European Union so as to discourage an independence bid by Catalonia. But in the period following Britain's decision at a referendum in 2016 to withdraw from the European Union, it was easier to imagine circumstances where a secessionist Scotland would no longer be part of an existing member state of the European Union. The stated objection to Scotland's membership in the European Union would therefore fall away. Indeed, Spanish ministers have recently denied that a veto would be applied to any Scottish application because any bid for Scottish independence would be based on a lawful referendum and the consent of the United Kingdom. On the other hand, it was highly unlikely that Spain would withdraw from the European Union, and its veto on any Catalan application would therefore be final.

When the Catalan separatists won regional elections in 2015, it was clear that the issue of independence was not going to go away. Undaunted by the Madrid government's hard line on independence, Catalonia's independence movement, led by Carles Puigdemont, the president of the government of Catalonia, pressed ahead with plans for a full referendum to be held on October 1, 2017. Again, Madrid declared any referendum to be illegal, but this time the central government's opposition was forcefully demonstrated by heavy-handed police tactics. The electoral turnout at 43 percent was much depressed by the decision of anti-independence parties to boycott the referendum, casting a shadow over the result, which suggested that 90 percent of votes cast were in favor of independence. Nevertheless, the Catalan government declared independence on October 27.

The reaction of the Spanish government of Prime Minister Rajoy to the declaration of independence was hardly surprising given Madrid's statements that a referendum would be illegal. Invoking emergency powers, Rajoy dissolved the Catalan parliament and imposed direct rule from Madrid. Nine of the ministers of Catalonia's government were arrested and in 2018 were charged with rebellion.[36] In 2019 they were convicted and sentenced to lengthy terms in prison, bringing about rioting in Barcelona. Puigdemont left the country before he could be arrested and at the time of writing remains effectively in exile in Belgium.

In the runup to the declaration of independence, representatives of Catalonia had begun to work on the possibility of introducing a national cryptocurrency. Discussions were held with the government of Estonia, which was similarly planning to introduce a cryptocurrency (although those plans were rejected by the European Central Bank). Specialist journals reported that the Catalans were also being advised by Vitalik Buterin, the founder of Ethereum cryptocurrency. Commentators observed that the introduction of such a currency would create an independent economic community "outside the regulatory eye of a central bank."[37] The introduction of a digital currency independent of a central bank would of course have had a particular attraction for Catalonia, which, had it secured independence from Spain, would have been deprived of the support of both the central bank in Madrid and the European Central Bank. An entirely new technology would have strong appeal for a new state in Catalonia's unique circumstances. Indeed, Spanish law-enforcement bodies alleged that the Catalan government made payment to technology companies in the cryptocurrency Bitcoin for services provided for the October 1 referendum to evade Madrid's attempts to block its financial transactions, showing how cryptocurrencies could be tactically useful.[38]

Could the adoption of cryptocurrencies by Catalonia go some way to asserting a form of independence—if only in monetary matters—from Madrid? A new cryptocurrency is in use in Barcelona, although the authorities do not claim that it is being used to prepare the ground for a monetary split with the rest of Spain. Nevertheless, cryptocurrencies may offer the Catalans a way of asserting one aspect of their independence in the same way that Palestinian authorities see digital currencies as a possible monetary expression of independence and rejection of the Israeli state's control. Without a doubt, though, an attempt to operate a parallel payment system would be seen as a highly provocative act by Madrid, which has already demonstrated its willingness to take severe action against separatists. As in the case of Palestine, an alternative and independent currency will not flourish absent the necessary political independence.

KURDISTAN

The Kurds, who live in northern Iraq and Syria, in western Iran, and eastern and southeastern Turkey, enjoy the unenviable reputation of being the largest ethnic group in the world without their own state. The turmoil in Iraq following the overthrow of Saddam Hussein in 2003 and in Syria as a result of attempts to overthrow the government of Bashar Al Assad since 2011 seemed to some to offer an opportunity. As Scotland prepared for its referendum in 2014, the political leadership of the Kurdish Autonomous Zone in northern Iraq also turned its attention to thoughts of independence. In July 2014 Massoud Barzani, the president of the Kurdish Regional Government (KRG), instructed his parliament to prepare for an independence referendum.

Circumstances at that time might have seemed propitious for the independence that many Kurds had fervently desired. The rapid development and expansion of the fundamentalist and militant Islamic State (IS) in Iraq and Syria had posed existential threats to the governments in both countries. The capture of Mosul, Iraq's second largest city, provided IS fighters with a springboard to invade the Kurdish areas in northern Iraq. In neighboring Syria, the fighting against IS brought together a number of states and ethnic groups that might ordinarily have been ranged against each other with a shared objective: the destruction of the Caliphate, the Islamic State. In both cases, Iraq and Syria, the Kurdish Peshmerga played a leading part in confronting IS on the ground, providing much of the frontline infantry for the conflict while other participating states provided air support, intelligence, logistics, special forces, and technology.

In northern Iraq, the success of the Peshmerga in holding off and then pushing back IS in the absence of an effective defense by the Iraqi army in the summer of 2014, resulted in the Kurds holding 40 percent more land than before, including the important city of Kirkuk and its oilfields. Kurds had enjoyed similar successes in Syria with allied support, freeing a large part of the northeast of the country so that there were now Kurdish controlled zones abutting each other either side of the Iraq and Syria border. Kurds were able to cross from one Kurdish-controlled area in Iraq into another in Syria without having to present a valid visa. However, Kurdish hopes of American support for the creation of a new state were to be disappointed. There was no indication on the part of the administration of President Obama that Washington was willing to endorse a new state, thereby compromising existing borders and possibly causing a further fragmentation of the fragile state of Iraq. Without a powerful patron and protector, the prospects for statehood now seemed uncertain. Even the benefit of control of the oil fields around Kirkuk was hedged with doubt. To export oil to the world, the Kurds would have to arrange transit via Iraq, from which presumably the Kurds' secession would have been acrimonious. Whether the Kurds considered it or not, there was a very close parallel with the situation in South Sudan in 2011 that was dependent on Sudan for the export of its oil. Cautious counsels prevailed. By January 2015 the Iraqi Kurdish leadership had decided not to make a push for independence but rather to "give Iraq another chance to be a democratic state."[39]

And yet, later that year, at the height of the conflict with IS, some Kurds were discussing the merits of an independent Kurdish currency in place of the Iraqi dinar on grounds that it would deliver a measure of autonomy, could stoke economic growth, and might offer a stronger currency than the dinar, which had significantly lost value during the conflict with the IS. Because the northern Kurdish areas of Iraq had successfully operated a different currency from that of the Saddam-controlled rest of the country between the first Gulf War in 1990–1991 and the Iraq war of 2003, experience seemed to show that a separate currency for the Kurdish region would not be difficult to manage. Although those who promoted the idea of an independent currency could see difficulties—not least, the challenge of launching a currency during a war and with an empty treasury—the supposition was that an independent country would need to have its own currency.[40] But, because Ecuador, El Salvador, and East Timor had all adopted the dollar, rather than maintain an independent currency of their own, there had been ample evidence in recent times that an independent currency was not a prerequisite for national sovereignty. It had become only one of the menu options available to national legislators. In any case, experience had also shown that currencies introduced during a period of conflict—for example, in Mexico and in Bosnia during civil war—often failed.[41]

This remained a matter of no pressing importance for the time being, but underlying support for independence remained high and eventually led to a referendum on the question of secession from Iraq on Monday, September 25, only a week before Catalonia's own. Indeed, in March of that year, the Scottish Nationalist Party had submitted a request for referendum powers to the government in London. Although the request was rejected, it seemed as though secession movements in Catalonia, Scotland, and Kurdistan were moving in synch, an echo of the widespread waves of decolonization and secession in previous decades. In contrast to the referendum in Catalonia, however, the overall turnout was strong and estimated at 72 percent of the electorate. Of the votes cast, 92 percent were in favor of independence. As with the Catalonian referendum, the central government in Baghdad rejected the result. The Supreme Court had issued an order blocking the referendum, and Haider al-Abadi, the prime minister of Iraq, demanded that the referendum and its result be cancelled.[42] The government in Baghdad also announced its intention to block foreign currency transfers and sales of US dollars to banks in the Kurdish regions in response to the referendum. These penalties were subsequently eased in what was interpreted as a first step in deescalating the tensions between Baghdad and the Kurdish regional government.

Kurdish aspirations for an independent homeland have been dealt a further hard blow by the decision of the Trump administration to withdraw the remaining US troops out of northern Syria, exposing the Kurds in that region to military operations by Turkey, which is intent on creating a buffer zone between its southern borders and the Kurds. Any prospect for an independent Kurdish state and an independent currency remains at present remote.

Will new technologies that operate beyond the oversight of national institutions offer aspiring independence movements an opportunity to detach themselves from existing currency regimes? Technically, yes, assuming their popular adoption, but such a move would no doubt attract the ire of the governments in, for instance, Spain or Israel. There would be unpleasant consequences, perhaps along the lines of internal economic sanctions. Other than demonstrate a symbolic intention, a monetary unilateral declaration of independence would do little to secure political independence and would almost certainly attract internal economic sanctions. While political independence is necessary to secure some degree of monetary sovereignty, the opposite is not true.

NOTES

1. Adel Darwish, "Arafat to Demand Palestine's Gold," *The Independent* December 13, 1993, https://www.independent.co.uk/news/world/arafat-to-demand-palestine-s-gold-1467152.html.

2. Law No. 2 of 1997 on the Palestinian Monetary Authority, https://www.pma.ps/Portals/0/Users/002/02/2/Legislation/Laws/Law_No_2_of_1997_on_Palestinian_Monetary_Authority.pdf.

3. "Paris Protocol on Economic Relations between the Government of the State of Israel and the PLO representing the Palestinian People," Article IV.7.6.2, April 29, 1994, Israel Ministry of Foreign Affairs, https://mfa.gov.il/MFA/ForeignPolicy/Peace/Guide/Pages/Gaza-Jericho%20Agreement%20Annex%20IV%20-%20Economic%20Protoco.aspx.

4. Arie Arnon and Avia Spiva, "Monetary Integration between the Israeli, Jordanian and Palestinian Economies," Discussion Paper 95.11, 1, December 1995, Bank of Israel, https://www.boi.org.il/en/Research/Pages/papers-dp9511.aspx.

5. "A Case for a Palestinian Currency," *The Palestine-Israel Journal* 6, no. 4 (1999), http://pij.org/articles/244.

6. Arnon and Spivak, "Monetary Integration," 3; and WorldData inflation rates, https://www.worlddata.info/.

7. Sever Plocker, "Dollarization in Israel-Palestine," Analysis Paper No. 5, May 2005, V–XI, The Saban Center for Middle East Policy at the Brookings Institution, https://www.brookings.edu/wp-content/uploads/2016/06/plocker20050501.pdf.

8. Ibid.

9. Ibid.

10. David Cobham, "Alternative Currency Arrangements for a New Palestinian State," in *The Economics of Palestine: Economic Policy and Institutional Reform*

for a Viable Palestinian State, ed. David Cobham and Nu'man Kanafani (London: Routledge, 2004), 21.

11. Jonathan Schanzer, "Palestine: Gaining Currency?," September 17, 2010, *The National Interest*, https://nationalinterest.org/commentary/palestine-gaining-currency-4093.

12. Nasouh Nazzal, "Palestinians Plan to Ditch Israeli Currency, Gradually," *Gulf News*, April 20 2016, https://gulfnews.com/world/mena/palestinians-plan-to-ditch-israeli-currency-gradually-1.1717766.

13. Naomi Zevelof, "Is a Palestinian Bitcoin on the Way?," May 14, 2017, *Forward*, https://forward.com/fast-forward/371882/is-a-palestinian-bitcoin-on-the-way/; and "Palestine Hopes to Launch New Digital Currency in Five Years," *The New Arab*, https://www.alaraby.co.uk/english/news/2017/5/14/palestine-hopes-to-launch-national-digital-currency-in-five-years.

14. Daoud Kuttab, "Palestine May Replace Israeli Currency to Reduce Dependency," *Arab News*, February 18, 2018, https://www.arabnews.com/node/1248701/middle-east.

15. I. F. Grant, *The Social and Economic Development of Scotland before 1603* (London: Oliver and Boyd, 1930), 120.

16. Glyn Davies, *A History of Money*: *From Ancient Times to the Present Day* (Cardiff: University of Wales Press, 2002), 209.

17. "20 Years Today since the Scottish Devolution Referendum," Scottish Political Archive, September 11, 2017, https://www.scottishpoliticalarchive.org.uk/2017/09/11/20-years-today-since-scottish-devolution-referendum/.

18. "Timeline Scottish Independence Referendum," *BBC News Scotland*, October 15, 2012, https://www.bbc.co.uk/news/uk-scotland-scotland-politics-19907675.

19. Andrew Black, "Scottish Independence: Currency Debate Explained," *BBC News*, January 29, 2014, https://www.bbc.co.uk/news/uk-scotland-scotland-politics-25913721; and Patrick Brione, "The Great Scottish Currency Debate and an Important Note on Methodology," Survation, February 19, 2014, https://www.survation.com/the-great-scottish-currency-debate-an-important-note-on-methodology/.

20. Nick Robinson, "Scotland Currency: George Osborne Rules Out Union," *BBC News*, February 13, 2014, https://www.bbc.co.uk/news/av/uk-26179434/scotland-currency-george-osborne-rules-out-union. For further detail on the "difficulties," which might involve the full range of responsibilities of the Bank of England, see Brian Quinn, "Scottish Independence: Issues and Questions: Regulation, Supervision, Lender of Last Resort and Crisis Management," The David Hume Institute, August 2013, 7.

21. Alan Trench, "Scottish Independence: Does Taking a Sterling Currency Union Off the Table Change the Game?," UK Constitutional Law Association, February 13, 2014, https://ukconstitutionallaw.org/2014/02/13/scottish-independence-does-taking-a-sterling-currency-union-off-the-table-change-the-game/.

22. Quinn, "Scottish Independence: Issues and Questions," 4–5.

23. Angus Armstrong and Monique Ebell, "Scotland's Currency Options," Discussion Paper, September 17, 2013, Centre on Constitutional Change, https://www.centreonconstitutionalchange.ac.uk/sites/default/files/migrated/papers/

scotlands_currency_options.pdf. But note on page 9 where UK seigniorage was thought to amount in 2014 to no more than 0.2 percent of GDP, so it was hardly a "game changer" for a newly independent economy.

24. "Report on the Scottish Government's Proposals for an Independent Scotland," Second Report of Scottish Parliament, Sections 94–96, 2014, https://archive2021. parliament.scot/S4_EuropeanandExternalRelationsCommittee/Reports/euR-14-02w-rev.pdf.

25. Armstrong and Ebell, "Scotland's Currency Options," 13; Angus Armstrong and Monique Ebell, "Which Currency Would an Independent Scotland Use?" in *Scotland's Decision: 16 Questions to Think about for the Referendum on 18 September*, ed. Charlie Jeffery and Ray Perman, E-monograph, National Library of Scotland, https://www.nls.uk/e-monographs/2014/ScotlandsDecision.pdf.

26. Gerry Mooney, "The Scottish Independence Referendum: Why Was There a No Vote?," The Open University, March 2, 2015, https://www.open. edu/openlearn/people-politics-law/the-2014-scottish-independence-referendum-why-was-there-no-vote; and Stuart Rodger, "Explained—9 New Independent Scotland Currency Options Revealed," Commonspace, July 26, 2016, citing a poll by Lord Ashcroft, https://www.commonspace.scot/articles/8920/explained-9-new-independent-scotland-currency-options-laid-out-new-report.

27. Nicholas Watt, Severin Carrell, Rowena Mason, and Libby Brooks, "Fate of Second Scottish Independence Referendum 'in Hands of the People,'" *The Guardian*, October 15, 2015, https://www.theguardian.com/politics/2015/oct/15/second-scottish-independence-referendum-hands-people-nicola-sturgeon-snp.

28. Elisabeth O'Leary, "Brexit Drives Support for Scottish Independence to 49 Percent—YouGov," *Reuters*, April 27, 2019, https://www.reuters.com/article/uk-britain-eu-scotland-poll-idUKKCN1S30CE; and Margaret Arnott, "Brexit and a Second Scottish Independence Referendum: What Happens Next?," Political Studies Association, February 22, 2019, https://www.psa.ac.uk/psa/news/brexit-and-second-scottish-independence-referendum-what-happens-next.

29. Philip Booth, "Solving the Scottish Currency Referendum," Institute of Economic Affairs, June 11, 2019, https://iea.org.uk/solving-the-scottish-currency-conundrum/.

30. Akash Paun and Jess Sargeant, "A Second Referendum on Scottish Independence," Institute for Government, May 30, 2019, updated November 23, 2020, https://www.instituteforgovernment.org.uk/explainers/second-referendum-scottish-independence.

31. "Scottish Independence: New Scots Currency Plan If Yes Wins New Vote," *Edinburgh News*, May 20, 2018, https://www.edinburghnews.scotsman.com/news/politics/scottish-independence-new-scots-currency-plan-if-yes-wins-new-vote-290099.

32. "Part C: The Monetary Policy and Financial Regulation Framework for an Independent Scotland," C1.23, May 2018, Sustainable Growth Commission, https://static1.squarespace.com/static/5afc0bbbf79392ced8b73dbf/t/5b06e8a56d2a73f9e0305ad9/1527179438303/SGC+Part+C+Currency+Monetary+Framework.pdf.

33. Quinn, "Scottish Independence: Issues and Questions," 5.

34. "Catalonia Vote: 80% Back Independence—Officials," *BBC News*, November 10, 2014, https://www.bbc.co.uk/news/world-europe-29982960; Liane Wimhurst,

"What an Independent Catalonia Could Look Like," *I News*, October 2017, https://inews.co.uk/news/world/independent-catalonia-look-like-519501; and Iain Goldie, "The Economics of Catalan Secession from Spain," *Global Politics*, August 4, 2017, https://global-politics.co.uk/2017/08/04/economics-catalan-secession-spain/.

35. Peter Lavelle, "What Currency Would an Independent Catalonia Have?" *Homage to BCN* (Blog), November 11, 2013, https://homagetobcn.com/catalonia-currency/.

36. Stephen Burgen, "Catalan Politicians Charged a Year after Independence Vote," *The Guardian*, November 2, 2018, https://www.theguardian.com/world/2018/nov/02/catalan-politicians-charged-a-year-after-independence-vote-referendum.

37. John Buck, "Catalonia Considering Cryptocurrency Post-Independence, Advised by Ethereum Creator," *Cointelegraph*, October 28, 2017, https://cointelegraph.com/news/catalonia-considering-cryptocurrency-post-independence-advised-by-ethereum-creator.

38. C. Edward Kelso, "Catalonia Referendum Allegedly Funded by Bitcoin," *Bitcoin News*, November 26, 2017, https://news.bitcoin.com/cryptos-revolutionary-moment-catalonia-referendum-allegedly-funded-by-bitcoin/.

39. Christian Caryl, "The World's Next Country," *Foreign Policy*, January 21, 2015, https://foreignpolicy.com/2015/01/21/the-worlds-next-country-kurdistan-kurds-iraq/; and Henry J. Barkey, "Op Ed: Kurdistan, Scotland and Catalonia: They Just Want to Be Free, or Do They?" *Los Angeles Times*, July 16, 2014, https://www.latimes.com/opinion/op-ed/la-oe-0717-barkey-kurdistan-scotland-catalonia-20140717-story.html.

40. Yara Kamaran Ismael, "Is It Time Just Yet for a Kurdish Currency?," *The Kurdistan Tribune*, July 19, 2015, https://kurdistantribune.com/is-it-time-just-yet-for-a-kurdish-currency/.

41. Wilson, *Hostile Money*, 50–51, 87.

42. Bethan McKernan, "Kurdistan Referendum Results: 93 Percent of Iraqi Kurds Vote for Independence, Say Reports," The Independent, September 27, 2017, https://www.independent.co.uk/news/world/middle-east/kurdistan-referendum-results-vote-yes-iraqi-kurds-independence-iran-syria-a7970241.html.

Chapter 9

Modern Multinational Monetary Unions

As we have already seen, some new states may choose to join others in creating a new state with a single currency (accession). In other cases, separate states may decide to share a currency or coordinate currencies in what is to all intents and purposes a currency union but without full political and legal union. In this respect, we make a clear distinction between national monetary unions, which include sterling, the US dollar, and the dirham of the United Arab Emirates, and international monetary unions, which include the Latin and Scandinavian Monetary Unions of the nineteenth century, operated by independent countries without the oversight of a single central bank. The use of the word "national" may not be strictly accurate in the case of, for instance, Britain, where four nations share the pound sterling, or the former Yugoslavia, which combined a number of nations in a single fiscal, political, and monetary union with a single central bank and currency, the dinar. The word nevertheless serves to describe a unified sovereign entity with a single monetary authority and a single currency. The euro and a few other currency unions form a third type that involves a number of sovereign states bound together by a shared currency, usually, but not in all cases, overseen by a single central bank. For the sake of convenience, we might call this third type a multinational monetary union.

EASTERN CARIBBEAN CURRENCY UNION

The Eastern Caribbean Currency Board is to a large extent the heir to the British Caribbean Currency Board, which was responsible from 1951 for currency issue for Trinidad and Tobago, Barbados, and British Guiana (all of which now issue their own separate currencies) as well as the countries forming the present Eastern Caribbean Currency Union (ECCU). By the mid-1960s, it was clear that the three countries named above would break away and plans were put in motion to create an Eastern Caribbean Currency authority. In June 1981, seven of the Eastern Caribbean countries, which were member states of the original British Caribbean Currency Board, came together to form the Organisation of Eastern Caribbean States (OECS) to foster a program of greater political and economic unity between those states. The founder members of OECS were Antigua and Barbuda, Dominica, Monserrat, Grenada, Saint Kitts and Nevis, Saint Lucia, Saint Vincent, and the Grenadines. Two British Overseas Territories—Anguilla and the British Virgin Islands—as well as Martinique and Guadeloupe, have joined as associate members of the OECS. Of these, the majority are considered to be "microstates" on the grounds of the countries' population.[1]

By June 2011, seven of the states concerned—Antigua and Barbuda, the Commonwealth of Dominica, Grenada, Montserrat, Saint Kitts and Nevis, Saint Lucia, and Saint Vincent and the Grenadines—had signed up to the Economic Union Treaty aimed at the free movement of capital, goods, and people within that group, guarantees that seem to take them closer to union along European lines.[2]

Eight of the OECS states—Anguilla, Antigua and Barbuda, Dominica, Grenada, Montserrat, Saint Kitts and Nevis, Saint Lucia, and Saint Vincent and the Grenadines—have formed the Eastern Caribbean Central Bank (ECCB), issuing the Eastern Caribbean dollar. Given that the ECCB comprises both independent states and United Kingdom Overseas Territories, it is uniquely interesting as a single central bank and currency operating across jurisdictions, some of which are fully independent from the original colonial power and some still not. The origins of the ECCB, which derive from the British Caribbean Currency Board of 1950, go some way to explain this seemingly unusual arrangement. As in other parts of the dissolving British Empire, newly independent states, such as Jamaica, Barbados, and Trinidad and Tobago replaced the currency board arrangement with their own independent central banks. The remaining members of the Caribbean Currency Board—some of them still British territories—simply remained together pragmatically in the newly formed ECCB in 1983.[3]

The Eastern Caribbean dollar was fixed to the US dollar at $2.7 to one even before the formal creation of the ECCB and has stayed at that rate for nearly forty years thanks to a system that has been described as that of a "quasi-currency board." While the bank does not operate on strict currency board standards, requiring a legal cover of 60 percent rather than 100 percent foreign reserves to back the issue of its currency, it has in fact adhered to very high levels of cover. In 2010–2011, the ECCB held foreign reserves equivalent to 95 percent of the value of its currency on issue. In 2014–2015 the foreign reserves held equated again to 95 percent of currency in circulation.

So, while legislation permits a reasonably generous approach to reserves backing currency on issue, the reality is that the ECCB has exercised discipline in keeping to almost classic levels of reserve cover, as they would be prescribed for a currency board. Like most of the classical currency boards of the empire in the nineteenth century, there is a legal limit on the total value of domestic assets that the ECCB may use to back the issue of currency. Indeed, the reserves backing the ECCB dollar are almost entirely US treasury gilts. The choice of US government debt denominated in what remains the world's premier reserve currency again demonstrates the ECCB's prudence. The inclusion of British Overseas Territories Monserrat and Anguilla in a currency system pegged to the US dollar, rather than sterling, acknowledges the regional trade realities. A third to a half of all imports to Caribbean states comes from the United States, and the dollar is the dominant currency of the region, being used to denominate tourism.[4] This adherence to a US dollar–backed monetary system also seems to hark back to the pragmatic adoption by Britain's colonies in the nineteenth century of currency arrangements that reflected regional trade realities, rather than loyalty to the currency system of the central government in London. That London has gone along with it in respect to its two participating overseas territories also says something about the United Kingdom's realism in such matters.

The disciplines of a quasi-currency board and, perhaps, its disadvantages are to be seen in regional performance. Consumer prices increased at the rate of 5 percent in 2010–2011 in the period shortly after the financial crisis of 2008 but slowed to 1.5 percent in 2014–2015. Average public debt across the Eastern Caribbean Monetary Union also declined during this period from an average of 80 percent to 76 percent, although this does not adequately represent the differing levels of budget deficit, which at the end of 2014 ranged from 3.7 percent in Montserrat to 99 percent in Grenada (2014 figures). The International Monetary Fund (IMF) has remarked on the financial and monetary stability of the Eastern Caribbean Monetary Union and in particular has highlighted the role of the ECCB in guaranteeing that stability.[5] But growth in real GDP averaged between only 0 and 1 percent per year over the same period. Stability had come at the cost of growth, but in comparison with some of Europe's economies in the period following the financial crisis of 2008, the ECCB's record was creditable.[6]

Eight small territories with economies that are heavily dependent on tourism and some other services but otherwise export little and vulnerable to natural shocks, such as hurricanes and even, in the case of Montserrat, volcanic eruption seem to operate a monetary union to the benefit of all. No single country of the ECCU so dominates the others economically that it attracts the suspicions and envy of the others. Questions of sovereignty do not appear to plague the internal politics of the ECCU as they do the euro, to the extent that

Britain accepts the leadership and decision-making of the ECCB in monetary matters relevant to Anguilla and Montserrat, which remain British territories. Differences of opinion between the constituent states on the relative merits of ECCB monetary policies and its constitutional and operational foundations do not seem to spill over into public disputes between states, as they do, for instance, in the franc zones of Africa.

One lesson above all would seem to be worth drawing from the ECCU. Of the eight states making up the union, six are recognized as microstates, and the remaining two would be if they were not British Overseas Territories. It would be impossible for any of them acting alone to operate a professional, well-resourced central bank or currency board; a challenge, as we have seen, that the IMF considered daunting for Timor-Leste, which by virtue of its colonial history was geographically and culturally isolated and therefore unable to team up with other partners to create a viable independent monetary institution. That the member states of the ECCU have relative proximity to each other, a shared language and history and similar political institutions and outlook, as well as a shared institutional background in the Caribbean Currency Board, has been to their advantage. And they have not failed to make it work.

THE MULTILATERAL MONETARY
AREA OF SOUTHERN AFRICA

If the ECCB operates as a "quasi-currency board," the Multilateral Monetary Area (MMA) compromising South Africa, Lesotho, Namibia, and Swaziland might be thought of as a "quasi-monetary union." Like the ECCB, the MMA has its origins in arrangements that stem from those that operated during British rule in the region. The South African rand became the only legal tender circulating in the MMA countries since 1921 when the South African Reserve Bank was created. (Extraordinarily, the South African Reserve Bank remains in private ownership, some seventy years after the Bank of England was nationalized.) This arrangement was maintained through a transitional period in the 1960s as countries became independent of Britain one by one. For all intents and purposes, Britain had in any case transferred responsibility for monetary matters to South Africa. The junior partners of Lesotho, Swaziland, and Namibia had no say in monetary policy decisions and obtained no seigniorage from South Africa's issue of the rand during this transitional period.

By 1974, Lesotho and Swaziland had gained their independence from Britain while Namibia remained under direct South African administration. But momentous developments were taking place in that year in the immediate region where wars of independence had been underway in Portugal's colonies

Angola and Mozambique since the early 1960s. The death of Portugal's authoritarian leader Antonio Salazar in 1970 had loosened the grip of the right in Portugal, and a military and left-wing coup installed a new government there in 1974. The new government in Lisbon promptly indicated its intention of granting independence to its colonies and began to wind down military operations in Angola and Mozambique. By mid-1975, both countries were independent, but not well disposed toward the regime in Pretoria, which had supported continuing Portuguese rule in the region as some form of stabilizing force. Indeed, after the independence of Angola and Mozambique, South African military forces carried out a series of operational incursions into both countries. In the case of Angola, the incursions from 1974 were primarily aimed at interdicting the operations of the South West Africa People's Organisation (SWAPO), which was seeking to free Namibia from South African control.

Increasingly isolated on the world stage and hemmed in by unsympathetic governments in countries bordering South Africa, the government in Pretoria pursued a series of policies addressing regional and domestic difficulties. The need to strengthen its local economic relationships led to the December 1974 Rand Monetary Area Agreement, formalizing the legacy monetary arrangements with Lesotho and Swaziland and making the rand legal tender in those two countries as well as in South Africa. Botswana (formerly Bechuanaland) had been a part of the informal rand area, but at this point withdrew to establish its own currency and central bank. Following Namibia's independence from South Africa in 1990, it too formally joined the rand area (which in 1986 had been renamed the Common Monetary Area) in 1992. The agreement was renamed the Multilateral Monetary Agreement to mark the accession of Namibia.[7]

All four countries possess a central bank, and all have a residual option to set interest rates, but the reality is that the South African Reserve Bank determines monetary policy for the MMA, albeit with input from representatives of the other countries. It is in view of this reality that the South African Reserve Bank can be construed as the central bank of MMA, with perhaps, those of Lesotho, Swaziland, and Namibia having associate status. These three countries do issue their own currencies: the lilangeni for Swaziland, the loti for Lesotho, and the Namibian dollar. Each national currency is valid as legal tender currency only in the country of its issue. In the case of the last two, the loti and the Namibian dollar, both have a fixed rate of exchange to the rand at one to one and are fully backed by assets denominated in rand. Their central banks are in effect currency boards, based on the rand as the anchor currency, and because the rand has legal tender status in both countries, they receive a share of seigniorage from the South African Reserve Bank (SARB) based on estimates of the amount of rand circulating in each country.

Other than Botswana's decision to go its own way, there has been no serious attempt to break away from the MMA. In 1986, the year in which Mswati III became king in succession to his father, Swaziland decided to cancel the formal legal requirement for a one-to-one exchange rate of the lilangeni with the rand. A decision was also made to deny the rand legal tender status in Swaziland, which, as a result, received no share of the seigniorage from SARB. When the local population elected to use the rand anyway, the government reversed its original decision and reinstated the rand's legal tender status to recover the seigniorage. The lessons of this episode were not missed by Lesotho, where a key source of national income was the remittance of rand by miners from Lesotho employed in South Africa. The foreign reserves that back the currencies of the MMA are pooled and held under the control of SARB.[8]

The MMA is often discussed as a possible nucleus for a wider regional currency. In these terms, but in the context of a national currency emergency, senior political figures in Zimbabwe considered the merits of joining the MMA in 2009. Analysis of the benefits focused on the free flow of capital across borders and the encouragement that would give to South Africans planning to invest in Zimbabwe. Commentators noted that the other members of the MMA that were consulted on monetary policy were able to maintain their own central banks but that, thanks to the fixed exchange rate to the rand, they enjoyed monetary stability. This was proposed as the solution to Zimbabwe's extreme inflation while at the same time preserving the symbol of sovereignty represented by the institution of a central bank. Zimbabwe elected to adopt the US dollar to replace the hyperinflating Zimbabwean dollar largely because the population of Zimbabwe had become aware of the steady decline in the value of the rand over the years.

However, as it became increasingly difficult for Zimbabwe to earn adequate amounts of dollars, bans were placed on the import of certain items from South Africa in July 2016 in order to save Zimbabwe's US dollars. Reacting to the threat to trade between the two countries, South African officials proposed that Zimbabwe adopt the South African rand. One of the benefits cited was again the suggestion that adoption of the rand would encourage large South African institutions to invest in Zimbabwe. At the same time, the use of US dollars was criticized as having a negative effect on Zimbabwe's balance of trade because it made its exports too expensive, one of the points made when experts debated a new currency for Afghanistan after the US-led invasion. According to one report, both the governor of the central bank and minister of finance of Zimbabwe were in favor of this proposal.

However, it was generally believed that President Robert Mugabe of Zimbabwe was opposed to the idea on the grounds that Zimbabwe would thereby be ceding its monetary sovereignty. Such a development in itself would have constituted recognition that his government was unable to manage the country's monetary system. Moreover, others in Zimbabwe were wary of South Africa's ultimate objectives in promoting the rand union, fearing that it could be the first step toward the absorption of Zimbabwe as South Africa's tenth province.[9]

Political uncertainties in South Africa and the weak rand exchange rate to the dollar, which in 1982 had been approximately one to one but by 2016 had fallen to one to fifteen, were beginning to raise questions on the part of other members of the MMA. In Namibia, the declining rand on the world markets dragged the Namibian dollar down with it. But as 80 percent of Namibia's imports came from South Africa, being fixed at par to the rand offered some relief. Bank of Namibia officials remained convinced that, until the volume of imports from South Africa reduced from their exceptionally high levels of 80 percent to, say, 10 percent, decoupling from the rand would make no sense, unless of course inflation were to pick up in South Africa, in which case it would be imported to Namibia. Unwise economic policies on the part of the senior partner could in those circumstances undo the presumed benefits of fixing the national currency to an underperforming anchor currency, as Ireland's experience with sterling showed in the 1970s. Over the past ten years the rand has lost half of its value against the US dollar, and this has been a major factor in the announcement by the South African government of its intention to nationalize the bank to bring it into line with almost all other central banks around the world.[10] Other South African government policies, in particular the planned expropriation of land without compensation, threaten to deter inward investment, further damaging the South African economy. If the wider economy of South Africa does get dragged down into a spiral of decline redolent of that in Zimbabwe, the resultant inflation will be transferred to the other MMA states. Under those circumstances, officials at the Bank of Namibia and others may need to review their attachment to the MMA.

THE FRANC ZONE UNIONS OF WEST AND CENTRAL AFRICA

As France wound down its African Empire, attention was turned toward monetary arrangements for newly independent colonies. Two monetary unions were created, each with its own central bank and the colonies invited to choose whether they would participate or not. Initially, the two unions continued to use the legacy monetary unit of the CFA (Colonies Francaises d'Afrique) franc,[11] which had existed since 1945 and was originally pegged to the French franc at fifty to one. Backing for the CFA franc was in due course reduced below the requirement for 100 percent cover in gold, French francs, or other convertible currency so that securities issued by the local government were acceptable. A single currency was issued for each of the two zones, and although one of the central banks proposed individual currencies for each of the countries within its zone, the proposal met with no enthusiasm among the participating governments. With only a few exceptions, the political leadership of the newly independent states was generally conservative in outlook and not disposed toward a complete break with France.[12]

The Banque Centrale des Etats Africain de l'Ouest (BCEAO), based in Senegal, was created to issue the CFA franc on behalf of the West African Monetary Union (WAMU), which was established in 1973 and included Senegal, Cote D'Ivoire, Mali, Benin, Burkina Faso, Togo, and Niger. Guinea Bissau, a Portuguese colony until independence in 1974, joined the monetary union in 1997. Mauritania began as a member of WAMU, but subsequently withdrew. In 1994, WAMU became WAEMU, the West African Economic and Monetary Union, with an extended remit to set up a common market and coordinate national economic policies.

In parallel, the Banque des Etats de l'Afrique Centrale (BEAC), headquartered in Cameroon, was established in 1972 to serve the CEMAC—Central African Economic and Monetary Community (rather than union). It consists of Cameroun, Gabon, Chad, Central African Republic, Congo, and Equatorial Guinea, of which the last had been Spain's only Sub-Saharan colony. CEMAC's remit includes the harmonization of tax and the formulation of common policies on a range of sectors that have an economic significance. Neither WAEMU nor CEMAC are mandated to formulate diplomatic or military policies.[13] A further issuing bank was created for the Comoros isles.

Since the establishment of BCEAO and BEAC, there have been several withdrawals from the zones, one of which was only temporary. Guinea Conakry remained a member of the franc zone for only two years after independence but, led by the then Marxist president, Ahmed Sekou Toure, quickly severed its monetary link to France altogether. Mauretania and Madagascar both left the franc zone in 1973 and 1972, respectively. In Madagascar, the rupture with France was not only monetary but also military, resulting in the withdrawal of French military bases as well. And in Mauretania the government felt confident that, although it would be sacrificing French budgetary assistance in return for greater independence in monetary matters, it could nevertheless rely on earnings from its copper and iron mining operations to earn the hard currency to back its own national money. There was also a perception that it would be able to rely to a certain extent on support from Libya, which at that time was beginning to extend its financial influence in Sub-Saharan Africa. Announcing the withdrawal from the franc zone, President Ould Daddah explained that the country would have to make some economic sacrifices to achieve full monetary sovereignty.

The most pronounced case of a failed bid for monetary independence from the franc zone was that of Mali. In June 1962, less than two years after Mali had achieved independence from France, President Keita announced the decision to withdraw from BCEAO and, citing the view that true independence would always be linked to an independent currency, launched the Mali franc. Initially, an increased money supply seemed to work well, but before long Mali's foreign exchange reserves dwindled, causing its vital imports to dry up. Balance of payments crises in 1964 and thereafter were averted by assistance from Russia, China, the IMF and others, but inflation continued to rise, and the Malian franc declined in value. The support of Russia and China for Mali's new monetary independence may be seen in the context of the Cold War as an effort to disengage the former French colony from France's sphere of influence in totality. The fact that Mali's new currency was produced in communist Czechoslovakia serves to underline the geopolitical nature of the operation.[14]

While imports declined, the country's principal exports in peanuts and rice also fell, notwithstanding the weakness of the local franc, which should have boosted those exports. By 1967, the government accepted that it had reached an economic dead end. Negotiations with France led to Mali's reentry to the franc zone with a promise of convertibility of Mali's franc to the French franc. Political aspirations toward monetary sovereignty had been overwhelmed by economic realities.[15] But after five years of stagnation, reentry to the franc zone did not bring immediate relief to the economy. Indeed, returning to pre-independence levels of import would have further drained what little reserves Mali had left. The deal with France therefore imposed constraints on levels of imports. President Keita attempted to paper over the cracks in the economic reality of the situation in 1968 with a program of radical populist propaganda very much in tune with the leftist atmosphere of the time. But again, the economic realities swept all resistance aside. The population remained unsatisfied and in November 1968 Keita's government was toppled by the military.[16]

As with countries asserting their independence from Britain at the same time, possession of a central bank and the freedom to shape monetary policies was a major part of the move by Guinea and Mali toward monetary independence. In an oratorical flourish, Touré declared that the decision to assert monetary independence was "comparable, if not superior" to the move toward national independence itself.[17]

Remarkably, the headquarters of both banks were located in Paris until 1972, an indication of France's hegemony, but the participating banks were permitted increasing degrees of influence in the decision-making processes. The new central banks would legally possess the various former colonies' reserves, although those reserves would be held in French francs at the French

Treasury's Operations Account in the Banque de France in Paris. The reserves of all CFA participating countries would be "pooled." Until 1973, Paris held 100 percent of the national reserves of its former colonies used to back the two common currencies, the BEAC franc and the BCEAO franc. In 1973, the minimum proportion of foreign reserves held in Paris was reduced to 65 percent, and in 2005 that was further reduced to 50 percent. In reality the operational accounts are said to be holding in excess of 90 percent of the CFA countries' reserves. One report suggests that these CFA reserves are invested on the Paris stock exchange by the Banque de France "in its own name" and that high levels of reserves held in Paris deprive the participating countries of liquidity and credit at home.[18] Other reports suggest that French treasury officials are forbidden to reveal what proportion of the total pooled reserves belong to each of the CFA countries.[19]

The CFA (in 1958, renamed Communaute Francaise d'Afrique) had, upon the independence from France of the participating states, become the Communaute Financiere Africaine in West Africa and Cooperation Financiere en Afrique Centrale in Central Africa. Both francs would be fully convertible into French francs at a fixed parity and the convertibility guaranteed by the French government. Foreign exchange transactions conducted by exporters from the franc zone would be managed via the operational accounts in Paris. BCEAO rules stipulate that, if the operational accounts in Paris lack sufficient reserves to settle foreign transactions, those accounts must be topped up by the BCEAO, which will require public and private organizations to surrender their foreign currency holdings in return for CFA francs. This process replicates a similar arrangement that exists in metropolitan France and is known as ratissage,[20] a word that had originally been applied to French military raids in France's North African colonies, betraying, perhaps, a certain linguistic insensitivity.

The CFA system has certainly yielded currency stability, and this monetary stability is one of the principal benefits of membership of the franc zone as set out by the Banque de France. France additionally points out that a unified currency zone will promote intraregional trade. But there have also been economic disadvantages to pegging the CFA franc to the French franc. When the French franc appreciated strongly against other currencies in the second half of the 1980s, the CFA franc rose with it, and exports from the region were badly affected as a result. In an effort to counter this situation and following discussions with the IMF and France, the Franc zone countries decided to devalue against the franc in 1994 so that one French franc was now worth one hundred CFA francs, rather than fifty. However, this had the predictable effect of making imports much more expensive.[21] But this was no more than the experience of other countries that had pegged to other, apparently more stable, currencies. Both the Irish punt, pegged to sterling until 1979, and the

Argentinian peso, pegged to the dollar until 2002, were ultimately unable to remain pegged because of the excessive depreciation or appreciation of the anchor currencies.

Since France's accession to the Eurosystem, the CFA franc has been pegged to the euro, and the French treasury guarantees the convertibility of the CFA franc to the euro. But the CFA franc has been caught yet again by the same problem encountered in the immediate postwar period and the 1980s: it is pegged to a currency over which the CFA countries have no control. Depreciation of the euro against the US dollar, in which oil products are invoiced, clearly makes purchases of oil more expensive for franc zone territories.

But there were other benefits to CFA countries. The monetary aegis of France, which included the pegging of the CFA franc to the French franc (and now to the euro), has been part of a larger deal that offered France's former colonies bilateral development and military aid. Import duties on produce of the participating states were waived and higher prices paid for imports from participating states.[22]

Despite political clashes between France and its former colonies from time to time (most notably France's military intervention in the 2002 civil war in Cote d'Ivoire) the franc zone has by and large proven to be a remarkably solid institution, even though there have been expressions of dissatisfaction by political leaders of some of the CFA countries at the retention of CFA reserves in Paris. Abdulaye Wade, president of Senegal from 2000–2012, for instance, called for the repatriation of those reserves. And, regarding the benefits of remaining pegged to the euro, opinion is split. In late 2015, President Deby of Chad spoke out for a break with the euro and production of individual currencies for the CFA countries. Deby's argument was that being pegged to such a strong currency as the euro made Chad's exports uncompetitive. But this position was countered by Prime Minister Duncan of Cote d'Ivoire, who observed that other countries in the region not pegged to the euro were experiencing significant inflation compared to CFA countries. The president of Cote d'Ivoire, Alassane Ouattara, made the same point in early 2016. Thus, the problems of the 1980s and 1990s when pegging to the French franc, which were felt to render the CFA franc uncompetitive, have repeated themselves a generation later as a result of a global economic slowdown.[23]

But what benefits did France hope to accrue from the arrangement? Some observers point to France's desire to project political prestige and the francophone culture abroad. Some analysts in the period following the financial crash of 2008 suggested that the CFA reserves held by the Bank of France in the French treasury account were used by France as part of its contribution to the bailout of weaker euro country economies.

Others might point toward a more mercantile motive. In 1990 France was still the lead trading partner for all the CFA zone countries, although even at that point a continuous decline in France's trade with the franc zone had been noted. Twenty-five years later, it remains a lead source of imports to five out of the eleven former colonies. But as a destination for CFA country exports, its position has declined even more significantly, with China and the United States absorbing very high proportions of those countries' exports, particularly in raw materials.[24] All the same, France's military commitment to the region more than half a century after independence is undiminished, as proven by its current engagement in Operation Barkhane. This deployment of French forces supports counterinsurgency operations by Burkina Faso, Mali, Niger, Chad, and Mauritania, all of them except the last being members of the franc zone. Thus, there have been clear defense benefits for the former colonies to remain in the franc zone as an integral part of their close association with France.

And yet, since the paragraphs above were written, the franc zone has gone through another major development. In December 2019 the West African franc zone announced its decision to rename its currency the eco and to make other significant changes to the currency union. Although the eco, like the West African franc, would be pegged to the euro, reserves would no longer be held in Paris, and France would no longer have a representative on the governing board.[25] President Macron of France, who together with President Ouattara of Cote d'Ivoire announced the change in Abidjan, acknowledged that the CFA franc zone was associated with the "trappings of colonialism." At the same time, Bruno Le Maire, France's finance minister together with representatives of WAMU signed a new monetary cooperation agreement preserving France's monetary guarantee of unlimited convertibility of CFA currency into euros.

ECOWAS (Economic Community of West African States, to which all the West African CFA states belong) has reacted positively, encouraging its wider membership of fifteen countries to adopt a common currency for West Africa.[26]

Although some commentators in the region are not convinced the monetary break with France has gone far enough, there can be no doubt that the repatriation of reserves marks another—perhaps penultimate—stage in the relationship of the franc zone with France. One hundred percent of all reserves were held in France until 1973 when the new minimum level was then set at 65 percent. In 2005 the minimum held in Paris was further reduced to 50 percent of all reserves, a requirement that has now disappeared altogether. These figures, taken together with a decline in France's position among WAMU's trading partners, plot the reduction of France's economic influence in West Africa.

THE EUROSYSTEM

Sovereign debt and banking crises from 2008 in the eurozone have high-lighted the difficulty in managing a political and economic regime that binds constituent states with a single monetary regime but leaves significant differences in the tax and spending policies of a European Union, which is still only half formed and certainly not harmonized, much less unified.

As a monetary system shared by a number of countries that are not bound by a common government and fiscal policy, the euro is not a unique development. As we have seen, the ECCB, the Banque Centrale des Etats de l'Afrique de l' Ouest, the Banque des Etats de l'Afrique Centrale, and the Multilateral Monetary Area all preceded the European Central Bank and all continue to function on the same principle of monetary union without political and fiscal union. The difference, however, between these monetary unions and the monetary union of the euro is that the latter was devised as a conscious and seemingly necessary step toward political unification. It is this difference that confers on the euro the status of experiment because, while there have been many instances of monetary unions accompanying the creation of a new state, there are no instances where monetary unions were pursued as a necessary precursor to political union. In this regard, the international monetary unions of the nineteenth century also differed from the euro; they were never introduced as a measure to promote and support political union. Even in the case of Germany, where some degree of monetary harmonization preceded political unification, there is no evidence that monetary union was conceived as a vital preparatory step. The euro, therefore, is as much if not more a political experiment as it is a monetary one. Indeed, Axel Weber, the former president of Germany's Bundesbank, has clearly stated that it is a political, not an economic, project.[27]

The political environment in which the euro project incubated was created by visionary political leaders whose attitude toward international European cooperation had been shaped by the traumatic experience of the Second World War. Among them, a view developed that a shared monetary system would lead to pooled sovereignty and limitations on independent political decision-making. A joint monetary system would perform the same function that the European Coal and Steel Community had been designed to achieve; with France and Germany joined at the hip in such essential matters as the production of raw materials and money, there would be no chance of war.

Political considerations were not, however, the sole basis for the conception of the euro. Conditions in the economies of the developed world in the 1970s did of course concentrate minds on the potential economic benefits of monetary union: the decoupling of the dollar from the gold standard, oil shocks and double-digit inflation in many countries, and the appreciation of the Deutsche Mark against the dollar undermining German exports all combined to raise monetary union as a potential solution to economic problems. More broadly, some Europeans thought that a second powerful currency in the world would offer an economic counterweight to the dollar and, particularly in French minds, would dilute America's ability to exert monetary power in pursuit of its political and economic objectives.[28]

As the political interest in a European currency gathered pace, experts turned their attention to the mechanics. The best means of establishing a single currency for Europe was debated during the 1960s by academics whose eminence in the economic field and enthusiasm for the project had perhaps clouded their sense of what was politically acceptable. Thus, Robert Mundell, who conceived the idea of the optimal currency area, put forward the idea in 1969 of a "living currency" being adopted as the appropriate launch currency for the "euro zone." Over time, he became clear in his own mind about the currency best suited for this role. Mundell saw that the Deutsche Mark, a globally significant currency managed by an "experienced and capable bank," could emerge as the "pivot currency," temporarily acting as the first euro, with other European currencies fixed to it.[29]

THE WERNER REPORT

The earliest formulation of the euro project, the Report on Economic and Monetary Union, by Pierre Werner, prime minister and finance minister of Luxembourg, was produced in 1970 at the request of heads of government (and, in the case of France, the head of state) meeting in the Hague in 1969. The report began by recognizing that the "disequilibrium"—the differences—in the economies of the various European Union states would hinder integration. While the emphasis of Werner's end objective was economic, the report stated that transfers of responsibility "from the national plane to the Community plane" will be essential "to achieve economic and monetary cohesion," surrendering monetary sovereignty to a supranational authority. Furthermore, although his report suggested that the objective could conceivably be achieved either by retaining national currencies, but locking their exchange rates together, or by doing away with national currencies altogether, replacing them with a single currency, he clearly steers toward the latter option because it would secure the "irreversibility of the venture." Monetary policy would be centralized, in other words, would be set at a European Community level.

Werner's commitment to the economic unity of the European project (in which currency union was only one element) extended to the control of budgets, an objective that was seriously addressed only forty years later, after the sovereign debt crisis, which followed hard on the heels of (and as a result of) the banking crisis of 2008. A hierarchy for decision-making established a committee of governors of central banks that would make recommendations to the European Commission (the civil service) and the Economic and Financial Affairs Council. At this stage of "euro thinking," therefore, the role of the central bank governors was one of technical advice to elected ministers, circumscribing the autonomy of the banking technocrats and implicitly subordinating them to the political leadership, running counter to the principle now seen as best practice—central bank autonomy.

In his conclusion, Werner indicates that monetary and economic union is an indispensable "leaven" for the development of political union; that is, monetary union would perform a task in facilitating the development of political union. So, from the opening position of promoting monetary union as an economic objective, the report moves to a position where monetary and economic union will promote political union.[30] The promotion of the euro as a preparatory step toward political union can therefore be traced back, at least in its published form, to Werner.

Attempts to stabilize currencies of the core European Union countries were tried at a relatively early stage. The first of them, the so-called "snake" or the "snake in the tunnel," provided a framework for exchange rates between the currencies of the European Economic Community (the precursor of the European Union) using the dollar as a reference point. Established in 1971, the snake survived only a few years, collapsing as the short-lived Smithsonian Agreement failed, finally doing away with a fixed dollar to gold value. Thus, the first attempt to provide order to inter–European Union exchange rates by using the dollar failed precisely because the dollar's position as a stable reference point had been compromised. By 1977, a new mechanism was in place based on the Deutsche Mark, which was tracked by the currencies of the Netherlands, Luxembourg, Belgium, and Denmark.[31] By this time, then, the Deutsche Mark was starting to emerge as a more reliable "anchor" for some European states than either the dollar or sterling. Circumstances in Europe and further afield seemed to indicate that the time for a unified European currency was approaching.

When the independently minded Bundesbank leadership indicated opposition to the idea of monetary union, German Chancellor Helmut Schmidt appealed in 1978 to the sensitivity of the bank's council by reference to the war (in which he had served in the German army) and asserted the importance of monetary union as a vital element in postwar reconciliation.[32] Whether economic circumstances of the 1970s and subsequent periods were convincing arguments or not, it was this political, rather than economic, argument that was to feature time and time again in the efforts of German chancellors and other integrationists attempting to keep the project on track.

The creation of the European Monetary System in 1979, whereby European currencies stabilized their exchange rates to each other and the Deutsche Mark started to emerge as the principal reference point for those exchange rates, marked the next stage of development in the creation of what would become the Eurosystem.

THE DELORS REPORT

The next milestone in setting out the purpose of and transition to monetary union was the Report on Economic and Monetary Union, produced in 1989 by a committee chaired by Jacques Delors, a former senior official of the Banque de France and subsequently economics and finance minister in the socialist government of Francois Mitterrand. From 1985 to 1995, Delors was president of the European Commission, and it was during this period that the Delors report was compiled. As with so many other public figures of his generation, his personal experiences during the Second World War governed Delors's attitude toward European integration, which he saw as the most reliable means of preventing war in Europe. Monetary integration was, in his view, one of the steps on the road to this objective.[33] The development and implementation of the euro was for Delors and for others of a like mind and experience a means of achieving long-term peace in Europe. In this sense, monetary integration was one integral part of a project to bind Europe together in such a way as to guarantee peace. The value of money in this way as a means to a greater political end—peace—was more important from a political than an economic standpoint.

Delors's report began by summarizing the recent history of the European Union's development, citing the implementation of the common customs union and the common agricultural policy as evidence of progress in integration. It also pointed out that the Bretton Woods system had shown signs of "decline." The time had seemed to be right for a move toward monetary union. However, the report noted, progress had stalled, notwithstanding some preliminary success, because of the varying economic shocks of the 1970s, which included high inflation and oil embargoes by OPEC and differing approaches toward tackling those shocks. Noting that some progress had been achieved by the establishment of the European Monetary System and that the Deutsche Mark had proven a steady anchor against inflation, the report nevertheless found that progress fell far short of the target largely because some countries were not yet participating in the system or were running exceptional budget deficits. Individual monetary policies and, in particular, adherence to existing exchange rates were cited as part of the problem, and the report called for a more cooperative approach in policy making.

Despite this call for cooperation, Delors and his team accepted that the European Union would continue to consist of *"individual nations with differing economic, social, cultural and political characteristics"* and that it would be necessary for a *"balance to be struck between national and Community competences."* Recognizing thus that states would have different approaches to certain economic issues, but that monetary union would require a degree of economic cooperation, Delors's team recommended that an economic framework be established that would set the outer boundaries of economic decision-making while permitting autonomy within those boundaries.[34]

A principle of subsidiarity would be applied whereby only those issues that needed to be decided or agreed on at the European Community level would be referred to that level, while anything and everything else requiring a policy decision would rest at national, regional, and local levels. But there was a caveat in that only those decisions that would not have an adverse bearing on the work of the union as a whole would remain with the national authorities. This of course would leave open the question of what would and would not have an adverse economic or monetary effect on the work of the union as a whole.

Delors shared Werner's view that the adoption of a single currency would secure the irreversibility of the monetary union project, but, perhaps because of his own background in central banking, Delors's report clearly proposed an autonomous central bank with full authority over the formulation and implementation of monetary policy. Moreover, the European Central Bank was to be independent of instructions issued by national governments and European Community authorities. This last proposal was indeed adopted and included as article 107 in the Maastricht Treaty. One important suggestion of the Delors report was, however, not advanced successfully. Parallelism was the principle by which economic union would be developed alongside monetary union. In this area, Delors observed that further progress in economic union would be necessary to secure the success of monetary union. Delors had identified a clear weakness in the area of economic union; some euro countries were able to run up unmanageable sovereign debts without central supervision and constraint that almost led to the collapse of the euro after 2008. And when the crisis did finally come, it evoked policy proposals from some leading European political figures that would have posed a severe challenge to Delors's original principle of subsidiarity. Among those proposals was, for instance, the suggestion by Olli Rehn, the European Commissioner for Economy and Finance, that national budgets should be cleared by the commission before being presented to national parliaments.[35]

Although Delors, as a lead proponent of integration, was seen as the bogey-man by some Eurosceptics in, for instance, the United Kingdom, in other ways he was not as doctrinaire as he was made out to be (suggesting, for instance, in 2012 that, if the United Kingdom could not entertain integration, an alternative relationship based on a free trade agreement would be viable). As events of 2008 and afterward were to show, on the subject of the necessity for parallel economic and monetary union for euro member states, he was, however, right. And, as events in Britain following the 2016 referendum on withdrawal from the European Union showed his comments in 2012 had real merit and would seem to be the basis of a relationship between the United Kingdom and the European Union that would be satisfactory to many.

But the drive toward monetary union was to lie in the hands of elected officials, rather than technocrats. Germany's unification in 1989, making it by far the largest single country in Europe in terms of population, further concentrated French minds. The French were now outnumbered in Europe by Germans, and there were reasonable grounds to assume that West Germany's highly successful exporting economy could only grow stronger by the addition of another sixteen million citizens. Monetary union would be one means of managing the nightmare of a resurgent Germany. This is not to say that Europeans saw no economic benefits in the euro. Germany's reputation for monetary discipline and the effectiveness of its autonomous central bank would be, they thought, the models for an effective monetary system to be shared by other European states. These were then among the economic benefits of a common monetary system to be obtained in return for pooling, or even surrendering, monetary sovereignty.

And then there were the other benefits that were political rather than economic. Germany's Chancellor Helmut Kohl and Francois Mitterrand, president of France, the combined driving force behind the introduction of the euro, both had a sense of destiny that carried the project to fruition. For both, the defining experience of life was the 1939–1945 war that had torn Europe apart. On more than one occasion, Kohl had stated that "the euro is a question of war and peace."[36] From the perspective of a later generation—particularly those in the Western European core countries—this might have seemed little more than political hyperbole. But for those countries, notably the Baltic states, which in 1991 had only just succeeded in exiting the Soviet Union after nearly fifty years of occupation, Kohl's warning carried more weight. Membership of the euro would further bind them to Europe and make it more difficult for Russia to regain control over them. Membership of the European Union and consequently of the euro offered political reinsurance.

In time, then, the euro project had come to be seen not as a purely economic project, but more fundamentally as a prerequisite for a federation of states of Europe. Indeed, the euro became so inextricably a part of the wider

European project that political leaders saw it as one of the foundation stones of the project of political unification, rather than the final coping stone.[37] The political significance of the euro over and above its economic role was such that, during the period of intense sovereign debt crisis in the period 2010–2013, political leaders spoke in terms of the preservation of a unified currency as necessary to preserve European unity. The most extreme predictions threatened bloodshed and instability in the event of a collapse of the euro.[38]

Transitional arrangements for the introduction of the euro were set out in the Maastricht Treaty of 1992 and included the creation of the European Monetary Institute, which would carry the burden of preparing for the euro until handover to the European Central Bank. From January 1, 1994, central banks were to work toward independence from operational interference by national governments, a position that was to be achieved by January 1, 1999, the date for the establishment of the European System of Central Banks (ESCB). This system would include the European Central Bank, central banks of countries joining the euro, and the wider group of European Union central banks not yet ready to join the euro. All these banks would work to coordinate monetary policies. From January 1, 1999, conversion rates—prescribed as *"irrevocable"* by Article 3a.2 of the Maastricht Treaty—for the various currencies participating in the euro came into force, and the euro was launched. The combination of the European Central Bank and the participating central banks (now numbering eighteen) is known as the Eurosystem. Recognizing the fact that the euro area contains a wide variety of banks with different linguistic, cultural, and operational traditions, national central banks were preserved as the point of contact and supervisory body for commercial banks in each country.[39] The principal decision-making body of the Eurosystem consists of the executive board of six of the most senior officials of the European Central bank and the governors of the national central banks. The presence of the representatives of the national central banks defines the European Central Bank as a federal institution.

The Maastricht Treaty and the Stability and Growth Pact, adopted at the European Summit in Dublin in December 1996, established boundaries for fiscal and political probity, including national public debt to GDP ratios and limits on budget deficits.[40]

Conservative German opinion, strongly adherent to the idea of a robust and stable Deutsche Mark, had felt particular concern through the 1990s at the fact that the unified currency would be introduced without the stable platform of political and fiscal union.[41] Set against Germany's own monetary experience in the nineteenth century, when the currencies of different German regions were fixed against each other prior to unification, but a single national currency emerged only after full political unification, it is easy to understand the historical basis of German concerns. From the launch of the euro until

2008, these concerns seemed to be unfounded. But, when the developed world was rocked in that year by a banking crisis, the knock-on effect on euro governments with high sovereign debt exposed the danger and threatened to bring down the euro.

European political leaders attempted to limit the influence of national politics in the monetary policies of the European project. Clause 107 of the Maastricht Treaty stipulated that national governments and other public and private institutions were not to lobby the European Central Bank.[42] This has always been seen as a requirement of the German political leadership, which sought to establish a politically independent, technocratic central bank analogous to the autonomy enjoyed by the Bundesbank. And yet much of the support for the creation of a European Central Bank came from southern European states wishing to exercise some degree of influence over monetary policy. Indeed, well before the sovereign debt crisis and before the introduction of the euro, Alain Juppe, prime minister of France, spelled out his objection to a politically autonomous European Central Bank: "We don't want decisions on economic, budgetary, fiscal and monetary policy to be shaped by a technocratically-driven, semi-automatic (*sic*) system under the sole authority of the ECB. That is not our concept of democracy."[43] Nor, some might have commented, was it France's way of shaping monetary policy.

Divergent views between the countries of North and South Europe over the question of political control over the ECB and therefore over the euro seem to echo, if not the question of the remit of a central bank, then at least a North–South tension as displayed during both the German and Italian monetary unifications over a century earlier. It was hardly then a surprise when, under the strains of the sovereign debt financial crisis from 2009–2010 onward, some euro states sought to change the ECB's terms of reference. Mediterranean countries gripped by a crisis of sovereign debt and banking failure fell into severe economic depression and urged the ECB to inject liquidity into the financial system by means of quantitative easing, which had been the method preferred by the US Federal Reserve, the Bank of England, and the Bank of Japan. Northern countries led by Germany, however, insisted that this was not within the ECB's remit.[44]

Political unity and the will of the constituent states to see the euro survive will be, in the view of Bordo and Jonung, the factor that determines the euro's success or failure in the long term. Moreover, a dominant state or combination of dominant states would need to emerge in order to provide a driving force able to see the monetary system through the shocks that would inevitably beset it. Again, Bordo and Jonung foretold that tensions between France and Germany as the European "motor" could lead to serious problems for the euro. France's influence and relative importance as a coequal partner alongside Germany in the Eurosystem had over time been seen to decline somewhat. At the time of writing, there are few who doubt that Germany is the economic hegemon of the Eurozone. But also, at the time of writing, it has become apparent that Germany's political leadership of the entire European Union has been somewhat on the wane as Angela Merkel's tenure as chancellor of Germany comes to an end and France's Emmanuel Macron exercises increasing influence and energy in internal and external affairs. It remains to be seen whether a relative shift in the balance of influence between France and Germany will have a significant long-term effect on the operations and survival of the euro. But there may be those who recall that France was the central power behind the Latin Monetary Union, which lasted no more than two generations.

North and south divisions in the European Union again rose to the surface under the dangers posed by the COVID-19 outbreak of 2020. The extraordinary impact of the virus and the countermeasures taken by European governments have threatened massive economic disruption. Italy, France, and Spain, with very high rates of infection and deaths, have called for European Union–wide support for their economies by means of the issue of European COVID-19 bonds, effectively sharing the burden of borrowing across the union. Germany and the Netherlands, with lower infection and mortality rates, as well as a traditionally different attitude toward economic management, have resisted the proposal.

When, intermittently, major threats to the European Union's economic management arise, the cohesion of the whole is put under extreme pressure, and the continuing participation of individual states may be threatened. It is difficult to see how the current arrangements—including the euro—can indefinitely survive repeated external shocks of this kind. And yet the Maastricht Treaty does not set out mechanisms for a country to leave the Eurosystem or for a majority of members in effect to expel a country that is unwilling or unable to conform to the qualifying requirements for membership. Indeed, the experience of Greece during and after its sovereign debt crisis demonstrates that euro states are so financially and economically intertwined that, even when it might be desirable for a country to leave the system in its own interests and in the interests of all the other members, it is difficult, if not impossible, to plot a path for them out of it.

At the peak of the sovereign debt crisis in Europe, when it seemed very possible that some countries might leave the Eurosystem or that the system could collapse altogether, some of Europe's most prominent political figures raised the specter of war should the system collapse. Whether or not they really believed that survival of the monetary system meant the difference between war or peace in Europe, this presentational position demonstrates that the decisions on a country's monetary regime are sometimes shaped by factors other than the purely economic. But need that be the case?

NOTES

1. "The World Bank in Small States: Overview" (see graphic for Micro States), World Bank, https://www.worldbank.org/en/country/smallstates/overview; W. F. Crick, *Commonwealth Banking Systems* (Oxford: Clarendon Press, 1965), 481; and "Member States," Organisation of Eastern Caribbean States, https://www.oecs.org/en/who-we-are/member-states.

2. "Revised Treaty of Basseterre Establishing the Organisation of Eastern Caribbean States Economic Union," https://drive.google.com/file/d/1287Ag0Tp3ZudDkGi0ztljE-2ZUPUzl_F/view.

3. "Economic Union Treaty, Frequently Asked Questions (FAQs)," Organisation of Eastern Caribbean States, April 2008, http://ctrc.sice.oas.org/CARICOM/OECS/FAQs_OECS_Integration.pdf; and DeLisle Worrell, "A Currency Union for the Caribbean," Working Paper WP 03/35, International Monetary Fund, February 2003, 4–6.

4. Worrel, "A Currency Union for the Caribbean."

5. "Eastern Caribbean Currency Union: Financial System Stability Assessment," International Monetary Fund, April 15, 2004, https://www.imf.org/external/pubs/ft/scr/2004/cr04293.pdf; "Annual Economic and Financial Review," Eastern Caribbean Central Bank, 2014, https://eccb-centralbank.org/documents/22.

6. Eastern Caribbean Central Bank, "Annual Report 2010–2011 and 2014–2015"; "Monetary Unions in the Caribbean Context: The Challenges Faced by the Eastern Caribbean Currency Union since the Financial Crisis," Eastern Caribbean Central Bank, March 2016, 20190118_monetary_unions_in_the_caribbean_context_ii.pdf (centralbank.cw).

7. Lambertus van Zyl, "South Africa's Experience of Regional Currency Areas and the Use of Foreign Currencies," in *Regional Currency Areas and the Use of Foreign Currencies*, Bank of International Settlements, Paper 17, May 2003, 134–36. https://www.bis.org/publ/bppdf/bispap17o.pdf; and Johannes Chiminya, "Sustainability of Rand Union?," *The Financial Gazette*, September 25, 2009.

8. "The Loti-Rand Peg: Benefits and Costs," Central Bank of Lesotho Economic Review, May 2006, https://www.centralbank.org.ls/images/Publications/Research/Reports/MonthlyEconomicReviews/2006/Economic_Review_May_06.pdf.

9. Chiminya, "Sustainability of Rand Union?"; Peter Fabricius, "SA Advises Zim to Join Rand Monetary Area," *Independent Online*, July 9, 2016, https://www.iol.co.za/news/africa/sa-advises-zim-to-adopt-the-rand-2043588; and "Zimbabwe Currency Crisis: The Rand and Long History of Trade with South Africa," *Zimbabwe Independent*, May 12, 2016 https://www.theindependent.co.zw/2016/05/12/55811/.

10. "Rand vs the Dollar: 1978–2016," *Businesstech*, March 13, 2016, https://businesstech.co.za/news/finance/116372/rand-vs-the-dollar-1978-2016/; "EFF's Plan to Nationalise South Africa's Reserve Bank Takes First Step," *Businesstech*, November 2, 2020, https://businesstech.co.za/news/banking/444996/effs-plan-to-nationalise-south-africas-reserve-bank-takes-first-step/.

11. "La Zone franc de 1939 à aujourd'hui," Direction générale du Trésor, https://www.tresor.economie.gouv.fr/tresor-international/la-zone-franc/la-zone-franc-de-1939-a-aujourd-hui.

12. Eric Helleiner, *The Making of National Money: Territorial Currencies in Historical Perspective* (New York: Cornell University Press, 2003), 210, 212, 213.

13. "Fact Sheet No. 127: The Franc Zone," Banque de France, July 2010, https://www.banque-france.fr/sites/default/files/media/2016/11/02/the_fact_sheet_n_127_july-2010.pdf.

14. Jonathan Kirshner, *Currency and Coercion* (Princeton, NJ: Princeton University Press, 1995), 152n.

15. Ibid., 152–53.

16. Ibid., 153.

17. Helleiner, *The Making of National Money*, 213.

18. Nicoletta Fagiolo, "The CFA Franc: Africa's Financial Anachronism," October 17, 2015, https://www.free-simone-and-laurent-gbagbo.com/single-post/2017/12/12/the-cfa-franc-africa-s-financial-anachronism.

19. Jay Wamey, "Devaluation Jitters Grip CFA Franc Zone," *Cameroon Post*, December 4, 2011, https://cameroonpostline.com/devaluation-jitters-grip-cfa-franc-zone.

20. "Fact Sheet No. 127: The Franc Zone."

21. "A Brief History of the CFA Franc, "*African Business*, February 19, 2012, http://africanbusinessmagazine.com/uncategorised/a-brief-history-of-the-cfa-franc/.

22. Alan Wheatley, "The Pretenders to the Dollar's Crown," in *The Power of Currencies and Currencies of Power*, ed. Alan Wheatley (London: International Institute for Strategic Studies, 2013), 49; Kirshner, *Currency and Coercion*, 150; and "Fact Sheet No. 127: The Franc Zone."

"A Brief History of the CFA Franc"

23. Assandé des Adom, "Beyond the CFA Franc: An Empirical Analysis of the Choice of an Exchange Rate Regime in the UEMOA," *Economic Issues* 17, Part 2 (2012): 76; Emilie Lob, "Have West, Central Africa Outgrown the CFA Franc?," Voice of America, April 26, 2016, https://www.voanews.com/africa/have-west-central-africa-outgrown-cfa-franc; and Issiaka Coulibaly, "Costs and Benefits of the CFA Franc," World Policy, February 28, 2017, http://worldpolicy.org/2017/02/28/costs-and-benefits-of-the-cfa-franc/.

24. World Integrated Trade Solution, http://wits.worldbank.org/#, and Trading Economics, https://tradingeconomics.com/; and Allechi M'Bet and Amlan Madeleine Niamkey, "European Economic Integration and the Franc Zone: The Future of the CFA Franc after 1996," African Economic Research Consortium, Research Paper 19, July 1993, http://opendocs.ids.ac.uk/opendocs/bitstream/handle/123456789/2046/No%2019.pdf?sequence=1.

25. Ange Aboa, "West Africa Renames CFA Franc but Keeps It Pegged to Euro," *Reuters*, December 21, 2019, https://www.reuters.com/article/us-ivorycoast-france-macron-idUSKBN1YP0JR; and "New Currency '' to Replace CFA Franc but Will Remain Pegged to Euro," *France 24*, December 22, 2019, https://www.france24.com/en/20191222-cfa-franc-to-be-replaced-by-the--but-will-stay-pegged-to-euro.

26. Laura Angela Bagnetto, "End of CFA Franc in West Africa 'Only a Symbolic Change': Economist," Radio France International, December 22, 2019, https://www.rfi.fr/en/africa/20191222-end-cfa-franc-west-africa-only-symbolic-change-economist.

27. "European Banks and the Eurozone Crisis: Keynote Speech by Axel Weber," The Policy Exchange, Westminster, London, September 5, 2013, https://www.youtube.com/watch?v=_oLSagYc8uU. The author was present.

28. The prospects for the euro as a global alternative to the US dollar have been well tested in recent times by US sanctions on Iran, which were reimposed by the Trump administration in May 2018. When US and European foreign policies on Iran diverged as a result, the existence of a currency alternative in the form of the euro made little difference to preserving European trade with Iran in the face of European banks' unwillingness to incur US wrath by trading with the sanctioned country.

29. Robert Mundell, "Money and the Sovereignty of the State," paper presented at the International Economic Association Conference, Trento, September 4–7, 1997, 37–38, accessed January 9, 2020, https://www-ceel.economia.unitn.it/events/monetary/mundell14.pdf.

30. "Report to the Council and the Commission on the Realisation by Stages of Economic and Monetary Union in the Community, Werner Report," Council/Commission of the European Communities, 1970, http://aei.pitt.edu/1002/1/monetary_werner_final.pdf.

31. Kwasi Kwarteng, *War and Gold* (London: Bloomsbury, 2014), 263.

32. Barry Eichengreen, *Exorbitant Privilege* (Oxford: Oxford University Press, 2011), 82; and Wheatley, "The Pretenders to the Dollar's Crown," 46.

33. Eichengreen, *Exorbitant Privilege*, 84.

34. Jacques Delors, "Report on Monetary and Economic Union in the European Community," April 17, 1989, http://aei.pitt.edu/1007/1/monetary_delors.pdf.

35. Eichengreen, *Exorbitant Privilege*, 133.

36. Wheatley, "The Pretenders to the Dollar's Crown," 45.

37. Kwarteng, *Gold and War*, 277.

38. "Merkel Warns of Europe's Collapse," *European Union Times*, May 18, 2010, https://www.eutimes.net/2010/05/merkel-warns-of-europes-collapse/; and Michael Bordo and Lars Jonung, "The Future of EMU: What Does the History of Monetary Unions Tell Us?," working paper, National Bureau of Economic Research, 1999, 26 n56, https://www.nber.org/papers/w7365; Kwarteng, *War and Gold*, 262.

39. "Economic and Monetary Union (EMU)," European Central Bank—Eurosystem, https://www.ecb.europa.eu/ecb/history/emu/html/index.en.html; "European System of Central Banks," Eesti Pank (Bank of Estonia), https://www.eestipank.ee/en/eesti-pank/european-system-central-banks; and "Eurosystem," Eesti Pank (Bank of Estonia), https://www.eestipank.ee/en/eesti-pank/eurosystem.

40. Harold James, "Monetary and Fiscal Unification in Nineteenth-Century Germany: What Can Kohl Learn from Bismarck?" Princeton Department of Economics, 1997, 28, https://ies.princeton.edu/pdf/E202.pdf.

41. Kwarteng, *War and Gold*, 274–75.

42. Council/Commission of the European Communities, "Treaty on European Union," February 7, 1992, https://europa.eu/european-union/sites/europaeu/files/docs/body/treaty_on_european_union_en.pdf.

43. James, "Monetary and Fiscal Unification," 30, citing the *Financial Times* of December 14 1996.

44. James, "Monetary and Fiscal Unification," 30–31.

Chapter 10

Monetary Sovereignty and the Making of the State

Whenever new states emerged from larger unions in the second half of the twentieth century and the beginning of the twenty-first, the establishment of a central bank usually accompanied the creation of other governmental organs as an indispensable tool of national administration as well as a symbol of sovereignty and self-determination. The second half of the twentieth century had already seen the creation of dozens of newly independent states as the lingering empires of Britain, France, Belgium, and Portugal were dissolved. The fragmentation in the early 1990s of the Soviet Union into fifteen separate states added to these numbers when in each case the birth of new republics was accompanied by the creation of a separate central bank for each, most if not all of which had previously been branches of the Central Bank of the Soviet Union. When Yugoslavia, also in the early 1990s, dissolved into the five states of Slovenia, Croatia, Macedonia, Bosnia Herzegovina, and Serbia Montenegro, all immediately established their claims to independent control of their own currency by creating a central bank. Even Timor-Leste and Ecuador, which both use the US dollar, have institutions called central banks, even though they do not have the range of powers and autonomy of a true central bank. Some states that have not yet fully achieved recognition as sovereign in the wider world—Somaliland, for instance, which issues its own currency, and Palestine, which does not—have a central bank and a monetary authority, respectively. The possession of something called a central bank or currency board in no way points toward full monetary sovereignty. However, possession of a central bank (or for that matter a currency board) does preserve a residual sense of monetary independence separate from whichever currency is in use—an independence that can be revived when necessary. When a country decides to adopt another country's currency, thereby relinquishing its monetary independence, it does not surrender its sovereignty—the ultimate right and ability to reverse that decision and adopt a different currency regime.

In his 1997 paper "Money and the Sovereignty of the State," Robert Mundell, the Nobel Prize–winning economist, wrote:

> *The right to produce and control money is a clear-cut test of a country's independence and sovereignty. The most important dimension of this monetary sovereignty, however, is the right of a state to declare that which counts as legal tender. This principle, called the Law of Payment, goes back to ancient times.*[1]

He went on to write:

> *Monetary sovereignty can be broken into three parts: (a) the right to determine what constitutes the unit of account—the commodity or token in which price lists are specified; (b) the right to determine the means of payment—legal tender for purposes of the discharge of debt; and (c) the right to produce money—or else determine the conditions under which it is to be produced by others.*

Mundell asserts that the *right* to produce and control money is a test of sovereignty. But this is not to say that the country *must* always exercise that right by issuing its own money. As we have shown, the decision by some countries to compromise that right does not compromise the wider issue of its sovereignty because, retaining its independence of action in such matters, that is, its sovereignty, the country may always chose to adopt a different currency. He goes on to say that monetary sovereignty consists of the right to decide on the unit of account and to determine what constitutes legal tender. So, in these terms, a country can exercise its right by deciding to adopt the currency of a different country, rather than issue its own. In essence, monetary sovereignty does lie in the right of the country to produce its own national currency if it considers the circumstances right to do so, but, equally, it leaves open the right to forgo production of its own currency should there be good grounds for doing so.

Indeed, events subsequent to the publication of Mundell's paper have led some countries to abandon a national currency when it has clearly failed—Ecuador in 2000, Bosnia in 2004, and Zimbabwe in 2009—or to adopt another country's currency as an act of expediency—Timor-Leste in 2000 and Montenegro in 2002. But unilateral adoption of another country's currency can bring with it difficulties. In October 2007 finance ministers of the eurozone challenged Montenegro's unilateral decision to use the euro as "incompatible with the EU's treaty on monetary union which foresees the eventual adoption of the euro as the endpoint of a structured convergence process within a multicultural framework."[2] As Montenegro was preparing to move toward membership of the European Union and eventual adoption of the euro, European Union ministers sensibly stopped short of forbidding its use of the euro, which it would eventually be required to adopt. The European Union was simply objecting to the circumstances in which Montenegro had decided unilaterally to adopt the euro.

Some legal analysis asserts that, while a state issuing currency may enact laws forbidding the use of its currency in another country or may "make representations on the matter" to another country, as the European Union was prepared to do to Montenegro, there is no reason to believe that the issuer's laws would have authority in the other jurisdiction. This same analysis concludes, therefore, that the laws of one country on the issue of its money would have no extraterritorial effect in another country[3] (unless of course the latter were to pass laws accepting that position, but why would it need to do so if it had no intention of adopting the other country's currency, nor indeed if it intended to adopt it without approval of the issuing state?). If this analysis is correct, there would appear to be no means in international law of preventing, for example, an independent Scotland from using sterling without the blessing of the Bank of England. The only question for the Scots to consider is, would that be the best solution for Scotland's currency requirements in the short to medium term?

Relinquishing monetary rights of issue by choice is now well accepted as an alternative to issue of a national currency to the extent that it has been recommended by the International Monetary Fund in cases such as that of Timor-Leste. Britain has permitted monetary issue for some of its overseas territories, such as Montserrat and the British Virgin Islands, to be passed to the Eastern Caribbean Central Bank and the US Federal Reserve Bank, respectively, for the sake of convenience. In the most striking of all examples of the surrender of national issuance of currency, nineteen European countries have pooled their sovereignty in adopting the euro, which works on a supranational set of policies and consequently reflects a supranational identity. But temporary suspension of those rights does not mean that it has been surrendered in perpetuity. As long as the country concerned reserves the right to reverse any decision to forgo full control of currency production and issue, it retains the essence of its monetary sovereignty. Any independent country that chooses to surrender some degree of independence in its issue of currency in one of these ways might be said to have passed its monetary sovereignty or some degree of it to another country or countries "on loan."

Beyond the question of the limits and exercise of a state's rights, there is the question of practicalities and outcomes. When experts assert the importance of monetary sovereignty, it is usually because they expect governments and central banks to use that sovereignty to implement policies that will deliver the best outcomes for the country concerned. But, as we all know, there have been too many examples of countries and their central banks that fail to manage the national currency effectively. In the most extreme of cases (for instance, in Zimbabwe), the population will turn away from the national currency in favor of some other currency that does what they need from it: provide a stable currency that will be acceptable in transactions and will, to a reasonable degree, hold its value. In such cases, it seems that the population will assert its sovereignty of choice in the marketplace, a choice that would have been illegal under the laws of ancient Rome but that has been seen in multiple cases of monetary collapse since then. The population asserts, as it were, a higher sovereignty of choice above that of the law. Monetary sovereignty as expressed by a government's imposition of legal tender laws in such cases is empty if the national currency does not do what it should do. Indeed, a currency that to some extent is designed to convey a sense of national pride quite clearly achieves the opposite if it is seen to be an abject failure. Recent history demonstrates that the effective economic functioning of a currency is now of greater importance than its significance as a pure symbol of national sentiment and that the latter will be sacrificed in favor of the former (as in the case of Ecuador, for instance). Moreover, as demonstrated in other cases (notably, that of Estonia), monetary sovereignty might be traded in return for some other benefit, such as security.

Mundell, describing the sharing of monetary sovereignty by members of the euro (although he does point out that they retain a share in the decision-making process), repeats the assumption that the act will be irrevocable.[4] Given that the monetary unions of the Soviet Union and Yugoslavia had both dissolved less than ten years before his comments, this was a strange belief to repeat. At the peak of the sovereign debt crisis in the eurozone, commentators reminded people of the collapse of the Latin Monetary Union and sought to draw lessons from it for the European Union and the euro. It was perfectly possible, according to historical precedent, for monetary unions of one sort or another to be dissolved. It was simply the case that the European Union had not explicitly provided for this possibility in the Maastricht Treaty, perhaps because to provide for it might have encouraged people to consider it possible and that in turn possibilities might become realities. So long as the constituent members of the European Union retain ultimate control of their own fate, they will retain the de facto ability to exit the euro even though, as we have already seen in the case of Greece, it is difficult to take the leap.

Indeed, Britain's 2016 decision to leave the European Union makes withdrawal from the euro system by one or more members more "thinkable." If a country is able to withdraw altogether from a federation to which it was bound by treaty, it is also perfectly possible for a country to withdraw from a monetary system whether it had acceded to that system by treaty or not. And, even though some European states have ceded their monetary sovereignty to the European Central Bank as part of the euro project, they have yet to dissolve their individual central banks. Neither fully independent, because they have pooled the setting of interest rates, nor yet fully integrated into a single institution, because they continue to represent the monetary interests of nation-states that seek to negotiate within the European Central Bank monetary policies specifically favorable to themselves, national central banks remain just that—national, rather than supranational, institutions.

If it is true that member states of the Eurosystem may withdraw from that system at will, is it also conceivable that some constituent states of the United States might consider the benefits of withdrawal from the Federal Reserve System? In 2013, the State Senate and House of delegates of the Commonwealth of Virginia created a subcommittee to look into the possibility of introducing an alternative currency to the US dollar.[5] While the prospects for a withdrawal from the US dollar system by one of the states of the union looks extremely remote, the fact that at least one state has debated the possibility demonstrates that it is not unthinkable.

There is no single formula governing the monetary path of a country from constituent and subordinate element of a union to an independent, sovereign, and internationally recognized state with full monetary sovereignty exercised by its own central bank. Nor need there be a single model for an independent state in forming a monetary union with other states. Rather than a straightforward, binary question of sovereignty or no sovereignty, history shows that, when it comes to money, there is a sovereignty spectrum, at one end of which some states conclude that the right thing for them to do is to adopt the currency of another state or fix their currency to that of another state through a currency board mechanism. Yet others on a different point of the sovereignty spectrum choose to pool their monetary sovereignty with that of other states, while some, such as Britain, Japan, and Switzerland, continue to operate with the apparatus of classical monetary independence (even if independence has to operate in a monetary universe molded by the actions of other monetary authorities, above all, the Federal Reserve).

And, at the further end of the spectrum, a currency—currently the dollar—achieves, by virtue of its strength and reliability and the geopolitical clout of the country that issues it, what is in effect extraterritorial sovereignty: a currency used by other states and possessed of a political power that goes beyond its own borders. In this respect there has been much speculation surrounding the possibility of China's renminbi as a future world reserve currency. However, Zhou Xiaochuan, the former governor of the People's Bank of China, decried the idea of basing the international monetary order on a single national currency (code for the US dollar). But Xiaochuan also warned against encouraging the emergence of the renminbi as a leading international currency. Indeed, he urged the international community to devise an international reserve currency that is disconnected from national domestic interests.[6]

Long term, Xiaochuan is surely right: the increasing globalization of world economic activity should be supported by forms of money that are insulated from shocks or distortions generated by a single country's domestic policies. The emergence of a truly internationalized reserve currency—internationalized in the sense that it is based on a variety of currencies or indeed a new monetary unit and is removed from the control of a single state—would supply the requirement for a reserve currency resistant to political influence and manipulation. This would of course require the creation of an international institution to act as the guarantor of such a system, a successor to the role played by gold during the era of the gold standard. The logical starting point for the creation of such an institution and an internationalized reserve currency would, Xiaochuan suggested, be the International Monetary Fund and its existing system of special drawing rights. A detailed investigation of this idea is, however, beyond the scope of this book.

Some economists go further and propose that money can and should cease to be a matter for central governments and central banks altogether. In one version of this, money is viewed as just another commodity that can be supplied by private entities acting in competition with each other.[7] This idea had appeared in China among Confucian thinkers in the second century before the Christian Era. So it is not entirely new. While the idea might have its attractions today for many when confidence in central banks has been severely damaged by the financial crash of 2008 and the European sovereign debt crisis following it, it would require a daring government to take the plunge and entirely abdicate its responsibility for supervision of the national monetary architecture and issue of currency. Populations tend to be conservative in monetary matters (so long as their money is working adequately). They expect governments to use monetary policy actively and effectively, or, if an independent monetary policy cannot be efficiently managed, then at least stable alternatives must be adopted. As we have seen, history records many examples of periods when a currency issued by one country freely circulated in another, but these have usually ended by the government of the latter asserting or reasserting its control. Similarly, devolution of monetary issue rights within a state has all too often led to confusion and resulted in a reversal of policy. This was so in the Netherlands in the sixteenth century, in the United States in the nineteenth century, and in the Latin Monetary Union in the late nineteenth century.

In this respect, it is possible, as some people propose, that an altogether more libertarian and yet in some ways more robust approach would be better—that private moneys should be allowed to circulate freely, but that governments should resist the temptation to bail out the issuer at the time of crisis. The premise on which this idea is based is that this would induce a more cautious set of behaviors on the part of the commercial issuers. The threat of moral hazard—the temptation to take injudicious risks knowing that another will pick up the bill—would be removed by the prospect of the commercial issuer having no safety net in the form of a government bailout. In the extreme, the directors of a failing commercial currency issue would be personally liable to creditors for their failure. But, for this to work, requires not only a certain amount of fear-induced prudence on the part of the commercial parties (a prudence that all too often is shown to be lacking in the most enterprising of risk takers, even when the consequences are clearly severe), but also a political courage rarely found among officials and political figures. This courage means not only a willingness to let a commercial currency fail with serious consequences for a limited number of directors of the company concerned, but also and more seriously, a willingness to allow all those holding the money issued by that company to be left holding worthless currency. If the amount of currency on issue is relatively small, it is possible to imagine a government allowing it to fail. But what if it amounts to a very large value such that its failure might prove a threat to the livelihood of a large part of the population? And what would this mean for the ability of those affected to pay their taxes? While a government is responsible for the issue of legal tender, it must accept that currency in settlement of taxes. But it would surely be impossible to accept commercially issued currencies in settlement of taxes when those currencies have collapsed in value, perhaps due to mismanagement by the commercial issuer. It is easy to see how governments would do everything possible to avoid being put in such a position.

Nevertheless, new challenges to the orthodox forms of monetary sovereignty always emerge, and quite often they take the form of innovation. In our own era it is conceivable that, should commercial activity on a variety of private digital currency platforms, such as Bitcoin, develop critical mass to the extent that it starts to crowd out nationally issued currencies, then the national monopoly of money issue may well start to decline as the accepted norm. The question of private digital currencies in settlement of taxes is even more problematic given that they have been designed to operate outside of government regulation and scrutiny. Although the central banks of major developed countries do not see these new private digital trading tokens as genuine currency, but rather as speculative investments, they have recognized their emergence as a reality and in some cases see them as a direct threat to national (monetary) sovereignty. And because the proliferation of these private digital systems may threaten national monopolies of money, a number of national monetary authorities are responding by working on their own digital currencies, so-called central bank digital currencies.[8]

History shows that private sector monetary innovations are often taken over or at least regulated by the public sector, usually, because of some actual or potential threat of a major systemic breakdown in monetary activity or undermining of control. Whether this best serves the common good or not is open to debate, but it does seem to be the norm. This was the case with the introduction of paper notes by traders in China at the end of the tenth century, subsequently controlled and produced by regional governments. It was also the case with the later paper currency issued in Sweden in the seventeenth century, initially issued by a commercial bank and then by the public Riksbank for very similar reasons.[9]

But the dramatic impact of the internet on trading habits may lead to changes in the national character of money that we can barely imagine today. The national symbols and culture that banknotes present to the public, for instance, will have little or no role to play in currencies that exist in purely digital form. In the absence of such overtly nationalist symbols, the compulsion to issue national currencies would be further diminished and leave the way open to a single digital currency serving a group of countries that have closely interlinked economies. Some commentators assert, however, that new nationally issued digital currencies will continue to reflect national interests and that there will be competition between the leading currency issuers to be leaders in the new centrally issued digital currency world.[10]

Currencies will certainly reflect national economic and even political interests. But we must beware of unfounded claims for the political powers of currency: it does not confer international recognition on a country aspiring to independence. It is not true that the collapse of a monetary system must lead to war. The sharing of a currency by two states does not mean that they are necessarily politically conjoined. The attribution of such powers to currency is at worst political legerdemain and, at best, ignorance. Currency is essentially a tool to support trade and maintain value earned. The acceptance of this simpler characterization of money will liberate governments and central banks to adopt the monetary regime that best works for their countries, free of the mystique of nationalism.

For individual nations, there is a range of currency regime options from which to choose without fear of compromising national sovereignty in the political sense. Governments should be willing to abandon the obsolete belief that every independent country must have its own currency; they should dare to adopt the currency regime that will best serve their countries by ensuring monetary stability and facilitating trade. The idea of monetary sovereignty seen in black and white terms of a country either having monetary sovereignty or not having it is becoming a thing of the past. Increasingly, when it comes to money, people are coming to understand that there are shades of sovereignty.

NOTES

1. Robert Mundell, "Money and the Sovereignty of the State," paper presented at the International Economic Association Conference, Trento, September 4–7, 1997, accessed January 9, 2020, https://www-ceel.economia.unitn.it/events/monetary/mundell14.pdf. This paper provides a very detailed history of the matter of monetary sovereignty in Europe and America.

2. Lucia Kubosova, "EU to Question Montenegro's Use of the Euro," *EU Observer*, October 8, 2007, https://euobserver.com/enlargement/24924.

3. Francois Gianviti, "Current Legal Aspects of Monetary Sovereignty," paper presented at the International Monetary Fund Seminar on Current Developments in Monetary and Financial Law, May 24–June 4, 2004, Washington, DC, https://www.imf.org/external/np/leg/sem/2004/cdmfl/eng/gianvi.pdf.

4. Mundell, "Money and the Sovereignty of the State," 5.

5. "House Joint Resolution No. 590," January 2013, LIS (Virginia's Legislative Information System).

6. Paola Subacchi, *The Cost of Free Money* (New Haven, CT: Yale University Press, 2020), 67, 99–100.

7. F. A. Hayek, "Denationalisation of Money," Institute of Economic Affairs, accessed January 7, 2020, https://iea.org.uk/wp-content/uploads/2016/07/Denationalisation%20of%20Money.pdf.

8. "Retail CBDCs: The Next Payments Frontier," Official Monetary and Financial Institutions Forum and IBM, 4, https://www.omfif.org/wp-content/uploads/2019/11/Retail-CBDCs-The-next-payments-frontier.pdf.

9. William N. Goetzmann and Geert K. Rouwenhorst, *The Origins of Value: The Financial Innovations That Created Modern Capital Markets* (Oxford: Oxford University Press, 2005), 68.

10. Philip Middleton, "Prepare for Digital Currency Wars," Official Monetary and Financial Institutions Forum, October 21, 2020, https://www.omfif.org/2020/10/prepare-for-digital-currency-wars/.

Bibliography

PRIMARY SOURCES

Basic Law of the Hong Kong Special Administrative Region of the People's Republic of China.

Council/Commission of the European Communities. "Report to the Council and the Commission on the Realisation by Stages of Economic and Monetary Union in the Community, Werner Report." http://aei.pitt.edu/1002/1/monetary_werner_final.pdf.

Council/Commission of the European Communities. "Treaty on European Union." February 7, 1992. https://europa.eu/european-union/sites/europaeu/files/docs/body/treaty_on_european_union_en.pdf.

Dail in Committee (Irish Free State). Coinage Bill, 1926. Second-stage debate, January 27, 1926.

Delors, Jacques. "Report on Economic and Monetary Union in the European Community." April 17, 1989. http://aei.pitt.edu/1007/1/monetary_delors.pdf.

Hamilton, Alexander. "The Report of the Secretary of the Treasury, Alexander Hamilton, on the Subject of a National Bank: Read in the House of Representatives, Dec. 13th, 1790." https://fraser.stlouisfed.org/title/report-secretary-treasury-alexander-hamilton-subject-a-national-bank-3677.

Indian Councils Act, 1861. https://archive.org/details/indiancouncilsac00grearich/page/20/mode/2up?q=currency.

Israel Ministry of Foreign Affairs. "Paris Protocol on Economic Relations between the Government of the State of Israel and the PLO Representing the Palestinian People." Article IV, Paris, April 29, 1994. https://mfa.gov.il/MFA/ForeignPolicy/Peace/Guide/Pages/Gaza-Jericho%20Agreement%20Annex%20IV%20-%20Economic%20Protoco.aspx.

Law No. 2 of 1997 of the Palestinian Monetary Authority. https://www.pma.ps/Portals/0/Users/002/02/2/Legislation/Laws/Law_No_2_of_1997_on_Palestinian_Monetary_Authority.pdf.

League of Nations. "Mandate for Palestine and Memorandum by the British Government Relating to Its Application for Transjordan" and "Article 25 of the Palestine Mandate Memorandum by the British Representative." September 16, 1922. https://dl.wdl.org/11572/service/11572.pdf.

Ministry of Foreign Affairs of the People's Republic of China. "The Chinese Government Resumed Exercise of Sovereignty over Hong Kong." Accessed March 28, 2021. https://www.fmprc.gov.cn/mfa_eng/ziliao_665539/3602_665543/3604_665547/t18032.shtml.

Organisation of Eastern Caribbean States. "Economic Union Treaty: Frequently Asked Questions (FAQs)." April 2008. http://ctrc.sice.oas.org/CARICOM/OECS/FAQs_OECS_Integration.pdf.

Scottish Parliament. "Report on the Scottish Government's Proposals for an Independent Scotland," Second Report, https://archive2021.parliament.scot/S4_EuropeanandExternalRelationsCommittee/Reports/euR-14-02w-rev.pdf.

Sustainable Growth Commission. "The Monetary Policy and Financial Regulation Framework for an Independent Scotland," C1.23. May 2018. https://static1.squarespace.com/static/5afc0bbbf79392ced8b73dbf/t/5b06e8a56d2a73f9e030 5ad9/1527179438303/SGC+Part+C+Currency+Monetary+Framework.pdf.

UK Government National Archives. "Beith, J. G. S. (Foreign Office) to Higham, J. (Colonial Office)." 18 March 1948, Cabinet Office File 537/3878, The National Archives, Kew.

UK Government National Archives. "Future of the Palestine Currency Board." Cabinet Office File CO 537/2307 The National Archives, Kew.

UK Government National Archives. "Letter from Egyptian Ministry of Finance, Cairo to Foreign Office." August 24, 1951, Foreign Office File FO 371/91388, The National Archives, Kew.

UK Government National Archives. "Letter from Foreign Office to Bank Leumi." June 20, 1951, Foreign Office File 371/ 91388, Palestine Currency Board, The National Archives, Kew.

UK Government National Archives. "Palestine Currency Board to Under-Secretary of State." Colonial Office 11 June, Cabinet Office File 537/3878, The National Archives, Kew.

UK Parliament. Debate of March 2, 1948, on Sterling Balances (Palestine). https://www.theyworkforyou.com/debates/?id=1948-03-02a.205.10&s=Sterling+balances+Palestine#g207.5.

UK Parliament. Debate of July 12, 1949 on Sterling Balances (Palestine). https://www.theyworkforyou.com/debates/?id=1949-07-12a.202.3.

United Nations. Joint Declaration of the Government of Great Britain and Northern Ireland and the Government of the People's Republic of China on the Question of Hong Kong, 3(2), https://treaties.un.org/doc/Publication/UNTS/Volume%201399/v1399.pdf.

United Nations Conciliation Commission for Palestine. "Note on Palestine Assets." https://www.un.org/unispal/document/frozen-assets-of-the-palestine-currency-board-unccp-working-paper/.

United Nations Conciliation Commission for Palestine. "Status of the Question of Unfreezing of Assets (Report of M. Servoise)." November 23, 1949. https://www.un.org/unispal/document/auto-insert-211947/.

United Nations Conciliation Commission for Palestine. "Summary Record of the Two Hundred and Sixth Meeting." https://unispal.un.org/DPA/DPR/unispal.nsf/0/B9B43F8E135A5C7585256BE9006C6E04.

United Nations General Assembly. "Resolution 181." https://www.trumanlibrary.org/israel/unres181.htm.

United Nations Missions in Sudan. "Comprehensive Peace Agreement—Naivasha." May 26, 2004, Part V Schedules, Schedule A—National Powers.

United Nations Palestine Commission. "Communication Received from the Jewish Agency for Palestine Concerning Currency Arrangements." March 18, 1948. https://www.un.org/unispal/document/un-palestine-commission-currency-arrange-ments-communication-from-the-jewish-agency-for-palestine/.

United Nations Palestine Commission. "Communication Received from the United Kingdom Delegation Concerning the Palestine Currency Board." https://www.un.org/unispal/document/un-palestine-commission-palestine-currency-board-letter-from-united-kingdom.

United Nations Palestine Commission. "First Special Report to the Security Council: The Problem of Security in Palestine." https://unispal.un.org/DPA/DPR/unispal.nsf/5ba47a5c6cef541b802563e000493b8c/fdf734eb76c39d6385256c4c004cdba7?OpenDocument.

United Nations Palestine Commission. "Report from the Advance Party Concerning Discussion with Finance and Currency Officers." March 10, 1948. https://www.un.org/unispal/document/un-palestine-commission-finance-currency-report-from-the-advance-party/.

United Nations Palestine Commission. "Report of the Palestine Commission to the Second Special Session of the General Assembly of the United Nations: Introduction." Paragraph F3. https://unispal.un.org/DPA/DPR/unispal.nsf/0/BCE2BD823185E523802564AA0056DAEA.

United Nations Transitional Administration in East Timor (UNTAET). "Explaining the Currency of East Timor: Questions and Answers about Using the United States Dollar (US$)." https://peacekeeping.un.org/mission/past/etimor/untaetPU/currency.pdf.

Yale Law School. "The Palestine Mandate, Article 2." http://avalon.law.yale.edu/20th_century/palmanda.asp.

SECONDARY SOURCES

Abdelal, Rawi. "Contested Currency: Russia's Ruble in Domestic and International Politics." *Journal of Communist Studies and Transition Politics* 19, no. 2 (2003): 55–76.

Aboa, Ange. "West Africa Renames CFA Franc but Keeps It Pegged to Euro." *Reuters*. December 21, 2019. https://www.reuters.com/article/us-ivorycoast-france-macron-idUSKBN1YP0JR.

des Adom, Assandé, "Beyond the CFA Franc: An Empirical Analysis of the Choice of an Exchange Rate Regime in the UEMOA," *Economic Issues* 17, Part 2 (2012): 76.

Ahamad, Liaquat. *Lords of Finance: The Bankers Who Broke the World.* London: Windmill Books, 2010.

Amum, Pagan. South Sudan's Minister for Peace, quoted by the BBC. *BBC Africa*, July 25, 2011.

Armstrong, Angus, and Monique Ebell. "Scotland's Currency Options." Discussion Paper. September 17, 2013. Centre on Constitutional Change. https://www.centreonconstitutionalchange.ac.uk/sites/default/files/migrated/papers/scotlands_currency_options.pdf.

Arnold, Matthew, and Matthew LeRiche. *South Sudan: From Revolution to Independence*. London: C. Hurst and Co. Ltd., 2012.

Arnon, Arie, and Avia Spiva. "Monetary Integration Between the Israeli, Jordanian and Palestinian Economies." Discussion Paper 95.11. Bank of Israel. https://www.boi.org.il/en/Research/Pages/papers-dp9511.aspx.

Arnott, Margaret. "Brexit and a Second Scottish Independence Referendum: What Happens Next?" Political Studies Association. February 22, 2019. https://www.psa.ac.uk/psa/news/brexit-and-second-scottish-independence-referendum-what-happens-next.

Aucoin, Louis, and Michele Brandt. "East Timor's Constitutional Passage to Independence." In *Framing the State in Times of Transition: Case Studies in Constitution Making*, edited by Laurel Miller, 245–274. Washington, DC: United States Institute of Peace Press, 2010.

Bagnetto, Laura Angela. "End of CFA Franc in West Africa 'Only a Symbolic Change': Economist." Radio France International. December 22, 2019. https://www.rfi.fr/en/africa/20191222-end-cfa-franc-west-africa-only-symbolic-change-economist.

Bakke, Elisabeth. "The Principle of National Self-Determination in Czechoslovak Constitutions, 1920-1992." https://www.researchgate.net/publication/342572105_The_principle_of_national_self-determination_in_Czechoslovak_constitutions_1920-1992.

Ball, Laurence. "Hard Currency Pegs." In *Handbook of Monetary Economics*, Vol. 3B, edited by Benjamin M. Friedman and Michael Woodford, 1328–31. Amsterdam: North-Holland, 2011.

Barkey, Henry J. "Kurdistan, Scotland and Catalonia: They Just Want to Be Free, or Do They?" *Los Angeles Times*, July 16, 2014. https://www.latimes.com/opinion/op-ed/la-oe-0717-barkey-kurdistan-scotland-catalonia-20140717-story.html.

Basch, A. "Development Projects in Jordan." International Bank for Reconstruction and Development, June 25, 1951.

Bernanke, Ben, and Harold James. "The Gold Standard, Deflation, and Financial Crisis in the Great Depression: An International Comparison." In *Financial Markets and Financial Crises*, edited by R. Glenn Hubbard, 43. Chicago: University of Chicago Press, 1991.

Biryabarema, Elias. "East African Trade Bloc Approves Monetary Union Deal." *Reuters*, November 30, 2013, https://www.reuters.com/article/us-africa-monetaryunion-idUSBRE9AT08O20131130.

Black, Andrew. "Scottish Independence: Currency Debate Explained." *BBC News*. January 29, 2014. https://www.bbc.co.uk/news/uk-scotland-scotland-politics-25913721.

Blanchard, Ben, Michael Holden, and Venus Wu. "China Says Sino-British Joint Declaration on Hong Kong No Longer Has Meaning." *Reuters*. June 30, 2017. https://www.reuters.com/article/us-hongkong-anniversary-china-idUSKBN19L1J1.

Bokarev, Y., V. Kuchkin, and V. Stepanov. *History of Monetary Circulation of Russia.* Moscow: Bank of Russia, 2010.

Booth, Philip. "Solving the Scottish Currency Conundrum." Institute of Economic Affairs. June 11, 2019. https://iea.org.uk/solving-the-scottish-currency-conundrum/.

Bordo, Michael, and Lars Jonung. "The Future of EMU: What Does the History of Monetary Unions Tell Us?" Working paper, National Bureau of Economic Research, 1999. https://www.nber.org/papers/w7365.

Bosco, Joseph. "What China's Stance on Hong Kong Means for US–Taiwan Relations." The Diplomat, July 2017. https://thediplomat.com/2017/07/what-chinas-stance-on-hong-kong-means-for-us-taiwan-relations/.

Bridge, Adrian. "Czechs and Slovaks Split Their Currency." *The Independent*, February 3, 1993. https://www.independent.co.uk/news/business/czechs-and-slovaks-split-their-currency-1470651.html.

Brione, Patrick. "The Great Scottish Currency Debate and an Important Note on Methodology." Survation, February 19, 2014. https://www.survation.com/the-great-scottish-currency-debate-an-important-note-on-methodology/.

Buck, John. "Catalonia Considering Cryptocurrency Post-Independence, Advised by Ethereum Creator." *Cointelegraph*, October 28, 2017. https://cointelegraph.com/news/catalonia-considering-cryptocurrency-post-independence-advised-by-ethereum-creator.

Buksbaum, Noam. "Israel Prints First Money Using Ceylon Template." *Haaretz*, April 13, 2018. https://www.haaretz.com/israel-news/business/forgotten-stories-from-70-years-of-israeli-economic-history-1.5994597.

Burdekin, Richard C. K. "Currency Boards vs. Dollarization: Lessons from the Cook Islands." *Cato Journal* 28, no. 1 (2008): 101–15. https://www.cato.org/sites/cato.org/files/serials/files/cato-journal/2008/1/cj28n1-7.pdf.

Burgen, Stephen. "Catalan Politicians Charged a Year after Independence Vote." *The Guardian*, November 2, 2018. https://www.theguardian.com/world/2018/nov/02/catalan-politicians-charged-a-year-after-independence-vote-referendum.

Butlin, S. J. "Foundations of the Australian Monetary System 1788–1851." University of Sydney Library, 2002. http://setis.library.usyd.edu.au/pubotbin/sup2pdfall?id=sup0003.

Businesstech. "EFF's Plan to Nationalise South Africa's Reserve Bank Takes First Step." November 2, 2020. https://businesstech.co.za/news/banking/444996/effs-plan-to-nationalise-south-africas-reserve-bank-takes-first-step/.

Businesstech. "Rand vs the Dollar: 1978–2016." March 13, 2016. https://businesstech.co.za/news/finance/116372/rand-vs-the-dollar-1978-2016/.

Carapico, Sheila. "The Economic Dimension of Yemeni Unity." *Middle East Report* 184, no. 5 (1993): 9–14.

Caryl, Christian. "The World's Next Country." *Foreign Policy*, January 21, 2015. https://foreignpolicy.com/2015/01/21/the-worlds-next-country-kurdistan-kurds-iraq/.

Cermakova, Klara. "Brief History of Currency Separation: Case Study of Czech and Slovak Koruna." *International Journal of Economic Sciences* VI, no. 2 (2017): 30–44.

Chalmers, Robert. *A History of Currency in the British Colonies*. London: HM Stationery Office, 1893.

Chernow, Ron. *Alexander Hamilton*. New York: Penguin Press, 2004.

Chiminya, Johannes. "Sustainability of Rand Union?" *The Financial Gazette*, September 25, 2009.

Chiu, Priscilla. "Hong Kong's Experience in Operating the Currency Board System." International Monetary Fund, 2001. https://www.imf.org/external/pubs/ft/seminar/2001/err/eng/chiu.pdf.

Chown, John F. *A History of Money from AD 800*. New York: Routledge, 1996.

Cobham, David. "Alternative Currency Arrangements for a New Palestinian State." In *The Economics of Palestine: Economic Policy and Institutional Reform for a Viable Palestinian State*, edited by David Cobham and Nu'man Kanafani, 38–59. London: Routledge, 2004.

Copnall, James. *A Poisonous Thorn in Our Hearts: Sudan and South Sudan's Bitter and Incomplete Divorce.* London: Hurst, 2014.

Coulibaly, Issiaka. "Costs and Benefits of the CFA Franc." *World Policy*. February 28, 2017. http://worldpolicy.org/2017/02/28/costs-and-benefits-of-the-cfa-franc/.

Crick, W. F. *Commonwealth Banking Systems*. Oxford: Clarendon Press, 1965.

Dabrowski, Marek. "The Reasons of the Collapse of the Ruble Zone." Center for Social & Economic Research, 1995. http://case-research.eu/sites/default/files/publications/3460035_058e_0.pdf.

Darwish, Adel. "Arafat to Demand Palestine's Gold." *The Independent*, December 13, 1993. https://www.independent.co.uk/news/world/arafat-to-demand-palestines-gold-1467152.html.

Davies, Glyn. *A History of Money: From Ancient Times to the Present Day*. Cardiff: University of Wales Press, 2002.

Deane, Marjorie, and Robert Pringle. *The Central Banks.* New York: Viking Press, 1995.

De Brouwer, Gordon. "Currency and Monetary Arrangements for East Timor." Australian National University, April 5, 2001. https://crawford.anu.edu.au/pdf/staff/gordon_debrouwer/GdB01-01.pdf.

Del Mar, Alexander. *Barbara Villiers: A History of Monetary Crimes*. Hawaii: University Press of the Pacific, 2004.

Deyell, John S. "The Development of Akbar's Currency System and Monetary Integration of the Conquered Kingdoms." In *The Imperial Monetary System of Mughal India*, edited by John F. Richards, 13–67. Delhi: Oxford University Press, 1987.

Durand, Frederick. "Three Centuries of Violence and Struggle in East Timor." SciencesPo. October 14, 2011. https://www.sciencespo.fr/mass-violence-war-massacre-resistance/en/document/three-centuries-violence-and-struggle-east-timor-1726-2008.

Eastern Caribbean Central Bank. "Monetary Unions in the Caribbean Context: The Challenges Faced by the Eastern Caribbean Currency Union since the Financial Crisis." March 16, 2016. 20190118_monetary_unions_in_the_caribbean_context_ii.pdf (centralbank.cw).

Edinburgh News. "Scottish Independence: New Scots Currency Plan If Yes Wins New Vote." May 20, 2018. https://www.edinburghnews.scotsman.com/news/politics/scottish-independence-new-scots-currency-plan-if-yes-wins-new-vote-290099.

Eichengreen, Barry. *Exorbitant Privilege*. Oxford: Oxford University Press, 2011.

Elligett, Patrick. "From Treasure Island to World's Newest Nation: What Is Happening in Bougainville?" *Sydney Morning Herald*, December 11, 2019. https://www.smh.com.au/world/oceania/from-treasure-island-to-world-s-newest-nation-what-is-happening-in-bougainville-20191127-p53eph.html.

Fagiolo, Nicoletta. "The CFA Franc: Africa's Financial Anachronism." October 17, 2015. https://www.free-simone-and-laurent-gbagbo.com/single-post/2017/12/12/the-cfa-franc-africa-s-financial-anachronism.

Fessehazion, Tekie. "Eritrean and Ethiopian State of Economic Relations: A Nakfa/Birr/LC Analysis." Denden Media. http://www.denden.com/Conflict/newscom/com-tek98.htm.

Fidrmuc, Jan, Julius Horvath, and Jarko Fidrmuc. "The Stability of Monetary Unions: Lessons from the Breakup of Czechoslovakia." *Journal of Comparative Economics* 27(1999): 753–81. http://cms-content.bates.edu/prebuilt/fidrmuc,horvath&fidrmuc.pdf.

Foot, Michael, and Isaac Kramnick, eds. *The Thomas Paine Reader.* London: Penguin, 1987.

Foreman-Peck, James. "Lessons from Italian Monetary Unification." Working paper 113, Austrian National Bank, 2006. https://www.researchgate.net/publication/4801732_Lessons_from_Italian_Monetary_Unification.

Gallarotti, Giulio M. "The Scramble for Gold: Monetary Regime Transformation in the 1870s." In *Monetary Regimes in Transition*, edited by Michael D. Bordo and Forrest Capie, 15–67. New York: Cambridge University Press, 1994.

Gianviti, Francois. "Current Legal Aspects of Monetary Sovereignty." Paper presented at the International Monetary Fund Seminar on Current Developments in

Monetary and Financial Law, May 24–June 4, 2004, Washington, DC. https://www.imf.org/external/np/leg/sem/2004/cdmfl/eng/gianvi.pdf.

Girmay, Haile Selassie. "Ethiopia-Eritrea Border Conflict: The Role Nakfa Played." Ethiopian Embassy to the United Kingdom, 2010.

Goetzmann, William N., and Geert K. Rouwenhorst. *The Origins of Value: The Financial Innovations That Created Modern Capital Markets*. Oxford: Oxford University Press, 2005.

Goldie, Iain. "The Economics of Catalan Secession from Spain." *Global Politics*. August 4, 2017. https://global-politics.co.uk/2017/08/04/economics-catalan-secession-spain/.

Grant, I. F. *The Social and Economic Development of Scotland before 1603*. London: Oliver and Boyd, 1930.

Habte Selassie, Bereket. "Dreams That Turned to Nightmares: The Ethio-Eritrean War of 1998-2000 and Its Aftermath." In *The Search for Peace: The Conflict between Ethiopia and Eritrea.* Proceedings of Scholarly Conference on the Ethiopia–Eritrea Conflict, Oslo, July 6–7, 2006.

Hainsworth, Paul. "From Occupation and Civil War to Nation-Statehood: East Timor and the Struggle for Self-Determination and Freedom from Indonesia." Institute for British–Irish Studies, IBIS Discussion Paper No. 5, University College Dublin. Accessed January 7, 2020. https://www.ucd.ie/ibis/filestore/p_hainsworth.pdf.

Hanke, Steve. "Argentina's Peso: Nothing but Trouble." *Forbes*, March 16, 2019. https://www.forbes.com/sites/stevehanke/2019/03/16/argentinas-peso-nothing-but-trouble/?sh=32f1789c2a9a.

Hanke, Steve. "Argentina Should Scrap the Peso and Dollarize." *Forbes*, June 29, 2018. https://www.forbes.com/sites/stevehanke/2018/06/29/argentina-should-scrap-the-peso-and-dollarize/?sh=5ad2ffad393e.

Hanke, Steve, and Kurt Schuler. "Currency Boards and Currency Convertibility." *Cato Journal* 12, no. 3 (1993), 687–727. Accessed January 7, 2020. http://latlibre.org/wp-content/uploads/2019/02/99Schuler02.pdf.

Hanke, Steve, and Kurt Schuler. "Currency Boards for Developing Countries: A Handbook." Institute for Contemporary Studies. Accessed January 7, 2020. https://sites.krieger.jhu.edu/iae/files/2017/06/Currency_Boards_for_Developing_Countries.pdf.

Hanson, Ardo H. "Transforming an Economy While Building a Nation: The Case of Estonia." Working Paper 113, World Institute for Development Economics Research, United Nations University, July 1993. https://www.wider.unu.edu/sites/default/files/WP113.pdf.

Hayek, F. A. "Denationalisation of Money." Institute of Economic Affairs. Accessed January 7, 2020. https://iea.org.uk/wp-content/uploads/2016/07/Denationalisation%20of%20Money.pdf.

Helleiner, Eric. *The Making of National Money: Territorial Currencies in Historical Perspective.* New York: Cornell University Press, 2003.

Henze, Paul. "Introduction." In *Eritrea's War: Confrontation, International Response, Outcome, Prospects*. Addis Ababa: Shama Books, 2001.

Herbert, Ross. "The End of the Eritrean Exception?" Country Report No. 8, South African Institute of International Affairs, 2002.

Ho, Stephanie. "History of Singapore Currency." https://eresources.nlb.gov.sg/infopedia/articles/SIP_2016-03-09_114438.html.

Honohan, Patrick. "Currency Board or Central Bank? Lessons from the Irish Pound's Link with Sterling 1928-1979." Economic and Social Research Institute, 1994. Accessed January 7, 2020. https://www.researchgate.net/publication/4836435_Currency_Board_or_Central_Bank_Lessons_from_the_Irish_Pound%27s_Link_with_Sterling_1928-79.

Horesh, Niv. *Chinese Money in Global Context: Historic Junctures between 600 BCE and 2012.* Stanford: Stanford University Press, 2014.

Huang, Michael Lee, and Auke Leen. "How a Free Market System Resulted in Hegemony and a Magnificent Era: The Case of Nobunaga Oda, 16th Century Japan." Archives of Economic History. Accessed January 7, 2020. http://www.vonmisesinstitute-europe.org/wp-content/uploads/2018/10/article-A.-R.-Leen-met-M.-Huang-about-Japan.pdf.

Inbaraj, Sonny. "East Timor: Language, Currency a Sore Point for New Nation." *Inter Press Service*, January 21, 2000. http://www.ipsnews.net/2000/01/east-timor-language-currency-a-sore-point-for-new-nation/.

Isaacson, Walter. *Benjamin Franklin: An American Life.* New York: Simon & Schuster, 2003.

Ismael, Yara Kamaran. "Is It Time Just Yet for a Kurdish Currency?" *The Kurdistan Tribune*, July 19, 2015. https://kurdistantribune.com/is-it-time-just-yet-for-a-kurdish-currency/.

James, Harold. "Monetary and Fiscal Unification in Nineteenth-Century Germany: What Can Kohl Learn from Bismarck?" Princeton Department of Economics, 1997. https://ies.princeton.edu/pdf/E202.pdf.

Jefferis, Keith. "Monetary and Exchange Rate Management: Policies and Processes for Stability and Growth." International Growth Centre. October 8, 2015. http://www.theigc.org/event/monetary-and-exchange-rate-management-policies-and-processes-for-stability-and-growth/.

Karmin, Craig. *Biography of the Dollar*. New York: Three Rivers Press, 2008.

Keller, Arnold, and John Sandrock. "The Significance of Stamps Used on Banknotes." *The Currency Collector*, http://thecurrencycollector.com/pdfs/The_Significance_of_Stamps_Used_on_Bank_Notes.pdf.

Kelso, C. Edward. "Catalonia Referendum Allegedly Funded by Bitcoin." *Bitcoin News*. November 26, 2017. https://news.bitcoin.com/cryptos-revolutionary-moment-catalonia-referendum-allegedly-funded-by-bitcoin/.

Keynes, John Maynard. *Indian Currency and Finance.* Cambridge: Cambridge University Press for the Royal Economic Society, 2013.

Kheng, Cheah Boon. "The Separation of Singapore." Malaysian Bar, July 25, 2007, https://www.malaysianbar.org.my/article/news/legal-and-general-news/general-news/the-separation-of-singapore.

Khourry, Garrett. "The Original Sin of Yemen." Medium Corporation. March 26, 2015. https://medium.com/the-eastern-project/the-original-sin-of-yemen-fde04ab298e6.

Kifle, Temesgen. "Can Border Demarcation Help Eritrea to Reverse the General Slowdown in Growth?" Institute of World Economics and International Management, University of Bremen, 2004.

Kindleberger, Charles P. *A Financial History of Western Europe*. London: Routledge, 2006.

Kirshner, Jonathan. *Currency and Coercion*. Princeton, NJ: Princeton University Press, 1995.

Kubosova, Lucia. "EU to Question Montenegro's Use of the Euro." *EU Observer*. October 8, 2007. https://euobserver.com/enlargement/24924.Kuttab, Daoud. "Palestine May Replace Israeli Currency to Reduce Dependency." *Arab News*. February 18, 2018. https://www.arabnews.com/node/1248701/middle-east.

Kwarteng, Kwasi. *War and Gold*. London: Bloomsbury, 2014.

Kwon, Goohoon. "Experiences with Monetary Integration and Lessons for Korean Unification." Working Paper 1997/65. International Monetary Fund, May 1997. https://www.imf.org/external/pubs/ft/wp/wp9765.pdf.

Lainela, Seija, and Pekka Sutela. "Introducing New Currencies in the Baltic Countries." Bank of Finland, Institute for Economies in Transition, October 8, 1993.

Lata, Leenco. "The Causes, Mediation and Settlement of the Ethio-Eritrea Conflict." In *The Search for Peace: The Conflict between Ethiopia and Eritrea*. FAFO Report 2007/14.

Lavelle, Peter. "What Currency Would an Independent Catalonia Have?" *Homage to BCN* (Blog), November 11, 2013. https://homagetobcn.com/catalonia-currency/.

Li, Jiang. "Analysis of the Czech and Slovak Different Strategic Choices towards the Eurozone." *Romanian Journal of European Affairs* 16, no. 1 (2016): 73–77.

Lim, Edmund. "Behind the Scenes: What Led to Separation in 1965." *The Straits Times*, August 5, 2015.

Lob, Emilie. "Have West, Central Africa Outgrown the CFA Franc?" *Voice of America*. April 26, 2016. https://www.voanews.com/africa/have-west-central-africa-outgrown-cfa-franc.Lo Cascio, Elio. "The Function of Gold Coinage in the Monetary Economy of the Roman Empire." In *The Monetary Systems of the Greeks and Romans*, edited by W. V. Harris, 161. Oxford: Oxford University Press, 2010.

Marshall, Jonathan. "Dirty Wars: French and American Piaster Profiteering in Indochina, 1945-75." *The Asia-Pacific Journal* 12, no. 32 (2014): 3–10.

Martin, Felix. *Money: The Unauthorized Biography*. London: The Bodley Head, 2013.

Mason, R. H. P., and J. G. Caiger. *A History of Japan*. North Clarendon, VT: Tuttle Publishing, 1997.

Mauri, Arnaldo. "Eritrea's Early Stages in Monetary and Banking Development." Working paper 28, University of Milan, 2003.

M'Bet, Allechi, and Amlan Madeleine Niamkey. "European Economic Integration and the Franc Zone: The Future of the CFA Franc after 1996." African Economic Research Consortium, Research Paper 19, July 1993. http://opendocs.ids.ac.uk/opendocs/bitstream/handle/123456789/2046/No%2019.pdf?sequence=1.

McKernan, Bethan. "Kurdistan Referendum Results: 93% of Iraqi Kurds Vote for Independence, Say Reports." *The Independent*, September 27, 2017. https://www.independent.co.uk/news/world/middle-east/kurdistan-referendum-results-vote-yes-iraqi-kurds-independence-iran-syria-a7970241.html.

Melliss, C. L., and Mark Cornelius. "New Currencies in the Former Soviet Union: A Recipe for Hyperinflation or the Path to Price Stability?" Working Paper 26, Bank of England, September 1, 1994. https://www.bankofengland.co.uk/working-paper/1994/new-currencies-in-the-former-soviet-union-a-recipe-for-hyperinfla-tion-or-the-path-to-price-stability.

Mencinge, Jože. "Financial Regulation in Slovenia." http://www.sinteza.co/wp-con-tent/uploads/2016/01/Zakaj-je-potrebna-revizija5-MENCINGER-ENG.pdf.

Metzler, Mark. *Lever of Empire: The International Gold Standard and the Crisis of Liberalism in Prewar Japan.* Berkeley: University of California Press, 2006.

Middleton, Philip. "Prepare for Digital Currency Wars." Official Monetary and Financial Institutions Forum, October 21, 2020. https://www.omfif.org/2020/10/prepare-for-digital-currency-wars/.

Middleton, Philip, and Saket Sinha. "Retail CBDCs: The Next Payments Frontier." OMFIF. https://www.omfif.org/wp-content/uploads/2019/11/Retail-CBDCs-The-next-payments-frontier.pdf.

Mooney, Gerry. "The Scottish Independence Referendum: Why Was There a No Vote?" The Open University, March 2, 2015. https://www.open.edu/openlearn/people-politics-law/the-2014-scottish-independence-referendum-why-was-there-no-vote.

Morris, Ewan. "Devilish Devices or Farmyard Friends?" *History Ireland* 12, no. 1 (2004). Accessed January 9, 2020. https://www.historyireland.com/20th-century-contemporary-history/devilish-devices-or-farmyard-friends/.

Morys, Matthias. "Was the Bundesbank's Credibility Undermined during the Process of German Reunification?" Working Paper No. 74/03, 2003. London School of Economics. http://eprints.lse.ac.uk/22355/1/wp74.pdf.

Mosel, Irina, and Emily Henderson. "Markets in Crises: South Sudan Case Study." Working Paper, Humanitarian Policy Group, October 2015. https://cdn.odi.org/media/documents/9920.pdf.

Mrak, Mojmir, Matija Rocek, and Carlos Silva-Jauregui. *Slovenia: From Yugoslavia to the European Union.* Washington, DC: The World Bank, 2004. http://documents.worldbank.org/curated/en/197621468776951986/pdf/283760PAPER0Slovenia.pdf.

Mundell, Robert. "Money and the Sovereignty of the State." Paper presented at the International Economic Association Conference, Trento, September 4–7, 1997. Accessed January 9, 2020. https://www-ceel.economia.unitn.it/events/monetary/mundell14.pdf.

Nazzal, Nassouh. "Palestinians Plan to Ditch Israeli Currency, Gradually." *Gulf News*, April 20, 2016. https://gulfnews.com/world/mena/palestinians-plan-to-ditch-israeli-currency-gradually-1.1717766.

Neill, R. "Central Banking and Government Policy: Canada, 1871." University of Prince Edward Island. Accessed November 21, 2020. http://people.upei.ca/rneill/web_papers/1871_notes.html.

Noth, Martin. *The History of Israel*. London: Adam and Charles Black, 1972.

Nunes, A. B., C. Bastien, N. Valerio, R. M. de Sousa, and S. D. Costa. "Banking in the Portuguese Colonial Empire (1864–1975)." Working paper 41, Office of Economic and Social Research, University of Lisbon, 2010. https://ideas.repec.org/p/ise/gheswp/wp412010.html.

O'Leary, Elisabeth. "Brexit Drives Support for Scottish Independence to 49 Percent—YouGov." *Reuters*. April 27, 2019. https://www.reuters.com/article/uk-britain-eu-scotland-poll-idUKKCN1S30CE.

Oreskovic, Luka. "Slovenia's Membership of the Euro Is Only Partly to Blame for the Country's Economic Problems." *London School of Economics and Political Science Blog.* December 5, 2012. Accessed January 9, 2012. http://blogs.lse.ac.uk/europpblog/2012/12/05/slovenia-eu-economy/.

Oresme, Nicholas. *De Moneta*. London: Thomas Nelson and Sons Ltd., 1956.

Ow, Chwee-Huay. "The Currency Board Monetary System: The Case of Singapore and Hong Kong." PhD diss., John Hopkins University, 1985.

Pamuk, Şevket. *A Monetary History of the Ottoman Empire*. Cambridge: Cambridge University Press, 2000.

Paun, Akash, and Jess Sargeant. "A Second Referendum on Scottish Independence." May 30, 2019. Updated November 23, 2020. https://www.instituteforgovernment.org.uk/explainers/second-referendum-scottish-independence.

Pintev, Svetoslav. *Currency Board Arrangements: Rationale for Their Introduction, Advantages and Disadvantages: The Case of Bulgaria.* Diplomica Verlag, 2002.

Pisha, Arta, Besa Vorpsi, and Neraida Hoxhaj. "Albania: from 1920–1944." In *South-Eastern European Monetary and Economic Statistics from the Nineteenth Century to World War II*, 355–378. https://www.bnb.bg/bnbweb/groups/public/documents/bnb_publication/pub_np_seemhn_02_09_en.pdf.

Plocker, Sever. "Dollarization in Israel-Palestine." May 2005. The Saban Center for Middle East Policy at the Brookings Institution. https://www.brookings.edu/wp-content/uploads/2016/06/plocker20050501.pdf.

Political Economy Research Institute. "Modern Conflicts: East Timor-Indonesia (1975–1999)." University of Massachusetts Amherst. http://www.peri.umass.edu/fileadmin/pdf/Easttimor.pdf.

Powell, James. "A History of the Canadian Dollar." Bank of Canada, 2005. https://www.bankofcanada.ca/wp-content/uploads/2010/07/dollar_book.pdf.

Prakash, Om. "Foreign Merchants and Indian Mints in the Seventeenth and the Early Eighteenth Century." In *The Imperial Monetary System of Mughal India*, edited by John F. Richards, 184. Delhi: Oxford University Press, 1987.

Pratschke, J. L. "The Establishing of the Irish Pound: A Backward Glance." *Economic and Social Review* 1, no. 1 (1969): 51–75. http://www.tara.tcd.ie/bitstream/handle/2262/68789/v1n11969_3.pdf?sequence=1&isAllowed=y.

Quinn, Brian. "Scottish Independence: Issues and Questions: Regulation, Supervision, Lender of Last Resort and Crisis Management." The David Hume Institute, August 2013, 5.

Quinn, Frederick. *The French Overseas Empire.* Westport: Praeger Publishers, 2000.

Raza, Saima. "Italian Colonisation and Libyan Resistance: The Al-Sanusi of Cyrenaica." *Journal of Middle Eastern and Islamic Studies* 6, no. 1 (2012), 87–120. http://mideast.shisu.edu.cn/_upload/article/43/90/71b453574410bb697d5 766774f85/11caa68a-4eae-413c-a0ce-8c6101d7dd85.pdf.

Redish, Angela. "The Latin Monetary Union and the Emergence of the International Gold Standard." In *Monetary Regimes in Transition*, edited by Michael D. Bordo and Forrest Capie, 68–85. New York: Cambridge University Press, 1994.

Reece, Richard. *The Coinage of Roman Britain.* Stroud: Tempus Publishing, 2006.

Rena, Ravinder. "Historical Development of Money and Banking in Eritrea from the Axumite Kingdom to the Present." *African and Asian Studies* 6, no. 1–2 (2007): 10.

Richards, John F. *The Mughal Empire.* Cambridge: Cambridge University Press, 2008.

Robinson, Nick. "Scotland Currency: George Osborne Rules Out Union." *BBC News.* February 13, 2014. https://www.bbc.co.uk/news/av/uk-26179434/ scotland-currency-george-osborne-rules-out-union.

Rodger, Stuart. "Explained: 9 New Independent Scotland Currency Options Revealed." July 26, 2016. https://www.commonspace.scot/articles/8920/ explained-9-new-independent-scotland-currency-options-laid-out-new-report.

Sandrock, John E. "Italy's Colonial Empire: A Paper Money Trail." *The Currency Collector.* http://www.thecurrencycollector.com/pdfs/Italys_Colonial_ Empire_-_A_Paper_Money_Trail.pdf.

Sargent, Thomas J., and Francois R. Velde. *The Big Problem of Small Change.* Princeton, NJ: Princeton University Press, 2002.

Şaul, Mahir. "Money in Colonial Transition: Cowries and Francs in West Africa." University of Illinois. http://faculty.las.illinois.edu/m-saul/documents/ SaulMoneyinColonialAA.pdf.

Schanzer, Jonathan. "Palestine: Gaining Currency?" *The National Interest*, September 17, 2010. https://nationalinterest.org/commentary/palestine-gaining-currency-4093.

Schuler, Kurt. "Episodes from Asian Monetary History: A Brief History of Hong Kong Monetary Standards." *Asian Monetary Monitor*, September–October 1989.

Sepp, Urmas, Raoul Laettemae, and Marrti Randveer. "The History and Sustainability of the CBA in Estonia." University of Munich, 2002. Accessed January 9, 2020. https://econwpa.ub.uni-muenchen.de/econ-wp/mac/papers/0212/0212002.pdf.

Sinclair, David. *The Pound, a Biography.* London: Arrow Books, 2000.

Šiška, Marko. "Twenty Years of National Currency." http://www.twenty.si/ first-20-years/overview/before-and-now/twenty-years-of/.

Soerg, M. "Estonian Currency Board and Economic Performance." University of Tartu Estonia, 1998.

Spufford, Peter. *Money and Its Use in Medieval Europe.* Cambridge: Cambridge University Press, 1988.

Stiglitz, Joseph. *Globalisation and Its Discontents*. London: W. W. Norton and Company, 2002.

Strangio, Donatella. *The Reasons for Underdevelopment: The Case of Decolonisation in Somaliland*. Berlin-Heidelberg: Physica Verlag, 2012.

Subacchi, Paola. *The Cost of Free Money*. New Haven, CT: Yale University Press, 2020.

Swee, Goh Keng. "Why Singapore Chose a Currency Board over a Central Bank." EconomyNext. November 6, 2015. https://economynext.com/why-singapore-chose-a-currency-board-over-a-central-bank-3071/.

Sy, Amadou. "The Implications of South Sudan's Decision to Float Its Currency." *Africa in Focus* (blog). Brookings Institute. December 18, 2015. https://www.brookings.edu/blog/africa-in-focus/2015/12/18/the-implications-of-south-sudans-decision-to-float-its-currency/.

Sytas, Andrius. "Lithuania Joins Euro as Tensions with Neighboring Russia Rise." *Reuters*, December 31, 2014. https://www.reuters.com/article/us-lithuania-euro-idUSKBN0K918E20141231.

Talts, Mait. "Euro Debate in Estonia: Pros and Contras in Estonian Press." Paper presented at *Estonia and Finland in the Process of Eurointegration Seminar*, Laulasmaa, Estonia, November 6–7, 1998. https://www.ies.ee/061198paper.html.

Tesfay, Seyoum Yohannes. "Eritrea-Ethiopia Arbitration: A 'Cure' Based on Neither Diagnosis nor Prognosis." *Mizan Law Review* 6, no. 2 (2012): 164–199.

Toniolo, Gianni, and Piet Clement. *Central Bank Cooperation at the Bank for International Settlements, 1930-1973*. Cambridge: Cambridge University Press, 2005.

Trench, Alan. "Scottish Independence: Does Taking a Sterling Currency Union Off the Table Change the Game?" UK Constitutional Law Association, February 13, 2014. https://ukconstitutionallaw.org/2014/02/13/scottish-independence-does-taking-a-sterling-currency-union-off-the-table-change-the-game/.

Tsoi, Benjamin. "The Constitutions (Founding Laws) and Comparable Features of Select Currency Boards in the Former British Empire." Working paper, Johns Hopkins University, October 2014. https://sites.krieger.jhu.edu/iae/files/2021/02/Benjamin-Tsoi-Working-Paper-2-21.pdf.

Turnell, Sean. *Fiery Dragons: Banks, Moneylenders and Microfinance in Burma*. Copenhagen: Nordic Institute of Asian Studies Press, 2009.

Uche, Chibuike U. "Banks and the West African Currency Board." In *Money in Africa*, edited by Catherine Eagleton, Harcourt Fuller, and John Perkins, 50. London: British Museum Press, 2009.

Valdivieso, Luis, Toshihide Endo, Luis Mendonca, Shamsuddin Tareq, and Alexandro Lopez-Mejia. "East Timor: Establishing the Foundations of Sound Macroeconomic Management." International Monetary Fund, 2000, https://www.imf.org/external/pubs/ft/etimor/timor.pdf.

Van Zyl, Lambertus. "South Africa's Experience of Regional Currency Areas and the Use of Foreign Currencies." Bank of International Settlements, Paper 17. https://www.bis.org/publ/bppdf/bispap17o.pdf.

Wamey, Jay. "Devaluation Jitters Grip CFA Franc Zone." December 4, 2011. https://cameroonpostline.com/devaluation-jitters-grip-cfa-franc-zone.

Watt, Nicholas, Severin Carrell, Rowena Mason, and Libby Brooks. "Fate of Second Scottish Independence Referendum 'in Hands of the People.'" *The Guardian*, October 15, 2015. https://www.theguardian.com/politics/2015/oct/15/second-scottish-independence-referendum-hands-people-nicola-sturgeon-snp.

Westerman, Ashley. "Trying to Form the World's Newest Country, Bougainville Has a Road Ahead." National Public Radio. December 30, 2019. https://www.npr.org/2019/12/30/789697304/trying-to-form-the-worlds-newest-country-bougainville-has-a-road-ahead?t=1577958856861.

Wheatley, Alan. "The Pretenders to the Dollar's Crown." In *The Power of Currencies and Currencies of Power*, edited by Alan Wheatley, 45–74. London: International Institute for Strategic Studies, 2013.

William, Jonathan, ed. *Money: A History*. London: British Museum Press, 1997.

Williams, Kieran. *The Break-Up of Czechoslovakia and Scottish Independence*. London: History & Policy, 2013.

Wilson, Paul. *Hostile Money: Currencies in Conflict*. Cheltenham: The History Press, 2019.

Wimhurst, Liane. "What an Independent Catalonia Could Look Like." *I News*. October 4, 2017. https://inews.co.uk/news/world/independent-catalonia-look-like-519501.

World Bank. "Inflation in South Sudan." South Sudan Economic Brief Issue No. 1, 2012. http://documents1.worldbank.org/curated/en/833711468169442089/pdf/774280BRI0SS0e00Box377296B00PUBLIC0.pdf.

Worrell, DeLisle. "A Currency Union for the Caribbean." Working Paper, International Monetary Fund, February 2003.

Yam, Joseph. "Review of Currency Arrangements in Hong Kong." Hong Kong Monetary Authority, December 5, 1998. https://www.hkma.gov.hk/media/eng/publication-and-research/reference-materials/monetary/rcbahke.pdf.

Zevelof, Naomi. "Is a Palestinian Bitcoin on the Way?" *Forward*. May 14, 2017. https://forward.com/fast-forward/371882/is-a-palestinian-bitcoin-on-the-way/.

Zimbabwe Independent. "Zimbabwe Currency Crisis: The Rand and Long History of Trade with South Africa." May 12, 2016. https://www.theindependent.co.zw/2016/05/12/55811/.

WEBSITES

Central Banks

Bank of Ghana. www.bog.gov.gh.

Bank of Israel. "History." https://www.boi.org.il/en/AboutTheBank/History/Pages/Default.aspx.

Bank of Italy. www.Bancaditalia.it.

Banque de France. "Fact Sheet No. 127: The Franc Zone." July 2010. https://www.banque-france.fr/sites/default/files/media/2016/11/02/the_fact_sheet_n_127_july-2010.pdf.

Central Bank of Lesotho. "The Loti-Rand Peg: Benefits and Costs." May 2006. https://www.centralbank.org.ls/images/Publications/Research/Reports/MonthlyEconomicReviews/2006/Economic_Review_May_06.pdf.

Central Bank of Sri Lanka, "The Bank's Beginning," https://www.cbsl.gov.lk/en/about/about-the-bank/bank-history.

Eastern Caribbean Central Bank. "Annual Economic and Financial Review, 2014." https://www.eccb-centralbank.org/documents/19.

Eastern Caribbean Central Bank. "Annual Report 2010-2011 and 2014-2015." https://www.eccb-centralbank.org/documents/19.

European Commission. "Slovenia Joins the Euro Area." http://ec.europa.eu/economy_finance/articles/euro/slovenia_joins_the_euro_area_en.htm.

Hong Kong Monetary Authority. "How the Link Works." https://www.hkma.gov.hk/media/eng/publication-and-research/background-briefs/hkmalin/06.pdf.

Hong Kong Monetary Authority. "Review of Currency Board Arrangements in Hong Kong." https://www.hkma.gov.hk/media/eng/publication-and-research/reference-materials/monetary/rcbahke.pdf.

International Monetary Fund. "Eastern Caribbean Currency Union: Financial System Stability Assessment." April 15, 2004. https://www.imf.org/external/pubs/ft/scr/2004/cr04293.pdf.

International Monetary Fund. "East Timor: Recent Developments and Macroeconomic Assessment." Section VI, Paragraph 18. November 30, 2000. https://www.imf.org/external/np/et/2000/eng/113000.htm.

International Monetary Fund. "Eritrea: Selected Issues and Statistical Appendix." IMF Country Report 03/166, 2003, International Monetary Fund. https://www.imf.org/external/pubs/ft/scr/2003/cr03166.pdf.

International Monetary Fund. "The Federal Democratic Republic of Ethiopia: Selected Issues and Statistical Appendix." IMF Country Report No. 05/28, 2005. https://www.imf.org/external/pubs/ft/scr/2005/cr0528.pdf.

International Monetary Fund. "Jordan: Selected Issues." IMF Country Report, 08/291, August 2008. https://www.imf.org/external/pubs/ft/scr/2008/cr08291.pdf.

International Monetary Fund. "World Economic Outlook." October 1992. https://www.elibrary.imf.org/doc/IMF081/14367-9781451944563/14367-9781451944563/Other_formats/Source_PDF/14367-9781455261710.pdf.

International Trade Centre. "Timor-Leste: Country Brief." Accessed November 29, 2020. http://www.intracen.org/country/timor-leste/sector-trade-performance/.

Reserve Bank of Australia: www.rba.gov.au.

Reserve Bank of New Zealand. www.rbnz.govt.nz.

St. Louis Federal Reserve Bulletin, 1948. https://fraser.stlouisfed.org/files/docs/publications/FRB/pages/1945-1949/30313_1945-1949.pdf.

World Bank. "GDP Per Capita (Current US$)—Timor-Leste." Accessed November 29, 2020. https://data.worldbank.org/indicator/NY.GDP.PCAP.CD?locations=TL.

World Bank GDP Rankings 2017. https://databank.worldbank.org/data/download/GDP.pdf.

World Bank. "The World Bank in Small States: Overview." https://www.worldbank.org/en/country/smallstates/overview.

World Bank, World Integrated Trade Solution. "East Timor Trade Balance, Exports, Imports by Country and Region 2017." Accessed November 29, 2020. https://wits.worldbank.org/CountryProfile/en/Country/TMP/Year/LTST/TradeFlow/EXPIMP.

MEDIA

African Business. "A Brief History of the CFA Franc." February 19, 2012. http://africanbusinessmagazine.com/uncategorised/a-brief-history-of-the-cfa-franc/.

BBC News. "Catalonia Vote: 80% Back Independence—Officials." November 10, 2014. https://www.bbc.co.uk/news/world-europe-29982960.

BBC News Scotland. "Timeline Scottish Independence Referendum." October 15, 2012. https://www.bbc.co.uk/news/uk-scotland-scotland-politics-19907675.

European Union Times. "Merkel Warns of Europe's Collapse." May 18, 2010. https://www.eutimes.net/2010/05/merkel-warns-of-europes-collapse/.

The New Arab. "Palestine Hopes to Launch New Digital Currency in Five Years." May 14, 2017. https://www.alaraby.co.uk/english/news/2017/5/14/palestine-hopes-to-launch-national-digital-currency-in-five-years.

The Straits Times. "Second Separation: Why Singapore Rejected a Common Currency with Malaysia." May 14, 2016. https://www.straitstimes.com/singapore/second-separation-why-singapore-rejected-a-common-currency-with-malaysia.

OTHERS

Dominica, Office of the President, Commonwealth of Dominica, Address by President Liverpool June 19, 2011.

Economic Cooperation Foundation. "Termination of the Mandate for Palestine." https://ecf.org.il/issues/issue/945.

Estonian World. May 1, 2014.

Focus Economics. "Slovenia." https://www.focus-economics.com/countries/slovenia.

Hashemite Kingdom of Jordan. History. "The Making of Jordan" http://www.king-hussein.gov.jo/his_transjordan.html.

Macrotrends. "U.S. Dollar Index—43 Year Historical Chart. Accessed November 29, 2020. https://www.macrotrends.net/1329/us-dollar-index-historical-chart.

The Palestine–Israel Journal, "The Case for a Palestinian Currency" 2019 http://pij.org/articles/244.

Republic of Slovenia. "Euro: 10 Years of the Single Currency in Slovenia." December 23, 2016. https://www.stat.si/statweb/en/news/index/6414.

Trading Economics. "Australian Dollar to US Dollar Exchange Rates." https://tradingeconomics.com/australia/currency.

Treasury Vault Blog. "All About the Jordan Dinar." April 2, 2015. https://treasuryvault.com/blog/all-about-jordan-dinar/.

University of Quebec at Montreal, "Currency, French Indochina." http://indochine.uqam.ca/en/historical-dictionary/333-currency-french-indochina.html.

US Congress Federal Research Division, Library of Congress, Country Studies, "Singapore: The Road to Independence."

US Department of State, Office of the Historian. "Creation of Israel 1948." https://history.state.gov/milestones/1945-1952/creation-israel.

Warwick and Warwick Auctioneers. "Extremely Rare Palestine 1947 1 Mil Coin." https://www.warwickandwarwick.com/latest-news/extremely-rare-palestine-1947-1-mil-coin-to-be-offered-in-our-19th-june-2019-auction.

TALK

"European Banks and the Eurozone Crisis: Keynote Speech by Axel Weber." The Policy Exchange. Westminster, London. September 5, 2013. https://www.youtube.com/watch?v=_oLSagYc8uU.

Index

al-Abadi, Haider, 190
Abdallah (King of Jordan), 102
accession: Hong Kong, 167–70; with
    Yemen and unification, 166–67
Act of Union (1707), 179
Adams, John, 18
Adams, John Quincy, 20
Afewerki, Isaias, 139–40
Affair of the Piastres (1945–
    1954), 108–10
Afghanistan, 148, 176, 200
Africa, 2, 5, 70; east, 77–79, 104–5;
    Ethiopia and Italian east, 77–79;
    franc in Sub-Saharan, 110–12; franc
    zone unions of West and Central,
    201–6; Italy with empire in, 74–75;
    multilateral monetary area of
    Southern, 198–201; west, 65–68,
    103–4, 201–6
Africa Orientale Italiana (AOI)
    lira, 78–79
Akbar (Mughal Emperor), 50, 51
akçe, Ottoman Empire, 48, 49
Albania, 79, 129
Algeria, 110
Algiers, 69
American Banknote Company, 98

American colonies, 4, 18; currency
    problems, 10–13, 14; paper money
    in, 11–13, 15–17, 19, 21
anchor currency, 95, 201; currency
    boards and, xi–xii, 72, 102, 127, 153,
    199; gold standard era and, 107
Anglo-Palestine Bank, 98–99
Angola, 72, 73, 74, 199
Anguilla, 196, 197, 198
Ansip, Andrus, 128
Antigua, 196
AOI (Africa Orientale Italiana)
    lira, 78–79
Arab League, 99–100
Arafat, Yasser, 174
arbitrage, xi, 23, 39, 42–44
Argentina, 68, 147
Armenia, 123, 124, 155n9
Al Assad, Bashar, 188
Atlee, Clement, 6, 102
Aurangzeb (Mughal Emperor), 54–55
Australia, 49, 66, 78, 147; gold and,
    61–62; paper money and, 59–60;
    with sterling or dollar, 59–62
Australian Notes Act (1910), 62
Austria, 25–27, 32, 38–40, 62,
    75, 129, 136
Austro-Italian War (1859), 26
Azerbaijan, 123, 124, 155n9

Bagehot, Walter, 30
Balkans, 32, 48, 79, 129
Bamberger, Ludwig, 31–32
Banca di Napoli, 28, 74
Banca di Sicilia, 28, 74
Banca d'Italia, 28, 74, 76–77, 106–7
Banco di Napoli, 74, 76
Banco di Roma, 74, 77
Banco di Sicilia, 74, 77
Banco Nacional Ultramarino (National
    Overseas Bank), 72–74
the Banco Nationale nel Regno d'Italia
    (Bank of the Kingdom of Italy,
    BNR), 27–29
Bangladesh, 117
Bank Charter Act (1844), 53,
    63–64, 180
bank money, 10
Bank Negara Malaysia, 119–20
banknote issue, 18, 55, 72, 77, 98;
    Canada, 52–53; China and, 58, 169;
    Hong Kong and, 58, 169, 180; with
    monopoly reversal in New Zealand,
    64; politics and, 21; Portuguese
    Banknote Crisis, 73; by private
    banks, 25; reform, 27–28; Scotland
    and, 179–80; Singapore and, 121.
    See also paper money
Bank of Amsterdam, 10, 16
Bank of Canada, 54, 67
Bank of Canada Act (1934), 54
Bank of England, 13, 16, 23, 29, 33,
    120, 180; gold and, 57; interest rates
    and, 181; on legal tender, xii–xiii;
    power of, 185
Bank of International Settlements
    (BIS), 126
Bank of Israel Law, 100
Bank of Korea, 82
Bank of Mauritius, 63
Bank of Montreal, 52
Bank of New South Wales, 60–61
Bank of Prussia, 29–30, 32
Bank of Scotland, 179, 180, 184, 185
Bank of Slovenia, 131, 132

Bank of the Kingdom of Italy (the
    Banco Nationale nel Regno d'Italia,
    BNR), 27–28
Bank of the Papal States, 28
banks: banknote issue by private, 25;
    central, 173, 221; collapse of, 22;
    crisis, 184; ESCB, 213; Federal
    Reserve Bank, US, 94; free banking,
    xii, 32, 64–65, 184; Hamilton and,
    16–19; Israel with independent
    currency and, 100; "Report on the
    Subject of a National Bank," 16. *See
    also specific banks*
Bank Wars, 20–21
Banque de France, 33, 39, 41–42, 72,
    89, 204, 210
Banque de l'Afrique Occidentale, 70
Banque des Antilles, 70
Banque d'Indochine, 70
Banque Royale, 17
Barbados, 195, 196
Barbuda, 196
Barroso, Jose Manuel, 182–83
Barzani, Massoud, 189
Basic Law, Hong Kong and, 169–70
Belarus, 122, 123, 155n9
Belgium, 38, 40, 43, 105, 181, 221;
    Latin Monetary Union and, 39, 41;
    silver coinage, 25, 27
Belgrade, 129, 130, 131
Ben-Gurion, David, 97–98
Benin, 93, 202
Berlin Wall, fall of, 129, 130, 163
Biddle, Nicholas, 20–21
bimetallic system, xi, 26, 30, 31, 38–43
BIS (Bank of International
    Settlements), 126
Bismarck, Otto von, 30, 32, 41
Bitcoin, 188, 227
Blair, Tony, 180
Blumenthal, Erwin, 104, 105
Blythe, Ernest, 90–91
BNR (the Banco Nationale nel Regno
    d'Italia, Bank of the Kingdom of
    Italy), 27–29

Bohemia, 37
Bonaparte, Napoleon, 25, 39
Bordo, Michael, 44, 214
Bosnia, 152, 182, 190, 222
Bosnia Herzegovina, 221
Botswana, 199, 200
Bougainville, 153–55, 173
Bratislava, 136, 137
Brazil, 23
Bretton Woods agreement, xii, 103, 109–10, 210
Brioni Agreement, 130, 131, 132
Brisbane, Thomas, 60
British Coinage Act (1816), 62
British Virgin Islands, 196
Brunei, 66, 119, 120
Brussels Conference (1920), 5
Bulgaria, 39
Bundesbank, 178, 207
Burkina Faso (West Volta), 71, 93, 202, 206
Burma, 55, 93, 94–95, 108, 109
Burundi, 104
Buterin, Vitalik, 188

Caisse Centrale de la France Libre, 71
Cameroon, 93, 202
Camphausen, Otto von, 32
Canada, 52–54, 60, 66–68
capital, free movement of, 2, 196
Carausius (Roman admiral), 3–4
Caribbean, 2, 5, 66, 173, 195–98, 223
"Carnation Revolution," Portugal, 143
Catalonia, 186–88, 190
Central Africa, 201–6
Central African Republic, 93, 202
Central Bank of Jordan, 102, 176
Ceylon (Sri Lanka), 66, 93, 94, 103, 113n21
CFA (Colonies Francaises d'Afrique) franc, 110–11, 201–2, 204–6
Chad, 93, 202, 206
Charles I (King of England), 10
Chernomyrdin, Viktor, 123

China, 82, 173, 228; Hong Kong and, 58–59, 167–70; renminbi, 225–26
Christian Democratic Party, Czechoslovakia, 135
Civic Democratic Party, Czechoslovakia, 135
Civil War, US, 22, 55
civil wars: Bosnia, 152, 182, 190; Papua New Guinea, 153; South Sudan, 152, 153, 167; Tajikistan, 124; Yemen and Shia Houthi people, 167
Clinton, Bill, 143
Clydesdale Bank, 180
coinage: British Coinage Act, 62; copper, 51, 63, 81–82; debasing, 9–11, 22–23; England, 179; Federal Coinage Act of 1850, 24; Germany, 31; gold, 23, 24, 31, 37, 39–40, 41, 44, 48–49, 54, 57, 58, 61–62, 63, 65, 79, 82, 179; India, 50, 54; Irish Free State and, 90–91; Israel, 4; issuance of, 3, 24, 55; Mughal Empire, 54–55; Munich Coinage Treaty of 1837, 28; nickel, 81–82; Ottoman Empire, 48–49; overvaluation, 49; retiring of, 26; Rome, 4; Scotland, 179; security and distribution of, 51; shortage, 34n4; sikka, 3, 55; silver, 22–23, 24, 25, 27, 30, 31, 37, 39–40, 41, 43, 44, 48–49, 51, 53, 56, 60–62, 65, 179; Turkey and, 3; withdrawal from circulation, 30, 41–42, 179
Coinage Act of 1792, US, 19
Coinage Act of 1926, Ireland, 91
Colonial Bank of Issue, 63, 64
colonies. *See* American colonies
Colonies Francaises d'Afrique (CFA) franc, 110–11, 201–2, 204–6
Commercial Bank, Mauritius, 63
Congo, 69, 93, 202
Constitutional Congress, 14–16, 24
Consumer Price Index, xii
convenience, monetary issue and, 222, 223
convicts, 59, 62, 187

Cook Islands, 147
copper, 44, 51, 63, 81–82
Cote D'Ivoire, 93, 202, 205, 206
counterfeits, in American colonies, 11
COVID-19 infection rates, 215
Crimea, 39, 48, 49
Cripps, Stafford, 96, 97
Croatia, 130, 221
cryptocurrencies, 6, 188, 227. *See also* digital currencies
Cunliffe, Walter, 36n59
currencies: American colonies and problem of, 10–13, 14; anchor, xi–xii, 72, 95, 102, 107, 127, 153, 199, 201; digital, 6, 173, 177, 188, 227; francs as model, 24–25, 26, 27; state authority with, 3–4; surrogate, 155n9; trade and, 55, 228; US federal control of, 14–19. *See also* independent currencies
currencies, in waiting: Catalonia and, 186–88; Kurdistan and, 188–91; Palestine and, 174–79; Scotland and, 179–86
"Currency, Economic and Social Union between the German Democratic Republic and the Federal Republic of Germany," 163
Currency Act of 1764, Great Britain, 13, 16
Currency Act of 1927, Ireland, 91–92
currency adoption (dollarization), xi, 90, 146–48, 170, 175–76
currency boards: anchor currency and, xi–xii, 72, 102, 127, 153, 199; Burma, 95; East African, 104–5; empire and, 64–65; establishment of, 65, 66; Palestine, 97; Transjordan, Israel and Palestine, 95–100; West African, 65–68, 103–4
currency unions: Germany, 163–66; Luxembourg and Belgium, 181; Mundell's principle and, 2; with Sweden, Denmark and Norway, 44
Customs Unit (Zollverein), 28

Cyprus, 93
Czechoslovakia, Velvet Divorce and, 134–39

Daddah, Ould, 202
Dai-ichi Bank, 81, 87n81
dam, Mughal Empire, 51
debasing, 9–11, 22–23
De Brouwer, Gordon, 146
debts: gold and, 23; silver and, 22; sovereign crisis of 2009–2010, 45, 92, 138, 181, 209, 213–15, 226
Deby, Idriss, 205
decentralization, banknote issue, 55
De Gaulle, Charles, 111
Delors, Jacques, 210–15
Delors Report, 210–15
Democracy in America (De Tocqueville), 19
Deng Shao Peng, 168
Denmark, 24, 43, 44, 46n20, 180
Derg Forces, 139, 141
Deutsche Marks, 127–28, 164–65, 182, 208–10, 213
devaluation, 7, 110, 120, 136
digital currencies: cryptocurrencies, 6, 188, 227; Palestine and, 177; private, 6, 173, 227
digital private currencies, 173
dinars: Jordan, 175, 177; Yugoslavia, 131–32
"Dissertations on Government, The Affairs of the Bank and Paper Money" (Paine), 17
dollar, US, 67; adoption of, 89, 176, 177, 182, 190; Hong Kong and, 168–69; influence of, 7, 53, 164, 166–67, 175; Palestine and, 175; withdrawal from, 225
dollarization (currency adoption), xi, 90, 146–48, 170, 175–76
dollars: Australia, 59–62, 147; Canada, 52–54; Hong Kong, 168–69; Maria Teresa, 74; Namibia, 199; Singapore, 121

Dominica, 196
dong, Vietnam, 108
Dresden Convention (1838), 28–29
ducat, Venetian, 37, 48–49
Duncan, Daniel Kablan, 205
Dutch East India Company,
 54–55, 59, 142

East Africa, 77–79, 104–5
Eastern Caribbean, 195–98
Eastern Caribbean Central Bank
 (ECCB), 173, 196, 197, 207, 223
Eastern Caribbean Currency Union
 (ECCU), 195, 197–98
East Germany, 163–65
East Timor, 134, 144, 176, 190
ECB (European Central Bank), 7,
 214, 224–26
ECCB (Eastern Caribbean Central
 Bank), 173, 196, 197, 207, 223
ECCU (Eastern Caribbean Currency
 Union), 195, 197–98
Economic Community of West African
 States (ECOWAS), 206
Economic Union Treaty, 196
ECOWAS (Economic Community of
 West African States), 206
Ecuador, 134, 148, 176, 190, 221, 222
Eden, Anthony, 77–78
Edward IV (King of England), 51
Eesti Pank, 126, 127
Egypt, 48, 76, 80, 100, 150
Elizabeth I (Queen of England), 179
El Salvador, 134, 148, 176, 182, 190
empire, end of: Britain and wind
 of change, 93; Burma, 94–95;
 dissolution and, 221; East African
 currency board, 104–5; France, 89,
 221; franc in Sub-Saharan Africa,
 110–12; Indochina (1945–1954),
 108–10; Irish Free State and Irish
 Republic, 90–93; Israel, Transjordan
 and Palestine currency board,
 95–100; Italy with trusteeship in
 Somalia, 105–8; Sri Lanka, 94;

Transjordan, 101–2; West African
 currency board, 103–4. *See also*
 money, empire and
England, 6, 10, 22, 179
EPLF (Eritrean People's Liberation
 Front), 139
Equatorial Guinea, 202
Eritrea, 74, 77; money, empire and,
 75–76; in 1997, 139–42
Eritrean People's Liberation Front
 (EPLF), 139
ESCB (European System of Central
 Banks), 213
Estonia, 2, 125–28, 176, 182
Ethereum, 188
Ethiopia, 77–79, 141
EU. *See* European Union
euro: adoption of, 133, 182, 183,
 218n28, 222–23; Denmark and,
 46n20; rejection of, 148
Europe: currency union and, 2;
 liberalism, gold and nation
 building in, 22–24
European Central Bank (ECB), 7,
 214, 224–26
European Coal and Steel
 Community, 164, 207
European Commission, 186–87
European Exchange Rate Mechanism, 6
European Monetary System, 92, 210
European System of Central Banks
 (ESCB), 213
European Union (EU), 5, 92; Delors
 Report and, 210; as mediator, 130–
 31; membership, 128, 132, 137–38,
 163, 182–84, 186–87, 222–23, 224
Eurosystem, 207–8
eurozone, trade and, 176
Exchange Fund, 168–69
Exchange Rate Mechanism, 6, 132
exchange rates: defined, xii; fixed, xii,
 29, 127, 131, 200; floating, xii, 146;
 pegged, xii, 106, 176
extreme inflation, xii, 200

farmers, 21, 22, 23
farmyard animals, 90
Faroe Isles, 180
Federal Coinage Act (1850), 24
Federal Constitution (1850), 24
Federalist Papers, 14–16, 18
Federal Reserve Bank, US, 94
Federal Reserve System, US, 7, 22, 182, 214, 223, 225
First Bank of the United States, 18, 19, 20
First Opium War (1842), 167
fixed exchange rate, xii, 29, 127, 131, 200
floating exchange rate, xii, 146
florins, 37
forced circulation, 27, 175
Ford, Gerald, 143
Foreman-Peck, James, 33
France, 32, 105, 203; Banque de France, 33, 39, 41–42, 72, 89, 204, 210; bimetallic system in, 38, 41; currency system, 24–25, 26, 30; with dissolution of empire, 89, 221; Gaullist Party, 110; Germany and, 69, 163, 164; with gold standard, 42; Italy and, 26–27, 38, 41; Latin Monetary Union and, 39; with loss of power and influence, 25; money and empire of, 69–72; paper money and, 40; revolutionary wars, 23, 24; silver coinage, 25; Vietnam and, 108–9
Franco-Prussian War (1871), 28, 30, 69
francs, Albania, 79
francs, CFA, 110–11, 201–2, 204–6
francs, France, 61, 70; currency modeled on, 24–25, 26, 27; Federal Coinage Act of 1850 and, 24; in Sub-Saharan Africa, 110–12; zone unions of West and Central Africa, 201–6
Franklin, Benjamin, 9, 12, 13, 16
free banking, xii, 32, 64–65, 184
free minting, xii, 19, 41, 56

free movement: of capital, 2, 196; of goods and people, 140, 196; of labor, 2, 135
Fretilin, Timor-Leste, 143

Gabon, 93, 202
Gallatin, Albert, 19
Gambia, 104
Ganghwa incident (1876), 81
Garang de Mabior, John, 149–50
Garibaldi, Giuseppe, 25
Gaullist Party, 110
GDP. *See* gross domestic product
Genoa Conference (1922), 5
George, Lloyd, 36n59
Georgia, 122, 123
Germany, 24, 25, 38, 105, 121, 131, 178, 209–10; coinage, 31; COVID-19 infection rates, 215; east, 163–65; France and, 69, 163, 164; Germania sui generis, 28–34; gold standard and, 30, 43; gulden, 28, 165; independence and, 4–5; reunification of, 163–66; Russia and, 32; west, 163–67, 212
Ghana, 93, 103–4
Giolitti, Giovanni, 77
Glass, Carter, 22
Glenelg (Lord), 61
globalization, 226
gold: American empire and, 80; banknote issue covered by, 52; Bank of England and, 57; coinage, 23, 24, 31, 37, 39–40, 41, 44, 48–49, 54, 57, 58, 61–62, 63, 65, 79, 82, 179; debts and, 23; Europe with liberalism and, 22–24; exchange standard and Japan, 5, 81–84; loss of, 78; over silver, 23, 30, 55–56; production, 52; ratio of silver to, 27, 31; reserves and Palestine, 174; rush, 29, 61
gold exchange standard, xii
gold standard, xii; adoption of, 30, 31, 40, 42, 43, 56; era and anchor currency, 107; Great Britain and,

52; rejection of, 64; return to, 27; withdrawal from, 68, 78
goods, free movement of people and, 140, 196
Gorbachev, Mikhail, 121
Great Britain, 62, 105, 224–25; Bank Charter Act of 1844, 53, 63–64, 180; Currency Act of 1764, 13, 16; with currency problem in American colonies, 10–13; with dissolution of empire, 221; empire, monetary system and, 51–52; gold standard and, 43, 52; Hong Kong and, 167–68, 169; pound sterling, 6–7; wind of change and, 93
Greece, 3, 39, 224
Grenada, 196, 197
Grenadines, 196
Gresham's law, 17, 39
groschen, 37
gross domestic product (GDP): Czechoslovakia, 137, 138; ECCB, 197; Estonia, 128; EU membership and, 187; Italy, 25; Scotland, 185; Slovenia, 133; Timor-Leste, 145–46; Yemen, 167
Guadeloupe, 196
Guinea, 93, 111, 202
gulden, 28, 165
Gulf War (1990–1991), 166, 190

Haaretz, 113n21
Habibie, Jusuf, 143–44, 154
Hadi, Abdrabbuh Mansur, 167
Hadrian (Emperor), 4
Haile Selassie (Emperor of Ethiopia), 139
Hainsworth, Paul, 159n59
Hamilton, Alexander, 4, 12, 14, 16–20
Hanke, Steve, 147
Hashemite Kingdom of Jordan, 101–2, 114n29
Ho Chi Minh, 108
Holland, 24

Hong Kong, 49, 52, 57, 64, 66; accession, 167–70; banknotes, 58, 169, 180; Basic Law and, 169–70; with lease of New Territories, 167; silver and, 58–59, 71; as Special Administrative Region, 168, 169, 170; US dollar and, 168–69
Hong Kong Monetary Authority, 169, 170
Horesh, Niv, 87n81
Houthi people, 167
Hungary, 37, 48, 129
Hussein, Saddam, 188
hyperinflation, xi, xii, 125

Iceland, 131
Ilkhanid dynasty, Persia, 47–48, 51
IMF. *See* International Monetary Fund
independence: Bougainville and, 173; Catalonia and, 186, 190; Germany and, 4–5; independent currencies and, 4, 48, 84, 89, 123, 134, 138, 175, 177–79, 188, 190, 191, 203; Scotland, 180–84, 186, 189, 190; Timor-Leste, 142, 159n59; UK Independence Party, 5; War of Independence, 4
independent currencies: with common standards, 28; during conflict, 190; digital private and, 173; independence and, 4, 48, 84, 89, 123, 134, 138, 175, 177–79, 188, 190, 191, 203; Israel with bank-funded, 100; Ottoman Empire and, 48; Palestine and, 175, 177–79, 188; problem of, 11; reintroduction of, 2, 72, 84, 89, 123; shekel and, 175, 177; SNP and, 182, 183; Somalia and, 106; surrogate and, 155n9
India, 49, 52, 67, 93; coinage, 50, 54; Dutch East India Company, 54–55, 59, 142; Mughal Empire and, 50–51; rupee, 51, 55–56, 63; silver and, 54–57, 71
Indian Councils Act (1861), 3

Indochina, 70, 108–10

Indonesia, 108, 142, 143, 159n59

infection rates, COVID-19, 215

inflation rates: extreme, xii, 200; hyperinflation, xi, xii, 125; rising, 141–42, 175

insurrection coins, 4

interest rates: Bank of England and, 181; policy of European Central Bank, 7; rising, 165

INTERFET, 144, 147

International Monetary Fund (IMF), 126, 127, 144–45, 156n17, 176, 197, 223, 226

international monetary unions, in nineteenth century: Latin, 25, 34, 38–43; Scandinavian, 34, 43–45; trade and, 37–38, 46n20

Iran, 68, 167, 218n28

Iraq, 166, 188, 189, 190

Iraq war of 2003, 190

Ireland, 89, 91–92, 169, 182

Irish Free State, 66, 90–93

Irish Republic, 90–93

IS (Islamic State), 189, 190

Islam, 3

Islamic State (IS), 189, 190

Israel, 4, 113n21, 191; banknote issue and, 98; with banks and independent currency, 100; Palestine and, 175, 177, 188; shekel, 174–78; Transjordan, Palestine currency board and, 95–100; US and, 176–77

Italy, 24, 150; with African empire, 74–75; with East Africa, 77–79; France and, 26–27, 38, 41; GDP, 25; Latin Monetary Union and, 39; lira, 26, 27, 28, 77, 78; paper money and, 40, 75; Somalia and trusteeship of, 105–8; unification of, 25–28, 29

Jackson, Andrew, 20–21

Jamaica, 196

James VI (King of Scotland), 179

Japan, 72, 108–9, 119, 121, 225; in Burma, 94; Dai-ichi Bank, 81, 87n81; gold exchange standard and, 5, 81–84; Yokohama Specie Bank, 82–83

Jefferson, Thomas, 4, 18, 19

Jewish Colonial Trust, 98

"The Joint Declaration of the Government of the United Kingdom of Great Britain and Northern Ireland and the Government of the People's Republic of China on the Question of Hong Kong," 169

Jonung, Lars, 44, 214

Jordan, 101, 102, 174, 175, 176, 177

Juppe, Alain, 214

Kazakhstan, 123–24, 156n17

Keita, Ibrahim Boubacar, 202

Kenya, 104, 149–50

Keynes, J. M., 56, 57

Kiir, Salva, 152

Kirshner, Jonathan, 78

Klaus, Vaclav, 138

Kohl, Helmut, 163, 212

Korea, 81–82, 87n81

Kosovo, 129

KRG (Kurdish Regional Government), 189–90

kroon, Estonia, 2

Kuala Lumpur, 118, 119

Kurdish Autonomous Zone, 189

Kurdish Regional Government (KRG), 189–90

Kurdistan, with currency in waiting, 188–91

Kuwait, 166

Kyrgyzstan, 123, 155n9

labor, free movement of, 2, 135

Labour Party, England, 6, 180

Lamont, Norman, 6–7

Latin Monetary Union, 25, 34, 38–43, 44, 224, 226

Latvia, 125, 127

laurel, 179
Law, John, 17, 126
Law of Payment, 222
League of Nations, 77–78, 95, 101, 105
Lee Kuan Yew, 119
legal sovereignty, 1, 178
legal tender, xii–xiii
lek, Albania, 79
Le Maire, Bruno, 206
Lesotho, 198, 199
Lex Cornelia (testamentaria nummaria), 3
liberalism, Europe with gold and, 22–24
Libya, 74, 76–77, 202
lilangeni, Swaziland, 199
lira, Italy, 26, 27, 28, 77, 78
Lisbon, 199
Lithuania, 122, 125, 127
London Imperial Economic Conference (1923), 68
loti, Lesotho, 199
Luxembourg, 181

Maastricht Treaty, 187, 211, 213–14, 224
Macau, 73
Macedonia, 221
Machar, Riek, 152
Macmillan, Harold, 89, 93
Macquarie, Lachlan, 60
Macron, Emmanuel, 206, 215
Madagascar, 69–70, 93, 111, 202
Madison, James, 4, 14–16, 18, 19, 20
Malaya, 118, 119
Malaysia, 57, 66, 93, 119–20
Mali, 93, 111, 202, 203, 206
Malta, 49
Marape, James, 154
Maria Teresa dollars, 74
Martinique, 196
Mas, Artur, 186
Mauretania, 111, 202
Mauritania, 93, 202, 206
Mauritius, 62–63, 64, 65
May, Theresa, 184

Mendonca, Luis, 144
Mengistu Haile Mariam, 139, 140
Merkel, Angela, 215
Mexico, 56, 70, 190
Middle Ages, 22, 23, 37
Mint Bill (1870), 51
minting, 9, 10; authority over, 24; coinage shortage with, 34n4; facilities consolidation, 50; free, xii, 19, 41, 56; with recoinage, 179
Mitterand, Francois, 210, 212
MMA (Multilateral Monetary Agreement), 199–201
"A Modest Enquiry into the Nature and Necessity of a paper currency" (Franklin), 12, 13
Mogadishu, 76, 106, 107
Moldova, 122, 123, 155n9
monetary issue, US Federal Reserve System, 223
monetary sovereignty, 1, 2, 190; cryptocurrencies threatening, 6; state and, 221–28
monetary system, British Empire and, 51–52
money, 10, 14–16. *See also* paper money
money, empire and: Australia with dollar or sterling, 59–62; Canada and dollar, 52–54; currency boards and, 64–65; Eritrea, 75–76; Ethiopia and Italian East Africa, 77–79; France, 69–72; gold and American, 80; gold exchange standard and Japan, 5, 81–84; Hong Kong and silver, 58–59; India and silver, 54–57; India under Mughals, 50–51; Italy and African empire, 74–75; Libya and, 76–77; Mauritius, 62–63; monetary system and British, 51–52; New Zealand and, 63–64; Ottoman, 47–49; Portugal abroad, 72–74; power and, 3; Somalia and, 76; West African currency board and, 65–68

money, of nation builders: American colonies and problem of, 10–13, 14; Bank Wars, 20–21; with Europe, liberalism and gold, 22–24; Federal Reserve System, 22; Germania sui generis, 28–34; Italy and unification, 25–28; Switzerland and unification, 24–25; United Provinces of the Netherlands, 9–10; US federal control of, 14–19

"Money and the Sovereignty of the State" (Mundell), 222

Montenegro, 79, 182, 222–23

Montserrat, 196, 197, 198, 223

moral hazard, xiii, 32, 227

Mozambique, 73, 199

Mswati III (King of Swaziland), 200

Mugabe, Robert, 200

Mughal Empire, 50–51, 54–55, 67

Multilateral Monetary Agreement (MMA), 199–201

multinational monetary unions, modern: Delors Report, 210–15; Eastern Caribbean, 195–98; Eurosystem, 207–8; franc zone unions of West and Central Africa, 201–6; Southern Africa, 198–201; Werner Report, 208–10

Mundell, Robert, 1–2, 208, 222, 224

Munich Coinage Treaty (1837), 28

Mussolini, Benito, 28, 76, 78

Naivasha Comprehensive Peace Agreement, 150

Namibia, 198, 199, 201

Napoleonic Wars, 23, 38, 62

Napoleon III (Emperor), 27, 30, 39, 40, 42

National Bank of the Sardinian States, 28

National Overseas Bank (Banco Nacional Ultramarino), 72–74

nation building, 22–24, 33, 38

NATO, 132, 176

Netanyahu, Benjamin, 176–77

Netherlands, 22, 38, 78, 209, 215, 226; with Indonesia, 142; South Sudan and, 150; United Provinces of the Netherlands, 9–10, 24

New York Times (newspaper), 98

New Zealand, 63–64, 66, 67, 153

nickel coinage, 81–82

Niger, 93, 202, 206

Nigeria, 93, 103, 104

Norman, Montagu, 36n59

North Africa, 49, 77, 204

North Borneo, 118, 119

Northern Ireland, 92, 169

Norway, 40, 43, 44, 150

Novo, Estado, 143

Obama, Barack, 176, 177, 189

OCA (Optimal Currency Area), 2, 208

OECS (Organisation of Eastern Caribbean States), 196

oil, 124, 146, 148, 151–52, 189, 208, 210

Optimal Currency Area (OCA), 2, 208

Organisation of Eastern Caribbean States (OECS), 196

Orhan Bey (Ottoman Sultan), 47, 49

Osborne, George, 181

Oslo Accords, 174

Ottawa Conference (1932), 68

Ottoman Empire, 47–49, 67, 101

Ouattara, Alassanne, 205, 206

overvaluation, coinage, 49

Paine, Thomas, 17

Pakistan, 93, 117

Palestine, 102, 105, 114n29; Anglo-Palestine Bank, 98–99; without central bank, 221; Conciliation Commission for Palestine, UN, 99, 101; with currency in waiting, 174–79; digital currency and, 177; gold reserves and, 174; independent currency and, 175, 177–79, 188; Paris Protocol on Economic

Relations and, 174–78; pound, 177, 179; security and, 96
Palestine Currency Board, 95–100, 174, 176
Palestine Liberation Organization (PLO), 174
Palestinian Monetary Authority, 174, 176, 177
Palestinian National Authority, 174, 177–78
Palmer Rule, 52
Pamuk, Şevket, 48–49
Panama, 80
Panama Canal, 80
PAP (People's Action Party), Singapore, 118
Papal States, 25, 26, 28, 39
paper money: in American colonies, 11–13, 15–17, 19, 21; Australia and, 59–60; expansion of, 40; Prussia and, 29; refusal to use, 75–76; regions or circles issuing, 55; rights with, 58
Papua New Guinea, 146–47, 153–54
parallelism, 211
Paris Protocol on Economic Relations (1994), 174–78
Parker-Willis, Henry, 91
pegged exchange rate, xii, 106, 176
people, free movement of goods and, 140, 196
People's Action Party (PAP), Singapore, 118
perestroika (restructuring), 121
Persia, 47–48, 51
Peshmerga, 189
Philippines, 80, 108
Piastre de Commerce, 70
pine tree shilling, 10–11, 34n4
PLO (Palestine Liberation Organization), 174
Plocker, Sever, 175–76
Poland, 37, 48, 78, 129
political sovereignty, 1, 5, 93
politics, banknote issue and, 21
Portugal, 72–74, 142–43, 221

Portuguese Banknote Crisis, 73
pound, Palestinian, 177, 179
pound sterling: adoption of, 185; devaluation of, 6; dominance, 67–68; resistance to using, 49
power, ancient Rome and, 3–4
Prague, 136, 137–38
private currencies, digital, 6, 173, 227
Prodi, Romano, 183
Prussia, 31, 33, 124; Bank of Prussia, 29–30, 32; Franco-Prussian War of 1871, 28, 30, 69
Puerto Rico, 80
Puigdemont, Carles, 187–88

Qing Empire, 82
quantitative easing, 214

Rahman, Tungku Abdul, 118, 119
Rajoy, Mariano, 187
Rand Monetary Area Agreement (1974), 199
Rehn, Olli, 211
Reichsbank, 30–33, 124
Renaissance, 22–23
renminbi, 225–26
"Report on the Subject of a National Bank" (Hamilton), 16
Reserve Bank of India, 67
Reserve Bank of New Zealand, 64, 67
reserve currency, 7, 67, 89, 94, 103, 110, 225–26
restructuring (*perestroika*), 121
Rhodesia, 66
Richter, Eugen, 32, 33
rigsdaler, 43
riksdaler, 43
Risorgimento, 25, 26
riyal, 166–67
Robert the Bruce, 180
Rome, ancient, 3–4, 22, 25, 48, 50, 224
Royal Bank of Scotland, 180, 184, 185
ruble zone: collapse of, 121–24, 155n9; Estonia in 1992 and end of, 125–28
rupee, India, 51, 55–56, 63

Russia, 32, 66, 81, 124–26, 155n9, 176
Rwanda, 104

Saint Kitts and Nevis, 196
Saint Lucia, 196
Saint Vincent, 196
Salazar, Antonio, 199
Saleh, Ali Abdullah, 167
Salmond, Alex, 183
Sarawak, 118, 119
SARB (South African Reserve
    Bank), 199, 200
Saudi Arabia, 166, 167
Scandinavian monetary
    union, 34, 43–45
Schacht, Hjalmar, 124
Schlesinger, Helmut, 165
Schmidt, Helmut, 209–10
Scotland: Act of Union and, 179;
    banknote issue and, 179–80; Bank
    of Scotland, 179, 180, 184, 185;
    Clydesdale Bank, 180; coinage, 179;
    with currency in waiting, 179–86;
    in EU, 182–84, 187; GDP, 185;
    independence, 180–84, 186, 189,
    190; Royal Bank of Scotland, 180,
    184, 185; taxes and, 180
Scottish National Party (SNP), 180–
    83, 185, 190
Second Bank of the United
    States, 19–21
Second Opium War (1860), 167
security: with coinage distribution,
    51; monetary sovereignty and, 224;
    Palestine and, 96
seigniorage, xiii, 9–11, 39–40, 62–65,
    91, 198–200
Senegal, 70, 202, 205
Serbia Montenegro, 221
Sha'ath, Nabeel, 177
shahi, Ottoman Empire, 49
shekel, Israel, 174–78
Sierra Leone, 104
sikka, coinage and, 3, 55

silver, 52; coinage, 22–23, 24, 25,
    27, 30, 31, 37, 39–40, 41, 43, 44,
    48–49, 51, 53, 56, 60–62, 65, 179;
    debts and, 22; demonitizing, 58;
    depreciation of, 56; gold over, 23,
    30, 55–56; Hong Kong and, 58–59,
    71; India and, 54–57, 71; pound
    sterling, 3–4, 6, 49, 67–68, 185; ratio
    of gold to, 27, 31
Singapore, 57; sovereignty and reserves
    in 1965, 118–21; Straits Settlement,
    65, 118–19
Slovenia, 131, 132, 133, 134, 221
SNP. *See* Scottish National Party
Solomon Isles, 153, 154
Somalia, 76, 105–8, 117
Somaliland, 74, 77, 150, 221
somalo, 107–8, 151
South Africa, 66, 68, 198
South African Reserve Bank
    (SARB), 199, 200
Southern Africa, 5, 198–201
South Sudan, 104; civil war, 152, 153,
    167; in 2011, 149–53, 189
South West Africa People's Organisation
    (SWAPO), 199
sovereign debt crisis of 2009–2010, 45,
    92, 138, 181, 209, 213–15, 226
sovereignty: legal, 1, 178; political, 1,
    5, 93; in Singapore and reserves in
    1965, 118–21. *See also* monetary
    sovereignty
Soviet Union, 2, 221, 224
Spain, 9, 186–88, 191, 202
Special Administrative Region, Hong
    Kong as, 168, 169, 170
specierigsdaler, 43
Sri Lanka (Ceylon), 66, 93, 94,
    103, 113n21
Stability and Growth Pact, 213
state authority, with currency, 3–4
states: monetary sovereignty and
    making of, 221–28; rights of, 223
Straits Settlement (1897), 65,
    66, 118–19

Stringher, Bonaldo, 74
Stringher, Bonert, 106
Sturgeon, Nicola, 183
Sub-Saharan Africa, 110–12
Sudan, 104, 149–53, 167, 176, 189
Suharto, 143
Sulla (81–80 BC), 3
surrogate currencies, 155n9
Sustainable Growth Commission, SNP and, 185
SWAPO (South West Africa People's Organisation), 199
Swaziland, 198, 199, 200
Sweden, 4, 22, 24, 40, 43–44, 131, 228
Swee, Goh Keng, 120–21
Switzerland, 27, 43; bimetallic system in, 38; Latin Monetary Union and, 39, 41; monetary independence and, 225; unification of, 24–25
Syria, 105, 188–89, 190

Taha, Ali, 149
Tahiti, 69
Taiwan, 82, 168
Tajikistan, 123, 124, 155n9
Tanganyika, 104
taxes, 11, 71, 180
testamentaria nummaria (Lex Cornelia), 3
thaler, 28, 75
Thatcher, Margaret, 168
Tigrean People's Liberation Front (TPLF), 139, 140
Timor-Leste, 222, 223; with central bank, 173, 221; GDP, 145–46; independence, 142, 159n59; in 1999, 142–49
De Tocqueville, Alexis, 19, 20
Togo, 93, 202
Toure, Ahmed Sekou, 202
TPLF (Tigrean People's Liberation Front), 139, 140
trade, 96, 146; currency and, 55, 228; eurozone and, 176; international monetary unions and, 37–38, 46n20

Transjordan, 105, 114n29; end of empire, 101–2; Israel, Palestine currency board and, 95–100
Treaty of Turin, 27
Trinidad and Tobago, 196
Truman, Harry S., 98
Trump, Donald, 190, 218n28
Turkey, 3, 49, 105, 188, 191

Uganda, 104, 150
UK. *See* United Kingdom
UK Independence Party, 5
UMNO (United Malays National Organisation), 118
unemployment, 137–38, 164–65
unification: of Germany, 163–66; Italy and, 25–28; Switzerland and, 24–25; of Yemen, 166–67
Union Bank of Burma, 95
Union of the Crowns (1603), 179
Union of Utrecht (1575), 9
United Arab Emirates, 195
United Kingdom (UK), 5, 97, 150, 169, 183–84
United Malays National Organisation (UMNO), 118
United Nations (UN): Conciliation Commission for Palestine, 99, 101; General Assembly Resolution 181, 95, 96, 174; peacekeeping forces, 141; Security Council Resolution 390A, 139; UNTAET, 144, 145, 148
United Provinces of the Netherlands, 9–10, 24
United States (US), 56, 80, 113n21, 150, 218n28; banks, 18, 19–21, 94; federal control of currency, 14–19; Federal Reserve System, 7, 22, 182, 214, 223, 225; Israel and, 176–77. *See also* American colonies; dollar, US
UNTAET (UN Transitional Administration in East Timor), 144, 145, 148
Uzbekistan, 123, 124, 155n9

Van Rumpuy, Hermann, 183
Velvet Divorce (1993), 134–39
Venetian ducat, 37, 48–49
Victor Emanuel (King of Piedmont), 25
Victor Emanuel II (King of Piedmont), 27
Victoria (Queen of England), 55
Vietnam, 69, 108, 109

Wade, Abdulaye, 205
Wales, 180
WAMU (West African Monetary Union), 202, 206
War of 1870–1871, 30, 33
War of Independence, American colonies, 4
Warsaw Pact, 129
Wars of the Roses, 51
Washington, George, 18
Werner, Pierre, 208, 209, 211
Werner Report, 208–10
West Africa: currency board, 65–68, 103–4; franc zone unions of central and, 201–6

West African Monetary Union (WAMU), 202, 206
West Germany, 163–67, 212
West Volta (Burkina Faso), 71, 93, 202, 206
William IV (King of England), 55
Wilson, Woodrow, 22
"Wind of Change Speech" (Macmillan), 89, 93
World Bank, 146, 152

Yeltsin, Boris, 126
Yemen, 25, 48–49, 166–67
yen, Japan, 81
Yi dynasty, Korea, 87n81
Yokohama Specie Bank, 82–83
Yugoslavia, 131–32, 195, 221, 224
Yugoslavia-Slovenia, 129–34

Zanzibar, 104
Zenawi, Meles, 139–40
Zhou Xiaochuan, 225–26
Zimbabwe, 200–201, 222
Zollverein (Customs Unit), 28